Silk
Roads

Silk
Roads

Sue Brunning, Luk Yu-ping,
Elisabeth R. O'Connell and Tim Williams

University of Washington Press / Seattle

Supported by

the
HUO FAMILY
FOUNDATION

Additional supporters
James Bartos
The Ruddock Foundation for the Arts

With further support from
The Ministry of Culture, Sports and Tourism of the Republic of Korea, Unicorn
Publishing Group, International Foundation for Arts and Culture Japan,
the National Museum of Tajikistan, Rodolphe Olard and Susan Sinclair,
The Huang Yao Foundation and Dr Michael Watts and Jolanda Watts.

This exhibition has been made possible as a result of the Government
Indemnity Scheme. The British Museum would like to thank HM Government
for providing Government Indemnity, and the Department for Culture, Media
and Sport and Arts Council England for arranging the indemnity.

Published to accompany the exhibition *Silk Roads* at the
British Museum from 26 September 2024 to 23 February 2025.

First published in the United Kingdom in 2024
by The British Museum Press

US edition published by
University of Washington Press
uwapress.uw.edu

Silk Roads
© 2024 The Trustees of the British Museum

Designed by Studio Noel
Colour reproduction by Altaimage
Printed in Italy by OGM

Images © 2024 The Trustees of the British Museum, courtesy of the British
Museum's Department of Photography and Imaging, unless otherwise
stated on page 299.

Further information about the British Museum and its collection can be
found at britishmuseum.org.

The papers used in this book are natural, renewable and recyclable, and the
manufacturing processes are expected to conform to the regulations of the
country of origin.

Frontispiece
Travelling monk, *c*. 851–900. Cave 17, Mogao Caves, Dunhuang, China.
Ink and pigments on paper. H. 41.1 cm, W. 30 cm. British Museum, London,
1919,0101,0.168. Stein collection.

Note to the reader
This catalogue gives a general overview of the Silk Roads, 500–1000.
A select bibliography can be found on page 296 and more detailed
references can be found in the notes to the chapters.

Diacritics have been removed from some transliterated words
for accessibility; the 'ayn and hamza have been retained in Arabic
transliterations.

Dates with dashes indicate a range (570–75); dates with slashes indicate
that something happened between two different years (570/75). Dates
after the year 500 do not include 'CE'. Islamic AH dates are not given in
chapters 4, 5 and 6.

Caption dimensions are given as maxima. An object's place of production or
origin is omitted if unknown.

References in chapters 1 and 2 use simple or complex Chinese characters
depending on their original source.

Contents

Director's foreword

Dr Nicholas Cullinan OBE

Silk Roads is an ambitious and exciting project, which explores the interlocking networks that stretched across Asia, Africa and Europe, from Japan to Ireland, through a series of extraordinary objects.

The sprawling extent of Silk Roads routes is evident in such artefacts. A tranquil figure of the Buddha was likely made in what is now Pakistan but was found thousands of kilometres away on the island of Helgö, Sweden. Paintings found at Dunhuang in China portray faceted glass of the kind made in the Sasanian empire, suggesting that such vessels travelled across West and Central Asia. Unassuming objects can reveal much about how people lived, such as a Tibetan phrasebook explaining how to say 'chopsticks', 'beer' and 'be quiet!' in Chinese, or the letters and contracts stored by the medieval Jewish community of Fustat-Cairo, which bring to light the everyday exchanges at a bustling cosmopolitan hub.

All the empires and regions along the Silk Roads during the period 500 to 1000 were comprised of diverse groups of people with numerous languages and different faiths. A series of case studies highlights a small selection of some of these groups – seafarers in the Indian Ocean, Sogdians in Central Asia, Vikings on the 'eastern way', Aksumites of northeast Africa and peoples of al-Andalus – to reveal the key roles they played in exchange. By situating their activities within the context of a much larger story, the curators of *Silk Roads*, Sue Brunning, Luk Yu-ping and Elisabeth R. O'Connell, have cleverly drawn out the nuanced nature of cross-cultural exchange to reveal its profits and perils, practicalities and pain. They, along with all colleagues involved in this impressive and complex exhibition, have my sincere thanks.

This exhibition would not have been possible without spectacular loans from twenty-nine institutions across the globe, some of which are on display in the United Kingdom for the first time. These include the Ashmolean Museum, University of Oxford; Asian Civilisations Museum, Singapore; Bute Museum; Bodleian Libraries, University of Oxford; The British Library, London; Gyeongju National Museum, Korea; Historiska Museet, Stockholm; Jarrow Hall, Tyne and Wear; Kunsthistorisches Museum, Vienna, Collection of Greek and Roman Antiquities; Lichfield Cathedral; Musée du Louvre, Paris; Musée national des arts asiatiques – Guimet, Paris; Museo Arceológico y Etnológico de Córdoba; Museo Archeológico Nacional, Madrid; Museum für Asiatische Kunst, Berlin; Museum für Byzantinische Kunst, Berlin; Museum für Islamische Kunst, Berlin; National Museum of Tajikistan; National Museums Scotland; Parker Library, Corpus Christi College Library, University of Cambridge; Petrie Museum, University College London; Samarkand State Historical, Architectural and Art Museum-Reserve; Southend Museums; State Museum of Arts of Uzbekistan, Tashkent; The Syndics of Cambridge University Library; Tokyo National Museum, Japan; University of Aberdeen, Scotland; Victoria and Albert Museum, London; and the Wyvern Collection. I would like to thank them for their collaboration in bringing this project to fruition.

Finally, we are enormously grateful to this exhibition's lead supporters – the Huo Family Foundation, James Bartos, and The Ruddock Foundation for the Arts – and thankful for the generosity of our other supporters.

Opposite
Shoulder-clasp in two halves, *c.* late 500s–early 600s. Found at Sutton Hoo, Suffolk, England. Gold, garnet and glass. L. 12.7 cm (halves joined), W. 5.6 cm (each). British Museum, London, 1939,1010.5 and 5.a. Donated by Mrs Edith M. Pretty.

Introduction

Sue Brunning, Luk Yu-ping and
Elisabeth R. O'Connell

The figure gazing gently from the facing page takes the unmistakable form of the Buddha (fig. 0.1). Just over 8 centimetres high, it was originally burnished gold, the natural colour of the copper alloy from which it was cast a millennium and a half ago. The Buddha is shown seated, poised in perfect calm on a double lotus flower with legs crossed and feet upturned. His right hand rests against his knee in *varadamudra*, the Buddhist gesture of wish fulfilment, palm out with fingers pointing downwards. His left hand, raised by a propped arm, grasps his *sanghati*, a monastic robe, which drapes around his form. The Buddha's expression is a portrait of serenity, with smiling lips and eyes gazing softly ahead. The metalworker picked out these features in silver, tin and black niello, contrasting with the once gold-coloured skin, as if to emphasise the Buddha's tranquil aspect. The eyes themselves may originally have glittered between the half-closed lids, hinted at by copper and glass residues found within. On his forehead, the raised dot or *urna*, an auspicious mark, was also accentuated with a layer of precious metal, apparently gold, that still shimmers today.[1]

Iconographically, the figure belongs to the artistic tradition of the Swat Valley in present-day Pakistan, where it was probably made between the late sixth and mid-seventh centuries. The valley was a major centre of early Buddhism, a faith that spread from the Indian subcontinent to China in the first centuries CE.[2] The figure, however, was not found in the Swat Valley, nor in any other Buddhist centre known in the world at the time. It was found on the small lake island of Helgö in Sweden, nearly 5,000 kilometres away. The startling discovery, made during archaeological excavations of buildings dating to around 800, poses searching questions about the true extent of interconnectedness in the past, and the place of the so-called 'Silk Road' in this story.

The 'Silk Road(s)': a modern concept

The lakes and forests of Sweden are a world away from the popular image of the Silk Road, which typically involves snaking trains of camels bearing silk westward from China along desert paths, or multicoloured spices for sale in Samarkand, or Marco Polo (1254–1324) trading tales with Kublai Khan (1215–1294) at the Mongol court. In fact, this vision is a modern concept that first appeared in writings during the nineteenth century. The geographer Ferdinand von Richthofen (1833–1905) is often credited with the invention of the term in German ('Seidenstrasse'; plural, 'Seidenstrassen') in 1877, although recent findings reveal that it was already in use before then.[3] Nevertheless, Richthofen provided a more precise definition of the term based on historical sources.[4] It appeared in his multivolume *China* series, in the text proper and on the legend of a fold-out 'Map of Central Asia: Overview of transport connections from 128 BC to 150 AD ...' (fig. 0.2). Two lines in red and

0.1

Buddha figure, late 500s–mid 600s. Probably made in the Swat Valley, Pakistan, found on Helgö, Uppland, Sweden. Copper alloy, silver, glass, tin, niello and probably gold. H. 8.4 cm, W. 6.4 cm. Historiska Museet, Stockholm, 108115_HST.

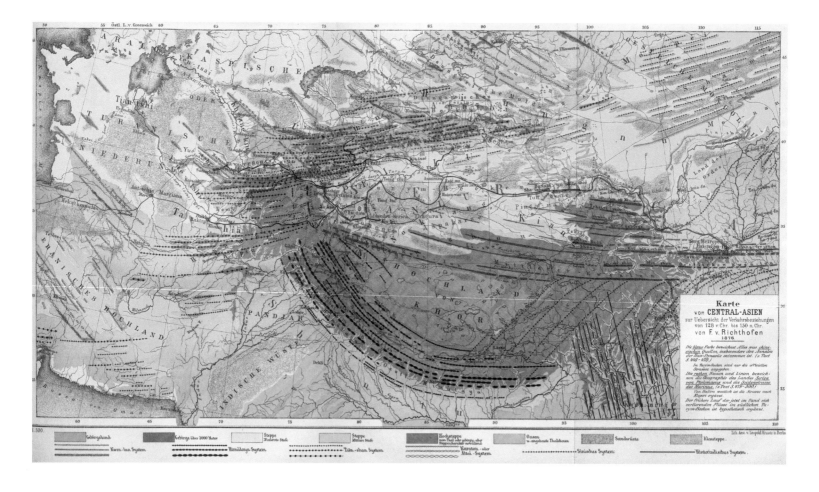

0.2

'Map of Central Asia'. From Ferdinand von Richthofen, *China: Ergebnisse eigener Reisen und darauf gegründeter Studien* (Berlin, 1877).

blue were drawn on the map to distinguish his conjectured routes, based on Greek and Chinese sources, respectively.[5] The red line, which was identified as 'die Seidenstrasse', stretched from Chang'an (Xi'an in present-day China) to the left edge of the map, reaching what is now Iran. Richthofen's definition of the term 'Silk Road' was narrow. It referred primarily to trade routes along which silk moved west from Han-dynasty (206 BCE–220 CE) China to Central Asia and beyond.[6]

Richthofen was writing at a time of imperial rivalry between Britain and Russia in Central Asia, and when there was an interest in exploiting commercial opportunities in the newly reconquered western regions of China.[7] Behind his map and surveys was a potential transcontinental railway that would connect Europe to China.[8] In the early twentieth century, foreign explorers and archaeologists such as Marc Aurel Stein (1862–1943) embarked upon expeditions around the Tarim Basin.[9] They collected large quantities of artefacts that would end up in museum collections around the world, including the British Museum, and would come to represent key aspects of the Silk Road in later publications and exhibitions.[10] This book and the exhibition that it accompanies are no exception. Travel writings in the 1920s and 1930s, notably Sven Hedin's *The Silk Road* (first published in 1936 in Swedish then quickly translated into German and English), helped bring the term to wider audiences. From this time onwards, 'Silk Road' began to be translated into non-European languages as well. Another contributing factor to its growing popularity was the tourism industry. Railways, steamships and motorways made long-distance travel more available to European and American tourists, fuelling interest in the Silk Road and its romantic association with adventure in exotic lands.

However, it was not until the latter part of the twentieth century that the term 'Silk Road' truly reached global recognition.[11] In the aftermath of the Second World War and then the Cold War, and with the formation of new, decolonised sovereign states in Asia, the Silk Road gained significance in the development of national identities and the reimagining of interregional and international relations. The United Nations Educational, Scientific and Cultural Organization (UNESCO), established in 1945, played a key role in promoting the Silk Road as a means of encouraging mutual appreciation and exchange between countries. Japan was an early proponent of these initiatives as it sought to rebuild its international image and diplomatic ties with its neighbours after the Second World War.[12] The concept of a 'Maritime Silk Road' became part of these wider discussions.[13] Interest in the Silk Road continued to grow in the 1980s, supported by publications, conferences, exhibitions, study tours, conservation projects, documentary films, and other arts and cultural events. This extended to government policies on cross-border trade and investment. The United States proposed a New Silk Road Initiative in the 2010s for engagement with Afghanistan and Central Asia. In 2013 China launched policies that were to become the Belt and Road Initiative, which reimagines the historical land and maritime Silk Roads as a major global infrastructure development strategy.[14] The Initiative has additionally promoted heritage diplomacy in the form of cultural collaboration programmes and intergovernmental cooperation in the nomination of historic Silk Road sites to the World Heritage List administered by UNESCO.[15]

This brief history of the term 'Silk Road' shows that, since the late 1800s, it has been deeply entangled in shifting economic and geopolitical agendas. Concurrently, the concept has expanded far beyond the red line across Richthofen's map. A major recent book on the topic, covering Afro-Eurasia from roughly 200 BCE to 1400 CE, opens with a map that could scarcely look more different from the German geographer's, showing a web of routes sprawling west to Britain and Ireland, south to Madagascar, east to Japan, and north to Scandinavia and Siberia.[16] The Helgö Buddha is one pixel in this expanded concept of the 'Silk Roads', which styles them as a transcontinental network stretching out in all directions.

The 'Silk Road(s)': a useful concept?

As a modern invention with shifting meanings, the analytical usefulness of the term 'Silk Road(s)' has been called into question.[17] Critics have pointed out its limitations and shortcomings, in that it overemphasises silk as a commodity at the expense of the myriad objects – as well as people and ideas – that were conveyed, while also giving a false impression of a fixed land route that stretched neatly and continuously across Eurasia. The focus, especially in early scholarship, on east–west exchange and the conventionally understood termini of the Silk Road(s) in China and Europe have meant that north–south interactions and regions of significant connectivity, such as Central Asia and India, have been overlooked.

The uncertain chronology of the Silk Road(s) poses additional challenges for interpretation. Chinese accounts tend to begin with the expedition of the Han-dynasty imperial envoy Zhang Qian (c. 167–114 BCE) to Central Asia, starting in 138 BCE.[18] Others may look further back to the military campaigns of Alexander III (Alexander the Great, r. 336–323 BCE) into Central Asia and the northwestern Indian subcontinent, or to the millennia-old movement of Indo-European nomadic groups as part of the story of the Silk Road(s).[19] Timelines of the Silk Road(s) can stop at different historical periods or continue up to the 1800s and beyond.[20]

Nonetheless, the term 'Silk Road(s)' has survived scholarly challenges due to its iconic status and convenience, akin to a shorthand for cross-cultural exchange in this part of the world.[21] This broad understanding of the term also lends itself to current interest in scholarship on human histories that emphasise contact and connections as opposed to depicting societies in isolation, maintaining disciplinary divides.[22] Its popular recognition and continued appeal can help to bring new ideas, perspectives and cross-disciplinary discoveries about connected histories to a wider audience.[23] Scholarship has also demonstrated that focused 'Silk Road(s)' studies can be nuanced and productive.[24] While the term might, for some, conjure clichéd images of camels and spices, it also arouses notions of transcontinental exchange, which are core principles within today's more complex conceptualisation. Consequently, despite its limitations, the term remains a touchpoint for curious audiences and summons up ideas that are both relevant and evocative. Its application seems likely to persist, albeit in a slightly different guise: recent works tend consistently to use the pluralised term 'Silk Roads', a simple tweak that evokes the greater intricacy with which the concept is now presented and understood.[25]

Expanding horizons: pluralising the 'Silk Road'

In an expanded understanding of the Silk Roads, Afro-Eurasian connections are not confined to desert sands or even to land in general. Maritime routes are now viewed as critical arteries, exemplified by significant studies on the Baltic Sea as a European gateway to the east, and on the Red Sea and Indian Ocean linking East Asia to Africa, Mediterranean Europe and beyond.[26] Rivers were also pivotal connectors, such as the waterways of Eastern Europe, Russia and Ukraine, which facilitated transformative exchanges between northern Europe and the Byzantine and Islamic worlds from at least the seventh century (see pp. 138–45).[27] North–south connections, particularly the relationship between pastoral nomadic or semi-nomadic and sedentary societies, were just as important as journeys moving east–west.

Routes of all kinds merged to provide astonishing transcontinental coverage, with goods often transferring between different paths to reach their final destination. Visualisations of neatly intersecting lines on maps can make it seem as though traversing geographical expanses in the past was straightforward and

0.3
Peacock remains, *c.* 900. Ship burial, Gokstad, near Sandefjord, Vestfold, Norway. Animal bone and feather. L. 9.5 cm, W. 4.2 cm (approx., largest piece). Kulturhistorisk Museum, Oslo, C10466.l.

routine – one reason why indicative routes have been omitted from the main map of this book (see pp. 8–9).[28] In fact, there is little evidence to suggest that individuals personally journeyed from one end of the map to the other, and only certain groups appear to have travelled significant distances themselves. Recent research into mechanisms of exchange and interconnectivity has characterised travel routes as building blocks within regional networks that intersected with each other at key hubs such as urban centres, ports and markets. Here, goods could be exchanged by relay, from one network to another, creating a chain of segmented journeys that added up, eventually, to a far-flung passage. Therefore, those operating along the networks may not have travelled very far themselves, but what they handled could cross the known world. Long-distance exchange, the glamour of which has traditionally attracted disproportionate attention, was really driven by regional and local exchange.[29]

Individual networks were subject to fluctuations over time. Segments closed, opened, expanded, contracted and alternated in response to impactful events, most notably the transcontinental spread of Islam from the seventh century, but also the end of the Western Roman empire in fifth-century Europe. Studies have shown that not all networks across Afro-Eurasia were connected in the same way at the same time, and exchange impacted regions differently based on factors including distance and physical accessibility.[30] While routes drawn upon maps are helpful for visualising connectivity, they also create the illusion that such routes were monolithic and permanent rather than variable and organic. Accordingly, one scholar has proposed reimagining the Silk Roads less as a constellation of lines and more as interwoven landscapes.[31] Another approach identifies major nodes (large settlements), segments of routes between them and broader corridors of 'movement and impact'.[32] Combining these ideas could help to nurture a sense that the world of the Silk Roads was connected by, but not confined to, the routes that traversed it.

As mentioned above, it is also now widely understood that silk was just one of the commodities exchanged across Afro-Eurasia, and not necessarily the most significant.[33] A plethora of materials, objects, people and ideas traversed geographical and cultural boundaries and changed hands in a range of contexts including trade, but also warfare, diplomacy, learning, pilgrimage and more. Among the tangible survivals are the shadows of countless intangible exchanges, whose passages are more difficult to reconstruct.[34]

Archaeological and documentary evidence, together with scientific analysis, have revealed a host of raw materials on the move along criss-crossing pathways by land, river and sea: precious and semi-precious gemstones, like sapphire and garnet; minerals, including jade and rock crystal; resins, such as amber; animal products, like ivory, pearl, shell and fur; base and precious metals; raw glass; dyes and pigments; food and drink, such as spices, nuts, fruits, wine and honey; aromatic and medicinal substances; and plants, crops, trees, timber and seeds. Crafted objects known to have travelled include coins; vessels for food and drink; garments and dress accessories, including head- and footwear, jewellery and other adornments; architectural elements; artworks, such as sculptures, carvings and figures; religious paraphernalia; and literary and documentary texts. Animals were also exchanged, notably horses, elephants, hunting dogs, birds of prey, ornamental fowl such as peacocks (fig. 0.3), and other desirable creatures destined for aviaries and menageries. While luxury goods have drawn the most attention, humbler goods, notably everyday pottery, are now highly valued as evidence for exchange. Not only do they survive in large numbers, but they often preserve residues of consumables that indicate changing foodways and cooking methods, or surface treatments like glazing, suggesting technological and stylistic transfers (see chapters 1, 4, 5 and pp. 232–43).[35]

Many items exchanged along the Silk Roads were made for specific functions, such as paying for goods or storing food, or they carried intended meanings, such as evoking a spiritual figure. However, these values did not necessarily travel with them. In some cases, visible signs of repurposing or adaptation signal a change in use or meaning. Other cases require a greater degree of speculation, particularly where an object has moved far from its place of origin and into a different cultural context. A case in point is the Buddha statue that opened this book. What meaning did it have for its owners in Scandinavia? What kinds of stories did they tell about it? A post-excavation photograph tantalises with possibilities. It shows that the figure was found with thick leather bands around its neck and left wrist, thought to have been added after its arrival in Sweden (fig. 0.4). Initially, the bands were interpreted as straps for suspending the Buddha from a wall or a person's body, hinting that it was treated primarily as an exotic curio or display piece whose original meaning did not survive the long journey north. However, a recent reading has likened the leather bands to those found with wooden idols of deities excavated from Scandinavian wetlands, raising the possibility that some knowledge of the Buddha's spiritual significance was transmitted and 'repackaged' for a Norse religious context.[36]

Unfortunately, the Helgö Buddha's leather bands were not preserved and further clues, for instance via scientific analysis, are now beyond reach. Nonetheless, instances such as this pose questions about the intersection between tangible and intangible exchanges along the Silk Roads, some of which are explored later in this book. In general, however, ideas moved along networks just as physical objects did. Faiths of all magnitudes crossed continents, the largest being Buddhism, Islam and Christianity. So did political systems and hierarchies; spiritual and cultural customs; languages and scripts; knowledge, such as science, medicine, geography and law; styles, iconographies and other arts, like music and poetry; economic methods, from coinage to weights and measures; fashions, hairstyles and cosmetics; and technologies, including metalworking, glassmaking, papermaking and hydraulics, and, of course, moriculture and sericulture, namely the cultivation of mulberry trees and domesticated silkworms fed with mulberry leaves to produce silk.

People travelled in their own right, too. Research into human mobility and migration has painted a nuanced portrait of people on the move across Afro-Eurasia. Socio-economic, political and other structures interplay with individual agency in histories of migration.[37] The numbers involved ranged from individuals to entire populations. Those who may have moved by choice include traders, artisans, pilgrims, missionaries, scholars, explorers, diplomats and mercenaries. Others were forced to move, for instance by natural disasters, climate change, war, persecution and state coercion, such as the expulsion of political rivals or the marriage of elite women into allied families.[38] Arguably, the most significant group in this category was enslaved human beings who, as the historian Susan Whitfield poignantly explains, were bought and sold in markets across Afro-Eurasia.[39] This trade was endemic, involving – and consuming – millions of individuals throughout the period. Its prevalence can be explained, at least in part, by its incredible value not only to merchants who performed the transactions, but to many polities and regions who benefited from the proceeds of the trade, its taxation and the labour supplied by enslaved peoples themselves.[40]

Received wisdom has long maintained that the business of slavery is 'archaeologically invisible' and is best observed through documentary evidence, ranging from annals and biographies to charters, contracts and bills of sale (see chapters 2, 5 and pp. 138–45). Recent studies, however, have added new insights by approaching the issue from novel angles: for instance, through comparisons with the later Transatlantic trade; examination of suspected market sites; burials

0.4

Photograph of the Helgö Buddha figure after discovery, showing leather bands around the neck and wrist. Published in Wilhelm Holmqvist et al., *Excavations at Helgö I: Report for 1954–1956* (Uppsala, 1961), p. 112, fig. 18.

of individuals in perceived 'subordinate', restrained or malnourished states; and the commodities for which the enslaved were probably exchanged, notably Islamic silver coins and glass beads in the Viking world. Meanwhile, analysis of large fortified sites in Eastern Europe, together with unusual cemetery demographics indicating a dearth of adolescents, appear to support written and linguistic evidence that highlights Slav regions, and their peoples, as a special target for captive-takers, especially in the tenth century (see pp. 143–5).[41] Other research has emphasised an appreciable religious dimension to the medieval trade, in theory if not always in practice: for instance, legislation surrounding the seizure and sale of co-religionists required Byzantine and Islamic authorities to seek populations to enslave from beyond Christian and Muslim lands respectively.[42] Such important work has forged a more tangible impression of this core facet of exchange on the Silk Roads.

All those who moved were potential vectors for another major traveller: disease. Waves of bubonic plague swept along the Silk Roads networks, originating possibly in Asia and conveyed most likely by fleas that infested rodents aboard merchant, military and food supply transports. Indeed, the so-called Plague of Justinian was first recorded in 541 at a key port, Pelusium in Egypt, which linked the Mediterranean and Red Sea (see p. 191). References in China to an illness with symptoms very similar to those of the bubonic plague appear in a medical compendium dated *c.* 610.[43] Chilling written accounts chart the plague's spread throughout the Mediterranean world, West Asia and Europe, as far west as Ireland, into the eighth century. Its inescapability even in remote rural areas is highlighted by the discovery of *Yersinia pestis*, the bacterium responsible for bubonic plague, in human remains from Spain, Germany, France and England.[44] These unfortunate individuals demonstrate, in a macabre way, how even local communities were deeply connected to the wider world.

Archaeological science has made some of the most dramatic contributions to Silk Roads studies. Analytical techniques that reveal the identity, composition, date and provenance of materials, artefacts and human remains have been able to indicate movement, recycling, adoption, adaptation and other behaviours associated with cultural interactions. In some cases, they have confirmed information previously known only from written and other non-archaeological sources. For instance, X-ray fluorescence (XRF) and laser ablation techniques have shown that the metal used in Viking silver jewellery was recycled Islamic silver dirhams (coins), echoing contemporary Arabic references to Scandinavian traders making neck rings for their wives whenever they acquired enough of these coins.[45] Scientific analysis has also confirmed that glass from the Sasanian empire reached Japan.[46] In other cases, archaeological science has uncovered new stories that might otherwise have gone untold, often challenging received wisdom about the limits and directions of exchange. A notable example concerns a young girl buried during the early seventh century in Updown, southeastern England. Her body was laid to rest with typically local accoutrements, but ancient DNA extracted from her skeleton indicated 33 per cent West African ancestry, suggesting that members of her family had arrived in England as transcontinental migrants.[47] These powerful scientific techniques, and others still to be developed, could yield the greatest advances in knowledge about the Silk Roads in the years to come.[48]

500 to 1000

In order to address such a vast subject, this book cuts a narrow slice through the Silk Roads' long history, focusing on the five centuries between the years 500 and 1000.[49] This may be an unfamiliar period for some readers acquainted with the topic, as it pre-dates Marco Polo's travels in Asia by several centuries.[50] But there are compelling reasons to adopt this chronology.[51] It roughly coincides with the presence of several major polities – including China's Tang dynasty (618–907); newly emerged Islamic states, starting with the Rashidun caliphate (632–61); a resurgent Byzantium from the reign of Justinian I (d. 565) to Basil II (d. 1025); and the Carolingian empire (800–87) particularly under Charlemagne (d. 814) – which provide historical markers as well as some cohesion across large territories. These empires, and many other smaller polities on the Silk Roads at this time, were home to different peoples interacting with one another, speaking numerous languages and practising various faiths. Indeed, also during this time, the major universalising religions of Buddhism, Christianity and Islam spread and were adopted by various rulers, connecting even Eurasia's island extremities, Britain and Japan, to the continent.[52] Furthermore, the scale of organised trade during this period exceeded that of previous times, while sustained and large-scale movement of people in response to diverse stimuli helped to reconfigure the mosaic of cultures across the map. The arrival of Scandinavian Vikings in Newfoundland around the year 1000, bringing the Americas into Afro-Eurasia's reach, offers a fitting terminus to the timeline, after which a new phase of connectivity began.[53]

It is, admittedly, impossible to capture the full extent and complexity of the Silk Roads in a single publication, even within a limited timeframe. Within its approximate chronology from 500 to 1000, this book inevitably simplifies and highlights selected sites and narratives for the sake of clarity and to enable discussion of objects in their specific contexts. In West Asia, for instance, the rise of Islam and the Arab conquest form the key headline of chapter 4, while the Sasanian empire, which survived until 651, is introduced and addressed in terms of its legacy. Furthermore, practical considerations such as the availability and accessibility of objects and written sources, as well as the authors' own interests and expertise, have shaped the story told here.

An epic journey

The book is structured as a journey that broadly progresses east to west across the Silk Roads map. Each of the main chapters focuses on a particular geographic zone, and is connected by shorter case studies that either introduce groups of people who travelled widely or significant sites notable for their hybrid contexts and intense cultural interactions. The case studies are located at the intersections of the geographic zones, underscoring the connections that existed across Afro-Eurasia long before today's globalised world. Divergences along the way highlight the multidirectionality of these networks, while maritime and riverine moments emphasise the plurality of landscapes and modes of transport involved.

Chapter 1 begins in East Asia, focusing on three capital cities: Heijō-kyō (Nara) in Nara Japan (710–94), Geumseong (Gyeongju) in Silla Korea (57 BCE–935 CE) and Chang'an (Xi'an) in Tang China. The Tang capital is renowned for its cosmopolitan culture. But the Silk Roads network also extended east, as imports from distant lands reached Nara Japan and Silla Korea. This part of the world was further connected to wider networks through interregional contacts and the spread of Buddhism (figs 0.5–0.6). The journey then moves south towards the ocean, to the first case study, which explores a remarkable shipwreck salvaged off the coast of Belitung, an island of present-day Indonesia. Carrying some 60,000 pieces of Tang Chinese ceramics and other objects, the vessel is believed to have sunk in the ninth century on its return journey to Arabia or the Persian Gulf, revealing the extent of maritime activity across the Indian Ocean.

Chapter 2 continues from Southeast Asia, covering vast and diverse territories to reach the desert oases of the Tarim Basin in present-day Xinjiang Uyghur Autonomous Region, China. It introduces contacts and exchanges in parts of

0.5
Statues of foreign envoys, now headless, *c.* 684–708. Qianling mausoleum, built for Emperor Gaozong and Empress Wu Zetian. Stone. H. 155–177 cm. Qian County, Shaanxi province, China.

0.6
Borobudur Temple, Central Java, Indonesia, built around the late 700s or early 800s.

0.7 opposite top

Buddhist cave temple complex in the Bamiyan Valley, Afghanistan, once home to two colossal Buddha statues dating to the 500s.

0.8 opposite bottom

Jokhang Temple, Lhasa, Tibet or Xizang Autonomous Region, China, first built in 652 by King Songtsen Gampo.

0.9 above

Site of the ancient oasis city of Gaochang (Kocho), Xinjiang Uyghur Autonomous Region, China.

0.10 right

Turkic-period temple complex Kagan at the Eleke Sazy Valley, East Kazakhstan, 600–700.

Southeast Asia and the Indian subcontinent, as well as the Tibetan empire (Chinese: Tubo) across the Himalayas, with an emphasis on Buddhism that continued to spread across Asia (figs 0.7–0.8). Moving northeast, the narrative dwells on the extraordinary finds from the 'Library Cave' (Cave 17), Dunhuang, that offer insights into life along the Silk Roads. From there, the journey goes west around the Tarim Basin and the Taklamakan Desert, encountering the oasis kingdoms of Gaochang (Kocho, fig. 0.9) and Khotan. To the west of the Tarim Basin lies Central Asia, and the second case study introduces the Sogdians, who were renowned long-distance traders. Objects from Afrasiab (Samarkand) in present-day Uzbekistan reveal the Sogdians' prosperity, skill and outward-looking worldview.

The journey remains in Central Asia for chapter 3, focusing on the presence of Turkic pastoral nomads who dominated the steppe and expanded beyond it. Important archaeological finds from present-day Kazakhstan, Kyrgyzstan and Tajikistan reveal their development of settlements that became stopping points along the Silk Roads (fig. 0.10), and the different religious beliefs that coexisted under their dominance. The steppe region brings contacts with Scandinavian travellers popularly known today as Vikings, who from the later eighth century increasingly crossed the Baltic Sea to exploit, and settle along, the well-connected rivers of Eastern Europe, Ukraine and Russia (fig. 0.11). Their consequential exchanges with peoples on the steppe, in the northern Caucasus and, further east, Islamic lands, form the focus of the third case study.

Chapter 4 concentrates on journeys across Central Asia to Arabia. It considers the changes and continuities that resulted from the expansion of the Islamic empire from the seventh century, which brought different people and cultures into contact (fig. 0.12). It is followed by a case study of northeast Africa and the kingdom of Aksum. Through its cosmopolitan port, Adulis, this Christian ally of Byzantium periodically dominated maritime trade and expanded its territory across the Red Sea to the southwest tip of the Arabian Peninsula.

0.11 *below*
Volga River, Russia, a critical conduit for Vikings travelling eastwards.

0.12
Qusayr 'Amra, Jordan, built *c.* 723–43 during Umayyad caliphate rule.

0.13
View of a rocky Mediterranean coast, which posed the risk of shipwreck.

From here, sea routes offer westward passage into chapter 5, which explores connections in the Mediterranean (figs 0.13–0.14), where the Byzantine empire was repeatedly challenged by both Christian kingdoms and, in time, by Muslim polities that expanded across northern Africa and soon revitalised routes across the Sahara Desert (fig. 0.15). The final case study turns northward, disembarking onto the Iberian Peninsula to consider the arrival of Islam through the experiences of those living in al-Andalus, an Umayyad emirate that, in time, became a flourishing independent caliphate (fig. 0.16). Pyrenean passes, at last, bring the journey to its

end in chapter 6, focusing on northwest Europe (fig. 0.17). It stops first in Francia, exploring the imperial activities of its redoubtable ruler Charlemagne, before crossing to Britain and Ireland, where rich evidence belies the traditional view of the region's remoteness after Roman rule ended in the early fifth century CE.

Through a dazzling array of objects, this book challenges the romanticised image of the 'Silk Road' by revealing the myriad networks and types of exchange that conveyed people, objects and ideas across continents. By taking readers on their own Silk Roads journeys, from East Asia to northwest Europe, it attempts to capture a sense of the true scale of past connections by adopting a panoramic view of Afro-Eurasia, enlarging the traditional 'Silk Road' map to encompass the region bounded by Japan to the east, Scandinavia to the north, Ireland to the west and Madagascar to the south.[54] The inclusion of key objects from Kazakhstan, Kyrgyzstan, Tajikistan and Uzbekistan also highlights a region that may be less familiar to some readers but was central to the history of the Silk Roads.[55]

Six key themes that are pertinent to cross-cultural connections are woven throughout the book: diplomacy and military conquest; the movement of various groups of people; objects in transit, both as raw materials and as finished goods; the adoption and adaptation of cultural elements; religious encounters; and the transmission of ideas, knowledge and technology. Readers are introduced to individuals who themselves travelled the Silk Roads for different reasons, some swashbuckling and others tragic. The findings of innovative scientific research, so vital to Silk Roads studies, are also included, demonstrating how knowledge relating to past connectivity continues to evolve and reveal ever more astonishing stories. Together, these narratives, and the peoples encountered, highlight the profits and perils of cultural exchange during these five centuries, while encouraging readers to reflect upon their own connected lives in today's globalised world.

0.14

An aerial view of modern Istanbul, formerly the Byzantine capital Constantinople, strategically located on the Sea of Marmara, linking the Mediterranean and Black Sea.

0.15

View down the Essouk Valley, Mali, where the ruins of the trans-Saharan entrepôt of Essouk-Tadmekka are located.

0.16

Ruins of Madinat al-Zahra, palace complex of Caliph 'Abd al-Rahman III of al-Andalus, built from 936 near Córdoba, Spain.

0.17 *below*

A view of the Northumberland coast and the North Sea, northeastern England. Early medieval art, literature and archaeology from the region demonstrate its links to the wider world.

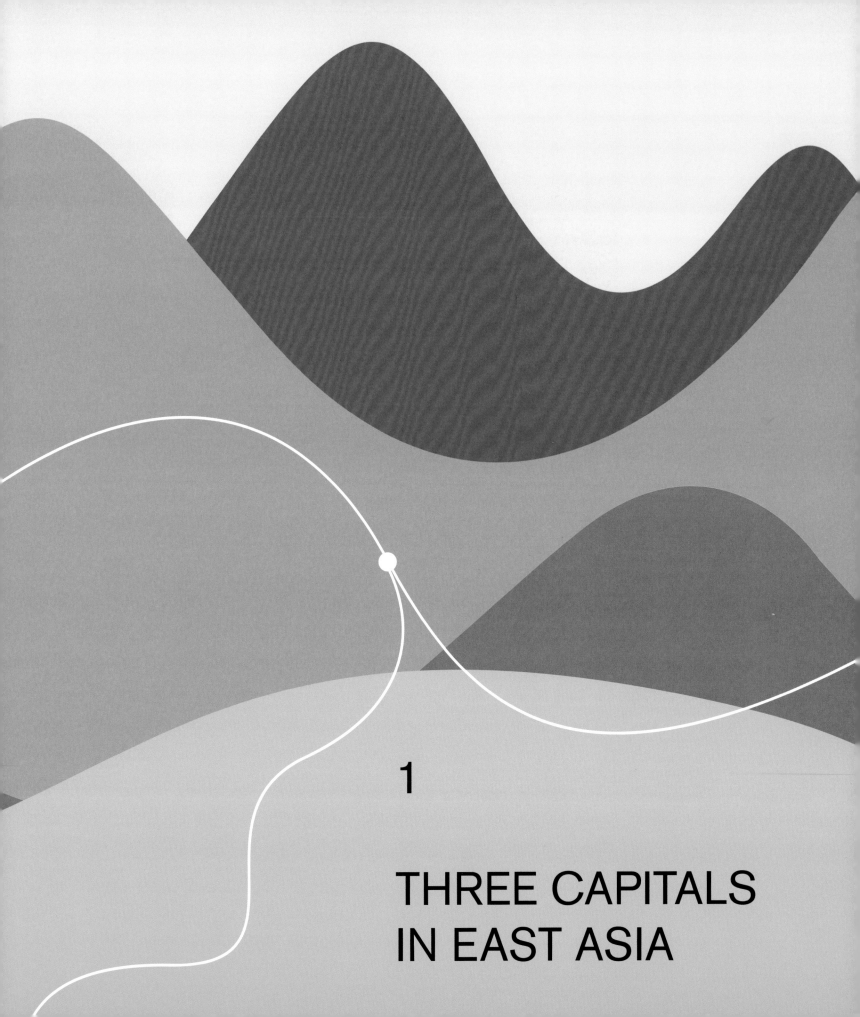

1

THREE CAPITALS
IN EAST ASIA

Three capitals in East Asia

Luk Yu-ping

At the eastern ends of the Silk Roads lie the Japanese archipelago, the Korean Peninsula and mainland China.[1] As neighbours, the polities in this region have long interacted with one another. During the period 500 to 1000, their exchanges entered a new phase when China was reunified under the Sui (581–618) and then the Tang (618–907) dynasties, forming a powerful presence in the region. The Korean Peninsula was divided into three main kingdoms until the 660s, when much of it came under the rule of Silla, while Japan moved from a confederacy towards a more centralised court.

The impact of cross-cultural exchanges between Japan and the continent during this period can be observed in the widespread adoption of Buddhism, and the centralisation and strengthening of the imperial court based on a Chinese-style model of administration. The timeline encompasses the Asuka period (538–710) of the Yamato confederacy, as well as the courtly age of the Nara (710–84) and early Heian (794–1185) periods.[2] Such developments were most clearly articulated during the Nara period, when the city of Nara, historically known as Heijō-kyō, on Honshū, the main island of Japan, became the capital. Luxury objects from distant lands also reached the imperial court located there.

The kingdom of Silla, founded around 57 BCE in the southeast of the Korean Peninsula, defied the odds when it conquered its larger neighbours through an alliance with Tang China in the 660s. By 676 Silla had managed to consolidate its control over much of the peninsula, beginning a period known as Unified Silla that would continue until 935.[3] Excavations of elite burial mounds from before this time have revealed a taste for luxury imports. Such lavish burials disappeared from the first half of the sixth century following Silla's acceptance of Buddhism and changes in tomb designs. As in Japan at this time, the rulers of Unified Silla looked to Tang China for models of sociopolitical and cultural practices that helped them to centralise power and elevate their status in the wider region. These changes, however, took their own form in Silla Korea.

Across the sea to the west, the extensive territories of Tang China meant that its rulers were engaging with different neighbours in multiple directions.[4] To the east and south lay a lengthy coastline, while to the north it shared borderlands with pastoral nomads of the steppe, to the west with the Tibetan empire (c. 600–866; Chinese: Tubo), and further regimes to the southwest. Early Tang rulers took an expansionist approach, seeking to extend their territories into the Korean Peninsula, Mongolia, northern Vietnam and Central Asia. During the 600s Tang China triumphed over the Eastern and Western Türks from the Mongolian Plateau and established the Anxi ('Pacifying the West') protectorate, with garrisons reaching as far as Suyab (present-day Ak-Beshim in Kyrgyzstan, see chapter 3). Tang China's nominal influence extended even further, reaching Uzbekistan and Afghanistan. In 751 Tang forces fought and lost against an army of the ʿAbbasid caliphate at Talas near the modern border of Kyrgyzstan and Kazakhstan. Neither side pressed further, and the moment may be seen as a symbolic end to Tang expansion.[5] More significant to Tang China was the rebellion from 755 to 763 of An Lushan (703–757) – a general of Turko-Sogdian background – which substantially weakened the central government. Furthermore, a campaign of persecution against foreign religions, including Buddhism, took place in the 840s under Emperor Wuzong (r. 840–46).[6] Following these events, the demographic, cultural and economic centre increasingly shifted towards cities in southern China (see pp. 63–71).

The expansion of Tang China into Central Asia, coupled with its later turn towards maritime interactions along the coast, led to a period of heightened developments in regional as well as long-distance activities. The emergence of new political centres in the Korean Peninsula and the Japanese archipelago introduced new contexts for the Silk Roads that extended to the eastern extremities of Eurasia. Through the lens of their three capital cities – Heijō-kyō (Nara) in Nara Japan, Geumseong (Gyeongju) in Silla Korea and Chang'an (Xi'an) in Tang China – it is possible to uncover nuanced and intriguing interactions between these three states in East Asia, as well as their connections with the wider world.

Nara Japan

In the eighth century, Nara Japan's capital Heijō-kyō was an important stop along the Silk Roads. The city is home to an extraordinary collection of objects preserved in the Shōsōin Imperial Treasury, which includes imported luxury items and motifs from the distant lands of Byzantium and the Sasanian empire in West Asia, as well as from Central Asia and, in closer proximity, Tang China and Silla Korea.[7] Mostly dating to the 600s and 700s, objects in the Shōsōin (meaning a storehouse of an important establishment) originated from the personal collection of Emperor Shōmu (r. 724–49). After his death in 756, his consort Empress Kōmyō (701–760) dedicated treasured items of his to the Buddha Vairocana at the Tōdai-ji Temple. The collection has remained almost intact and preserved in remarkable condition to the present day. Dating from the mid-700s, the original storehouse holding the empress's donations still stands in the Tōdai-ji complex in Nara.

The objects in the Shōsōin Imperial Treasury are diverse, ranging from religious implements and musical instruments to manuscripts, textiles, furnishings and accessories. It is generally believed that most of the imported objects in the repository arrived in Japan through diplomatic and religious channels via Tang China. Among them are at least two glass vessels of West Asian origin: a hemispherical bowl with hexagonal faceted sides (fig. 1.1) and a transparent white glass ewer with a handle.[8] The glass bowl has been dated to the sixth century and so it was already an antique piece when it entered the repository, while the ewer may be from a later date.[9] By the time of Shōmu's reign, glass carried Buddhist associations. When the Chinese monk Jianzhen (688–763; Japanese: Ganjin) travelled to Japan, he brought with him ritual objects, including Buddhist relics kept in a greenish glass bottle probably from a western country.[10] It is possible that the glass bowl in the Shōsōin also arrived in Japan in a Buddhist context.[11] A similar faceted glass bowl is depicted on a Buddhist banner painting of a bodhisattva from Dunhuang in northwest China (see fig. 2.24). Actual West Asian glass vessels dated to the Sasanian and Islamic periods have been discovered in northwest China, suggesting the overland routes along which such objects may have been transported eastward.[12] Another possibility is that West Asian glass arrived in Japan through Indian Ocean maritime interactions, together

with ceramic jars with a turquoise glaze from Iraq, sherds of which have been discovered in northwest Kyūshū and southern Honshū.[13]

Indeed, imports from distant lands have been found not only in the Shōsōin, but at other sites in Japan as well. A similar type of faceted glass bowl, with nearly identical dimensions to the one in the imperial repository, was excavated from the mausoleum of Emperor Ankan (r. 531–6) in Osaka.[14] Fragments of Sasanian glass vessels have also been excavated from shrines of Japan's native Shintō belief system in Kyōto and in Okinoshima, off the coast of Kyūshū.[15] Apart from vessels, West Asian glass beads have also been found in archaeological contexts in Japan, including a string of blue beads dating to the 500s (fig. 1.2). Seventeen of these beads have recently undergone non-destructive scientific analysis at the British Museum.[16] The results indicate that fourteen were made of a plant-ash glass composition (consistent with Sasanian production), while the other three have characteristics suggesting that they were not Sasanian but of another high-potash type found in many parts of Asia, pointing to the existence of several different sources of glass in Japan.[17]

Interregional trade and diplomatic exchanges

Since ancient times, people from the mainland have moved to Japan, bringing with them artisanal skills and other knowledge.[18] Silla's conquest in 660 of the Baekje kingdom in the southwestern part of the Korean Peninsula, in an alliance with Tang China, resulted in a new wave of migration to Japan. Among those who sought refuge were members of the Baekje aristocracy who were familiar with the language of the elites of China.[19] They became advisors to Japanese rulers and contributed to the spread of culture from the mainland to Japan.[20] Diplomatic missions were also exchanged between Japan, the polities in the Korean Peninsula and China. Envoys presented goods to their host and received gifts in return as a material expression of the diplomatic relationship. 'Exotic' animals were appreciated as special gifts.[21] For instance, in 599 an envoy from Baekje presented a camel, a donkey, two sheep and a white pheasant to the Japanese ruler.[22] Ginseng, honey and animal furs came from envoys from a new kingdom known in Chinese sources as Bohai (Korean: Balhae), which emerged to the north of Silla from 698 to 926.[23] Silk in different forms was the main gift that the Japanese court gave in return.[24] The relationship between Japan and Silla Korea had been uneasy since the latter's conquered Japan's closest ally, Baekje, thereby becoming a rival in the region.[25] However, despite the tension, frequent trade missions were exchanged between them. A Japanese account from 752 mentions goods purchased from Silla, including plant, animal and mineral substances used for medicines, perfumes and dyes, as well as everyday items and ritual instruments.[26]

By the 600s Japan's direct links with Sui-Tang China grew in importance as Japanese rulers sought to adopt Chinese models of administration and learning.[27] From 630 to 894, the Japanese court sent multiple diplomatic missions to the Tang dynasty, fifteen of which reached the capital Chang'an.[28] By the 700s a mission was typically made up of around 500 people travelling on four ships.[29] They included the ambassador and other officials, accompanied by scholars, monks, sculptors and various craftspeople, as well as the crew of the ships.[30] Early voyages took a 'northern' route that passed along the west coast of the Korean Peninsula to arrive in Dengzhou in Shandong province, China.[31] Later, when the political situation changed, the missions travelled south before crossing the East China Sea to reach the mouth of the Yangzi River. The journey was arduous. As many as twelve vessels sent by the Japanese court were shipwrecked.[32] Upon arrival, some members of the mission continued the journey to the Tang capital, while others stayed in the port city, where their activities were supervised by local authorities.[33] Scholars and monks on these missions may have chosen to stay behind in China for longer.[34]

One of the Japanese representatives to Tang China was Mino no Okamaro (662–728), whose bronze epitaph was discovered in the foothills of Mount Ikoma in the Nara prefecture (fig. 1.3). According to this epitaph, he was an official who was appointed to be an envoy to Tang China in 701.[35] On the same mission was the monk Dōji (d. 744; Chinese: Daoci) who ended up staying in Chang'an for sixteen years.[36] After his return to Japan, Dōji became a high-ranking monk in charge of rebuilding the major Buddhist Daian-ji Temple in Nara. By 716 Mino had also returned to Japan, becoming a government official and serving as Director of the Bureau of Palace Equipment and Upkeep in the Ministry of the Imperial Household.[37] Crucially, the promotion of envoys to important positions after their return facilitated the transmission of culture from Tang China. Mino's epitaph was created in 730, two years after his death. It is written neatly in Chinese in columns, arranged vertically from right to left following Chinese convention. The first half of the text records key moments in his career, while the second half highlights his qualities of caution and loyalty to the emperor based on the *Classic of Filial Piety* (*Xiaojing*), a Chinese text dating to the fourth or third century BCE. It is not surprising that Mino's epitaph would show strong connections with Tang China given his role as an envoy, but it also demonstrates how figures in Japanese society were adopting Chinese cultural conventions.

The goods that Japanese envoys presented to the Tang court included amber, agate, crystal, silver, silk fabric and floss, other textiles and camellia oil.[38] In return, according to one account in 805, they received silk, perfumes and medicines.[39] Books were also in high demand.[40] In addition, envoys made purchases in markets in Chang'an and coastal cities.[41] The collection of the Shōsōin provides an indication of the types of object that Japanese envoys may have brought back with them. Official visits also went in the other direction. In the 660s, during its attempted expansion into the Korean Peninsula, the Tang court sent several ambassadors to Japan.[42] Later on, it occasionally dispatched officials and other individuals to accompany Japanese missions on their return journey.[43] Additionally, Japanese envoys actively sought to persuade talented individuals to go to Japan.[44] The Chinese monk Jianzhen was invited to travel there to spread Buddhist teachings and perform ordinations. He managed to reach Japan in 753 on his sixth attempt, the previous five having been foiled by internal disputes or poor weather conditions.[45] In 736 a return mission from China included three Tang subjects and one Persian, as well as Chinese and Indian monks, bringing further international connections to Japan.[46] The inscription on a wooden tablet dated to 765, excavated from the site of the palace in Nara, indicates that there was an official at the Japanese court who came from Persia (*hashi*).[47]

Diplomatic relations between China and Japan ceased after 839 because of the weakening of the Tang central government and political unrest. Nevertheless, networks between the two states and the flow of goods continued through private traders as well as Buddhist monks who, on one reported occasion, travelled to Tang China on a merchant ship with financial support from the Japanese court.[48]

Heijō-kyō (Nara) and the formation of Nihon

Japan's adoption and adaptation of Tang Chinese models in the seventh and eighth centuries is given its most visible form in the construction of the capital Heijō-kyō, later known as Nara, which emulated the layout of Chang'an, the main capital of Tang China (see fig. 1.21). It was not the first Chinese-style capital in Japan – that had been Fujiwara-kyō, located not far from Nara and the

使人　　　　　　　　以
于甲　　　　　　　　短
唐　　　　　　　　　天
生　国平城官　　　　務
平　　　　　　　　　定
□　歳次丙辰　　　　　
□　　五　　　　　　　
公天　生歳次八　　　　
　平　　　　　　　　　
　　　午花五　　　　　

任□殿二年寮頭神龜五生歳次八　事壽多才
　　　　　　　　亀　　　　　　　　
　　　　　　　　五　　　　　　　　

卑春秋六十心能秀其巨爲人　　成功屬興観書
　　　　　　　　　下成　　　　　　　　
　　　　　　　　　　功　　　　　　　　
　　　　　　　　　　屬　　　　　　　　

定忠前帝顯親遺不懲之長示
高榮揚名作斯之納□中臺
庚無窮伊天平二年歳次戊辰午

capital from 694 to 710 – but Heijō-kyō is better known, and institutions there have, remarkably, survived to the present day.[49] Heijō-kyō measured around 4.8 kilometres north–south and 5.7 kilometres east–west (fig. 1.4).[50] A conservative estimate of its population in the 700s is 70,000 to 100,000.[51]

Like Chang'an, Heijō-kyō was laid out in a grid fashion, with the imperial palace located to the north and centre of the city. The ceremonial buildings of the palace followed the Chang'an model, with bays and wooden pillars supporting large tiled roofs.[52] This is reflected in the Kōdō (lecture hall) of the Buddhist Tōshōdai-ji Temple that was originally part of the palace (fig. 1.5).[53] However, the layout of Nara differed from Chang'an in several ways, notably the absence of a surrounding city wall.[54] Another difference is that, while both Chang'an and Heijō-kyō were built to be permanent capitals, the older tradition of moving courts from site to site persisted in Japan.[55] Tang Chinese models were adapted to suit the needs of the Japanese context.

This approach extended to many other aspects of society during the Nara period, including the legal system, government administration and the written language. As Tang China extended its reach into the Korean Peninsula in a coalition with the Silla kingdom in the 660s, the process of reform and centralisation accelerated and intensified in Japan.[56] The earliest native histories of Japan were written during the Nara period. These were the *Records of Ancient Matters* (*Kojiki*), compiled in 712, and the *Chronicles of Japan* (*Nihon shoki* or *Nihongi*), completed in 720 (fig. 1.6). References to Chinese models are clear in both books. The *Records of Ancient Matters* were written using Chinese characters to convey

1.3 *opposite*

Epitaph of Mino no Okamaro, envoy to Tang China, 730. Excavated at Aoyamadai, Ikoma-shi, Nara, Japan. Bronze. H. 29.7 cm, W. 20.9 cm, D. 0.2 cm. Important Cultural Property. Tokyo National Museum, Tokyo, J-39204.

1.4 *top*

Map of Heijō-kyō.

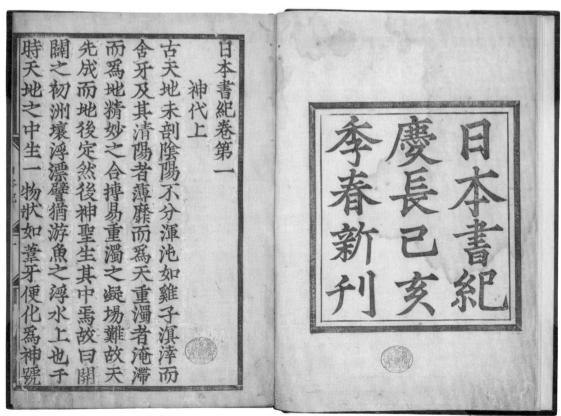

日本書紀卷第一

神代上

古天地未剖陰陽不分渾沌如雞子溟涬而含牙及其清陽者薄靡而爲天重濁者淹滯而爲地精妙之合搏易重濁之凝竭難故天先成而地後定然後神聖生其中焉故曰開闢之初洲壤浮漂譬猶游魚之浮水上也于時天地之中生一物狀如葦牙便化爲神號

1.5 *top*

Kōdō (Lecture Hall), Tōshōdai-ji, Nara, built during the Nara period.

1.6 *left*

Chronicles of Japan (Nihon shoki), Keichō edition, 1599. Japan. Ink on paper. H. 28.6 cm, W. 20.6 cm (each page). The British Library, London, Or 59.bb.5.

the sounds of Japanese words, but the *Chronicles of Japan* were composed entirely in Chinese in the manner of Chinese historical annals. Combining myth and historical narratives, these texts elevated and legitimised the imperial family by tracing their ancestry to the gods.[57] The latter work highlights the newly adopted name for Japan, Nihon (also Nippon) in its title, replacing the older written name of Wa.[58] With characters meaning 'Origin of the Sun', this remains the Japanese name for the country today. Japanese rulers at this time also adopted the written title of *tennō* or 'Heavenly Sovereign', based on the title of the Chinese emperor.[59] It is clear that the adoption of Chinese conventions in Japan was not a straightforward acceptance of an imported culture, but rather was aimed at transforming Japan into a regional power.

The spread of Buddhism

Buddhism, one of the major religions that travelled along the Silk Roads, provided another link between Japan and the continent. According to the *Chronicles of Japan*, Buddhism was formally introduced to Japan in 552 when the king of Baekje sent a gift of a statue of Shakyamuni Buddha, ritual banners and canopies, sutras and commentaries.[60] Initially opposed by the ritualists of Shintō, Buddhism found official support from the late 500s onwards, although it had probably reached Japan earlier through unofficial channels.[61] Remarkably, acceptance of Buddhism grew at a time when a darker consequence of the Silk Roads was felt in Japan – the spread of disease. In 735, starting from Kyūshū in the south, Japan suffered from a smallpox epidemic that had spread from the continent. The disease reduced the overall population by around 30 per cent.[62] In the midst of this devastation, Emperor Shōmu, to whom the Shōsōin repository would later be dedicated, turned to Buddhist ritual and prayers to provide solace and hope to the people.[63] In the aftermath of the epidemic, Shōmu commissioned the Great Buddha Hall at Tōdai-ji in Nara to house a colossal image of the Buddha Vairocana, as well as other temples in the provinces.

The Buddhist connection between Japan and Korea can be observed in the earliest extant Buddhist sculptures in Japan, some of which are believed to have been imported from the Korean Peninsula.[64] Gilt-bronze images of a seated bodhisattva with one ankle resting on a knee, often referred to as the meditating or pensive bodhisattva, were popular and typically associated with Maitreya, the Buddha of the next age, in both regions.[65] One example from the 600s was found on Mount Nachi, Wakayama, to the south of the Nara prefecture (fig. 1.7). Some scholars have suggested that it came from the Korean Peninsula based on its style and physical properties.[66] Tang China was another major source of Buddhist teachings and art for Japan.[67] The monks Saichō (767–822) and Kūkai (774–835), who studied there, brought the Tiantai and Zhenyan traditions of Buddhism to Japan. These became the Tendai and Shingon schools, respectively, and are still active in Japan today.

Sovereigns in Japan adopted Buddhism and utilised it to consolidate their power. In addition to the building of temples, another large-scale state-sponsored Buddhist project was the 'One Million Pagodas and *Dharani* Prayers' (*Hyakumantō darani*), commissioned by Empress Shōtoku (r. 749–58 as Kōken, r. 764–70 as Shōtoku) (fig. 1.8). Each of the miniature wooden pagodas encased a printed and rolled-up Buddhist invocation (*dharani*) in Chinese taken from the *Sutra of the Dharani of Pure Unsullied Light* (Chinese: *Wugou jingguang da tuoluoni jing*) (fig. 1.9).[68] One hundred thousand of them were distributed among ten major monasteries. This is the earliest record of printing in Japan, a new technology that had also spread from the continent. The copying and placement of the *dharani* in miniature pagodas was believed to have the power to prolong life. However, the large scale of the commission indicates other motivations – the commission took

place after Shōtōku's victory over her main rival in 764 and demonstrates her control of resources and her role as protector of the state through her patronage of Buddhism. Intriguingly, Shōtōku may have been inspired by Wu Zetian (also known as Wu Zhao, r. 690–705) in China, who also used Buddhism to legitimise her position as a female emperor (see p. 53). Under Wu's reign, the aforementioned sutra was translated into Chinese from Sanskrit. Evidence of similar acts of piety is also seen in Silla Korea. For instance, 157 miniature clay pagodas (not containers) were discovered inside the stone Kilsangtap pagoda, dating to 895, at the Haeinsa temple. According to a pagoda record, they were enshrined along with a copy of the sutra.[69] The veneration of this *dharani* is another example of shared Buddhist interests across East Asia during this period.

Silla Korea

Silla has been described as a 'kingdom of gold'.[70] Its royal capital was located in the southeast and known by various names, including 'Geumseong'.[71] Archaeological excavations of large royal burial mounds (dating from the 300s CE to the first half of the 500s) at the site (present-day Gyeongju) have uncovered spectacular gold objects. One example is an ornate necklace comprised of small leaf-shaped pieces attached to openwork beads (fig. 1.10). Dated to the early 500s, it exemplifies the luxury enjoyed by the royalty of Silla and the connection between gold and power in the kingdom at the beginning of this period. The curved jade pendant hanging from the necklace also points to a link between the Korean Peninsula and the Japanese archipelago. While the origins and ancient meanings of such 'comma-shaped' ornaments are debated, it seems that during the fourth to sixth centuries, examples made of jade were only produced in these regions.[72] Jade (specifically jadeite) was also one of the materials that was traded from Japan to the Korean Peninsula.[73]

The construction of these Silla burials, consisting of a wooden chamber covered with stone then an earthen mound, resembles the funerary practice of pastoral nomads in the steppe.[74] Foreign imports were among the burial goods found in these tombs, particularly beads and vessels made of glass which, together with examples from Japan discussed earlier, suggest trading networks for this material in both raw and finished form in the East Asia region.[75] At least twenty-six glass vessels have been excavated from the royal tombs of Silla.[76] Judging by their shape and technique, most of them are of the late Roman type originally produced in the eastern Mediterranean, such as in present-day Israel, Lebanon and Syria, in the 300s and 400s CE.[77] One dark-blue glass cup excavated from the Cheonmachong (Heavenly Horse Tomb) dates from the early sixth century (fig. 1.11).[78] It has a honeycomb-patterned decoration that was produced using a mould-blowing technique. This type of glass vessel has been found across Roman territory, as well as in the Caucasus and Black Sea region.[79] Recent scientific analysis indicates that the vessel was most likely produced in Egypt, which had a major centre of glassmaking in Alexandria.[80] Cheonmachong was the resting place of a royal male figure whose burial goods also included a gold crown, accessories, swords and a saddle flap decorated with the image of a flying horse (the namesake of the tomb).[81]

Luxury imported objects have not only been found in large royal tombs. An exceptional example is an iron dagger encased in a richly decorated wooden scabbard from Gyerim-ro Tomb 14, a relatively small burial from the early 500s (fig. 1.12).[82] The dagger has corroded but inorganic parts of the sheath and hilt remain well preserved.[83] The gold surface is decorated with cells in a variety of shapes inset with garnets and glass, known as the cloisonné technique. The lower part of the sheath has a distinctive trapezoid shape. The form and crafting of this object, as well as the composition of the gold, which has been scientifically analysed, indicate that it was not made in Silla.[84] Instead, it combines a popular shape from northwest China and Central Asia with the cloisonné technique that may have developed in the Black Sea, Caucasus or West Asian region. And so it is possible that the dagger and sheath were also produced at this likely source of the technique and then brought to Silla.[85] Another possibility, however, is that they were commissioned by a patron from northwest China or Central Asia and made by an artisan from there who was familiar with garnet cloisonné.[86] The garnets on the dagger may also have come from afar, since South Asia and Central Europe were known to be sources for this gemstone. Gyerim-ro Tomb 14 was a joint burial for two men, one of whom was wearing the dagger on his waist.[87] Although the modest size of the tomb suggests that it was not a royal burial like Cheonmachong,

1.10 *above*

Necklace, early 500s. Excavated from Noseo-dong no. 215 Tomb, Gyeongju, Korea. Gold and jade. L. 30.3 cm, D. 1.1 cm (bead), L. 3.3 cm (magatama). Treasure. National Museum of Korea, Seoul, Bongwan13613, Sinsu1287.

1.11 *opposite top*

Cup, early 500s. Excavated from Cheonmachong Tomb, Gyeongju, Korea. Glass. H. 7.4 cm, D. 7.3 cm (mouth). Treasure. Gyeongju National Museum, Gyeongju, Gyeongju2386.

1.12 *opposite bottom left*

Dagger and scabbard, late 400s to early 500s. Excavated from Gyerim-ro Tomb no. 14, Gyeongju. Gold, garnets, glass, iron and wood. L. 36 cm, W. 9.05 cm. Treasure. Gyeongju National Museum, Gyeongju, Gyeongju42429.

1.13 *opposite bottom right*

Twin stone pagodas at the Gameunsa Temple, Gyeongju, Korea, where reliquaries were found.

the deceased were very likely of high status given the fine burial objects found in the tomb, which also included horse accessories and traces of silk clothing. The Gyerim-ro dagger offers a striking parallel with other garnet cloisonné artefacts that were also products of the Silk Roads network – these ones were found at the other end of Eurasia in a ship burial at Sutton Hoo, England (see p. 262).

Buddhism and relic worship

Intriguingly, luxurious goods, including imports from distant lands, disappeared from elite burials in Silla from the mid-500s onwards. As Buddhism became the state religion of Silla between 527 and 535, elites devoted resources to the patronage of Buddhist temples and other monuments instead of adorning themselves with gold and other precious objects to be interred with them in tombs.[88] This change can be observed in the use of imported glass for Buddhist worship, such as in a Buddhist reliquary dated to the 700s found in a pagoda, a structure derived from the stupa, at Songnimsa (Pine Forest Temple) in Chilgok to the northwest of Gyeongju.[89] The reliquary contains a green glass cup from Central Asia, inside of which is a small glass relic bottle. The latter could be from China given its high lead content, although another view suggests that it may have been made in the Korean Peninsula.[90] The relic bottle was intended to hold crystalline 'beads' that were found among the historical Buddha's ashes, known as *sharira*.

As in Nara Japan, Buddhism became a means for the rulers of Silla to stabilise society and strengthen their secular and divine authority. Many state-sponsored temples were built in or near the capital Geumseong, such as Gameunsa, which was constructed in 682 to commemorate King Munmu (r. 661–81), who had united the Three Kingdoms of Silla, Goguryeo and Baekje to form Unified Silla from 668. Gameunsa has a pair of stone pagodas, at 13 metres in height each, one to the east and one to the west of the complex, which are the oldest surviving twin pagodas from Silla (fig. 1.13).[91] Twin pagodas were also a Buddhist architectural format in China and Japan, but the style was particularly popular in Unified Silla, where it became connected to the protection of the state.[92] Reliquaries displaying sophisticated artistry were discovered inside the pagodas of Gameunsa during restoration projects in the twentieth century.[93]

The reliquaries consist of a square outer container made of gilt bronze to which images of the Four Heavenly Kings of the cardinal directions, separately cast, are attached (fig. 1.14).[94] On each panel of the container, the monster masks holding rings in their mouths suggest doorways at which the Heavenly Kings stand guard to protect the relic inside. The relic itself is meant to be stored in a small crystal bottle (fig. 1.15) set in an elaborate inner container shaped like a pavilion. The earliest extant example of a reliquary depicting the Four Heavenly Kings is made of stone and dated to 604 at Shendesi Temple, Shaanxi province, China.[95] It is likely that this type of reliquary spread from China to the Korean Peninsula, where it developed local characteristics. The representation of the Four Heavenly Kings on the reliquaries at Gameunsa, as well as at several other royal memorial temples, indicates that this group of deities had become associated with the protection of the state in Unified Silla.[96]

Originally, relics representing the cremated remains of the Buddha were placed in stupas and worshipped across the Indian subcontinent.[97] As more pilgrims travelled to venerate relics associated with the Buddha, distribution of such sacred items started to develop, as did the appearance of relics outside of India.[98] In 643 the monk Jajang (active late 500s–mid-600s) is said to have brought relics of the Buddha's skull and finger bone from Mount Wutai, a sacred Buddhist mountain in northern China, to Silla.[99] Jajang was one of many Silla monks who travelled to Tang China and beyond in search of Buddhist teachings. Another monk, Hyecho (704–787), supposedly reached as far as Arabia on his journey, crossing present-day China, Vietnam, Indonesia, Myanmar, India, Pakistan and Afghanistan.[100] Silla monks also contributed to the wider development of Buddhism. Wonhyo (617–686), who did not travel to Tang China, nevertheless established a system of Buddhist philosophy based on translated scriptures that was in turn transmitted outwards.[101]

Adapting Tang Chinese models

According to textual sources, the capital Geumseong was about 5.3 by 5.4 kilometres in size in its heyday, which made it slightly larger than Heijō-kyō in Nara Japan.[102] Unlike the latter, however, which was newly established in the 700s, the site of Geumseong had been the capital of Silla since the founding of the kingdom in 57 BCE. From the 670s, rulers of Silla expanded and made changes to the layout of the capital with reference to Chang'an, the capital of Tang China, signalling the new era of Unified Silla.[103] A grid pattern of roads was adopted in the city, forming rectangular residential blocks in a system known as *bangri* (Chinese: *fangli*).[104] However, the city was already centuries old by this time, and the changes had to be adapted to its pre-existing structures. As a result, the grid pattern of roads and residential blocks was less strictly and regularly laid out compared to Chang'an and Heijō-kyō.[105] As in Heijō-kyō, the residential blocks and the city itself were not surrounded by gated walls.[106] New developments took place to the north of the existing palace of Wolseong and the large royal burial mounds that had formed the centre of the city (fig. 1.16).[107]

Changes to the layout of the capital were part of Silla's wider interest in Chinese culture. From the 500s, the Chinese title *wang* (king) for the ruler was adopted, and there was expanded use of the Chinese writing system.[108] Although conflict in the Korean Peninsula resulted in a tense period between Silla and Tang China in the late 600s, relations had normalised by the early 700s.[109] King Seongdeok (r. 702–37) despatched a total of forty-six diplomatic missions to Tang China during his thirty-five-year reign.[110] Diplomatic gifts from Silla Korea typically included silk, precious metals, ginseng, animals and paper.[111] Like the envoys from Japan, Silla representatives were particularly interested in accessing Chinese culture and learning, and these ideas were further disseminated when the State Academy

1.14 *opposite*

Outer container of a reliquary, *c.* 682. From the East Pagoda at Gameunsa Temple, Gyeongju, Korea. Gilt bronze. H. 31 cm, W. 19.9 cm. Treasure. National Museum of Korea, Seoul, Sinsu16424.

1.15 *above*

Reliquary bottle and components for storing *sharira*, *c.* 682. From the East Pagoda at Gameunsa site, Gyeongju, Korea. Crystal and gilt bronze. H. 0.8 cm, W. 1.4 cm (bottle cap); H. 3.6 cm, W. 2.3 cm (crystal bottle); H. 1 cm, W. 1.3 cm (bottle holder). Treasure. National Museum of Korea, Seoul, Sinsu16432.

(Gukhak) was established in Geumseong in 682, modelled on the Tang Imperial Academy (Guozijian).[112] It taught mathematics and the classics associated with the philosopher Confucius (*c.* 551–*c.* 479 BCE), these being two of the six schools of the Tang equivalent.[113] The adoption of Chinese-style education was seen as an enhancement of the training of Silla's aristocratic youth within the existing 'bone-rank system', in which privilege and status were based on a person's relative hereditary proximity to the throne.[114] Additionally, Silla merchants were active in maritime trade between the Korean Peninsula, Japan and eastern China, which would have further contributed to cultural exchange in the region.[115]

New funerary practices

Connections to Tang China and Buddhism also led to the emergence of new burial customs in Silla during the sixth century. The large burial mounds with inaccessible wooden tomb chambers where imported glass vessels were found were replaced by smaller tombs consisting of stone chambers with an entrance.[116] From the eighth century, some royal tombs were arranged with pathways lined with stone sculptures representing civil and military officials as well as animals in a manner derived from Tang tomb structures. Several of these sculptures are notably idiosyncratic in their appearance. An example at the tomb of King Wonseong (r. 785–98) shows a stern-looking bearded warrior with exaggerated facial features holding a club or staff.[117] Some scholars have suggested that these sculptures are indications of contact between the people of Silla and Sogdians from Central Asia (see pp. 105–13) or West Asians.[118]

Another development in Silla at this time was the inclusion of ceramic figures in tombs to serve the deceased in the afterlife, following burial customs from China.[119] Many of the excavated examples are shown dressed in contemporary Tang-style costumes. For instance, a female figure dated to the 700s wears a skirt fastened just over the bust and a loose robe with wide sleeves (fig. 1.17, see fig. 1.24 for comparison), while a male figure is dressed in a robe with a round collar, belt and wide sleeves (fig. 1.18). His hair is wrapped in a kerchief known in Chinese as a *futou*, and he may be holding a tablet typically carried by Chinese officials when

1.17
Female figure, 700s. Excavated from Yonggang-dong Tomb, Gyeongju, Korea. Earthenware. H. 17.2 cm, D. 6.8 cm (base). Gyeongju National Museum, Gyeongju, Gyeongju7506.

1.18
Figure of a civil official, 700s. Excavated from Yonggang-dong Tomb, Gyeongju, Korea. Earthenware. H. 17.1 cm, W. 5.2 cm (shoulder). Gyeongju National Museum, Gyeongju, Gyeongju7499.

meeting the sovereign.[120] The bushy beard of this male tomb figure is a feature typically associated in the Tang context with non-Han Chinese people, but it is not clear whether this was also the case in Silla. These tomb figures corroborate the Silla court's official adoption of Tang dress for men in 649 and for women in 664 following a diplomatic mission by Kim Chun-chu (603–661), later King Muyeol, to Tang China.[121]

Additionally, a notable change in funerary practices in Silla during this time was the widespread adoption of cremation, which was related to the spread of Buddhism.[122] After the deceased were cremated, the ashes were placed in urns and installed in tombs. Ceramic vessels imported from China could be used as funerary urns. A three-footed jar from northern China dated to the first half of 700s was found near the tomb of King Seongdeok (fig. 1.19).[123] Its distinctive splashed glaze belongs to the category of *sancai* ('three-coloured') wares that were often made for burial.[124] Such ceramic tripod jars could be used as incense burners in China but this example may have functioned as a burial object for the deceased to use in the afterlife. In Silla the status of the jar has been transformed into a container for ashes. It was given a silver dish as a cover and was placed into a stone container for burial. It is likely that this vessel was brought back to Silla by a visitor who had travelled to Tang China.[125] Another example of a Chinese ceramic used as a funerary urn in Silla is a celadon jar from the 800s (fig. 1.20). Produced in the Changsha kilns, Hunan province, the jar may originally have been a container for shipping tea in maritime trade.[126] Its cover is a ceramic tea bowl that came from a different kiln site – the Yue kilns in Zhejiang province (see p. 68).[127] It seems that these two objects were brought to the Korean Peninsula separately before they were put together. After being filled with ashes, the jar and cover were placed inside a locally produced earthenware

1.19 opposite top

Three-footed jar with lid, 700–750.
China. Excavated from near the tomb
of King Seongdeok, Gyeongju, Korea.
Earthenware with *sancai* glaze; silver lid.
H. 16.5 cm, Diam. 21.3 cm (jar, body);
Diam. 15.2 cm (jar, mouth), Diam. 16 cm
(lid). Gyeongju National Museum,
Gyeongju, Gyeongju1729.

1.20 opposite bottom

Jar with bowl cover (outer container not
shown), 800s. Changsha kilns, Hunan
province, China (jar); Yue kilns, Zhejiang
province, China (bowl). Excavated from
Samneung tombs, Bae-dong. Stoneware
with celadon glaze. H. 23.8 cm (jar),
Diam. 14 cm (inner container, bowl).
Gyeongju National Museum, Gyeongju,
Gyeongju494.

1.21 right

Map of Chang'an, with indicative
locations of religious sites of worship.

outer container for burial. The presence of these ceramic vessels from Tang China
in Silla Korea provides evidence of the movement of objects across the region, also
showing how they could be adapted and reused to suit local needs.

Tang China

The primary seat of government of the Tang dynasty was Chang'an (present-day
Xi'an) in northcentral China, with a second capital located to its east in Luoyang. In
Chinese historical narratives, the beginning of the Silk Roads is usually attributed
to the journey of the Han-dynasty envoy Zhang Qian, who travelled from the
capital (also called Chang'an, close to present-day Xi'an) to Central Asia and back
in the second century BCE.[128] Although it is situated inland, Chang'an was connected
to overland networks in the west through the flat basin known as the Hexi or
Gansu Corridor. A system of man-made mountain roads led to the southwest, and
riverways to coastal regions in southern China. It was a city of monumental scale,
measuring 9.7 by 8.6 kilometres, covering an inner surface area of about 84 square
kilometres.[129] At its height, it had a population of around one million.[130] The city was
rectangular in shape, with a symmetrical layout and grid plan on a north–south
axis (fig. 1.21). As discussed earlier, this formal grid layout and ward or block system
provided a model for Heijō-kyō (Nara) and, to an extent, Geumseong (Gyeongju).

● Buddhist
● Daoist
● Zoroastrian
● Church of the East

To Wei River

— Waterway
— Possible waterway

N

Daming Palace

Palace City

Eastern Palace

Imperial City

Xingqing Palace

Longshou Canal

Cao Canal

Western Market

Eastern Market

Qingming Canal

Yong'an Canal

Great Wild Goose Pagoda

Huang Canal

0   2 mile
0   2 km

Silk and horses

During the period 500 to 1000, silk from China was a valuable commodity, and the Tang court gave the material in its various forms as diplomatic gifts (see chapter 2). China has an ancient history of producing silk, a luxurious textile appreciated for its softness and strength. Evidence suggests that the breeding of domesticated silkworms (*Bombyx mori*) and the preparation of silk threads from unbroken cocoons may have started in China as early as 2700 BCE.[131] The labour-intensive and time-consuming process involved feeding silkworms large quantities of leaves of the white mulberry tree (*Morus alba*).[132] Sericulture or silk farming spread from China around 100 BCE and continued during the first millennium CE.[133] A wooden votive panel from Khotan, in present-day Xinjiang Uyghur Autonomous Region, records the legend of a 'silk princess', presumably Chinese, who introduced sericulture to the Buddhist kingdom (see fig. 2.43). By 1000, there were many centres of sericulture and silk weaving in Eurasia. Nevertheless, silk from China remained highly valued and sought-after, and it was traded as raw silk and in a variety of ready-made fabrics.[134]

Moreover, silk could be used as money along the Silk Roads. In China, silk, hemp and coins had been forms of currency since before the Qin dynasty (221–206 BCE).[135] Bolts of plain silk were collected from households as part of taxation. The standard bolt of plain silk for taxation payments during the Tang dynasty measured about 12 metres by 54 centimetres.[136] A smaller bolt of silk from Loulan, another site in Xinjiang, dating to the 200s to 300s CE, is a rare survival that gives an idea of the appearance of this valuable material (fig. 1.22). It may have been brought to Loulan as payment for soldiers who were stationed in Chinese garrisons.[137] The practice of paying troops with textiles continued in the Tang dynasty. In the 730s or 740s, the central government sent 900,000 bolts of silk to four military headquarters in the frontier regions of northwest China: Hami, Turpan, Beiting and Kucha.[138] The silk could then be used to pay salaries and to purchase food and equipment.[139] These payments injected money into local economies, which further stimulated commercial activities along the Silk Roads.[140]

One of the commodities that the Tang court coveted and paid for with silk in large quantities was horses. Horses were needed for the military, transport and communication, as well as pageantry and entertainment. While there were government ranches, the pastoral nomads in the northwest were a major source of horses for the Tang court.[141] A market register from Xizhou (Turpan), dated 742, shows the prices for different grades of horses at the time – for example, eighteen bolts of wide-loom tabby silk for an ordinary Turkic gelding (castrated male horse).[142] It is estimated that the total number of horses in use in Tang China during the early 700s was roughly several hundred thousand, while the number of replacement horses needed each year was probably in the tens of thousands.[143]

1.22 *opposite*

Bolt of silk, 200–400. Excavated from Loulan, China. H. 3.4 cm, W. 48 cm, D. 6.4 cm. British Museum, London, MAS.677.a–b. Stein collection.

1.23 *top*

Figure of a horse, 700–50. Northern China. Earthenware with *sancai* glaze. H. 76 cm, W. 84 cm, D. 28 cm. Victoria and Albert Museum, London, C.50-1964. Gift of Mrs Robert Solomon.

The Tang elite's appreciation for horses is evident in the many muscular and naturalistic ceramic horses that have been excavated from Tang tombs, often accompanied by figures of grooms or riders. One example shows the horse decorated with elaborate harness ornaments, including pendants called *xingye* ('apricot leaf'), which was an imported design, probably from the Sasanian empire (fig. 1.23).[144] Horse riding was popular among both elite men and women during the Tang dynasty. Aristocrats also enjoyed hunting on horseback as well as the game of polo, which may have been introduced from Persia or the Tibetan empire.[145] This equestrian culture was enjoyed by the imperial Li family, which had a mixed Chinese and Xianbei (Serbi or Särbi, a pastoral nomadic group) background.[146] Taizong (r. 626–49), the second emperor of the Tang dynasty who conquered the Eastern Türks, declared himself both a Chinese August Emperor (*huangdi*) and Heavenly Khagan, the supreme ruler of the Turko-Mongol peoples.[147] The eldest son of Taizong spoke the Turkic language and even set up a Turkic camp with tents in the imperial palace.[148] Tang elite women in wealthy households enjoyed relatively greater physical freedoms in comparison with other periods in China's history, and this has also been attributed to exposure to steppe customs.[149] Ceramic tomb figures include ladies dressed fashionably, such as with piled hair (fig. 1.24) or wearing men's riding costumes (see fig. 1.36). At the same time, the Tang period saw the establishment of standard editions of Confucian classics and official schools for teaching them, as well as the wider implementation of an examination system for entry into the civil service – developments that were adapted in Silla Korea and Nara Japan.[150] A set of ceramic tomb figures excavated from a general's tomb in Luoyang includes a large figure of a civil official dressed in ceremonial clothing (fig. 1.25). At its peak, the Tang dynasty not only was receptive to foreign elements but also developed institutions and cultural traditions that were rooted in the history of imperial China.

Foreigners in Chang'an

As the capital and a metropolis, Chang'an attracted people from all directions. The Eastern and Western Markets were the primary centres of commercial activity in the city and operated under the control of the central government. By the 700s the Eastern Market was surrounded by the homes of the nobility and high-ranking officials, while the Western Market was more raucous and attracted a greater number of foreign merchants.[151] The markets opened for business at midday, signalled by 300 drumbeats, and closed at dusk with 300 beats of gongs.[152] Trains of camels carrying a variety of products would have been a common sight at the height of the city's prosperity. Tang ceramic figures with *sancai* glazes made for burials include lively representations of camels carrying items that were imported to, and exported from, China. In one example, a Bactrian camel with two humps carries coiled silk, folded fabric, a West or Central Asian ewer and possibly a piece of rib meat next to bags covered with monster masks (fig. 1.26).[153]

1.24 *right*
Female figure, 700–50. Northern China. Earthenware with *sancai* glaze. H. 33.1 cm, W. 11.2 cm, D. 10.3 cm. British Museum, London, 1936,1012.135. Purchased from George Eumorfopoulos.

1.25 *far right*
Figure of an official, 728. From the tomb of Liu Tingxun, Henan province, China. Earthenware with *sancai* glaze. H. 107.3 cm, W. 29 cm, D. 29 cm. British Museum, London, 1936,1012.221. Purchased from George Eumorfopoulos.

1.26 *opposite*
Figure of a camel, 728. From the tomb of Liu Tingxun, Henan province, China. Earthenware with *sancai* glaze. H. 82.4 cm, W. 68.3 cm, D. 28.8 cm. British Museum, London, 1936,1012.228. Purchased from George Eumorfopoulos.

1.27 *left*
Mural from Li Xian's tomb showing foreign ambassadors at the Tang court, 706. Qianling Mausoleum, Shaanxi province.

1.28 *below*
Figure of a lion, *c.* 700–50. Possibly Gongxian kilns, Henan province. Earthenware with amber glaze. H. 26 cm. Private collection.

Diplomatic envoys from foreign lands paying tribute were a common presence in Chang'an. Missions came from as far away as West Asia, such as when Yazdegerd III (r. 632–51) of the Sasanian dynasty sought assistance from the Tang court to oppose threats from Türks and Arabs.[154] Wall paintings from the tomb of Li Xian (653–684), a crown prince of the Tang dynasty, in the Qianling Mausoleum in Shaanxi province depict foreign dignitaries being received by Tang officials (fig. 1.27). There has been much speculation about the ethnic identities of the foreigners depicted. In the scene on the east wall, the figure with feathers in his headdress is probably an envoy from Silla Korea, while the one wearing fur is very likely from the northeast of China. The interpretation of the third person's origins, with distinctly non-Han Chinese features, has ranged from Byzantium to the oasis kingdom of Kucha.[155] A range of 'exotic' gifts were presented at the capital by such envoys, including lions from Central and West Asia. In 719 one embassy presented two lions on behalf of 'Fulin', usually interpreted as Byzantium.[156] Lions became a common subject in Tang material and visual culture, as illustrated by a fierce-looking ceramic figure in a rare amber glaze that could have served as a guardian in a religious or ritual context (fig. 1.28).

It is not certain exactly how many foreigners lived in Chang'an, and the numbers must have fluctuated and at times been sizeable. Written records indicate that there was a significant number of people who came to Chang'an involuntarily, including many captives of war as well as refugees, who were brought to the capital during Tang China's military expansion. For instance, in 668, after the defeat of the Goguryeo kingdom in the Korean Peninsula, 200,000 people were resettled in and around Chang'an.[157] One of their descendants, Gao Xianzhi or Go Seonji (d. 756), became a Chinese military commander and fought in the Battle of Talas against Arab forces in 751.[158] Many Türks were taken captive during their conflict with Tang China. In 631, when Emperor Taizong overcame the Eastern Türks,

nearly 10,000 households were forced to move to Chang'an.[159] The Tang court also kept hostages from places that had pledged loyalty to them.[160]

One of the most notable foreigners to spend time in Chang'an was Firuz (also Peroz, d. 677), son of Yazdegerd III, the last ruler of the Sasanian dynasty. Firuz sought refuge in Chang'an in 674 after the fall of the Sasanian capital at Ctesiphon to Muslim forces, most likely accompanied by an entourage.[161] After Firuz's death in Chang'an, the Tang emperor bestowed his son Narsieh with the title of King of Persia (*Bosi wang*) and had him escorted to Tokharistan in Central Asia (see p. 54) where he was put under the protection of the local Türk ruler. In 708 Narsieh returned to Chang'an, where he died shortly afterwards.[162] Although no material trace of this royal line survives, a probable descendant of the Sasanian exiles has been identified on a bilingual Chinese–Pahlavi (Middle Persian) tomb epitaph excavated at Chang'an. The epitaph commemorates Mawash (849–874), known in Chinese as Lady Ma, who was a follower of Zoroastrianism.[163] Mawash was a member of the Suren clan, as was her husband, who held the position of honorary commander of the imperial guards known as the Shence Army, a post granted to foreign princes and envoys.[164] Dated to 874, this bilingual epitaph shows that descendants of Persian refugees held on to their identity and historical connections long after the fall of the Sasanian empire. The dating in the Pahlavi text uses Sasanian, Chinese and Islamic numbering systems, indicating the scribe's awareness of different cultural practices.[165]

Tang material and visual culture also include representations of people with foreign backgrounds, such as ceramic tomb figures that were meant to serve the deceased in the afterlife.[166] The majority of such figures have been unearthed from elite tombs in Chang'an and the eastern capital Luoyang, notably from the High Tang period, from the second half of the seventh century to the first half of the eighth century.[167] These figures are recognisable by stereotypical features

1.31

Southeast Asian figure, 618–750.
Northern China. Earthenware with glaze.
H. 30.2 cm, W. 13 cm, D. 8.3 cm. British
Museum, London, 1936,1012.288.
Purchased from George Eumorfopoulos.

of 'deep eyes' and 'high noses', beards and wavy or braided hair, characteristics associated with peoples from the north and west of Tang China, broadly referred to as *hu* in Chinese.[168] One example wears a riding costume with wide lapels and narrow sleeves as well as a distinctive tall hat (fig. 1.29). His posture, with both hands fisted, suggests that the figure was probably meant to be a groom and paired with a horse or camel, like the *sancai* example noted earlier (see fig. 1.26). *Hu* tomb figures are also portrayed as attendants, musicians and entertainers, merchants carrying goods for sale (fig. 1.30) and, less commonly, civil and military officials. They presumably reflect the typical roles of *hu* people in Tang China's major cities.

Another related group of Tang ceramic tomb figures depicts people with dark skin and wavy hair, some with their upper bodies exposed and trousers rolled up like a *dhoti* (long loincloth) (fig. 1.31). Since the third century CE, dark or 'black'-skinned people have been referred to in Chinese sources as *Kunlun* or 'enslaved people of *Kunlun*' (*Kunlun nu*), the meanings of which have been widely debated.[169] These terms became more prevalent during the Tang dynasty, particularly in reference to Southeast Asia.[170] Another term for dark-skinned people, *sengqi* (also *cengqi*), appeared in Tang and more frequently Song-dynasty (960–1279) sources. Polities in Southeast Asia (Chinese: *Nanhai*, 'southern seas') sent enslaved *sengqi* people, including women and boys, to the Tang court as tribute.[171] Some scholars relate this term to the Arabicised Persian *zanj* ('country of the blacks'), referring to regions in Africa.[172] It has also been suggested that there is a subgroup of Tang tomb figures that represent people from the African continent.[173] On the whole, most Tang tomb figures portrayed with dark skin are thought to represent enslaved people from Southeast Asia, such as the Malay archipelago, who were involuntarily taken to Tang China through trade or tribute (on slavery in Tang China, see pp. 88–9).

Interestingly, very few ceramic tomb figures depicting non-Han Chinese women have been discovered in Tang tombs. It has been estimated that, out of 700 archaeologically excavated non-Han Chinese Tang tomb figures, only 20 of them represent women, less than 3 per cent.[174] This is in contrast to the many references in Chinese poetry and written sources to foreign women, particularly Sogdians (*huji*), often in the context of female entertainers and drinking companions.[175] Perhaps owing to their low social status and association with entertainment districts, representations of foreign women may have been considered less appropriate for inclusion in elite tombs.[176]

Diverse religions in the capital

The early Tang government took a tolerant stance towards foreign religions, permitting followers to practise their faiths and to establish places of worship in the capital alongside the two dominant religions in China – Daoism and Buddhism. Daoism enjoyed special status during the Tang dynasty because the imperial Li family claimed to be descendants of Laozi, popularly known as the founder of Daoism who flourished in the sixth century and was later venerated as a supreme deity. At the beginning of the Tang dynasty, Emperor Gaozu (r. 618–26) decreed that Daoism ranked above Buddhism.[177] However, since its introduction to China in the early centuries CE, Buddhism had established itself among both the elite and ordinary people. As a result, it continued to enjoy popularity throughout much of the dynasty and competed with Daoism for imperial favour. The Japanese monk Ennin (794–864), who visited Chang'an, observed that the city boasted 300 Buddhist temples, each adorned with statues and other sacred objects.[178] Believers could also worship in their own homes, using small images. One such example depicts Padmapani ('Lotus Bearer'), a form of the bodhisattva Avalokiteshvara or Guanyin (fig. 1.32). This sculpture exhibits natural curves and flowing clothing that show the continuation of artistic elements from the Indian subcontinent, as adapted in Tang China.

Monks from Tang China travelled long distances in search of Buddhist teachings. One of the most famous was Xuanzang (c. 602–664). Ignoring a ban on foreign travel that Emperor Taizong had imposed on security grounds, he secretly set off in 629 on a trek to India via Central Asia.[179] His triumphant return to Chang'an in 645 was acknowledged and celebrated by the Tang court. He was invited to reside in the newly completed Ci'ensi Temple, which was dedicated to Empress Wende (601–636), the mother of the crown prince, the future Gaozong (r. 649–83).[180] The Buddhist scriptures, images and relics that Xuanzang brought back from his journey were intended for storage there. At the temple complex, the imperial court established a translation bureau with Xuanzang as its head.[181] Additionally, a stupa, standing approximately 53 metres tall, was built to house relics of the Buddha.[182] This was replaced in the 700s by a pagoda-style stupa known as Dayanta (Great Wild Goose Pagoda), which, after several reconstructions, still stands today (fig. 1.33).

Buddhism in Tang China flourished especially under the rule of Wu Zetian, the consort of Gaozong who took over the throne in 690 and temporarily established her own dynasty. Wu Zetian came from a Buddhist background and used Buddhism to legitimise her rule as the only female emperor in China's history. Her support of Buddhism attracted foreign monks from Central Asia, South and Southeast Asia, the Korean Peninsula and the Japanese islands to work on translation projects in Chang'an and Luoyang.[183] Later, during the reign of Emperor Xuanzong (r. 712–56), three masters of Esoteric Buddhism (see p. 82) arrived in the capital.[184] Shubhakarasimha (637–735; Chinese: Shanwuwei) and Vajrabodhi (671–741; Chinese: Jin'gangzhi) were both from India. The third, and eventually most powerful politically, was Amoghavajra (705–774; Chinese: Bukong). He may have arrived in China from Central Asia as a boy to become Vajrabodhi's student.[185] Held in high regard by successive Tang emperors, Amoghavajra was even bestowed with a ministerial position in the Court of State Ceremonial and elevated to the position of a duke of state (guogong). The teachings of these three masters subsequently spread from Tang China to Japan, providing the foundation for Shingon and Tendai Buddhism.

Manichaeism, Zoroastrianism (also known as Mazdeism) and the Church of the East (East Syriac Christianity, or 'Nestorianism'), belief systems that had spread from Central and West Asia, were the three main religions that communities of immigrants and expatriates practised in Chang'an. Manichaeism, which taught a dualistic cosmology of good and evil, was officially introduced to the Tang court in 694, when a Persian envoy presented Wu Zetian with a copy of a Manichaean scripture (on Manichaeism, see chapter 2).[186] Textual sources record the building of Manichaean places of worship in Chang'an, although their exact locations have not been identified.[187]

Zoroastrianism, the state religion of the Sasanian empire, and worshipped in a local form by Sogdians from Central Asia (see p. 108), may have reached the Chang'an–Luoyang region as early as the 300s CE.[188] Tombs of individuals of Sogdian background – dated to the second half of the 500s and the 600s, and discovered in northern China, including Chang'an – reveal stone funerary furniture carved with imagery that relates to Zoroastrianism.[189] A marble panel carved in relief, now in the Victoria and Albert Museum's collection, was originally the base of a Sogdian funerary couch. Such couches or beds for placing the deceased's remains derived from Chinese burial customs but also aligned with Zoroastrian practice, which avoided contact between the corpse and the sacred elements of earth and water.[190] Faintly visible in the lower centre of this example is a carving of a fire altar, with Zoroastrian 'bird-priests' on either side

1.32
Figure of the bodhisattva Padmapani, 700s. China. Gilt bronze. H. 16.4 cm, W. 6.6 cm, D. 4.7 cm (excl. stand). British Museum, London, 1970,1104.2. Purchased from Spink & Sons, funded by the Brooke Sewell Bequest.

1.33
Great Wild Goose Pagoda, Xi'an,
Shaanxi province, China.

1.34
Funerary couch panel, 550–77.
Northern China. Marble. H. 55.3 cm,
W. 249 cm, D. 11.8 cm. Victoria and
Albert Museum, London, A.54-1937.
Purchased from George Eumorfopoulos
with support from the Art Fund, the
Vallentin Bequest, Sir Percival David
and the Universities China Committee.

of it (fig. 1.34).[191] To the right of this scene are two male dancers with long hair, dressed in riding costume with extended sleeves, identified as Central Asians. This is balanced on the other side by the portrayal of two female dancers wearing long Chinese-style robes. On the two ends of the marble panel and in the upper row are guardian figures and musicians bearing resemblance to Buddhist imagery. The design of such funerary furniture reveals an adoption and adaptation of a variety of elements, and the development of burial practices that were unique to Sogdian immigrants in a Chinese context. By the 700s there were five recorded Zoroastrian establishments in Chang'an, four of them located around the Western Market where many foreign merchants conducted business.[192] Textual records clearly indicate that Sogdians established or frequented two Zoroastrian temples located in the Chonghua and Buzheng wards.[193] These places of worship could also have served the Persian communities in the capital, such as Firuz and his entourage, who sought refuge in Chang'an upon the fall of the Sasanian empire.[194]

The Church of the East, a branch of Christianity that originated in Syria and was established by the Sasanian empire, reached China in the seventh century. Its introduction and propagation in Chang'an is commemorated in a large stela dated 781, discovered in 1625 in the vicinity of the city and now kept in the Xi'an Beilin Museum. The inscribed stone slab of the stela sits on the back of a sculpted Bixi, a mythological dragon with the shell of a turtle, an established form in China. At the apex of the stela is a Christian cross and a title written in large Chinese characters referring to the Church of the East by its Chinese name, Jingjiao (Luminous Religion) (fig. 1.35). The main text carved on the stela is composed in Chinese script, with additional lines and names in Estrangela Syriac script along its base and sides.[195] According to the Chinese inscription, the presence of the Church of the East in Chang'an began in 635 when a priest named Aluoben (possibly the Chinese rendering of the Persian Ardaban) arrived at the capital from a place called Da Qin.[196] In sources from the fifth century CE, Da Qin generally referred to the eastern regions of the Roman empire.[197] There is much debate about the meaning of this term in the context of this stela. It may refer to a wide region that included Persia known in Chinese as *Bosi*, from where the religion spread eastwards.[198]

A priest named Adam in Syriac, or Jingjing in Chinese, is credited with composing the inscription, while the original calligraphy carved onto the stela was written by a Tang official named Lu Xiuyan (active eighth century). The writing highlights the support of successive Tang emperors for the Church of the East that had enabled the establishment of a place of worship in the Yining Ward

1.35

Rubbing of the Xi'an stela. Original stela
781, rubbing probably 1980s. Ink on
paper. H. 183.9 cm, W. 92.2 cm (stela
face). Rubbing: H. 54.6, W. 31.8 cm
(headpiece); H. 187.8 cm, W. 90.5 cm
(face); H. 181.1 cm, W. 27.3 cm (left
side); H. 75.1 cm; W. 26.9 cm (right
side). British Museum, London,
1989,1004,0.1–4. Bequeathed by
Basil Gray.

1.36
Figure of a woman in riding dress, 700–50. Northern China. Earthenware with *sancai* glaze. H. 33 cm, W. 12 cm, D. 7 cm. Victoria and Albert Museum, London, C.815-1936. Purchased from George Eumorfopoulos with support from the Art Fund, the Vallentin Bequest, Sir Percival David and the Universities China Committee in 1936.

and the initial ordination of twenty-one Christian followers.[199] The stela also emphasised the achievements of Adam's father Yazadbozid or Yisi (active mid-eighth century) who came from Balkh in present-day Afghanistan.[200] Yazadbozid received honours for aiding the Tang general Guo Ziyi (696–781) during the An Lushan rebellion.[201] However, the position of the Church of the East in the capital was under threat in 781 when the stela was erected, with high officials petitioning Emperor Dezong (r. 779–805) to impose restrictions on religious institutions to curb their political and economic power.[202] It has been argued that the stela was created as an act of self-promotion and self-protection by followers of Syriac Christianity in Chang'an.[203]

These foreign religions were suppressed alongside Buddhism during the reign of Emperor Wuzong in the mid-ninth century. One of the reasons for this suppression seems to be his fanatical support for Daoism. While Buddhism would subsequently recover, other religions eventually disappeared from Chang'an. Followers of Manichaeism escaped to the coastal provinces of southern China and the religion also found refuge in the Uyghur Kingdom of Kocho in the Tarim Basin to the west (see chapter 2).[204]

Cosmopolitan tastes

At the height of its prosperity, Tang China's urban centres exhibited a penchant for the foreign customs and goods that arrived with the many visitors and immigrants. As noted earlier, Tang elite men and women enjoyed horse riding and associated pastimes. They also adopted clothing that was suitable for equestrian pursuits, typically consisting of a narrow-sleeved robe, trousers, belt and boots. This type of attire was prevalent across Eurasia, developing local characteristics in each region. In Tang China, the robe was typically from mid-calf to ankle in length, with slits on both sides, and a round neckline that could be folded back to form wide lapels.[205] This style of clothing finds its immediate predecessor in the attire worn by the Xianbei peoples of the steppe.[206] A ceramic tomb figure, identifiable as a woman from her hairstyle, is shown wearing a riding dress (fig. 1.36). The deep blue of her robe, coloured with cobalt that was probably imported from Iran, further emphasises the foreign connections of her attire. During the Tang dynasty in the early 600s, this type of clothing, matched with a black headscarf (*futou*), was incorporated into the official sartorial system as everyday dress (*changfu*) for male officials.[207] Furthermore, the Tang court customarily bestowed silk robes and belts upon representatives of foreign states as a symbolic gesture of political bonding and Tang suzerainty.[208]

Apart from clothing, associations with the wider world could also be subtly suggested on the body, as well as in the surrounding spaces, through aromatics.[209] While there existed a range of scents native to China, these were enhanced by further varieties – sandalwood, aloe wood, camphor, frankincense and myrrh all arrived from South and Southeast Asia, as well as from West Asia.[210] The spread of Buddhism, which utilised incense in its rituals, was a conduit for the early import of incense to China from the Indian subcontinent.[211] Lightweight, portable spherical incense burners, crafted with delicate metalwork, emerged during the Tang dynasty (fig. 1.37). Made of two halves joined by a hinge and a bolt, these incense burners have a small bowl nested inside, suspended from two rings that turn on their own axis.[212] This ingenious design, invented during the Han dynasty, ensures that the bowl remains upright and the incense in the bowl does not spill, regardless of movement. Spherical incense burners could also serve as hand warmers or be hung indoors or placed on beds to warm bedding while exuding scent.[213] This type of incense burner would later spread to the Islamic world in the latter part of the twelfth century.

1.37 *left*
Censer, 618–907. China. Silver.
H. 4.3 cm, Diam. 7.5 cm. Victoria and
Albert Museum, London, M.98-1938.
Purchased from George Eumorfopoulos
with support from the Art Fund, the
Vallentin Bequest, Sir Percival David and
the Universities China Committee.

1.38 *below*
Flask showing a dancer and musicians,
500–700. China. Earthenware with
glaze. H. 11.9 cm, W. 9.5 cm, D. 5.6 cm.
British Museum, London, 1936,1012.3.
Purchased from George Eumorfopoulos.

Music and dance from the Tang empire's frontiers and beyond were performed in entertainment districts and at the imperial court in the capital. Poets wrote about beautiful foreign women, probably from Central Asia (*huji*), who captivated their customers with song and dance.[214] A particularly popular type of dance from Central Asia was the 'Sogdian whirl', known in Chinese as *huteng wu* ('foreign leaping dance') and *huxuan wu* ('foreign whirling dance').[215] The dancer would spin and leap while keeping to a small round carpet. A ceramic flask illustrates this type of performance (fig. 1.38). In the centre is a dancer with one arm and one leg raised as he whirls and spins. The small carpet has been transformed into a stylised lotus flower. Surrounding him are spectators as well as musicians playing different instruments. All the figures have exaggerated facial features that suggest they are *hu* people. The 'foreignness' of this object is further indicated by its flat bottle shape, which is derived from pilgrim flasks of West Asian origin.[216]

The two main musicians accompanying the dancer illustrated on the ceramic flask play a lute and a type of harp. A separate pair of ceramic figures of female musicians, intended for burial as part of a larger ensemble, are also shown playing these instruments (fig. 1.39). The pear-shaped lute known as a *pipa* was introduced into China from India and Central Asia by the time of the Han dynasty.[217] It was initially played using a large plectrum (plucking device), but during the Tang dynasty musicians increasingly adopted a finger-plucking technique that became the standard method.[218] The upright harp (*shu konghou*) was also introduced from the west before the Tang dynasty.[219] However, an important development during this period was the systematic integration into the court repertoire of non-Han Chinese music performed on these instruments. Seven out of the 'ten bureaus of performance' (*shibuji*) at the Tang court focused on imported music, from Kucha, Kashgar and Gaochang/Turpan (all in present-day Xinjiang Uyghur Autonomous Region); India; Kang State (Samarkand); An State (Bukhara); and Gaoli (Korean: Goguryeo).[220]

A variety of foreign foods was imported into Tang China because of the thriving Silk Road networks. Examples can be identified by the prefix *hu*,

1.39 *opposite*

Figures of musicians playing a lute and a harp, 671–730. Earthenware with pigment. H. 14.7 cm, W. 9.1 cm, D. 8.3 cm (lute player); H. 15.4 cm, W. 9.1 cm, D. 8.3 cm (harp player). Ashmolean Museum, University of Oxford, EA1991.58 and 59. Bequeathed by J. Gentilli in 1991.

1.40

Tripod dish, 619–907. Northern China. Earthenware with *sancai* glaze. H. 4.9 cm, Diam. 28.7 cm. British Museum, London, 1936,1012.208. Purchased from George Eumorfopoulos.

which broadly means foreign but more specifically from West and Central Asia. Sesame (*huma*), cucumber (*hugua*), walnut (*hutao*) and black pepper (*hujiao*) were all introduced during the Tang dynasty.[221] Other notable examples are the 'golden peaches of Samarkand', and spinach of Persian origin that was introduced to Tang China as a gift from the king of Nepal in 647.[222] 'Foreign cakes' (*hubing*) of various kinds that were baked or steamed were very popular (see p. 94 for examples). Those with meat fillings probably developed into *xianbing*, stuffed wheat-flour pockets that are still commonly eaten today. The popularity of *hubing* may have resulted in the development of larger platters with a flat, shallow surface, which were suited for serving such foods (fig. 1.40).[223]

Although grape wine was known in China from earlier periods, it was during the Tang dynasty that it became a popular beverage (see chapter 2). Sogdians, known for managing alcohol shops in the markets of Chang'an, sold wines imported from the west or made locally with adopted techniques.[224] Imported vessels associated with wine drinking have been discovered in China. A gazelle-headed rhyton (pouring vessel) made of carnelian with a gold muzzle, probably from Central Asia, was discovered in a famous hoard at Hejia Village in Chang'an.[225] Cups imitating the shape of rhyta, but without a spout at the bottom, were produced in ceramic, such as an example made of high-fired whiteware that only Chinese potters could produce at this time (fig. 1.41).[226] The beaded borders and figures wearing Central Asian costumes on each side further suggest the foreignness of its design. Other vessel shapes from the west that were imitated by craftspeople in China include small cups with ring handles that spread to Tang China from the Mediterranean region via the Sogdians of Central Asia (fig. 1.42).[227] A small goblet or stem cup was also based on models from the west, but its decoration of a detailed hunting scene against a ring-punched ground on a silver goblet was developed in China (fig. 1.43).[228]

Ewers derived from West and Central Asia, with their beak-like spouts, narrow necks, long handles and rounded bodies, were imitated in Tang China as well. In the case of a *sancai* ceramic phoenix-head ewer with relief decoration, the beak of the vessel is not perforated, so it could not be used as a pouring vessel (fig. 1.44).[229] Instead, it was meant to be a tomb object for the afterlife, which, like the figures of foreigners and camels, points to the connections with the wider

1.41 *opposite*

Cup in the shape of a rhyton, 618–907.
China. White stoneware. H. 9 cm,
W. 9.4 cm, D. 11.4 cm. British Museum,
London, 1968,0422.21. Bequeathed by
Mrs Walter Sedgwick.

1.42 *far left*

Cup with ring handle, 618–907. China.
Silver. H. 4.9 cm, W. 8.4 cm, D. 6.1 cm.
British Museum, London, 1938,0524.706.
Purchased from George Eumorfopoulos.

1.43 *left*

Stem cup, 618–907. China. Silver.
H. 9.8 cm, Diam. 7.7 cm. British
Museum, London, 1968,0422.10.
Bequeathed by Mrs Walter Sedgwick.

1.44 *below*

Phoenix-head ewer, 618–907. China.
Earthenware with *sancai* glaze.
H. 27.2 cm, W. 15 cm, D. 12.3 cm.
British Museum, London, 1936,1012.1.
Purchased from George Eumorfopoulos.

world that were expected to continue into the afterlife.[230] By the late Tang dynasty, functional ewers in ceramics were being produced and used.[231] This signalled a change in drinking habits, since pouring beverages from the spout of a ewer differed from the earlier practice in China, where alcohol was kept in a storage vessel and served into cups using a ladle.[232]

Archaeological findings from the three capitals of Nara, Geumseong and Chang'an, as well as from further afield, reveal a wide range of social, political and religious changes over the period 500 to 1000 – from trends in fashion and eating habits, to popular entertainment, to burial customs and the growth and spread of different religions. This evidence of exchange and mutual inspiration, as well as regional and longer-distance connections, demonstrates that Nara Japan, Silla Korea and Tang China were embedded in Silk Road networks, which led to significant societal changes with a lasting impact. Chang'an was a political centre and a major stop along overland Silk Road networks during this time, but other urban hubs in southern China, particularly along the coast, were also actively involved in trade and had foreign populations. The large-scale material evidence of the long-distance maritime movement of Chinese wares across the Indian Ocean, as seen in the so-called 'Belitung shipwreck', is the focus of the case study that follows.

Seafarers in the Indian Ocean

Luk Yu-ping

In 1998 a shipwreck with a cargo of over 60,000 pieces of Tang-dynasty (618–907) Chinese ceramics and other goods was discovered off the coast of the island of Belitung near Sumatra, Indonesia. Evidence suggests that the ship was on its return journey to Arabia or the Persian Gulf when it sank in the 800s (fig. 1.45). At the time, this region in West Asia was under the rule of the Islamic 'Abbasid caliphate (750–1258). This remarkable find provides large-scale physical evidence of the content and extent of international maritime connections across the Indian Ocean during the 800s that brought together two major empires – Tang China and the 'Abbasid caliphate – as well as other polities in between.[1]

The ship, crew and passengers

The keel of the *'Belitung'* (also called the Tang shipwreck or Batu Hitam shipwreck) measures 15.3 metres, while the widest point of the hull measures 5.1 metres.[2] The form of the ship and its technical features, including its construction using planks stitched together with rope, are consistent with shipbuilding traditions in India and West Asia, such as in Oman, where ships of this type were still built up until modern times.[3] Scientific analysis suggests that wood native to Africa was used in the ship, making it more likely that it came from an area in West Asia that depended on wood imports.[4] However, some of the wadding used on the hull and cordage are indigenous to Southeast Asia, which suggests that the ship probably spent time there during its journey for restitching and maintenance using local materials.[5] The recent study of another shipwreck from the 800s – *Phanom Surin,* discovered in Thailand with few surviving artefacts – found it to have a similar structure to the *Belitung,* although it was built using Southeast Asian timber.[6] This raises further questions about where the *Belitung* was constructed. Nevertheless, it is generally accepted that the ship and its cargo were intended for ports in West Asia, such as Siraf in Iran or Basra in Iraq.

In 2010 a modern reconstruction of the *Belitung* (fig. 1.46) successfully completed a sea voyage from Muscat, Oman, to Singapore in several legs. The voyage carried seventeen people, providing an indication of the comfortable capacity of a ship of this size. Isolated finds from the wreck of the original ship were probably personal belongings of its passengers and crew members, such as net weights for fishing or a die made of bone.[7] Some of these objects have a Southeast Asian provenance, including a grindstone and roller used for cooking, a scale and weights, aromatic resin, a bead-like gold coin (piloncito) and a bronze mirror from Sumatra (fig. 1.47).[8] Given the long and treacherous journey across the Indian Ocean, the ship likely stopped at ports along the way, not only to replenish supplies but also to recruit

Opposite

Detail of a pitcher with a feline-shaped handle, *c.* 830s (see fig. 1.54).

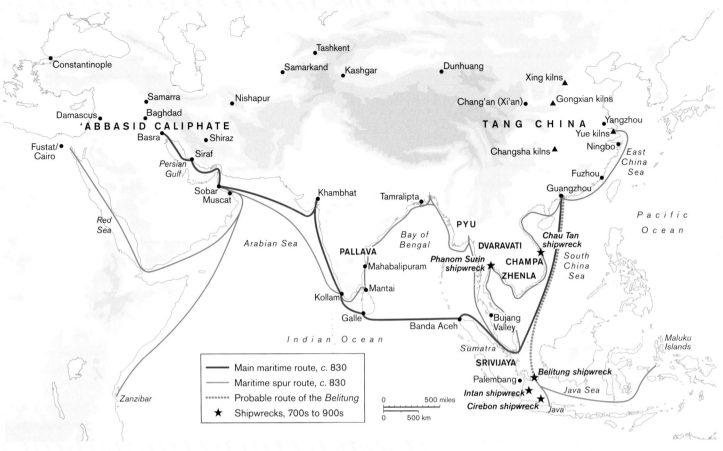

Constantinople

Tashkent
Samarkand   Kashgar   Dunhuang
                                                      Xing kilns ▲
                                                                        Gongxian kilns
                              Nishapur
Samarra   Chang'an (Xi'an) ●   ●   Yangzhou
Damascus ●   Baghdad ●   TANG CHINA   Yue kilns ▲
'ABBASID CALIPHATE   Basra ● ● Shiraz   Ningbo
Fustat/   ● Siraf   Changsha kilns ▲   Fuzhou   East
Cairo   China
              Persian   Guangzhou   Sea
              Gulf*   Sobar
                                Muscat   Khambhat   Tamralipta
Red   PYU   *Pacific*
Sea   *Ocean*
                          Arabian Sea   *Bay of   DVARAVATI   Chau Tan
              PALLAVA   *Bengal*   shipwreck
                                                    Phanom Surin   CHAMPA   *South*
                          Mahabalipuram   *shipwreck*   ZHENLA   *China*
                                                                                Sea
                          Mantai
              Kollam ●   *Maluku*
                    Galle ●   Banda Aceh   Bujang   *Islands*
                                                   Valley
                    Indian Ocean   *Java*
                                              Sumatra   *Sea*
                                        SRIVIJAYA
                                                        Belitung shipwreck
Zanzibar   Palembang ● ★
                                        Intan shipwreck ★
                                        Cirebon shipwreck ★ *Java*

──	Main maritime route, *c.* 830
──	Maritime spur route, *c.* 830
····	Probable route of the *Belitung*
★	Shipwrecks, 700s to 900s

0   500 miles
0   500 km

1.45
Map showing the probable route of the *Belitung*, as well as the location of other shipwrecks in Southeast Asia.

1.46
The *Jewel of Muscat*, a modern replica of a ship based on evidence from the *Belitung*, sailing near Oman, 2010. A gift of the Sultanate of Oman to Singapore, the ship is now displayed at the Maritime Experiential Museum, Singapore.

new crew members, which would explain the presence of these finds.[9]

Only a few objects of West Asian origin have been recovered from the shipwreck, even though the vessel probably came from the Persian Gulf. Examples include two turquoise-glazed ceramic amphorae that may have contained olive oil or date syrup (fig. 1.48).[10] This type of storage vessel was exported widely, and has been found in East Africa, Southeast Asia, China and Japan. Another item is a small glass bottle that might have been used for medicine or cosmetics (fig. 1.49).[11] These items could have been trade goods (or their containers) or the personal belongings of West Asian merchants who were presumably on board the ship.

It is also widely believed that there was a literate Chinese passenger on board, who was the owner of an inkstone incised with an insect (fig. 1.50), used for grinding inksticks for writing or painting.[12] Miscellaneous Chinese objects, such as bronze spoons and pieces of a lacquer dish, may have belonged to this person as well. Although it is speculative, these varied objects suggest that the crew and passengers of the *Belitung* came from different ethnic backgrounds, resulting in a multicultural environment on board the ship, reflecting the maritime networks in which it operated.[13]

The sea route

Objects with dated inscriptions recovered from the shipwreck help to narrow down the time frame of the ship's voyage to the period from 826 to 845.[14] When the *Belitung* left West Asia, it presumably carried a cargo of goods to maximise profits. These may have included aromatics, spices, ivory, glass, metal vessels and other items.[15] After offloading this cargo at its destination, it would have assembled a new set of goods for its fateful return voyage.

The ship's destination for its outbound journey and related port of departure for its return voyage remain a matter of debate. It is usually thought that the ship docked at either Guangzhou or Yangzhou in southern China.[16] Guangzhou had long been a major port in China for overseas trade, and from 661 had a maritime trade commissioner based there to supervise sea-related trade and diplomacy.[17] Yangzhou emerged as a major commercial centre in the Tang dynasty because of its location at the juncture of the Yangzi River and the north–south Grand Canal, which was constructed in the sixth and seventh centuries. Both cities attracted foreign merchants and settlers, including Persians, Arabs and others from West Asia.[18] Relationships between Chinese and foreign populations were not always peaceful. In 758 Arabs and Persians raided and briefly seized Guangzhou before leaving by sea.[19] In 760, during the political turmoil

1.47
Mirror, early 800s. Sumatra, Indonesia. Bronze. Diam. 10.5 cm. Tang Shipwreck Collection, Asian Civilisations Museum, Singapore, 2005.1.00834.

1.48
Amphora, *c.* 830s. Iraq or southwest Iran. Earthenware with turquoise glaze. H. 17.9 cm, Diam. 13 cm. Tang Shipwreck Collection, Asian Civilisations Museum, Singapore, 2005.1.00406.

of the An Lushan rebellion (755–63), a large number of Arab and Persian merchants in Yangzhou were massacred for their wealth by a Tang general.[20] However, both cities recovered sufficiently to continue to operate as major trading ports in the 800s. West Asian merchants of the *Belitung* would have found Arabs and Persians in both Guangzhou and Yangzhou to act on their behalf as procurement agents for Chinese products.[21]

The location where the *Belitung* sank is also intriguing, as it is well east of the expected route through the Strait of Malacca towards India. Was the ship simply blown off-course, or was the change in direction intentional? One possibility is that the ship was heading to a port in Java to top up spices during its return journey from China to West Asia.[22] Some have suggested that Southeast Asia played a bigger role in the *Belitung's* voyage. Specifically, the Srivijaya empire in modern-day Indonesia may have functioned as an entrepôt where the ship acquired and loaded its cargo of Chinese goods (see chapter 2); however, a recent study argues that this kind of trade at Srivijaya had not yet been established at the time of the *Belitung*.[23] The reason for the ship's final resting place remains unclear.

Nevertheless, it is generally accepted that the *Belitung's* intended return destination was Arabia or the Persian Gulf. By the 800s the nearly 10,000-kilometre-long sea route that linked ports in West Asia such as Basra to Guangzhou is documented in both Chinese and Arabic sources.[24] According to *Ancient Accounts of India and China (Akhbar al-sin wa'l-hind, c. 851)*, ships could travel from Muscat in Oman to Guangzhou in five months, not including stops, if they departed in October to take advantage of favourable winds.[25] The *Jewel of Muscat*, the reconstruction of the *Belitung*, took a comparable length of time when it sailed from Muscat to Singapore in stages from February to July 2010.[26] In Southeast Asia, the *Belitung* would have had to catch another set of monsoon winds between April and September to reach Guangzhou in a journey that took around thirty days. To travel in the opposite direction, the *Belitung* would have needed to set sail between November and January.[27] It is possible that

the ship stayed in China for longer than a year given the time required for the merchants to place their orders, and for the goods to be produced, transported and packed for loading at the port of departure.[28]

The cargo

In 1998–9 the *Belitung* cargo was salvaged by a German commercial company with the permission of the Indonesian government.[29] Most of the cargo was subsequently sold to Singapore, where it became part of the collection of the Asian Civilisations Museum. Of the approximately 60,000 pieces of Chinese ceramics that were recovered from the shipwreck, about 57,500 were made at the Changsha kilns in Hunan province in southcentral China.[30] Of these, about 55,000 pieces are bowls, while the remaining are ewers, jars and other forms. The vast quantity of Changsha ceramics on the *Belitung* show that potters in Tang China were able to cater to mass orders and production on an industrial

scale.[31] The bowls were either stacked and originally wrapped in straw 'cylinders', or packed in a helical fashion inside large stoneware jars that were made as containers in present-day Guangdong province, southern China (fig. 1.51).[32] Changsha bowls have a green-tinged glaze and painted decorations in brown, green and occasionally red, which are coloured using iron and copper pigments. Common decorative motifs include stylised birds, flowers, mountains, scrolls and fish that were freely and energetically painted. Some designs are more unusual, such as a bowl painted with the face of a curly-haired man with prominent features that may represent a Central or West Asian figure (fig. 1.52). Changsha bowls like those on the *Belitung* were probably commissioned for export since they were not the most commonly made wares at the kiln site.[33] There were also other kinds of vessels and objects from the Changsha kilns found in the shipwreck, such as a four-legged incense burner imitating metalware with a cover featuring a man wrestling a lion – an unusual subject in Chinese art (fig. 1.53).

Other types of ceramics in the *Belitung* include Chinese celadon wares, approximately 900 pieces, of which about 200 are from the Yue kilns in Zhejiang province (a type that was admired as tea vessels in China), while the others are primarily from kilns in Guangdong.[34] Besides these, there are about 300 pieces of white wares, as well as some 200 pieces of green-splashed wares or related monochrome-green wares with low-fired lead glaze, which probably came from the Xing and Gongxian kilns in Hebei and Henan provinces, northern China. One distinctive and unusually large example of a green-splashed ceramic is a pitcher with a feline-shaped handle and a spout in the form of a dragon's head (fig. 1.54).

In addition, an extremely rare group of ceramics consists of three white dishes painted with cobalt-blue decorations from the Gongxian kilns (fig. 1.55). They are among the earliest complete examples of 'blue-and-white' wares from China, which later became the most common type of Chinese porcelain exported around the world. The cobalt mineral used for the blue glaze was probably imported from Iran. However, unlike the underglaze blue porcelain that emerged during the Yuan dynasty (1271–1368), the decoration on these early pieces seems to be applied over the glaze.[35] Given that the blue-and-white colour palette was not popular in Tang-dynasty China, they were probably intended for the West Asian market.[36] Similarly, the lozenge motif surrounded by foliage adorning these dishes, also present on the green-splashed wares, does not come from the Chinese tradition of ornamentation but can be traced to pre-Islamic and Islamic West Asian designs.[37] (The artistic exchange in ceramics between Tang China and the Islamic world is discussed further in chapter 4.)

It is notable that ceramics on the *Belitung* came from a variety of kilns in northern, central and southern China, even though the overwhelming majority are from the Changsha kilns. Sherds of nearly the full range of Tang ceramics from the shipwreck have been found only in Yangzhou to date, providing clues that the city was the likely location where the bulk of the cargo was assembled, via the Grand Canal and tributaries of the Yangzi River, and then loaded on to the *Belitung*.[38] If the ship did not sail to Yangzhou, however, then the goods were probably shipped from Yangzhou to Guangzhou for loading, or

1.52
Bowl with a curly-haired man, *c.* 830s. Changsha kilns, Hunan province, China. Stoneware. H. 5.7 cm, Diam. 15.2 cm. Tang Shipwreck Collection, Asian Civilisations Museum, Singapore, 2005.1.00539.

1.53
Incense burner, *c.* 830s. Changsha kilns, Hunan province, China. Stoneware. H. 24 cm, Diam. 15.4 cm. Tang Shipwreck Collection, Asian Civilisations Museum, Singapore, 2005.1.00497-1/2 to 2/2.

part of the cargo could also have been sent directly from the kiln sites to Guangzhou.[39]

Apart from ceramics, the ship also carried an estimated 10 tonnes of lead ingots that were used as ballast and probably also as a trade item.[40] A few of these were found inside a ceramic spouted jar.[41] Some storage jars were also packed full of star anise, which was available in Guangzhou.[42] Other items in smaller quantities include gold and silver vessels, more than 2 kilograms of gold foil, bronze mirrors, Tang-dynasty coins, silver ingots, aromatics, lacquer and other items possibly belonging to the crew and passengers of the *Belitung* noted earlier. The cargo may also have included other goods known to be popular in West Asia, such as musk or silk, which would have disintegrated in the sea waters.[43]

Gold- and silverware

Among the non-ceramic items from China on the *Belitung*, the most spectacular are over thirty pieces of gold and silver vessels, most likely made in the Yangzhou region, which was a centre of gold- and silverware production in China during the mid- to late Tang dynasty.[44] One notable example from this collection is an octagonal gold cup (fig. 1.56). Each side of the cup is applied with an image of a non-Chinese figure, likely Central Asian, consisting of seven musicians and one dancer who has his arms and one leg raised, in the form of the 'Sogdian whirl' (see p. 57). The fluted shape of the cup, with a loop handle and a thumb rest decorated with back-to-back heads, along with the beading on the body of the cup, are elements inspired by Sogdian metalware.[45] Smaller cups in gold and gilded silver with similar shape and design have been discovered in the Hejia Village hoard in Chang'an (Xi'an), Shaanxi province, dated to the 700s (see chapter 1).

Other gold and silver vessels from the shipwreck include lobed oval drinking bowls, a shape that evolved in China from Sasanian models.[46] Two of these bowls in gold are decorated with a pair of geese, a symbol of fidelity and an appropriate wedding gift in China (fig. 1.57). Similarly, an ornately decorated wine flask, the largest silverware in the shipwreck at 38 centimetres in height, depicts a pair of mandarin ducks, a symbol

1.54
Pitcher with a feline-shaped handle, *c.* 830s. Perhaps Hebei province, China. Stoneware with green-splashed glaze. H. 32 cm, Diam. 18.5 cm. Tang Shipwreck Collection, Asian Civilisations Museum, Singapore, 2005.1.00403.

1.55
Dish, *c.* 830s. Gongxian kilns, Henan province, China. Stoneware with cobalt-blue decoration. H. 4.4 cm, Diam. 22.8 cm. Tang Shipwreck Collection, Asian Civilisations Museum, Singapore, 2005.1.00474.

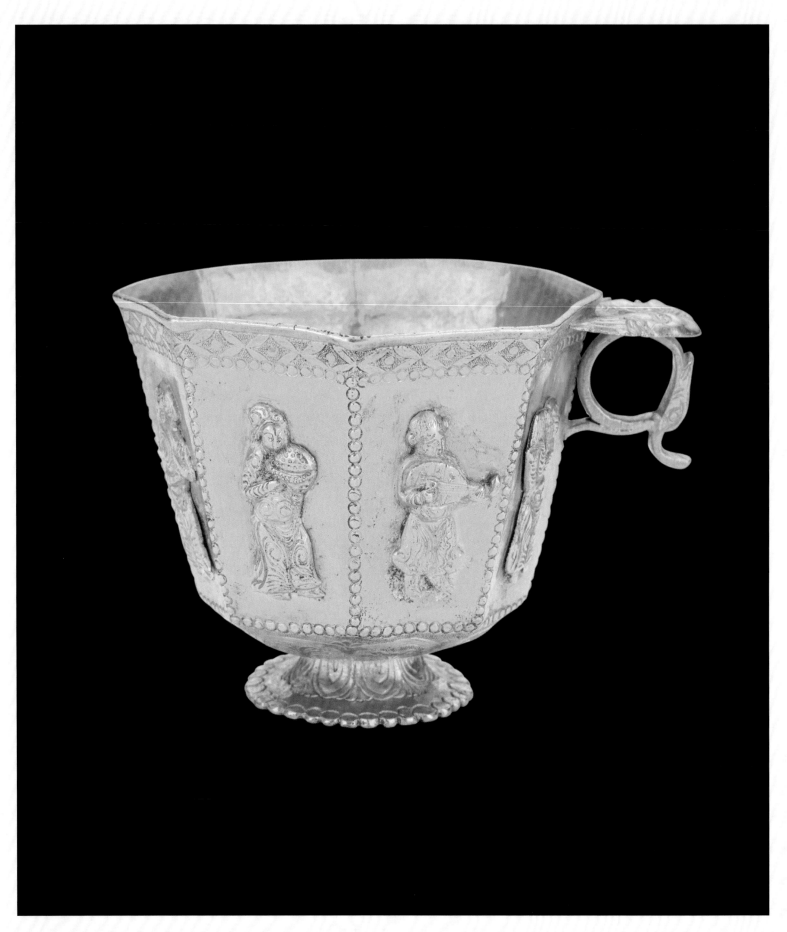

of marital bliss. One of the silver bowls, partially damaged, portrays a rhinoceros at the centre (fig. 1.58). This unusual design may refer to rhinoceroses that were sent to the Tang imperial court as diplomatic gifts from Southeast Asia and West Asia.[47] There are also silver boxes in a variety of shapes and gilded decorations, which could have been used to store cosmetics, incense or medicine.[48]

Objects in gold and silver were prestigious in Tang society, often associated with imperial patronage and gift-giving.[49] Examples from the shipwreck have been compared to wares excavated from the pagoda–stupa of the Buddhist Famensi Temple, around 120 kilometres west of Chang'an (Xi'an), which were gifts from the Tang imperial court and include a gilded silver basin decorated with a pair of mandarin ducks.[50] The special status of these gold and silver pieces has led to different theories about their purpose on the *Belitung*. It is possible that, together with some of the high-quality ceramics, they were meant as gifts for local authorities to facilitate negotiations along the journey.[51] Another possibility is that they may have been diplomatic gifts from the Tang court given in return to envoys from West Asia or Southeast Asia.[52] The likelihood of the *Belitung* having official connections is further suggested by two pieces of Chinese ceramics with inscriptions. One is a green-splashed dish incised with the word *jingfen* (tribute) while the other is a monochrome green bowl incised with the word *ying*, a reference to the Tang imperial storehouse.[53] While it is possible that they were purchased from the market, it is perhaps more likely that they were given by the Tang court to foreign merchants as return gifts. These objects offer further lines of enquiry about the nature of the *Belitung*, its voyage and the route that its passengers took. In the broader context of the Silk Roads, the discovery of the *Belitung* reveals the complexity and interconnectedness of regional and long-distance maritime activities, as well as the large-scale demand for Chinese ceramic exports that already existed at this time, but unresolved questions regarding the ship's itinerary and aspects of its cargo show that there is still much more to be learned about maritime networks in the period around 500 to 1000.

1.57

Lobed oval bowl with a pair of geese, *c.* 830s. Probably Yangzhou. Gold. H. 4 cm, W. 10 cm, L. 15.4 cm. Tang Shipwreck Collection, Asian Civilisations Museum, Singapore, 2005.1.00923.

1.56

Octagonal cup with musicians and a dancer, *c.* 830s. Probably Yangzhou. Gold. H. 9.2 cm, W. 10.8 cm, Diam. 13 cm. Tang Shipwreck Collection, Asian Civilisations Museum, Singapore, 2005.1.00918.

1.58

Lobed oval bowl with a rhinoceros, *c.* 830s. Probably Yangzhou. Silver, partly gilded. H. 2.5 cm, W. 14.1 cm, L. 10.5 cm. Tang Shipwreck Collection, Asian Civilisations Museum, Singapore, 2005.1.00888.

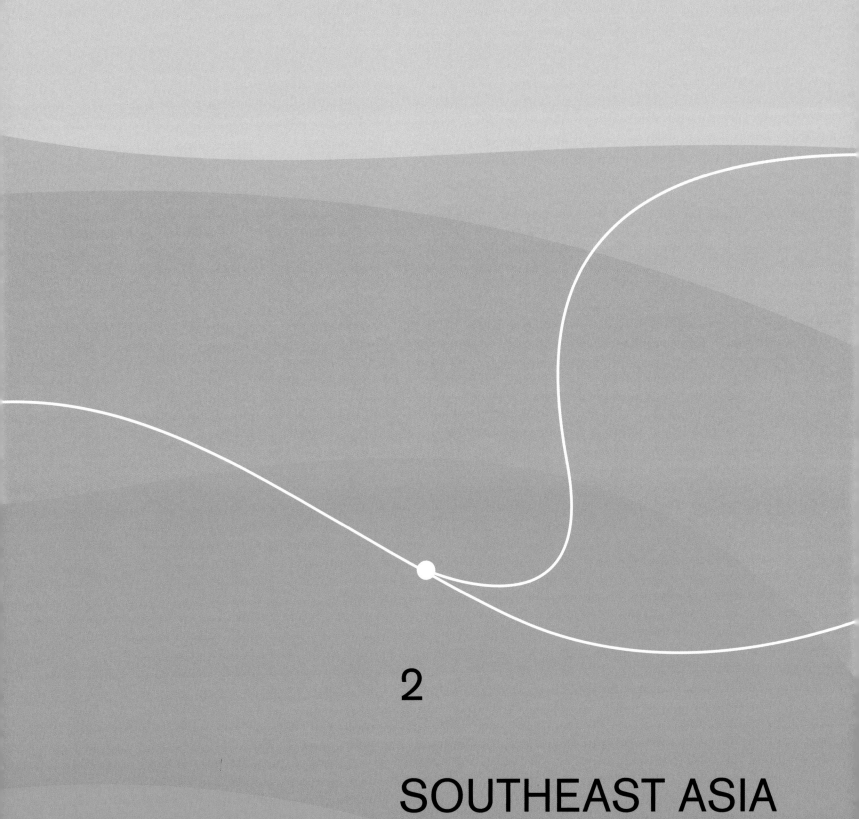

2

SOUTHEAST ASIA
TO THE TARIM BASIN

Southeast Asia to the Tarim Basin

Luk Yu-ping

When the *Belitung* sank near Sumatra, Indonesia, in the 800s, it was sailing in waters under the control of Srivijaya (600s–1100s), a major polity that had its capital at present-day Palembang in southern Sumatra.[1] Srivijaya was one of multiple regional powers located in Southeast Asia and the Indian subcontinent that were part of the Silk Roads network during this time. To the north, across the soaring mountain range of the Himalayas, was the Tibetan Plateau (Qinghai–Tibet Plateau), the centre of the Tibetan empire (Tubo, *c.* 600–866),[2] which at its peak extended north into the desert region of the Tarim Basin where the Tang dynasty had previously established protectorates. The oases settlements dotted near and around the Taklamakan and Lop deserts were stopping points for travellers and home to diverse communities. One of the sites was Dunhuang, the location of the Buddhist Mogao ('peerless') Cave temple complex. In 1900 Cave 17 (popularly known as the 'Library Cave') was discovered there, containing tens of thousands of manuscripts, paintings and other objects dated to before the early eleventh century. These finds provide remarkable evidence of languages and artistic production, as well as religious and secular life, along the Silk Roads.

2.1

Map of South and Southeast Asia, and parts of China, *c.* 700s–1000s.

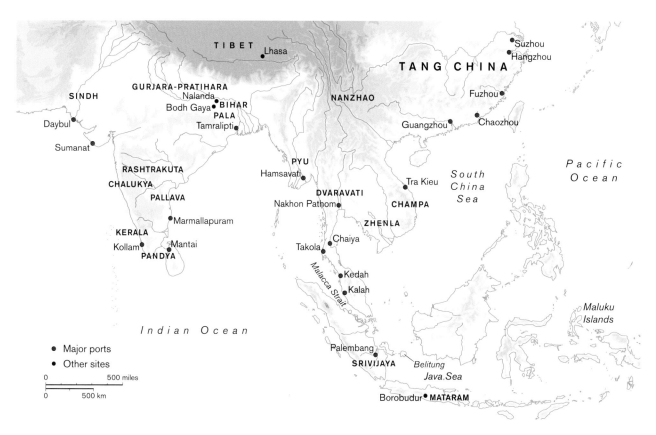

Empires in Southeast Asia

Srivijaya emerged as a polity in the river basin of southern Sumatra by the 670s.[3] Over time, it gained control of the key shipping channel of the Melaka (Malacca) Strait and seems to have extended its authority to the Malay Peninsula, including parts of present-day southern Thailand and Malaysia (fig. 2.1).[4] Srivijaya sent envoys to Tang China and capitalised on the commercial opportunities arising from the active maritime routes between China and the Indian subcontinent. Ships made stops at Srivijaya's ports for maintenance, to replenish supplies and to engage in trade of imported and local goods such as spices, woods, gold, tin, aromatics and resins.[5] It is likely that the *Belitung* did the same. Among the spices that were traded in this region were cloves, which grew only in the Maluku Islands (Moluccas) to the east of Sumatra but reached Europe during this period (see chapter 5).

Additionally, Srivijaya was a major Buddhist centre that attracted practitioners from abroad. The Chinese monk Yijing (635–713) visited the region as part of his journey from China to India, staying there for extended periods of time on his outbound and return journeys to study and translate texts.[6] The rulers of Srivijaya patronised religious building projects even from afar. In 860 King Balaputra funded the construction of a monastery at Nalanda in northeast India, the site of a major scholastic institution.[7] Buddhist sculptures from Srivijaya, such as a bronze figure of the compassionate bodhisattva Avalokiteshvara made in peninsular Thailand (fig. 2.2), drew inspiration from Indian models.[8] The multiple arms and hip wrap representing animal skin of this bodhisattva can be traced to images from southern India.[9] Small-size sculptures like these were easily transported, as demonstrated by a bronze sculpture of a Buddha seated on a throne, which was produced in present-day West Bengal, northeast India, but found in Java (present-day Indonesia) (fig. 2.3). Hinduism was also practised in Srivijaya.

Adjacent to Srivijaya in Central Java was another major power. Known as Mataram, this polity first appears in historical records in 732, becoming increasingly unified during the ninth century.[10] One theory suggests that the *Belitung* was on its way to this region, hence its final location some distance away from the expected route through the Malacca Strait (see pp. 65–6). The magnificent Borobudur monument, still the largest Buddhist site in the world, was built in Central Java around the late 700s to early 800s.[11] Carved out of the porous volcanic rock local to Java, a stone sculpture of the Buddha's head from the site (fig. 2.4) connects to images from the Indian Gupta period (300s–500s CE) through the use of 'snail-shell' curls and downcast eyes, but the rounded face and naturalistic features clearly identify it as from Java.[12] Among the reliefs that adorn the Borobudur monument are impressive representations of eleven seafaring ships (fig. 2.5).[13] They offer insights into the design of ships that were active in the Java Sea at this time, such as the use of rectangular sails and outriggers added for stabilisation. Moreover, their depiction as part of Buddhist narrative scenes at Borobudur highlights the close connection between seafaring activities in Southeast Asia and the transmission of Buddhism, as well as other ideas, materials and technologies.[14]

2.2 *top*
Figure of the bodhisattva Avalokiteshvara, 600–700s. Thailand. Bronze. H. 18.8 cm, W. 9 cm, D. 3.5 cm (excl. stand). Victoria and Albert Museum, London, IS.72-1993. Purchased from David Knight with Art Fund support.

2.3 *right*
Seated Buddha figure, 800–900. Made in West Bengal, found in Prambanan, Java, Indonesia. Bronze. H. 25.1 cm, W. 15 cm, D. 12.5 cm. British Museum, London, 1859,1228.1. Donated by Rev. William Charles Raffles Flint.

The Indian subcontinent

To travel to India, the Chinese monk Yijing first boarded a Persian ship to Srivijaya from the port of Guangzhou in southern China, then joined a merchant ship from 'Kacha', probably Kedah in northwest Malaysia, to reach his destination.[15] The sea route to Madhyadesha (India) took some thirty days.[16] Yijing stayed for eleven years in Nalanda in Bihar, northeast India (fig. 2.6). Other monks who travelled to Nalanda include Xuanzang (602–664) from Tang China, as well as Hyecho (704–787) from Silla Korea (see chapter 1).[17] Monks from Nalanda also journeyed outwards to spread Buddhist teachings, including Shubhakarasimha (637–735), who went to the Tang capital Chang'an (see chapter 1).

Following the collapse of the Gupta empire (320–550), Bihar was under the rule of regional powers, including the Pala dynasty (c. 750–1200) from the second half of the 700s. Rich in natural resources, it was the location of many holy sites associated with the historical Buddha, such as Bodh Gaya, where he attained enlightenment.[18] A sculpture from Bihar carved in schist depicts the seated Buddha delivering his First Sermon, over a lower frieze showing the Dharmachakra (Wheel of the Law) flanked by deer and monks (fig. 2.7).[19] On the back is an engraved stupa and an inscription of a statement in Sanskrit that encapsulates the fundamental teachings of the Buddha. This work exemplifies the Buddhist sculptural tradition that would continue to flourish and develop under the Pala dynasty.

While many travellers went to India in search of religious teachings, predominantly Buddhism and Hinduism, others brought foreign religions to the subcontinent. Communities of the Christian Church of the East (see p. 53) developed in Kerala along the southwest coast of India, as well as the southeast coast towards present-day Chennai and possibly other regions.[20] Cosmas Indicopleustes (active 500s), a merchant from Alexandria, Egypt who travelled to the Aksumite port city of Adulis on the Red Sea coast of Africa, records the presence of local Christians along the coast of Malabar in southwest India, whose priests had been sent there from Persia (see chapter 5).[21] He also notes that there were Christian churches in Sri Lanka, which points to the importance of maritime routes for the spread of Christianity to the Indian subcontinent.[22]

2.4

Figure of Buddha's head, late 700s or early 800s. Made in Central Java, Indonesia. Volcanic stone. H. 33 cm, W. 26 cm, D. 29 cm. British Museum, London, 1859,1228.176. Donated by Rev. William Charles Raffles Flint.

2.5

A seafaring ship depicted on a relief that adorns the Borobudur monument, Central Java, late 700s or early 800s.

2.6
Site of the Nalanda Mahavihara at
Nalanda, Bihar, northeast India.

2.7
Seated Buddha figure, *c.* late 600s.
Bihar, India. Schist. H. 34.5 cm,
W. 19.1 cm, D. 6.8 cm. British Museum,
London, 1854,0214.1. Purchased from
Robert Montgomery Martin.

As seen from the case of the shipwreck of the *Belitung*, Arab traders were active in the Indian Ocean by the 800s. Chinese and Arabic sources record the sea route from the ports of West Asia to Guangzhou, China, making stops along the way on the west coast of India, and in Sri Lanka and Southeast Asia. Arab merchants were also active in trade in South Asia. Spices, herbs and types of wood from India were shipped to the West Asian markets.[23] For instance, teak from South and Southeast Asia was used in the buildings of Samarra, the second capital of the ʿAbbasid caliphate (see chapter 4). Significant settlements of Arab Muslim merchants and their families appeared along the coast of India and Sri Lanka, such as in Malabar and Gujarat, where mosques were built.[24] Indo-Arab commercial ties along the Indian coast became the reason for military confrontation, leading to the Muslim conquest of Sindh (the southern part of modern Pakistan) in 711. One source records that the military campaign came about after the king of Sri Lanka arranged to send daughters of Muslim merchants who had died there back to West Asia, but the ship was attacked by pirates sailing out of Daybul (also Debal) in Sindh.[25]

Towards the east, polities in India and China saw an intensification of commercial and diplomatic exchanges in the 600s and 700s, following the reunification of the latter under the Sui and Tang dynasties. The courts in India and China exchanged over fifty embassies between the years 619 and 753.[26] It has been suggested that Sino-India relations during this period were underpinned by a shared interest in Buddhism, which had reached China in the early centuries.[27] Buddhist objects from India, as well as precious materials associated with Buddhism and other commodities, such as jewels, ivory, spices and incense, were in demand in Tang China.[28] Commodities from Tang China were imported to India for local consumption or re-export via its ports. Among them, silk was the most highly regarded.[29]

Tibetan empire

Across the mountain range of the Himalayas from the Indian subcontinent is the area now known as the Tibet or Xizang Autonomous Region, China. In the early 600s, rival clans based there were unified under Songtsen Gampo (r. 629–c. 649) of the Yarlung dynasty, forming an empire that lasted until the mid-800s.[30] The empire was known as 'Tubo' (also Tufan) in Chinese historical sources, and 'bod chen po' in Tibetan. Its relationship with Tang China was marked by periods of hostilities as well as peace and diplomatic engagement. At the height of its military might, the Tibetan empire contested regions that had been under the control of Tang China, taking over areas in modern Qinghai and Gansu provinces, and even occupied the Tang capital Chang'an (Xi'an) for fifteen days in 763 during the aftermath of the eight-year rebellion led by the general An Lushan (703–757).[31]

In the mid-600s, routes to Tang China through the Tibetan empire became accessible when the two established peaceful relations.[32] The Tang princesses Wencheng (d. 680) and Jincheng (698–739) were sent to the Tibetan court to establish marriage alliances.[33] A famous painting in the Palace Museum, Beijing, portrays the historic meeting between the Tang emperor Taizong (r. 626–49) and an envoy sent by Songtsen Gampo seeking the hand in marriage of Princess Wencheng.[34] Records of gifts from Tibetan rulers to Tang China repeatedly mention lavish gold and silver vessels.[35] The high quality of Tibetan metalware is corroborated in more recent archaeological finds and new studies.[36] Examples show a blending of artistic styles and metalworking techniques, such as a silver vase that has pairs of phoenixes (fig. 2.8), a motif found in Chinese art, but also a shape and beaded edge that were inspired by Sasanian models that had spread through Central Asia.[37]

After Buddhism became the official religion of the Tibetan empire in the 700s, its rulers began to draw on Buddhist artistic traditions from neighbouring regions in their own patronage projects.[38] The portability of certain Buddhist images, such as a bronze statue of the standing Buddha (fig. 2.9), produced at Bihar, facilitated the transmission of styles. So too did the movement of artisans who were summoned to work there. One nine-storey Buddhist temple in Ushangdo in central Tibet was constructed in the 800s reportedly with the involvement of not only local craftsmen but also those from Tang China, Khotan (see p. 99), the Indian subcontinent and the Himalayas.[39]

Tibet was also connected to the wider Silk Roads network through trade. A special commodity from there was musk, which became the most important aromatic in the Islamic world, enjoyed as a perfume and esteemed for its associations with the sacred.[40] Musk is produced from the glands of the male musk deer that inhabits the forested highlands of Eastern Eurasia.[41] The animal is recognisable by its distinctive protruding canine teeth, as depicted in a print made in Britain in the 1800s (fig. 2.10). Musk could be used in a granular form, or more commonly as oil, liquid, incense or powdered compounds.[42] It was so highly sought after from the region that scholars now use the term 'musk routes' to denote exchanges between Tibet and the Islamic world.[43]

Dunhuang and the hidden cave

The Tibetan empire's expansion north brought important towns and cities along the Silk Roads under its control. This included Dunhuang, which had been a part of Tang territories but came under Tibetan rule from 786 until 848. It was then taken over by the local Guiyijun ('Return to Allegiance Circuit') regime

2.9 *below*

Standing Buddha figure, early 600s. Made in Bihar, probably found in Tibet. Bronze. H. 38 cm, W. 17.8 cm, D. 12.1 cm. British Museum, London, 2004,0401.1. Purchased through Eskenazi Ltd with contributions from Heritage Lottery Fund, Art Fund (as NACF), Brooke Sewell Permanent Fund, Victoria and Albert Museum and Friends of the V&A.

2.10 *right*

William Home Lizars after John Stewart, *The Thibetian Musk*, 1866. Published in Edinburgh, Scotland. Etching with hand-colouring on paper. H. 10.3 cm, W. 10 cm. British Museum, London, 1983,U.691. Donated by Rev. Francis Palgrave.

(851–*c.* 1036), a military governorship that pledged allegiance to Chinese imperial dynasties.[44] Dunhuang is located at a strategic point that intersects the Hexi Corridor, a narrow stretch of flat land connected to Chang'an (Xi'an) and routes around the Tarim Basin that lead to Central and South Asia and beyond (fig. 2.11).

Around 25 kilometres southeast of the centre of Dunhuang are the Mogao Caves, a large Buddhist cave-temple complex. In 1900 a hidden cave known as the 'Library Cave' or Cave 17 was discovered there, containing some 70,000 manuscripts as well as paintings, textiles and other artefacts, most of which date to around the 800s and 900s.[45] In addition to Buddhist manuscripts written in Chinese and Tibetan, the cave revealed non-Buddhist and administrative documents, as well as writings in nearly twenty languages, including Sanskrit, Sogdian, Khotanese and Old Uyghur.[46] Many of the paintings and textiles also reflect the multicultural environment of Dunhuang. The discovery of Cave 17 has transformed our understanding of the history and culture of this region.

There is much debate about the purpose of Cave 17 and why so many manuscripts and other objects were kept there for centuries.[47] One view is that the contents of the cave belonged to the library of a monastery.[48] Another is that it served as a repository for 'sacred waste' – material too valuable to be discarded, similar to the Cairo geniza discovered in Fustat (Old Cairo) (see chapter 5).[49] A more recent assessment suggests the function of the cave may have changed over time and that some paper or silk items may have been intended for recycling.[50] During an expedition to Dunhuang in 1907, the British-Hungarian archaeologist Marc Aurel Stein purchased manuscripts as well as other items from Cave 17 from the self-appointed caretaker who had discovered the site.[51] A significant portion of the paintings, prints, textiles and two small wooden figures from this expedition are now in the British Museum collection.[52]

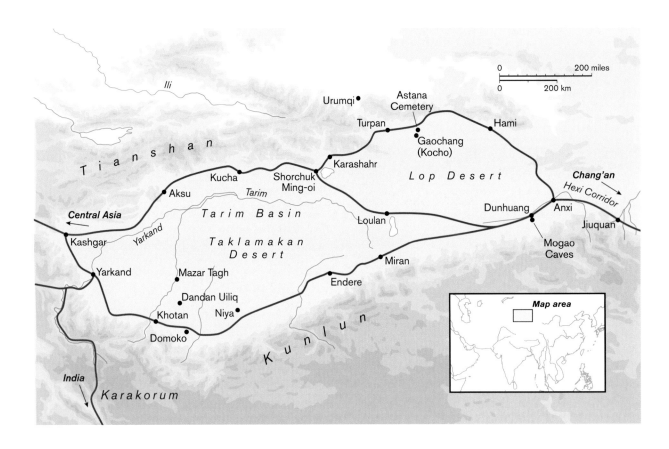

A Buddhist centre

One of the most impressive finds from Cave 17 is a silk embroidered textile nearly 2.5 metres in height (fig. 2.12) depicting a standing Buddha under a canopy accompanied by two bodhisattvas, the disciples Kashyapa (right) and Ananda (left), as well as *apsaras* (celestial nymphs) and lions.[53] At the bottom of the embroidery are male and female donor figures in small scale, including a monk, children and servants. Textiles like this may have been hung in shrines to be worshipped by believers.[54] Traces of embroidered text next to the donors, barely legible, records that the embroidery was commissioned by a *weina* (manager of a monastery's daily activities) at the Mogao Caves around the 700s, a time when the region was under Tang rule.[55] This is corroborated by the Tang-style dress of the donor figures. The embroidered scene represents the Miraculous Image of Liangzhou – a Buddha image that is supposed to have emerged from a rocky mountain in Liangzhou (in present-day Wuwei in the Hexi Corridor).[56] The image belongs to a new category of subject matter (termed *ruixiang*, 'auspicious images') that appeared at Dunhuang around this time and which depicted famous icons from India, Khotan and other sites in China.[57] The inclusion of the Miraculous Image of Liangzhou as one of the auspicious images distinguishes the Hexi region as a place where the Buddha could miraculously appear, and is an example of the localisation of Buddhism that had spread from the Indian subcontinent.

Many pilgrims and monks visited Dunhuang, including Xuanzang (mentioned earlier), who stopped there on his return journey from India to Chang'an. Intrepid travelling monks became a popular subject in paintings, as in an example where the figure is depicted with a wide-brimmed hat, holding a fly whisk and walking stick,

2.11

Map of the main routes around the Taklamakan and Lop deserts, showing the location of Dunhuang and other oases settlements.

2.12 *opposite*

Miraculous Image of Liangzhou, *c.* 700–800. Cave 17, Mogao Caves, Dunhuang, China. Silk thread on silk with hemp backing. H. 241 cm, W. 159 cm. British Museum, London, MAS,0.1129. Stein collection.

2.13

Travelling monk, *c.* 851–900. Cave 17, Mogao Caves, Dunhuang, China. Ink and pigments on paper. H. 41.1 cm, W. 30 cm. British Museum, London, 1919,0101,0.168. Stein collection.

2.14

Sketch of the Vajradhatu Mandala, late 800s or early 900s. Cave 17, Mogao Caves, Dunhuang, China. Ink on paper. H. 44.3 cm, W. 44 cm. British Museum, London, 1919,0101,0.173. Stein collection.

and carrying rolls of manuscripts in a backpack (fig. 2.13).[58] The monk's deep-set eyes and prominent nose suggest that he represents a non-Chinese person coming from a distant land. Notably, he is shown travelling on a cloud, as indicated in the damaged area of the paper, and is accompanied by a tame-looking tiger and an emanation of a Buddha seated on another cloud. Some of the other depictions of this subject from Cave 17 are inscribed with the name of a Buddha, 'Baosheng rulai', suggesting an identity that may have merged with the figure of the travelling monk over time.[59] The painters of these images have imagined a travelling Buddhist monk as a supernatural being, highlighting the special powers such individuals were thought to possess, perhaps unsurprising given the challenging journeys that they undertook.

Esoteric Buddhism, a newer form that focused on ritual programmes and techniques such as spells, incantations and mandalas (symbolic diagrams), is well represented in the material found in Dunhuang.[60] It was introduced there during Tibetan rule in the late 700s to the mid-800s.[61] One example of its spread is a sketch of a mandala that may have been used for visualisation or as a model for the physical layout of a ritual space (fig. 2.14).[62] Known as the Vajradhatu ('diamond realm'), it is derived from a text that appeared in India in the 600s and was translated into Chinese in 753, demonstrating the spread of this new knowledge.[63] The mandala depicts the Buddha Vairocana in the centre, surrounded by four buddhas of the cardinal directions and deities bearing offerings. In the outer band are the Four Heavenly Kings, as well as fierce guardians that are characteristic of Esoteric Buddhism.[64]

In addition to Buddhism, the presence of other religions has been identified in Cave 17. For instance, there are intriguing references to Christianity in a partially damaged painting that depicts a bodhisattva-like figure with a flaming halo among floating flowers (fig. 2.15). One of his hands is raised showing a version of the *vitarka mudra*, the gesture of discussion and the transmission of Buddhist teachings. Yet, when viewed closely, three crosses are visible on the figure – on his diadem, his necklace and chest.[65] The distinctive shape of the cross, with arms of equal length that taper to the centre, is associated with the Christian Church of the East that was present in the Tang capital Chang'an and southern India during this period (see pp. 53, 76). A similar image of the cross is seen carved at the top of the Church of the East stela (781) that was erected in Chang'an (see fig. 1.35). This painting is believed to represent either a Christian saint or a high-ranking clergyman, created by a painter accustomed to producing Buddhist images.[66] Such an image may have been intended for personal devotional use or for liturgical purposes by a member of the Church of the East in Dunhuang.[67] However, recent research suggests another possibility: that it may represent the cloaked figure of Jesus as a guide for the afterlife within the context of Manichaeism, a religion originating in Mesopotamia (see p. 95). This interpretation adds another layer of complexity to the religious encounters that form the basis of this painting.[68]

Multilingual environment

Manuscripts in more than one language can reveal the transmission of ideas and practices across cultures. For instance, comparable illustrated charts from this period featuring Chinese, Tibetan and Old Uyghur text explain moxibustion, a therapeutic practice that applies heat to points on the body. These charts have been discovered in Cave 17 and Turpan, northwest of Dunhuang, demonstrating the spread of medical knowledge.[69] Bilingual manuscripts from Cave 17 are particularly interesting examples of how people navigated a multilingual environment. The transmission of Buddhism from India throughout Asia necessitated the translation of teachings originally in Sanskrit and Pali into different languages, as well as the study of Sanskrit pronunciation. A concertina book from the 700s to 800s contains the Heart of the Perfection of Wisdom sutra (*Prajnaparamita hrdaya sutra*) in Sanskrit in the late Gupta script and Chinese transliterations written in alternating columns (fig. 2.16).[70] Sanskrit is read horizontally from left to right, while Chinese is traditionally read vertically from top to bottom, right to left. In this manuscript, the Sanskrit letters are arranged to match the orientation of the Chinese text. The use of brush for the writing also gives the Sanskrit text a flavour of Chinese calligraphy.[71]

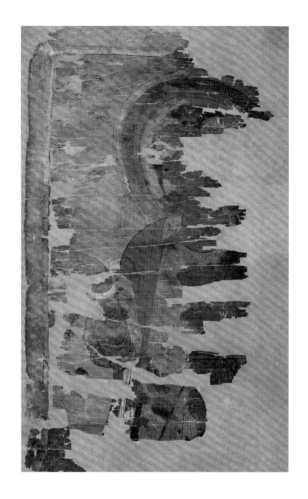

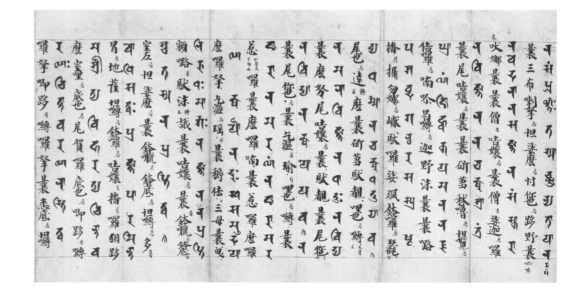

2.15 *top*
Bodhisattva-like figure with crosses, 800–900. Cave 17, Mogao Caves, Dunhuang, China. Ink and pigments on silk. H. 87.1 cm, W. 50.6 cm. British Museum, London, 1919,0101,0.48. Stein collection.

2.16 *right*
Heart of the Perfection of Wisdom sutra in Sanskrit with Chinese transliterations, 700–900. Cave 17, Mogao Caves, Dunhuang, China. Concertina manuscript, ink on paper. H. 26 cm, W. 99 cm. British Library, London, Or.8212/195. Stein collection.

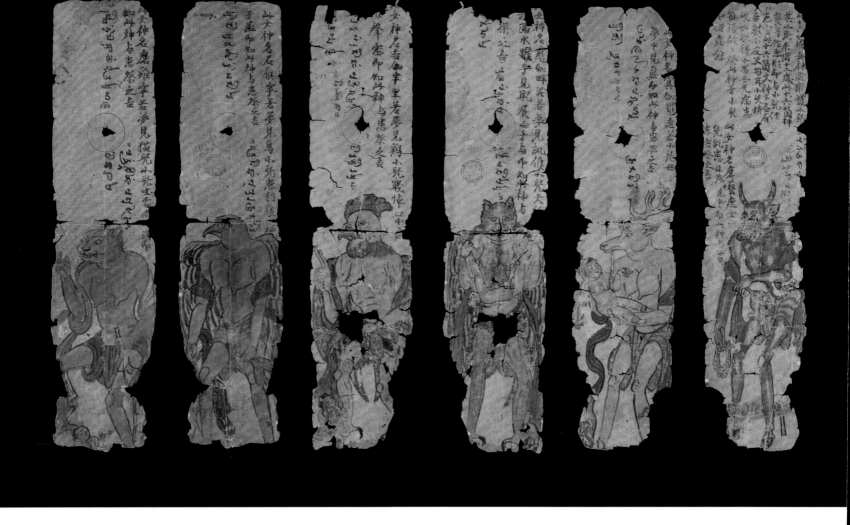

Another example of a bilingual manuscript is a set of three *pothi* leaves (oblong rectangular folia) with images and text written in Chinese and Khotanese on both sides (fig. 2.17).[72] The term *pothi* is derived from the Indian palm-leaf manuscript (Sanskrit: *pustaka*); the use of the *pothi* at Dunhuang is attributed to the presence of Tibetans, who used this format horizontally for writing.[73] This set of *pothi* may have functioned as an amulet, strung together by the holes in the paper sheets.[74] Khotanese, an Iranian language written in Brahmi script, was used in the Kingdom of Khotan in the southwest of the Tarim Basin. The Chinese text was written before the Khotanese and is oriented vertically, as are the images, so the reader would have to turn the leaves 90 degrees to read the Khotanese, which was written horizontally. The images depict figures with female bodies and animal heads, some of whom hold children in precarious positions. An introduction in Chinese on one of the leaves explains that originally the set depicted sixteen female spirits with animal heads, who could potentially bring harm to children before they reached the age of 12.[75] To protect the children, parents are advised to offer sacrifices to the relevant spirit. The animal-headed female spirits are thought to derive from yakshas (nature spirits) from Indian culture. Yakshas could be perceived as demonic or benevolent, suggesting further links to belief in protector deities in Khotan and Kizil in the Tarim Basin. This underlines the complex cultural mixing evident in this set of *pothi* leaves.[76]

2.17

Three *pothi* leaves (front and back) with images of animal-headed female spirits and children, and Chinese and Khotanese text, *c.* 800–900. Cave 17, Mogao Caves, Dunhuang, China. Ink and pigments on paper. H. 33 cm, W. 8 cm. British Museum, London, 1919,0101,0.177.1–3. Stein collection.

Bilingual phrasebooks and glossaries from Cave 17 also offer a glimpse into the concerns and interests of potential travellers encountering a multilingual context.[77] These manuscripts cover a wide range of scripts – Sino-Tibetan, Sino-Khotanese, Sanskrit-Khotanese and Turko-Khotanese – and would be useful for people needing to pick up some basic conversation and terms in an unfamiliar tongue. These documents may have been intended for merchants, but more recently they have been discussed in the context of diplomatic envoys and their long-distance journeys.[78] In a Sino-Tibetan example, Tibetan words and phrases are given with their Chinese equivalents written in Tibetan script (fig. 2.18). It must have been compiled by a person who knew Tibetan but not very much Chinese. The first two words in the document are 'chopsticks' and 'beer [in Tibetan]/barley wine [in Chinese]', and the last phrase is 'Be quiet!'[79] There are also concerns about being robbed and being wrongly accused, a reminder that journeys along the Silk Roads were a risky undertaking.

The multilingual context of Dunhuang applied not only to spoken and written languages but also to images and artistic traditions. This can be observed in a large painting portraying the Paradise of Bhaishajyaguru, the Medicine Buddha (fig. 2.19).[80] The Buddha is positioned in the upper centre of the painting, with two bodhisattvas and many other attendants on either side of him. Below the Buddha is a cartouche with writing, flanked by the bodhisattvas Samantabhadra and Manjushri, riding an elephant and a lion respectively. The lower part of the painting is damaged and missing, but different manifestations of the bodhisattva Avalokiteshvara remain visible. Notably, the two bodhisattvas next

2.18 *top*
Sino-Tibetan phrasebook, late 900s. Cave 17, Mogao Caves, Dunhuang, China. Ink on paper. H. 25 cm, L. 45.7 cm. The British Library, London, Or.8210/S.2736. Stein collection.

2.19 *left*
Paradise of Bhaishajyaguru, 836 or later. Cave 17, Mogao Caves, Dunhuang, China. Ink and pigments on silk. H. 153 cm, W. 178.4 cm. British Museum, London, 1919,0101,0.32. Stein collection.

to the Medicine Buddha are distinct in appearance from the other figures in the painting. They exhibit narrow waists, broad shoulders and elliptical halos, following a Himalayan-derived Tibetan type, as opposed to the rest of the painting, which follows a 'Chinese' manner.[81] Despite this difference, the painting maintains a consistent quality, indicating that the same painter or a group of painters produced the work and were able to confidently blend two artistic modes.[82] This familiarity is echoed in the Chinese and Tibetan inscriptions (now very faint). In this instance, the Chinese is written vertically from left to right, following in the direction of the Tibetan. The inscription records that the painting was commissioned by a Tibetan monk for the benefit of his mother's health. The date given has been interpreted as 836, during the Tibetan period in Dunhuang, although recent research suggests it could be later.[83]

The coexistence of different painting styles in Dunhuang has led to speculation as to whether works could have been produced elsewhere and then brought there. Ten banner paintings, three of which are in the British Museum, stand out as examples.[84] They have been linked to the artistic traditions of Khotan, Tibet, Kashmir and the Himalayas more generally, for reasons such as the representation of the bare chest, the crown with three peaks, and the *dhoti* (long loincloth) with colourful bands.[85] In addition, the images are painted on more densely woven silk and are narrower in width than other banners from Dunhuang.[86] They also do not have cartouches, which are typically included in compositions for writing Chinese inscriptions.[87] One of the ten banners has a Tibetan inscription on the verso identifying the bodhisattva as Vajrapani (fig. 2.20). Writing on the verso is a feature that can be found in Himalayan Buddhist paintings, leading to speculation that this group of paintings, especially the one of Vajrapani, may not have been produced in Dunhuang.[88] It has also been proposed that they could have been made during the Tibetan period at Dunhuang by a painter familiar with Khotanese and Himalayan artistic styles.[89]

Diplomatic envoys

Recent scholarship has highlighted the importance of diplomatic envoys in long-distance contact and exchange in Dunhuang during the Guiyijun period (851–c. mid-1000s).[90] It has been demonstrated that there was frequent and routine diplomatic engagement between Dunhuang and surrounding kingdoms in the Tarim Basin at this time, as well as with the 'Five dynasties' (907–60) and the Song dynasty (960–1127) after the fall of the Tang dynasty in 907.[91] At least forty missions from Dunhuang travelled to Chinese courts in the period from 850 to 1050.[92] The Ganzhou Uyghur Kingdom, located to the east of Dunhuang, sent at least seventy-nine diplomatic missions to the Chinese courts between 870 and 1030.[93] These journeys could involve a hundred or more people of different backgrounds, occasionally including women, such as the wives of envoys.[94] Moreover, interregional diplomatic relationships may have been be consolidated through marriage alliances, as was the case between the Cao family of Guiyijun Dunhuang and the ruling families of Khotan and the Ganzhou Uyghurs in the Tarim Basin.[95]

2.20

Bodhisattva Vajrapani, 801–50. Cave 17, Mogao Caves, Dunhuang, China. Ink and pigments on silk. H. 56.1 cm, W. 15.1 cm. British Museum, London, 1919,0101,0.103. Stein collection.

2.21

Envoys with horse and camel, 966. Cave 17, Mogao Caves, Dunhuang, China. Ink and pigments on paper. H. 31.5 cm, W. 86.3 cm. British Museum, London, 1919,0101,0.77. Stein collection.

A sketch from Cave 17 of a horse and camel with their grooms (fig. 2.21) has been interpreted as an energetic depiction of envoys with tribute animals, since the animals do not carry loads and the grooms wear the hats of government officials.[96] The hint of a whip still visible at the right end of the paper indicates the painting once depicted a longer procession. A sketch in a similar style of three more camels and two horses with grooms, now in the National Museum, New Delhi, may once have been part of the same composition.[97] In these sketches, the horse and camel are given equal emphasis by their matching size. Camels were vital for travel in the desert. The animal in the painting is a Bactrian camel with two humps (*Camelus bactrianus*), a more common species in this region than the single-humped Arabian camel (*Camelus dromedarius*).[98] Although horses were not so suitable for desert sands, they are faster on other terrains and were more valued as gifts than Bactrian camels.[99] It is not clear who the recipient of this tribute was, but the date of the sketch can be estimated from the writing on both sides of the paper, composed in the year 966 and thought to pre-date the image.[100] The writing records the restoration of a cave (Cave 96) sponsored by Cao Yuanzhong (d. 974), military commissioner of the Guiyijun, and his wife from the Zhai clan. The text refers to Cao Yuanzhong as a 'Great King' (*Da wang*) who ruled over Dunhuang. It also notes that he copied a sutra and disseminated it to seventeen temples, as well as one copy to the region of Xizhou (Turpan), then controlled by the Uyghurs, another example of diplomatic engagement.

Numerous documents from Cave 17 provide details of the experiences of diplomatic envoys, such as the customary exchanges of gifts between hosts and visitors. An incomplete document from Cave 17 lists the offerings from the ruler of the Ganzhou Uyghur Kingdom, his family and officials, to the Tang court, along with the corresponding return gifts from the Tang court for each item (fig. 2.22). It is impressed with the seal of the Tang commissioner of imperial manufacture.[101] As the Ganzhou Uyghur Kingdom was established in 894 and the Tang dynasty ended in 907, it can be dated to this short timeframe. The gifts from the Ganzhou Uyghurs included 'Persian' and other textiles, military equipment, ivory and antelope horns, as well as ammonium chloride (used as flux for metalwork and dyes), horses, food vessels, sable fur and jade belts.[102] Among the ruler's family

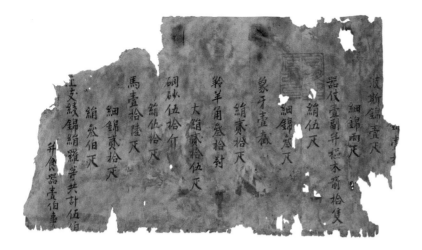

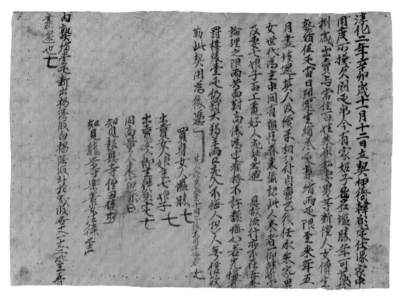

members who contributed was a princess who gave an unspecified token that came from the Uyghur queen. The return gifts from the Tang court were nearly all different types of silk textiles. For instance, a piece of ivory was reciprocated with twenty bolts of woven silk. This highlights once again the importance of textiles in diplomatic gift exchanges during this period, particularly those originating from China. Moreover, the variety of objects presented by the Ganzhou Uyghurs shows that diplomatic missions were one of the important ways through which luxury goods travelled at a courtly level.

Enslaved people could also be included as gifts of diplomatic envoys, a reminder of the human suffering that is a part of the history of the Silk Roads. On one occasion in the 900s, forty Sogdians were given by the ruler of the Ganzhou Uyghurs to Guiyijun Dunhuang.[103] Dunhuang manuscripts further indicate that there was an established trade of people in the city. One contract dated 991 records the selling of an enslaved woman in exchange for silk (fig. 2.23).[104] This agreement was made between a local official and his wife, and a monastery dependant and his family. Due to financial difficulties, the official decided to sell a woman called Xiansheng, who was 28 years old, for the price of three bolts of raw or un-degummed plain weave silk, payable immediately, and two bolts of degummed plain weave silk, payable in the following year. The contract was witnessed by two

monks, which may seem surprising. Surviving documents indicate that monks and nuns in Dunhuang and Turpan participated in the trade and possession of human beings, despite disapproval expressed in the Buddhist canon.[105] Xiansheng was apparently local to Dunhuang, but there is evidence that non-Han-Chinese people were traded in this region as well. For example, in another Dunhuang contract, from the mid-700s, an enslaved person probably from the west (*hunu*) called Duobao, aged 13, was sold for twenty-one bolts of silk, after having already been sold once before.[106] Both these contracts follow a standard format, suggesting the normalised practice of buying and selling of enslaved people, as well as the use of silk as a form of payment. In the case of Duobao, the contract emphasised the youth was of 'base' or 'mean' (*jian*) status as opposed to 'common' or 'good' (*liang*). This distinction follows the social organisation of Tang China, derived from earlier times, where commoners could not be enslaved unless they had been demoted to base status, such as by committing a crime.[107] Enslaved people held base status, although not all base people were enslaved.[108] The emphasis on Duobao as a 'base' person is assurance to his buyer that the transaction was lawful according to the Tang code.

Imported goods

Monastery inventories, found in Cave 17 and dating mostly from the Guiyijun period, provide evidence of imported objects in Dunhuang. Written in Chinese, these inventories record gifts from devotees, some of which were brought from elsewhere as indicated by the use of the term *hu* or *fan* in their description. These terms both broadly mean 'foreign', while *hu* tends to refer to West and Central Asia, specifically Sogdiana.[109] For instance, *hu* powder (*hufen*) refers to white-lead powder imported from the west of Tang China and used for wall paintings.[110] Sometimes, more specific sources are given for the objects, such as felt from Khotan, silver cups in a Byzantine style (*Fulin*, thought to be the ancient Chinese name for Byzantium) and items made of silk from Merv (*Molu*) in present-day Turkmenistan in Central Asia.[111] Unspecified gold and silver items, glass (*liuli*, could also mean crystal) vases, precious stones, incense and medicine are also assumed to have been imported.[112]

Depictions of glass can be seen on wall paintings as well as portable paintings from Dunhuang, usually carried in the hands of buddhas, bodhisattvas and monks. One example is a finely painted banner portraying a bodhisattva standing on a lotus while holding an alms bowl, translucent and of greenish tone, which clearly represents glass (fig. 2.24).[113] *Liuli* is considered one of the Seven Treasures of the Buddhist paradise and a symbol of clarity and purity.[114] The bowl in the banner painting is depicted with dots suggesting faceted sides, comparable to glass vessels associated with the Sasanian empire in West Asia (fig. 2.25).[115] A colourless Sasanian glass bowl with faceted decoration was excavated from a tomb near Datong, Shanxi province, China, dating to around the 400s CE.[116] A glass fragment of this type was also excavated by Stein in Loulan in the Tarim Basin and examples have been found as far east as Japan (see chapter 1).[117] However, based on comparable styles, the Dunhuang banner painting has been dated to 851–900, meaning it post-dates the production of Sasanian glass by two centuries or more.[118] While it is known that glass was brought to Dunhuang and gifted to monasteries, the question remains whether the painter had an opportunity to see antique examples of faceted Sasanian glass or if they were continuing a familiar depiction based on earlier painted models.

In one instance it is possible to match an extant example to a description in a monastery inventory. A manuscript from Cave 17, dated 873 and now in the Bibliothèque nationale de France (Pelliot chinois 2613), records a canopy made of red *fan jin* (*jin* is compound patterned woven silk) with roundels, each enclosing two lions and a pattern of birds in five colours.[119] The comparable design of confronting lions in a medallion can be observed along the silk border and tie of a sutra wrapper from Cave 17 (fig. 2.26). Several examples of textiles with a similar pattern are known, such as a sutra wrapper in the Musée Guimet, Paris, two in the Victoria and Albert Museum, London, and the shroud of Saint Columba and Saint Lupus in the cathedral treasury of Sens in France.[120] Another comparable textile, with confronting ibexes instead of lions, is the shroud of Saint Mengold in the Collegiate Church of Notre Dame at Huy in Belgium, which has been radiocarbon-dated with high probability to 780–980.[121] The Saint Mengold textile has an inscription written in Arabic identifying the owner and the amount he paid for it (38 gold dinars), suggesting that the purchase was probably made in Egypt or Syria, or possibly Iraq, although the textile may have originated further east.[122] Examples such as these show that textiles with confronting animals in a roundel design spread over long distances.

Scientific analysis can further help us identify possible imported materials by going as deep as the molecular level. It can also contribute to our understanding of production processes, such as the mixing of dyes and recycling in the case of textiles.[123] Dyes that were used to create the wide variety of colours in the Dunhuang textiles may have been local to the region or brought from elsewhere.[124] Recent scientific analysis has revealed that the green of the weft-faced compound twill (samite) border with the lion roundels on the sutra wrapper was obtained through a mixture of yellow larkspur and blue indigo.[125] Dye from the plant larkspur is rare in northwest China but common in Central Asia, which corroborates the theory that this textile was imported to Dunhuang and cut up for use in the sutra wrapper.[126] Data from this study has been used to aid in the reconstruction of several Dunhuang textiles to their original condition as far as is possible, taking into consideration colour fading and other changes over time.[127] One of the textiles involves the clamp-resist dyeing method, where the pattern is created using wooden clamps to reserve areas of the fabric, which is then dipped in the dye bath (fig. 2.27). Although the results are approximate, the reconstruction created by experts in China clearly shows the brightness and intensity of the original colours (fig. 2.28), pointing to the visual impact of these materials in their original state, as well as their contribution to a vibrant religious environment in Dunhuang.[128]

2.26
Sutra wrapper, late 700s–900. Cave 17, Mogao Caves, Dunhuang, China. Silk and hemp. H. 75.5 cm, W. 32 cm. British Museum, London, MAS.858 Stein collection.

2.27 *opposite left*
Clamp-resist dyed textile, 700–900. Cave 17, Mogao Caves, Dunhuang, China. Silk. H. 24.3 cm, W. 24.4 cm. British Museum, London, MAS.876. Stein collection.

2.28 *opposite right*
Work-in-progress modern replica of the textile shown in fig. 2.27 (MAS.876), 2024. Collaboration between the British Museum, the China National Silk Museum and Zhejiang University.

Gaochang under Tang rule

Dunhuang was close to the formidable Taklamakan Desert, which dominated the Tarim Basin. Travellers heading west could choose between northern and southern routes, both of which followed the rim of the desert, passing through oasis cities and towns before reaching the strategically located city of Kashgar (see fig. 2.11). During the period under discussion, this region was contested by Tang China and the Tibetan empire, as well as the Türk and Uyghur khaganates. Uyghurs of this period, one of the early Turkic peoples, may be considered among the ancestors of today's Muslim Uyghur population in Xinjiang.[129] Islamicisation of the region started after the early 1000s, with the arrival of Muslim Karakhanids from Central Asia.[130]

Situated along the northern rim of the Tarim Basin was the Kingdom of Gaochang, with its capital city around 30 kilometres southeast of modern Turpan. Gaochang had been under Chinese and Turkic control in the centuries preceding this period (see chapter 1). In 640 the Tang dynasty took control of the city, by which point the population was already predominantly Chinese.[131] This conquest led to further migration of Chinese people to the region, which is evident in the tomb finds from the Astana Cemetery, which served the population of Gaochang from the 200s to 700s. Epitaphs written in Chinese were placed at the entrance to the tombs. One example is the epitaph for Lady Qu, who died in 667 (fig. 2.29) and came from a major local clan that had ruled Gaochang from the early 500s until the Tang conquest.[132] Her husband Wang Huanyue, who was a military general of Gaochang, was granted a Tang official position as part of the Chinese government's policy of pacification.[133]

Paper manuscripts and other organic materials have survived from the Turpan region thanks to its arid conditions and the local practice of using recycled

大唐居運津被西州

驍騎之尉至都皆歸國

遷捅天山縣經一　　其夫

以斯晨殯葬於城西北原孔　其夫

逝即日媚居訓女教男聿巳成

年十二月九日卒於私第春

其月十一日春

2.29 *opposite*

Funerary tablet, 667. Astana Cemetery, Turpan, China. Clay. H. 36.2 cm, W. 37.5 cm, D. 4.3 cm. British Museum, London, 1928,1022.198. Stein collection.

2.30–2.32

Imitation Byzantine coin (left), Chinese coin (middle) and imitation Sasanian coin (right), 600–700 (left and right), 500–600 (middle). Found at Astana Cemetery, Turpan, China. Gold, copper alloy and silver. Diam. 1.6 cm, Weight 0.9 g (left), Diam. 2.2 cm, Weight 2.9 g (middle), Diam. 3.1 cm, Weight 3 g (right). British Museum, London, IA,XII.c.1, IA,XII.c.2, IA,XII.a.3. Stein collection.

paper to make funerary clothing.[134] From these manuscripts, it is known that Gaochang's population was nearly 40,000 shortly after the Tang conquest.[135] They also confirm the presence of different ethnic groups and languages in the region apart from Chinese, including Sogdians from Central Asia who settled in Turpan and dominated trade in these parts.[136] A collection of tax receipts, which has remarkably survived, records that over the course of a year some forty merchants, predominantly Sogdians, were trading in gold, silver, silk threads, aromatics and ammonium chloride.[137] There was also (less frequent) trade in brass, medicines, copper, turmeric and raw sugar.

Physical traces of long-distance trade in the Gaochang region can be found in the form of coinage: 130 Sasanian silver coins have been excavated from the Gaochang city site and about 30 from the Astana Cemetery.[138] This is out of about 1,300 examples that have been discovered in China, the majority in Xinjiang. In addition, at least nine Byzantine gold coins have been excavated from Turpan.[139] Sasanian and Arab-Sasanian coins were in circulation in Turpan from the late 500s to the early 700s – in one case, used in the purchase of an enslaved Sogdian for 120 silver (Islamic) dirhams.[140] The use of these coins in the Turpan region may have stopped partly due to Tang fiscal policies, including the spread of Chinese bronze coins and silk as a form of currency.[141] The question of money in use along the Silk Roads is complex.[142] Based on surviving documents, different forms of money seem to have been in circulation at different times.[143] As well as coins and silk, other textiles (hemp, cotton and wool), livestock and grain could be used for payment.[144]

Apart from their use in transactions, coins from the west were also imitated and incorporated into burial customs at Gaochang. In a tomb at the Astana Cemetery, the body of a man, an official from Dunhuang who died in 632, had a gold imitation Byzantine coin in his mouth (fig. 2.30).[145] The coin shows the head of Justinian I in three-quarter profile struck on the obverse. Lying next to him was a woman who had two Chinese bronze coins placed beside her head (fig. 2.31).[146] These have a standard square hole in the centre and bear the characters *wuzhu* ('five grains'), representing a coin type that was no longer produced from the year 621 but evidently still in circulation after that.[147] In another tomb, of a man and a woman, the man also had an imitation Byzantine gold coin in his mouth, while the woman had imitation Sasanian silver coins placed over her eyes (fig. 2.32).[148] The meaning and origin of this burial practice have been a matter of debate, but the presence of these coins certainly indicates the availability of foreign currency and the special value placed on them by local people.[149]

Due to the arid conditions, foodstuffs that were buried as offerings to the deceased are another rare survival from the Astana Cemetery. The discovery of rice grains (*Oryza sativa*) there offers clear evidence of the spread of this staple to northwest China from the Yangtze region in eastern China.[150] Considered alongside other archaeological finds, it points to the westward spread of rice into Central Asia, where it became more prevalent by the middle of the first millennium CE.[151] Rice was to become a major crop in southwest and Central Asia following the Arab conquests from the 600s, and dishes such as *plov* (related to pilau or pilaf in India and paella in Spain) are enjoyed today as a result of the transmission of rice along the Silk Roads.[152]

Another plant that spread along the Silk Roads was the grape vine. Examples of whole bunches or individual grapes have been preserved at the Astana Cemetery (fig. 2.33), along with pears and jujubes.[153] They were placed in vessels and trays as offerings to the deceased. Grapes were enjoyed across the ancient world, together with wine-drinking. Archaeological evidence indicates that grapes were already being cultivated in Xinjiang during the 300s to 200s BCE and wine from Central Asia was known in Han-dynasty China (206 BCE–220 CE).[154] However, it was during the Tang dynasty that wine gained wide popularity, facilitated by Sogdians who enjoyed, produced and traded the alcoholic drink (see p. 59).[155] The Tang conquest of Gaochang further contributed to the spread of viniculture to China. Records mention that a grape variety known as 'mare's teats' from Gaochang (still cultivated in Xinjiang today) was planted at the palace in Chang'an, and the technique for making wine was also transmitted there from the region.[156]

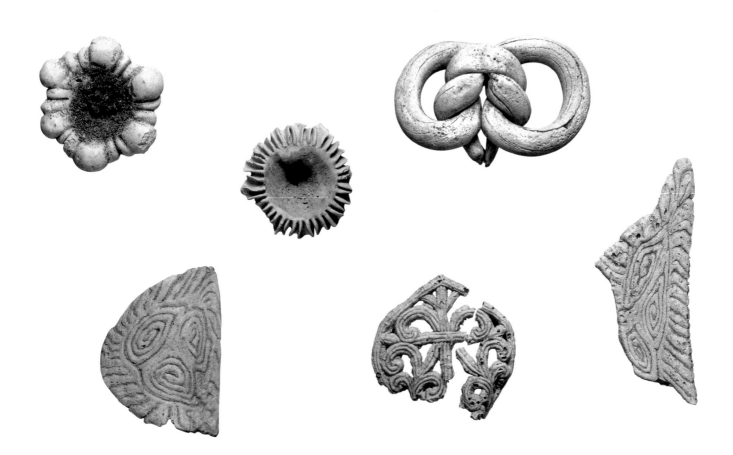

By comparison, the wider context for the astonishingly well-preserved small baked goods that were also offered to the deceased in the Astana Cemetery remains uncertain (fig. 2.34). Their similarity in appearance to treats commonly eaten today has prompted them to be identified as cookies, tartlets, pastries and wafers.[157] One of the small round examples has a granular substance in the centre containing a preserved grape, resembling a jam tartlet. Scientific analysis of similar examples found in Xinjiang has revealed that they were made of wheat flour (*Triticum aestivum*), a crop that became a staple in northern China during the Han dynasty.[158] So far, it has not been possible to convincingly match these food items to specific culinary records from the period, but they have been linked to *hubing* (baked bread, typically flattened), which was part of the wider non-Han Chinese cuisine that was imported from the west and embraced in Tang China.[159] The popularity of *hubing* in Tang China may have resulted in the wider use of shallow flat vessels that were more suitable for serving them (see chapter 1).

Kingdom of Kocho

After the retreat of Tang China from Central Asia, Gaochang was contested between Tibetan and Uyghur powers, until the latter secured it by the year 866 and established the Kingdom of Kocho (also Qocho).[160] The Uyghurs who settled in Kocho were fleeing from the fall of the Uyghur khaganate (744–840) based in present-day Mongolia. Another group of Uyghurs established the Ganzhou Uyghur Kingdom, located to the east of Dunhuang.

A particularly fine banner now in Berlin brings viewers face to face with an elite Uyghur from the tenth to eleventh centuries (fig. 2.35). Painted on both sides and on cotton, a material cultivated in Turpan, the main panel depicts an elegant and distinguished-looking man with a white beard, accompanied by two small figures.[161] Judging by his high crown, patterned red robe and belt with hangings, he must represent a figure of high rank, such as a Uyghur royal minister, as one interpretation suggests.[162] There are Old Uyghur scripts written at the top and bottom of the panel, the bottom inscription reading: 'For the soul of my father … Kara Totok.'[163] In Uyghur iconography, the tall flower stalk that he holds is a reference to a deceased person.[164] The format of this banner is similar to those found in Dunhuang, including the triangular upper part that depicts an image of a Buddha seated on a lotus pedestal. Yet, it features the portrait of a person, Kara Totok, as its primary subject, unlike Buddhist banners and hangings that typically focus on a divine being.[165] This and other pictorial elements have led to a reinterpretation of this work in relation to Manichaean funerary banners from Kocho.[166]

Established by the Parthian prophet Mani (216–274/77 CE), Manichaeism is a religion that originated in Mesopotamia in the 200s CE and found converts along the Silk Roads during the period 500 to 1000.[167] According to Manichaean teachings, the universe is divided between the benign and spiritual realm of light, and the dark and evil realm of matter. As the two have become intermingled in the present world, salvation is achieved through an understanding of this dualism and in seeking to free light from darkness.[168] This belief system reached Tang China in the 600s where it became known as Monijiao ('religion of Mani') (see chapter 1). In 762 the Uyghur ruler Bögü converted to Manichaeism through clerics from China.[169] Uyghurs continued to uphold Manichaeism as their state religion after their resettlement in Kocho. Some have suggested that the adoption of Manichaeism by Uyghur rulers was in part politically and economically motivated, enabling them to establish a distinct identity that unified the different tribes and to gain the support of Manichaean Sogdians.[170]

2.35 opposite
Memorial banner for Kara Totok, 900–
1100. Ruin Alpha, Kocho (Gaochang),
near Turpan, China. Pigments and
gold on cotton. H. 145 cm, W. 51.5cm,
D. 0.5 cm. Museum für Asiatische Kunst,
Staatliche Museen zu Berlin, III 4524.
First Turpan Expedition (1902–3).

2.36 above, left
Two Manichaean *electi*, 800–1000.
Ruin Alpha, Kocho (Gaochang), near
Turpan, China. Wall painting. H. 25.5 cm,
W. 39 cm , D. 3.5 cm. Museum für
Asiatische Kunst, Staatliche Museen zu
Berlin, III 4624. First Turpan Expedition
(1902–3).

2.37 above, right
Three Manichaean (?) women, 800–
1000. Ruin K, Kocho (Gaochang), near
Turpan, China. Wall painting. H. 27 cm,
W. 22 cm. Museum für Asiatische Kunst,
Staatliche Museen zu Berlin, III 6916.
Second Turpan Expedition (1904–5).

A wall painting fragment from the ninth to tenth centuries, excavated from
the ruins of Kocho, depicts two Uyghur Manichaean *electi* or clerics (fig. 2.36).[171]
It is painted with a degree of naturalism and concern for character that make it
comparable to the portrait of Kara Totok. In their dedication to the liberation
of light from darkness, Manichaean clerics practised celibacy and abstained
from eating meat and drinking wine.[172] Their garb consisted of tall headgear
and white priestly robes that covered their whole bodies, with only their faces
exposed – as can be glimpsed in fig. 2.36. A second wall painting fragment
from Kocho depicts women wearing headdresses of white cloth, who could be
Manichaean deities or perhaps laywomen (fig. 2.37).[173] The painting style of this
mural, including its blue background, has been compared to richly illustrated
Manichaean manuscript fragments on paper found at Kocho.[174] Even, fine lines,
bright colours and the use of gold are considered among the features of Uyghur
painting.[175] This particular example has also been categorised as an example
of 'Persian' or 'West Asian' style in Manichaean art, which scientific analysis
has confirmed to have been practised sometime between the late ninth and
early eleventh centuries.[176] This visual language with such distant origins raises
interesting questions as to how it was transmitted to, and preserved in, Turpan
after Manichaeism reached China.

Over time, however, Uyghurs came under the influence of local Buddhists and increasingly turned to their faith. By the early 1000s Uyghur rulers and most of their populace in the region were Buddhists.[177] The banner with the portrait of Kara Totok, discussed earlier, was probably produced at a time when the Uyghur elites were shifting their religious interests from Manichaeism to Buddhism.[178] Fragments from another wall painting also reflect Buddhism under Uyghur patronage (fig. 2.38). It was found at a low position on the back wall of the rear chamber of a temple complex that Stein called Ming-oi, about 60 kilometres south of Karashahr along the northern rim of the Tarim Basin.[179] Around the mid-800s, the Karashahr region came under the control of the Kocho Uyghurs.[180] Damaged in a fire in ancient times, the wall painting fragments once formed a continuous scene.[181] Kneeling young monks are depicted receiving instructions from their masters, while *apsaras* and Buddha-like figures descend from the sky. Notably, the figures in the scene on the far left are depicted using pens to write on *pothi* leaves that are held in the 'portrait' orientation. This would not suit Sanskrit but could accommodate Old Uyghur script, which was written vertically.[182] On the far right, a young man is shown kneeling in a posture of veneration, wearing a costume with patterns associated with Uyghur style.[183] This wall painting has been dated to the 900s, making it an early pictorial record of a Uyghur venerating Buddhism.[184]

2.38

Buddhist figures receiving instructions, c. 900–1000 or earlier. Ming-oi, near Karashahr, China. Wall paintings. Left to right: H. 72 cm, W. 47 cm; H. 68.5 cm, W. 39 cm; H. 73 cm, W. 50 cm; H. 48.5 cm, W. 17 cm; H. 66 cm, W. 17 cm; H. 56.5 cm, W. 43 cm. British Museum, London, 1919,0101,0.279d, c, b, a, l, m. Stein collection.

Shoe, late 700s–900. Excavated from
Mazar Tagh, China. Woollen felt, leather
and hemp. L. 25.5 cm, H. 9.9 cm,
W. 10.7 cm. British Museum, London,
MAS.495. Stein collection.

Khotan along the southern route

Gaochang or Kocho was a key settlement and stopping point for travellers along
the northern rim of the Tarim Basin. Along the southern route towards Kashgar,
travellers would encounter other communities, including the Buddhist Kingdom
of Khotan (see fig. 2.11). The heartland of Khotan lay between two rivers, the
Karakash and Yurungkash, and the region was famous for its jade (specifically
nephrite) sourced from these rivers.[185] Khotanese jade found a ready market in
China, which had long prized this mineral. Khotan was a thriving Buddhist centre.
The Tang monk Xuanzang stayed there for seven months during his journey to
India and noted the existence of more than a hundred monasteries with over 5,000
monks and nuns.[186] Like the settlements along the northern route, this kingdom
came under the control of different groups during the first millennium CE,
including Tang China and the Tibetan empire. However, it was to maintain its
own king and language, Khotanese, which was derived from Middle Persian and
written in a script related to Brahmi from India. An example of the script can be
seen in a Chinese–Khotanese *pothi* document from Cave 17, Dunhuang, discussed
earlier (see fig. 2.17). The rulers of Khotan and Guiyijun Dunhuang enjoyed close
ties until the Kingdom of Khotan was destroyed by the Muslim Karakhanids
around 1006.[187]

Khotanese materials have been found in sites around the modern city of Hotan
(Khotan, Hetian), such as silk textile fragments and woollen and felt items.[188] A
shoe made of woollen felt with leather patches, decorated with fan-pattern stitching
(fig. 2.39), from Mazar Tagh, north of Hotan, evokes daily life along the Silk Roads
and is a reminder of types of textiles other than silk that were used and traded.[189]

Important finds have been discovered at the ruins of Dandan Uiliq ('houses of ivory'), northwest of Hotan, abandoned by the end of the 700s. At one of the building structures at the site, Stein discovered part of a letter in New Persian written using Hebrew script, and with other elements, such as loan words, from Hebrew and/or Aramaic, as well as Middle Persian, Sogdian, Arabic and Chinese, reflecting a multilinguistic and multicultural context (fig. 2.40).[190] In 2004 a similar, almost intact, leaf was acquired by the National Library of China and appears to be the first page of the same letter. Its content relates to sheep trading and gifts needed to secure a deal, including silk, aromatics and sugar.[191] The second leaf also reports the defeat of Tibetan forces at Kashgar further west, presumably around 790. This makes the letter one of the earliest surviving Judaeo-Persian documents and therefore important in the understanding of the development of the Persian language.[192] Given the Sogdian elements in the text, it has been suggested that the writer of the letter was probably a Persian-speaking Sogdian who was possibly Jewish.[193] This two-page letter, together with a Jewish prayer document preserved in Cave 17, points to the possible existence of Jewish traders in the Tarim Basin.[194]

Also excavated at Dandan Uiliq were painted wooden votive panels, dated probably to the sixth to eighth centuries, that relate to the history of the Silk Roads. These panels were found inside buildings, along the base of walls and at the foot of pedestals, although some have holes on the back, suggesting that they may have once been fixed to the wall. Several of the panels, which may be painted on either or both sides, depict the Buddha as well as Hindu gods, highlighting connections with the Indian subcontinent. Other votive panels do not follow Buddhist or Hindu iconography and are more difficult to decipher. For instance, a rider on a spotted horse holding a bowl, accompanied by a black bird and a camel rider, has been interpreted in relation to the Buddhist Heavenly King Vaishravana, guardian of Khotan, and as a reference to the Turkic groups presenting diplomatic gifts to Khotan (fig. 2.41).[195] However, the recent discovery of wall paintings depicting similar imagery raises the possibility that the figures actually portray local deities.[196] Another example painted on both sides shows a combination of figures from Buddhist and local pantheons (fig. 2.42). One side of the panel shows a male figure holding a fan facing an animal-headed deity (identified by Stein as the 'rat king' who helped the king of Khotan defeat a nomadic group called the Xiongnu).[197] The deity may also be identified as a wolf-headed figure related to spirits who protected children. The third figure to the right has not been identified. The reverse of the panel depicts five seated buddhas.

Several other painted panels from Dandan Uiliq depict a popular legend of how silk production reached Khotan.[198] The story tells of a princess from the east, presumably China, who smuggled silkworm eggs and mulberry seeds in her headdress as she travelled to marry the king of Khotan. A monastery was later built on the spot where the mulberry seeds were planted. Versions of this legend can be found in Tibetan and Chinese sources, including an account by Xuanzang.

2.40

Letter in New Persian written in Hebrew script, c. 791. Dandan Uiliq, Khotan, China. Ink on paper. H. 45.5 cm, W. 38 cm. British Library, London, Or.8212/166. Stein collection.

2.41 *opposite*

Votive panel depicting horse and camel riders, probably 600–800. Dandan Uiliq, Khotan, China. Ink and pigments on wood. H. 38.4 cm, W. 18.1 cm, D. 1.7 cm. British Museum, London, 1907,1111.70. Stein collection.

In a panel now in the British Museum, the princess is portrayed in the centre, with perhaps a basket of silk cocoons next to her (fig. 2.43).[199] To the left is a female figure who seems to be gesturing towards the princess' headdress where the contraband is hidden. On her other side is another female figure with a loom who holds a comb beater used in weaving, an example of which was excavated from Mazar Toghrak near Hotan (fig. 2.44). Between them is a smaller figure, a male deity with four arms who has been identified as the patron deity of weaving. While the subject matter of the legend of the 'silk princess' is convincing, uncertainty remains over how to interpret the details of this painting. For instance, the women on both sides have been described as attendants, and yet they have halos, matching those of the princess and the god of weaving, indicating a level of importance if not divine status. Moreover, it is unclear whether the four-armed god is local to Khotan or a deity originating from elsewhere.[200]

The westward spread of silk technology from China had probably been taking place since the Han dynasty, when China expanded into the Tarim Basin.[201] For instance, silk produced at the site of Niya, east of Khotan, has been dated to the first to fourth century CE.[202] By the 600s Khotan had an established textile industry. In his travel records Xuanzang noted that Khotan produced woollen carpets, felts and floss silk that differed from spun silk from central China.[203]

2.42 *top*

Votive panel, possibly depicting the 'rat king', probably 600–800. Dandan Uiliq, Khotan, China. Ink and pigments on wood. H. 10.6 cm, W. 44.8 cm, D. 1.9 cm. British Museum, London, 1907,1111.68. Stein collection.

2.43 *bottom*

Votive panel depicting the 'silk princess', probably 600–800. Dandan Uiliq, Khotan, China. Ink and pigments on wood. H. 10.8 cm, W. 46 cm, D. 2.4 cm. British Museum, London, 1907,1111.73. Stein collection.

Unlike in Chinese practice, Khotanese textile makers did not kill the silkworms but left them to develop into moths and break from the cocoon, which resulted in shorter fibres. The same process was used in India, perhaps in consideration of the Buddhist prohibition on killing.[204] In the painted votive panels, the spread of sericulture has been elevated into the realm of legend.

Embedded in the story of the silk princess of Khotan is a history of royal women who travelled along the Silk Roads as part of marriage alliances and the role they played in the transmission of knowledge, shown in the diplomatic overtures surrounding the marriage of the Tang princesses Wencheng and Jincheng to Tibetan rulers. Notably, Jincheng is believed to have played an active role in negotiating peace between Tang China and the Tibetan empire. In 733 a stone stela marking the boundary between the two powers was erected upon her request following the signing of a peace treaty.[205] She asked for and received Chinese texts and products from the Tang court, and was presumably accompanied by an entourage who travelled with her from Tang China.[206] Women like her and their unnamed female attendants were also part of the history of the Silk Roads.

This chapter's journey, which started on the coasts of Southeast Asia and reached the desert oases of the Tarim Basin, highlights the great diversity of terrain that the Silk Roads covered, as well as the multidirectional nature of connections, which did not solely move east–west. Across this vast region, many peoples of different languages and beliefs, bringing with them a variety of objects and knowledge, came into contact with each other at times of war and of peace, particularly evidenced by the wealth of material discovered in Cave 17, Dunhuang. The Sogdians from Central Asia, who played a key role in this spread of goods and ideas across many parts of the region and beyond, will be the focus of the next section.

2.44
Comb beater, probably 700–800. Mazar Toghrak, China. Wood. H. 18.2 cm, W. 15.7 cm, D. 2.3 cm. British Museum, London, MAS.472. Stein collection.

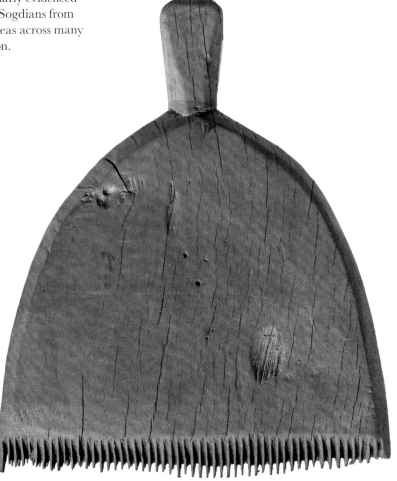

Sogdians from Central Asia

Luk Yu-ping

Sogdians were once among the great traders of the Silk Roads.[1] Setting forth from their homeland of Sogdiana (Sogd, Sogdia) between the two rivers Zeravshan and Kashkadarya (in present-day Uzbekistan and Tajikistan), they engaged in trade across thousands of kilometres, from the steppe to India, China to the Mediterranean.[2] Their widespread commercial activities are known from at least the 300s CE, reaching their peak in the 500s to around the mid-700s.[3] Mobile, adaptable and familiar with languages in addition to their native form of Middle Iranian, Sogdian traders took advantage of the opportunities that the Silk Roads presented.[4] They established diaspora communities particularly in China, which further facilitated the interaction of cultures (see p. 54).

Sogdiana consisted of a confederation of city-states or principalities, each with its own ruler. Historically, it was a region where different cultures came into contact: it was once a part of the Achaemenid Persian empire (550–330 BCE) before it was conquered by Alexander III, known as Alexander the Great, followed by successive nomadic groups.[5] In the 560s, it came under the rule of the Türks who expanded from the Mongolian Plateau. Many Sogdians participated in the administration as well as the military and diplomatic service of their new overlords, who in turn protected the Sogdian traders.[6] When the Türks in Central Asia were defeated by Chinese forces around 660, the city-states of Sogdiana become nominal vassals of the Tang dynasty, which lasted until the Arab conquest of the region in the early eighth century. Sogdiana flourished during the period of its alliance with the Türks and Tang China, and its urban centres prospered with the support of commerce and agriculture.

The reach of the Sogdians

Sogdian traders crossed mountains and deserts to reach China in the east. Historical records and archaeological finds indicate the presence of Sogdian communities stretching from the desert oases of the Tarim Basin (see chapter 2), across the Hexi Corridor to the capital Chang'an (Xi'an; see chapter 1) and the eastern capital Luoyang, on to Youzhou (Beijing) and Yingzhou (Chaoyang) in northeast China.[7] These communities were formed by merchant caravans of people, often with pack animals, travelling together for safety. They had chieftains known as *sartapao* (Chinese: *sabao* or *sapu*) who were given official government rank during the Tang dynasty.[8] There may have been Sogdian communities in southern China as well.[9] It is not certain if they went further east beyond China, although objects that passed through their hands did reach the Japanese archipelago: two pieces of aromatic sandalwood preserved in Hōryū-ji, a temple in Nara; they date to before 761 and bear a Sogdian mark and a Pahlavi (a form of Middle Persian) inscription.[10]

Opposite

Detail of south wall of the 'Hall of the Ambassadors', *c.* 660s (see fig. 2.53).

To the north, a Sogdian presence has been identified in the upper reaches of the River Yenisei in southern Siberia.[11] To the south, Sogdian inscriptions, dating probably from the 300s to 500s, appear on cliffs along the upper reaches of the Indus in northern Pakistan.[12] Although evidence is more limited after that, their involvement in trade with the Indian subcontinent most likely continued for some time.[13] There is also some indication that they were present in Southeast Asia.[14] To the west of their homeland in Central Asia, Sogdians reached Persia, the Black Sea region and as far as the Mediterranean world.[15] In 568 a Turkic and Sogdian embassy travelled to Constantinople, initiated by the Sogdians who sought to trade directly with the Byzantine Mediterranean, bypassing the Sasanian empire.[16] Additionally, there are intriguing mentions in Arabic and Persian sources of the movements of traders from Sogdiana after the Arab conquest of the region, including one individual from Samarkand who travelled to Guangzhou, China, via maritime routes. It is, however, impossible to know if they refer to Sogdians, Arabs or Persians living in Sogdiana after the conquest.[17]

Traders, makers and transmitters of ideas

The size of a Sogdian merchant caravan could range from just a few to several hundred people, and it may have been joined by travellers from other regions.[18] The Sogdians traded in a great variety of goods, from horses to gemstones, furs, textiles and even peaches.[19] Many of the western imports in Chang'an probably arrived there through the Sogdians (see chapter 1). Documents from Turpan in the Tarim Basin (see chapter 2) mention that items sold there by the Sogdians included gold, silver, brass, silk and aromatics. People were also traded, as attested in documents such as a sales contract, also found in Turpan, written in the Sogdian language and concerning an enslaved girl called Upach.[20] Born in 'Turkestan' (parts of Central Asia including Xinjiang) from a family that came from Samarkand, Upach was sold for 120 silver coins (drachms) of high purity that were minted in the Sasanian empire.[21]

Sogdians also traded wares that they produced. Sogdian metal vessels have been excavated from sites in China dated to the Tang dynasty and earlier.[22] One example is a silver bowl found in the western suburbs of Xi'an, which has a circular polylobed shape similar to a silver bowl excavated in Chilek, near Samarkand (fig. 2.45), from the sixth to seventh centuries.[23] The latter has a Sogdian inscription along its rim referring to the 'head of the community', indicating that it was once owned by a local leader.[24] A ceramic jug from Kafir Kala, dated to the same period, is another type of vessel form that spread to Tang China (fig. 2.46). The shape of

2.45 top
Bowl with Sogdian inscription, 500–700. Excavated at village of Chilek, Samarkand region, Uzbekistan. Silver. H. 3.8 cm, Diam. 16.5 cm (rim), 7 cm (base). Samarkand State Museum-Reserve, Uzbekistan, KP-2934/A; A-390-2; BS-2.

2.46 bottom
Jug, 500–700. Kafir Kala, Samarkand region, Uzbekistan. Fired clay with mica dressing. H. 24 cm, W. 14 cm. Samarkand State Museum-Reserve, Uzbekistan, A-183-814.

the jug imitates metalware, which is accentuated by the mica (a silicate mineral) dressing that gives it an almost metallic sheen. Its handle is attached to the top of the neck, as is more typical of Sasanian examples, rather than the shoulder.[25] A small ceramic tomb figure from the Tang dynasty depicting a Central Asian or Sogdian is shown carrying a similar type of jug (see fig. 1.30). Sogdian vessels inspired artisans in Tang China who adopted and adapted their forms and decorative elements (see chapter 1). Luxury metalware arrived in Sogdiana as well. The silver bowl from Chilek, noted above, was found with an earlier Sasanian silver dish showing a royal hunt and a bowl attributed to the Hephthalites, a tribal confederation in Central Asia, that may have been produced in areas south of Sogdiana.[26]

Apart from metalware, it is widely believed that the Sogdians excelled at making textiles.[27] Their richly patterned clothing, particularly with medallion designs, is represented on wall paintings in Central Asia. Comparable examples of archaeological textiles have been found in the Tarim Basin and nearby sites, including in Cave 17, Dunhuang, China (see chapter 2), although these may have been locally produced and inspired by imported designs or fashioned through a collaboration between makers of Chinese and Central Asian backgrounds.[28] Attributions are challenging since very few examples have been excavated from Sogdiana.

2.47 *above*

Textile with confronting ibexes in pearl roundels, 700s. Cave 17, Mogao Caves, Dunhuang, China. Silk. H. 28.5 cm, W. 26.2 cm (left); H. 22 cm, W. 8.3 cm (right). British Museum, London, MAS.876.a and b. Stein collection.

2.48 *left*

Map of key cities and settlements in Sogdiana.

A piece of textile kept in the Huy Cathedral, Belgium, was considered a representative example of Sogdian textile given its inscription, once thought to be Sogdian (see p. 90). The textile's repeated pattern of confronting animals with horns or antlers is similar to two fragments found in Cave 17, Dunhuang (fig. 2.47). However, the inscription turned out to be Arabic, so questions remain.[29] There is no doubt, however, that the Sogdians must have played a key role in the spread of textiles, styles and patterns, given the extent of their travels and their expansive mercantile activities.

As well as people and objects, Sogdian travellers facilitated the transmission of ideas. Based on documents found in northwest China and other archaeological finds, the Sogdian diaspora followed a form of Zoroastrianism (see below) as well as a variety of other religions, including Buddhism, Christianity, Manichaeism and possibly Judaism (see fig. 2.40), as well as participating in the translation of religious texts.[30] One of the legacies of the Sogdians is the transmission of their script, which originated from Aramaic. The Uyghurs adopted the Sogdian cursive script in the late 500s, and this became the basis for a form of writing known as 'Uyghur script' and later for writing Mongolian and Manchu.[31] The latter script was used by the Manchu rulers of the Qing dynasty (1644–1912) in China. Although Sogdian ceased to be used as a written language after the 1000s, it continued to be spoken. One dialect survives to the present day in a remote area of Tajikistan.[32]

Life and death in Sogdiana

Archaeological finds in the past century have revealed the richness of life and material culture in the city-states of Sogdiana (fig. 2.48), contrasting with stereotypical images of Sogdians from Tang China as pedlar-merchants and entertainers (see fig. 1.30). Impressive wall paintings from sites such as Panjikent, Samarkand, and Varakhsha relate to religious themes, narrative compositions, scenes of banquets and less common historical events (see below and chapter 3).[33] Carvings in wood and plaster have also been preserved. A notable example is from the citadel of Kafir Kala, located around 12 kilometres southeast of Samarkand at a meeting of routes that connected Samarkand to surrounding areas.[34] Discoveries there include four charred wooden panels, which were part of a large doorway from the 500s, preserved due to carbonisation (fig. 2.49). The panels were found inside a throne room in the citadel, which was presumably set on fire during the Arab conquest of the region (see chapter 4).[35] The panels portray two images of Nana, the supreme goddess of Sogdiana, accompanied by male worshippers carrying a variety of offerings, who may represent the heads of important

families in the city.[36] The image of Nana in the central panel is consistent with earlier depictions of the goddess from Bactria (now part of Afghanistan, Tajikistan and Uzbekistan), while the other Nana, at the top of the arch, has four arms, two holding the sun and moon, and is seated on a lion throne (fig. 2.50). The latter reflects a new image of Nana, incorporating borrowings from India that emerged in Sogdiana in the 500s, suggesting continued cross-cultural interactions.[37]

The worship of the goddess Nana was part of the Sogdians' religious beliefs before the arrival of Islam. There is also archaeological evidence of the spread of Christianity in Sogdiana.[38] Furthermore, Sogdians followed a local form of Zoroastrianism, a religion named after Zarathustra (Greek: Zoroaster, regarded as the founder) that originated from Central Asia and became the state religion of the Sasanian empire (224–651 CE).[39] The continuity of this religion among the Sogdians in Sogdiana can be observed in the widespread use of ossuaries for storing the bones of the deceased after the body had been defleshed by birds of prey, in accordance with Zoroastrian belief. An example from Mulla Kurgan, west of Samarkand, has moulded decorations that clearly depict two Zoroastrian priests facing a fire altar (fig. 2.51). They are wearing mouth-coverings to avoid polluting the sacred fire with their breath. Female dancers depicted on the pyramidal lid of the ossuary may represent figures from paradise or personified qualities of perfection and immortality.[40] Zoroastrian imagery, such as the sacred fire, also appears on funerary objects belonging to Sogdian immigrants in China who assimilated local burial practices (see fig. 1.34). Overall, the religious practices and pantheon of the Sogdians in Central Asia are difficult to ascertain due to limited textual sources from the region.[41]

Paintings in the 'Hall of the Ambassadors'

The leading city-state of Sogdiana was Samarkand, in present-day Uzbekistan. The Tang Chinese monk Xuanzang, who visited the city during his journey to Central Asia and India between 629 to 645, praised it as 'a great commercial entrepôt … very fertile, abounding in trees and flowers, and yielding many fine horses. Its inhabitants were skilful craftsmen, smart and energetic'.[42] The prosperity of Samarkand at this time can be

2.49 opposite left
Parts of a door with carvings showing Nana and worshippers, 500–600. Excavated at Kafir Kala, near Samarkand, Uzbekistan. Charred wood (reconstructed). H. 118 cm, L. 148 cm. Samarkand State Museum-Reserve, Uzbekistan, A-666-1 to 6.

2.50 opposite right
Line drawings of the door and a detail of Nana with worshippers. Drawings by M. Sultanova.

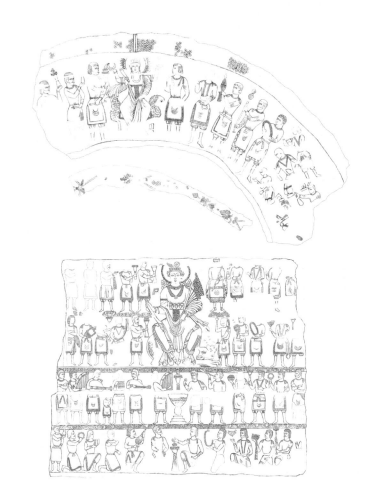

observed in the wall paintings that were excavated from a reception hall known as the 'Hall of the Ambassadors' in an aristocratic house in Afrasiab, the old city of Samarkand, in the 1960s. Although large parts of the wall paintings do not survive, the remaining sections reveal a complex composition that reflects the world view of the Sogdian elite.[43]

The reception hall derives its sobriquet from the depiction of representatives from foreign lands bearing gifts in the lower part of the wall painting of the main wall to the west (fig. 2.52). An inscription written in Sogdian records the words of envoys from two neighbouring principalities – Chach (present-day Tashkent) and Chaganian (a principality south of Samarkand) – addressed to the ruler of Samarkand, Varkhuman (r. *c.* 650–70). Based on their different dress and gifts they bear, the other envoys in the wall painting have been identified as representatives of Sogdian and nearby Tokharistani principalities, as well as from Tang China and the Tibetan empire. In addition, two men with feathers in their headdresses are believed to have come from as far away as the Korean Peninsula. Notably, the Tang envoys are depicted carrying cocoons and raw silk, highlighting the continued importance of China as a source of this luxury material in Central Asia.[44] Also portrayed among the figures are many Türks with long plaits, serving as guards and higher-ranking officers. These individuals presumably followed Varkhuman after their defeat in Central Asia by Tang China around the mid-600s.[45] The upper part of this wall painting is missing but it probably portrayed Varkhuman greeting the envoys. More recent research suggests that this gathering depicts Nowruz or Iranian New Year, a spring equinox festival celebrated by the Sogdians, when the ruler met with high-ranking figures and horsemen.[46]

The wall painting to the left of the main scene (on the south side of the hall) depicts a ritual procession held on the sixth day of Nowruz, when Varkhuman would have travelled to a shrine to perform sacrifices for his ancestors (fig. 2.53). He is accompanied by his consorts, guards, Zoroastrian priests wearing mouth-covers and high-ranking figures, some riding horses and camels. Three women riding side-saddle near the front of the procession are identified by an inscription as his secondary wives.[47] The woman riding an elephant at the front of the procession is thought to be Varkhuman's principal wife, while Varkhuman himself is the largest figure behind the group on horseback.

Opposite this (on the north side) is a wall painting that intriguingly portrays scenes from a Tang Chinese court (fig. 2.54). The scene on the left depicts women in a boat celebrating the Duanwu or Dragon Boat Festival, which coincided with Nowruz in 660 and within days of it in 663.[48] The right side of the painting depicts a hunting scene with a figure on a horse that is equivalent in size to Varkhuman in the procession on the opposite wall. It is thought that this figure represents the Tang emperor Gaozong (r. 649–83) and that the larger woman on the boat depicts his consort Wu Zetian, who would later take over the throne. The final wall painting on the entrance wall (east side) is badly damaged but the parts that survive suggest that it depicts legendary scenes associated with India.

The wall paintings in the 'Hall of the Ambassadors' are thought to have been created around the 660s, at a time of major changes in the region. The Sasanian empire collapsed in 651. In 657 Tang China defeated the last of the Western Türks and annexed their territory. The following year Gaozong sent an envoy to officially appoint Varkhuman as the governor of Samarkand and Sogdiana as part of the Tang protectorate in Central Asia.[49] The wall painting emphasises the importance of the alliance with Tang China to the Sogdians. Although the painting's commissioner and its intended audience are not known, it can be viewed as a form of royal propaganda that draws parallels between Varkhuman and the Tang emperor, as well as Nowruz celebrated by the Sogdians and the Duanwu festival in China. The remarkable survival of this set of wall paintings offers a window into the way the Sogdian elite wished themselves to be seen – not only as traders or intermediaries but as central to the context of the neighbouring region and the wider world.

During the 700s, Tang China retreated from Central Asia. The political unrest preceding the fall of the Tang dynasty in 907 impacted on the Sogdian diaspora in China.[50] Sogdiana itself was conquered by caliphate forces in the early 700s, after which it was gradually assimilated into the wider Islamic Iranian-speaking world.[51] The Sogdians, who were major participants along the Silk Roads, faded from the historical stage until archaeological discoveries and studies of manuscripts once more brought them to light. The transition of the city-states of Sogdiana to Islamic rule, and the resulting development of new elements in visual and material culture, are introduced in chapter 4, while the Türks who formed close alliances with the Sogdians are discussed further in chapter 3.

2.51

Ossuary, 600–800. Mulla Kurgan, Samarkand region, Uzbekistan. Fired clay. H. 69 cm, W. 53.2 cm, D. 25 cm. Samarkand State Museum-Reserve, Uzbekistan, A-436-1; KP-3582.

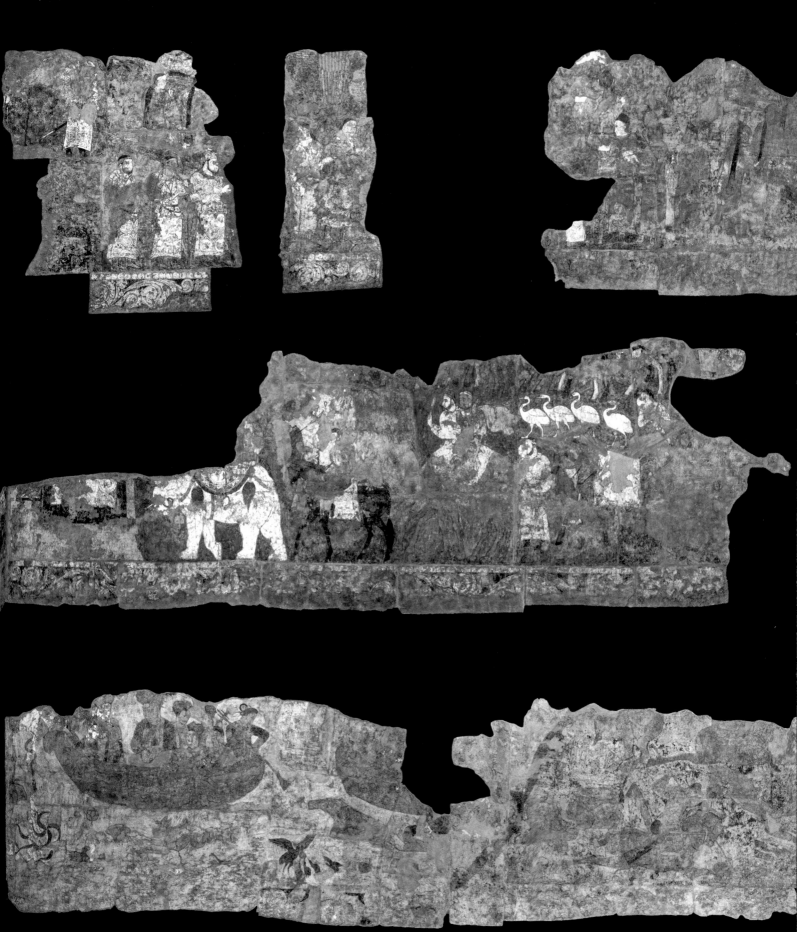

2.52 top

West wall of the 'Hall of the Ambassadors', showing representatives from foreign lands, *c.* 660s. Afrasiab (Samarkand), Uzbekistan. Wall painting. W. 11 m (approx., entire wall). Samarkand State Museum-Reserve, Uzbekistan, KP-6251.

2.53 middle

South wall of the 'Hall of the Ambassadors', showing the procession of Varkhuman and an entourage travelling to the shrine of his ancestors, *c.* 660s. Samarkand (Afrasiab), Uzbekistan. Wall painting. H. 250 cm, W. 670 cm (this section); W. 11 m (approx., entire wall). Samarkand State Museum-Reserve, Uzbekistan, KP-6251.

2.54 bottom

Detail from the north wall of the 'Hall of the Ambassadors', showing Tang court women in a boat (left) and a hunting scene (right), *c.* 660s. Samarkand (Afrasiab), Uzbekistan. Wall painting. W. 11 m (approx., entire wall). Samarkand State Museum-Reserve, Uzbekistan, KP-6251.

3

CENTRAL ASIA
AND THE STEPPE

Central Asia and the steppe

Tim Williams and Luk Yu-ping

The Eurasian steppe is a vast ecoregion of temperate grasslands, savannas and scrublands, depending on the season and latitude.[1] It stretches across present-day northeast China, Mongolia and the Xinjiang Autonomous Region to the plains of eastern Europe (fig. 3.1). The climate is too dry to support most trees, but not dry enough to create a desert. A complex region, the steppe cannot be considered in isolation from the mountain valleys, foothills and deserts to its south. Within such landscapes and ecosystems, societies emerged that developed into largely nomadic confederations and at times extensive empires. The highly skilled horse-riding people of these societies used their mobility to exploit scarce resources and to manage a peripatetic form of animal husbandry, with a tribal social organisation united by effective leaders. Additionally, the open terrain of the steppe, easily traversed on horseback, formed a corridor in the vast networks of the Silk Roads,[2] bringing nomadic groups into contact with settled communities, together with products that came from different ecologies.[3]

Between around 500 and 1000, early Turkic peoples, notably the Türks (also Göktürks; Chinese: Tujue), and later the Uyghurs, dominated the steppe.[4] Their

3.1

Map showing the Eastern and Western Türk khaganates and sites mentioned in the chapter.

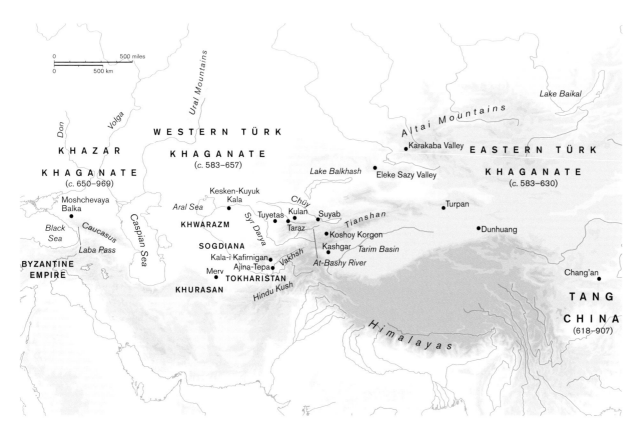

frontiers shifted in rhythm with waves of invasions and conflicts, interspersed with long periods of stability. Under the ruling Ashina clan in the mid-sixth century, the pastoral nomadic Türks rapidly expanded from the Altai Mountains at the western edge of the Mongolian Plateau, crossing the western Eurasian steppe to establish an empire that extended from northeast China to the frontiers of the Sasanian and Byzantine empires in the west (fig. 3.1).[5] In 569, the Türks defeated the Hephthalites in Central Asia to claim control over Sogdiana (see p. 105). The First Türk khaganate (552–630), ruled by a supreme leader known as a khagan, separated into the Eastern and Western Türk khaganates. Following defeats by Tang China, a Second Türk khaganate emerged in 682 and lasted until 744, when it was succeeded by the Uyghur khaganate (744–840). In the late sixth century, another Turkic group, known as the Khazars, established a major commercial empire in the northern Caucasus region, adjacent to Byzantium.

Spectacular archaeological finds, such as the dazzling gold artefacts belonging to the Scythians and Saka uncovered in present-day Ukraine, southern Russia and East Kazakhstan, have revealed the distinctive cultures that dominated the Eurasian steppe in earlier periods BCE. However, within the context of their participation in Silk Roads networks between 500 and 1000, the material culture of pastoral nomads is not well known in wider scholarship.[6] Recent archaeological discoveries have furthered understanding of Turkic societies not only along the steppe, but also in regions further south where they held sway. The Turkic elite's access to luxury material is suggested by a suite of gold belt fittings excavated in 2021 from a temple complex dating from around 600 to 700 at the Eleke Sazy Valley in eastern Kazakhstan (figs 3.2–3.3). These exquisite items comprise multiple rectangular mounts that would have adorned the length of a leather belt, and two scallop-edged buckles for fastening it. The most complete of these, measuring just 3.5 centimetres across, is thought to depict a crowned khagan, lavishly dressed and seated powerfully on a horse-headed throne while kneeling attendants, left and right, offer bowls of food and drink.[7] Gold-trimmed belts like this one were important symbols of power and status in Turkic communities for centuries. This example was probably an item of investiture that came from the Western Türk khagan.[8]

3.2

Belt plaque with the image of a Turkic khagan seated on a throne, *c.* 600–700. Excavated at Eleke Sazy, Kazakhstan. Gold. L. 3.3 cm, W. 2.8 cm, D. 0.2 cm. East Kazakhstan Regional Local Historical Museum.

3.3

Belt plaques, *c.* 600–700. Excavated at Eleke Sazy, Kazakhstan. Gold. L. 2.9 cm, W. 1.7 cm, D. 0.7 cm. East Kazakhstan Regional Local Historical Museum.

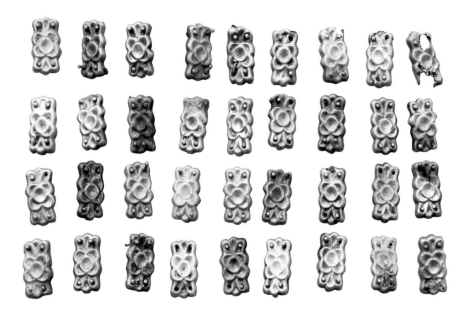

3.4

Statue, 700–900. Inner Tien Shan (Tianshan). Stone. H. 119 cm, W. 35 cm, D. 15 cm. National History Museum of the Kyrgyz Republic, Bishkek.

3.5

Lamp in the shape of a yurt, 900–1100. Excavated at the Taraz settlement. Clay. H. 14 cm, Diam. 18 cm (bottom). Zhambyl Regional Local Historical Museum, Kazakhstan.

Pastoral nomads and settlements

Pastoral nomadic peoples across Eurasia were reliant on the exploitation of mountain pastures and seasonal steppe grasslands. The animals they raised depended on local ecological conditions, but primarily horses and sheep, as well as goats, cattle and camels, were used for subsistence, exchange and transportation. These communities had interred their most important members in substantial burial mounds, known as kurgans, since ancient times. Thousands of them survive across the steppe, from Ukraine in the west to Mongolia in the east, leaving a highly visible legacy in the landscape. Other markers were also used, the most striking of which are perhaps anthropomorphic stone statues, traditionally known as *balbal*, that appear to have served as memorials and grave markers, placed on top of, or around, some kurgan burials.[9] The practice was inherited by Turkic nomads around the sixth or seventh century, developing a distinct iconography.[10] The example illustrated here (fig. 3.4), one of many displayed at the State History Museum in Bishkek, Kyrgyzstan, rests one hand upon a bladed weapon sheathed at the waist, and raises a globular vessel in the other.[11] These enigmatic stone figures were once thought to represent individual warriors. More recent research suggests that they were erected to honour the deceased, shown in a posture of ritual libation offered to a greater power.[12]

Steppe tribes were not exclusively nomadic. They developed important seasonal settlements, which might include agriculture, and increasingly populated cities, or had suzerainty over existing ones, such as the city states of Sogdiana. During

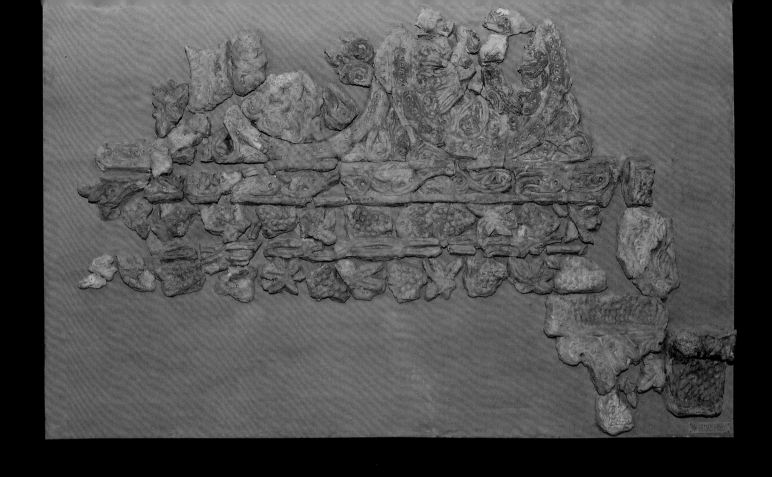

3.6

Carved wall decoration fragment, 700–800. Excavated at the Kulan settlement. Clay. H. 80 cm, W. 130 cm. National Museum of the Republic of Kazakhstan, Astana, Fragment no. 5.

the sixth to seventh centuries, Sogdians became willing collaborators and advisors to their Turkic overlords, who in turn protected and supported their trading activities. The overlap of nomadic and settled elements may be represented by a ceramic model that illustrates an essential part of nomadic life. It depicts a portable round tent, commonly called a yurt, transformed into a lamp indicated by traces of soot on its inner walls (fig. 3.5).[13] The model shows details of the tent, with a folding wooden lattice called a *kerege* serving as the foundation, covered and insulated with skins or felt, with ropes encircling the tent, and a smoke outlet at the top. It was found in Taraz, located near the southern border between present-day Kazakhstan and Uzbekistan. Taraz has been a major settlement since the first century CE, a connecting point along the Silk Roads that skirted the northern edge of the Chatkal and Kyrgyz mountain ranges, connecting with Burana (in present-day Kyrgyzstan) in the east, and Samarkand and Otrar (in Uzbekistan and Kazakhstan) to the west.[14]

In other instances, new settlements developed under Turkic rule, such as Kulan in southern Kazakhstan, inhabited from the seventh to the early thirteenth centuries.[15] The site had a citadel containing a palace dating to the eighth century with rooms richly decorated with carved clay friezes (fig. 3.6).[16] The clay was applied to a thick layer of plaster

and carved directly on location following a preliminary sketch, before the panel was painted in red or ochre.[17] Motifs on the walls of the palace at Kulan, such as large rosettes with intertwined vegetal elements featuring grapevines, are paralleled in West Asian art. The existence of viniculture at the site is indicated by the nearby remains of an agricultural estate with a workshop for the production of grape wine.[18] The Tang Chinese monk Xuanzang passed by Kulan in 730 during his journey to India, suggesting that it was a known stop for travellers from further east.[19]

Archaeological finds at other settlements also suggest the possible spread of objects, motifs or artisans. For instance, fragments of a striking censer (incense burner) dating to the eighth to tenth century (fig. 3.7) have been found at the Koshoy Korgon settlement in the mountainous At-Bashy Valley, Kyrgyzstan. Between the inner and outer rim of the vessel are openings for releasing burnt incense smoke. Its body is decorated with repeated stamped medallions encircling the bust of a crowned man. A similar motif in a roundel appears on a ceramic jar excavated at Yawuluk, Kashgar, in the Xinjiang Uyghur Autonomous Region, south of Koshoy Korgon and separated by mountain ranges.[20] These objects may be part of wider networks of transmissions via the Sogdians, as the crowned figure depicted on them is comparable to imagery found on Sogdian wall paintings and ossuaries near Samarkand, much further west.[21]

Incense was probably one of the commodities that Turkic tribes sought through trade. Archaeological evidence indicates that it was used in religious rituals. A ceramic censer in the shape of a boot was discovered at Kesken-Kuyuk Kala, near the Aral Sea in northwest Kazakhstan, at a temple site (fig. 3.8), along with other ceramic vessels, remains of animal sacrifices and an altar platform. Moreover, the settlement is known as one of the 'marsh towns' near the Aral Sea which may have functioned as an entrepôt that connected Central Asia to trade networks operating along east European river systems.[22] It is another example of a settlement under Turkic dominance that functioned as an important node along the Silk Roads in the period 500 to 1000. The number of these settlements across Central Asia raises questions about the degree to which the Turkic khaganates were 'nomadic', as opposed to urban, in character.

Buddhist art in Tokharistan

To the south, around 625, the Western Türk khaganate annexed the region of Tokharistan (formerly Bactria) that straddled northern Afghanistan, southern Uzbekistan and Tajikistan.[23] Buddhism, which is thought to have originated in northern India between the sixth and fifth centuries BCE, began to spread to Central Asia around the first or second century CE via Silk Roads routes through the chains of the Pamir Mountains and Hindu Kush. Many ancient cities testify to the spread of Buddhism in Central Asia, such as Merv in present-day

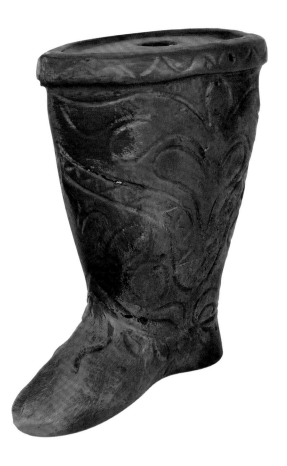

3.7 *opposite*
Censer, 700–1000. Excavated at Koshoy Korgon, Inner Tien Shan (Tianshan), Kyrgyzstan. Clay. H. 19 cm, W. 27.5 cm. National History Museum of the Kyrgyz Republic, Bishkek.

3.8 *right*
Censer in the form of a felt boot, 900–1100. Excavated at Kesken-Kuyuk Kala, Kazakhstan. Clay. H. 16.7 cm, W. 14 cm, D. 11.5 cm. National Museum of the Republic of Kazakhstan, Astana.

Turkmenistan, and Mes Aynak and Bamiyan in present-day Afghanistan (on Bamiyan, see chapter 4).[24] The religion was first adopted in Tokharistan during the second century when it was under the control of the Kushan empire (about 30–375 CE), formed by another group of pastoral nomads known as the Yuezhi.[25] Buddhism in Tokharistan fell into decline when the region was contested by the Sasanian empire and the Hephthalites, but experienced a revival when it came under Turkic dominance in the seventh century.[26] Pilgrims who travelled these regions included the Chinese monks Xuanzang and Yijing (see pp. 75, 108), as well as Hyecho from the Korean Peninsula (see p. 41).[27]

The complex beliefs of Turkic peoples included ancestral rites as well as a form of heaven worship in which Heaven (*Tengri*) is a supreme entity in relation to earth and humankind.[28] Turkic populations also began to adopt religions such as Buddhism, Manichaeism and Christianity, and later Islam, as these faiths spread along the Silk Roads. According to Xuanzang, the Western Türk khagan Tong Yabghu (r. 618–*c*. 630), who received him in 630, was apparently sympathetic to Buddhism.[29] Overall, the Türk khaganates demonstrated religious tolerance in the territories under their control.[30] It seems this tolerance enabled the revival of Buddhism in Tokharistan in the seventh century, but at the same time it left little trace of Buddhism in neighbouring Sogdiana, which was also under Turkic dominance.[31]

One of the Buddhist complexes in Tokharistan that developed during this period of Buddhist revival was Ajina-Tepa in the Vakhsh Valley in present-day Tajikistan.[32] Routes connected the valley to Sogdiana to the northwest, Afghanistan and the Indian subcontinent to the south and the oasis settlements of the Tarim Basin in the east. The complex included a monastery and an adjoining temple with a central stupa.[33] The discovery of coins, including one Sogdian coin, has helped to date the complex to the mid-to-second half of the seventh century.[34] It was abandoned and damaged as a religious site during the Arab conquest of this region around the mid-eighth century, but later it was once more occupied and used as workshops and living quarters.[35]

The walls of the Buddhist complex at Ajina-Tepa were decorated with colourful paintings, including the depiction of kneeling worshippers holding gold and silver vessels.[36] Many clay statues have been discovered at the site, the most impressive of which is an astonishing 12-metre-long clay statue of 'Buddha in Nirvana' or 'Sleeping Buddha', reclining on its right side on a pedestal with a headrest representing a cushion (fig. 3.9). It is located in the northwest corridor, which comes at the end point of ritual circumambulation around the main stupa.[37] Remains also point to another monumental Buddha image (4 metres high seated, 7 metres high standing).[38] The presence of colossal Buddha sculptures connects Ajina-Tepa to notable examples across Central Asia, such as those dated earlier in the Bamiyan Valley, and around and near the Tarim Basin, including Dunhuang, and further into China, such as at the Yungang and Longmen rock-cut temples. The latter were patronised by rulers of the Northern Wei dynasty (386–535), who also originated from the steppe. Much of the upper body of the reclining Buddha at Ajina-Tepa, including the head, was badly damaged and later reconstructed. An impression of its original appearance can be gained from other Buddha sculptures found at the site, such as one example created at larger than life size (fig. 3.10).[39] Despite it also being partially damaged, it is still possible to observe the arch of the eyebrows, the double curls in the centrally parted hair and the gentle expression of the image, all features comparable to examples from Afghanistan and the Tarim Basin.

Ajina-Tepa shows clear links to the Buddhist art and architecture of Gandhara,[40] a region in present-day northern Pakistan, with shared characteristics covering a wider region that includes the Swat Valley, the city of Taxila and parts of

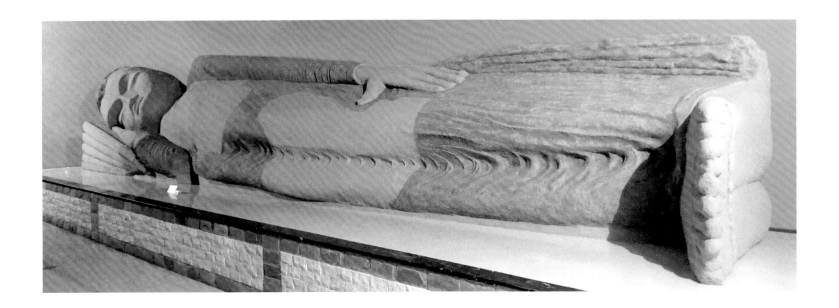

3.9

Replica of the 'Sleeping Buddha' from Ajina-Tepa, Tajikistan. Clay. L. 12 m. National Museum of Tajikistan, Dushanbe. The lighter restored section can be seen in the middle.

Afghanistan and Kashmir.[41] For instance, Ajina-Tepa's monastery is arranged in a quadrangular plan around a courtyard decorated with sculptures, similar to those found in Gandhara.[42] Sculptures at the site are also comparable to earlier Gandharan examples produced from the first or second century CE onwards. The latter is best known for its connection to the art traditions of ancient Greece and the Roman empire far away to the west, developing long after the Macedonian ruler Alexander III ('the Great') conquered Gandhara, as well as Sogdiana and Tokharistan.[43] A sculpture of a lay worshipper of the Buddha at Ajina-Tepa demonstrates the resemblance in the supple drapery of his robe, which clings to his form (fig. 3.11). The energetic treatment of the curly hair, once painted black, specifically recalls sculptures from Hadda in Afghanistan, part of the wider region associated with Gandhara.[44] The figure's outer garment, with its overlapping front panels folded to form lapels, is commonly known as a kaftan (also caftan) (see p. 137). It was a popular type of clothing across Eurasia, notably among the Turkic pastoral nomads and Sogdians that came under their sway. Another sculpture depicts the torso of a figure, perhaps a bodhisattva or a princely figure dressed like a bodhisattva (fig. 3.12). Once again, the naturalistic modelling of the body and clinging drapery recalls Gandharan art, while the depiction of the jewellery shows connections to Indian Gupta sculptures.[45]

In addition to Ajina-Tepa, Buddhist sculpture and wall paintings have been discovered at other sites along the Vakhsh and Kafirnigan (Kofarnihon) rivers. These include a head with a monster face found at Vakhsh Valley, probably representing the demon Mara (fig. 3.13), who, according to Buddhist tradition, was a malignant celestial king who strove to stop Prince Siddhartha from achieving Enlightenment, primarily by trying to seduce him with visions of beautiful women. Another torso, perhaps representing a Buddhist Heavenly King (Lokapala) or part of a noble retinue (fig. 3.14), was discovered at Kala-i Kafirnigan, an ancient town-site north of Ajina-Tepa, which was home to a Buddhist temple decorated with sculptures and murals. A painting was found near its entrance showing two female donor figures and a kneeling male donor preceded by a monk. Similar processions of worshippers are typically depicted in the wall paintings of rock-cut temples situated around the Tarim Basin and Dunhuang.

3.10

Head of a Buddha, 600s. Excavated at Ajina-Tepa, Tajikistan. Clay. H. 58 cm, W. 30 cm. National Museum of Tajikistan, Dushanbe, КV-13989.

3.11

Figure of a man wearing a kaftan, late 600s or early 700s. Excavated at Ajina-Tepa, Tajikistan. Clay. H. 70 cm, W. 44 cm, D. 13.5 cm. National Museum of Tajikistan, Dushanbe, КV-13990, RTL-79.

3.12

Figure of a prince, divine being or bodhisattva, late 600s or early 700s. Excavated at Ajina-Tepa, Tajikistan. Clay. H. 75 cm, W. 35 cm. National Museum of Tajikistan, Dushanbe, КV-14096, RTL-9.

3.13

Head of the demon Mara, 600s. Found in the Vakhsh Valley, Tajikistan. Clay. H. 28 cm, W. 24 cm. National Museum of Tajikistan, Dushanbe, КV-13971.

3.14

Figure of a Lokapala (Heavenly King), late 600s or early 700s. Excavated at Kalai-i Kafirnigan, Tajikistan. Clay. H. 35 cm, W. 23 cm. National Museum of Tajikistan, Dushanbe, КP-1912.3.

Co-existence of religions in the Chüy Valley

The Chüy Valley, part of present-day Kyrgyzstan and southern Kazakhstan, was a place where nomadic steppe and traditional agricultural regions met in the view of mountains. In the seventh century, the valley became the political centre of the Western Türk khaganate, and a network of settlements and cities rapidly appeared.[46] Archaeological finds suggest that, as in many places along the Silk Roads, different religions co-existed in this region, providing further evidence of tolerance and the spread of different faiths across Central Asia.

One of the ancient cities in the Chüy Valley, Suyab (present-day Ak-Beshim, Kyrgyzstan), represents a microcosm of the power struggles to control land and trade that took place along the Silk Roads (fig. 3.15). The valley offered excellent agricultural production, as well as being situated on vital east–west routes connecting western China and Central Asia. Agriculture provided sustenance for the large sedentary populations in towns and required the development of irrigation and farming technologies. The rare survival of a wooden plough from Suyab (fig. 3.16), dated to the eighth or ninth century, reflects the importance of the sown lands, and once again the overlap of steppe and farming worlds.

Suyab was probably founded as a Sogdian settlement by the sixth century.[47] Subsequently, it became the capital of the Western Türk khaganate. By 659, however, after the khaganate fell to Tang China, the city became the westernmost military outpost of the Tang dynasty, which was expanding into Central Asia. A significant archaeological find at Suyab is a stone fragment from a stela with a Chinese inscription, which states it was commissioned by the Chinese military official Du Huaibao (active *c.* 679) (fig. 3.17), who was stationed at Suyab to guard the city.[48] The discovery of this inscribed fragment in 1982 confirmed for the first

3.15 *opposite top*
Suyab (modern Ak-Beshim), in the broad and fertile Chüy Valley, Kyrgyzstan. The Tang fort is in the foreground, under excavation, and the Sogdian and later city lies in the background.

3.16 *opposite bottom*
Plough, 700–900. Excavated at Ak-Beshim, Kyrgyzstan. Wood. H. 94 cm, W. 46 cm (base), D. 20 cm. National History Museum of the Kyrgyz Republic, Bishkek.

3.17 *top*
Du Huaibao stela fragment, late 600s. Excavated at Ak-Beshim, Kyrgyzstan. Stone. H. 13.5 cm, W. 32.6 cm, D. 11 cm. Archaeological Museum at the Kyrgyz-Russian Slavic University, Bishkek.

3.18 *right*
Fragment of a Buddhist stela, 700–800. Excavated at Ak-Beshim, Kyrgyzstan. Stone. H. 67 cm, W. 47.5 cm, D. 12.5 cm. National History Museum of the Kyrgyz Republic, Bishkek.

time that Suyab was the city of Suiye referred to in Tang sources, and one of the Anxi Protectorates established by Tang China. Li Bai (701–762), one of the greatest poets in China's history, was born there before moving to present-day Sichuan province, China.[49] Subsequently, Suyab was further contested between Tang Chinese and Turkic forces, until Turkic groups held it from the late 700s onwards and the settlements persisted until the Mongol period.[50]

Architectural remains of three Buddhist complexes have been discovered at Suyab, with scholars proposing dates ranging from the sixth to the twelfth centuries.[51] One of the notable finds is a red stone fragment of a stela that clearly depicts the Buddha seated on a lotus pedestal accompanied by an attendant (originally presumably a pair) and lions (fig. 3.18).[52] The linearity of the carving and the style of the Buddha's robe suggest its derivation from China. Other interesting finds include a group of delicate bronze openwork plaques still bright with gilding (fig. 3.19). These were found in different locations in one of the Buddhist complexes.[53] Some of the plaques show a Buddha image with a fiery halo, sitting on a lotus pedestal and flanked by two kneeling worshippers. Another group shows a Buddha sitting between acanthus leaves, while a further example is inlaid with gemstone. The function of these plaques has not yet been determined. The largest plaque depicts a pair of figures seated on a throne, holding a small camel in their hands, recalling the journeys that facilitated the spread of religions.

Evidence indicates that Buddhism was newly established in Suyab in the seventh century.[54] Xuanzang, who stayed in the city when it was the capital of the Western Türk khaganate, did not mention the presence of the religion in the city or the Chüy Valley. It has been suggested that the expansion of the Tang dynasty into Central Asia probably led to the establishment of Buddhist complexes at Suyab and nearby areas, as well as the spread of Buddhist art styles from Tang China and the Tarim Basin.[55] Therefore, while Buddhism initially spread from the Indian subcontinent to China and beyond, over time it also moved in the opposite direction.

In addition to evidence of Buddhism, remains of two Christian church complexes have been found at Suyab, demonstrating the spread to Central Asia of the Church of the East that originated from Syria.[56] One of the churches had a wine cellar attached to it.[57] Among the finds are circular terracotta plaques with recessed images of Church of the East-style crosses, their shape characterised by flared arms (fig. 3.20).[58] A cross with Sogdian inscriptions has also been discovered there.[59] There are additionally indications of the presence of Zoroastrianism, as well as Islam, which arrived later with the rule of the Karakhanids, a Turkic Muslim dynasty, from the mid-tenth century.[60]

Beyond Suyab, traces of different beliefs have been found elsewhere in the Chüy Valley, such as objects bearing Hindu imagery from other settlements. Many are finely made and highly decorative, as illustrated by surviving bronze figures depicting the Hindu deities Shiva and Parvati (figs 3.21–3.22). Such objects demonstrate the work of skilled artisans, which in turn suggests that wealthy support for Hinduism existed in the area. The spread of Hinduism from South Asia into Central Asia, via the Pamir and Himalayan mountain chains, is another example of the role of the Silk Roads as a conduit for belief systems in the region. The presence of the Hindu Shahi dynasty (c. 822–1026) that ruled most of northern and northwestern Pakistan and parts of Afghanistan provides an explanation for the presence of Hindu artefacts in Central Asia.[61] It is interesting to note that similarly ornate and decorative portable altars relating to Jainism, one of the oldest religions still practised today, have also been found in the Chüy Valley and date to around the same time as the objects with Hindu imagery (figs 3.23–3.24). It seems that the interplay of beliefs, and the support for them among the elite and the populace, was complex – unsurprisingly so, given the interaction of people and ideas along the Silk Roads.

3.19 *opposite*

Plaques depicting Buddhist deities and symbols, 600–800. Excavated at Ak-Beshim, Kyrgyzstan. Gilded bronze and gemstone (?). Clockwise from top left: Diam. 11.2 cm; H. 8.3 cm, L. 11 cm; Diam. *c.* 11 cm; H. 8 cm, L. 9 cm. National History Museum of the Kyrgyz Republic, Bishkek.

3.20 *below*

Two plaques with recessed images of crosses, 700–800. Excavated at Ak-Beshim, Kyrgyzstan. Clay. H. 5 cm, Diam. 16 cm (top); H. 6.5 cm, Diam. 15 cm (bottom). National History Museum of the Kyrgyz Republic, Bishkek.

3.21

Statue of the Hindu deity Shiva, 800–1200. Found in the Chüy Valley, Kyrgyzstan. Bronze. H. 17 cm, W. 18 cm. National History Museum of the Kyrgyz Republic, Bishkek.

3.22

Statue of the Hindu deity Parvati, 800–1200. Found in the Chüy Valley, Kyrgyzstan. Bronze. H. 13.5 cm, W. 6 cm. National History Museum of the Kyrgyz Republic, Bishkek.

3.23

Jain portable altar, 800–1200. Excavated at the Ken-Bulun (Ken-Bulyn) settlement, Chüy Valley, Kyrgyzstan. Bronze. H. 10 cm, W. 5 cm. National History Museum of the Kyrgyz Republic, Bishkek.

3.24

Jain portable altar, 800–1200. Excavated at the Ken-Bulun (Ken-Bulyn) settlement, Chüy Valley, Kyrgyzstan. Bronze. H. 10 cm, W. 5 cm. National History Museum of the Kyrgyz Republic, Bishkek.

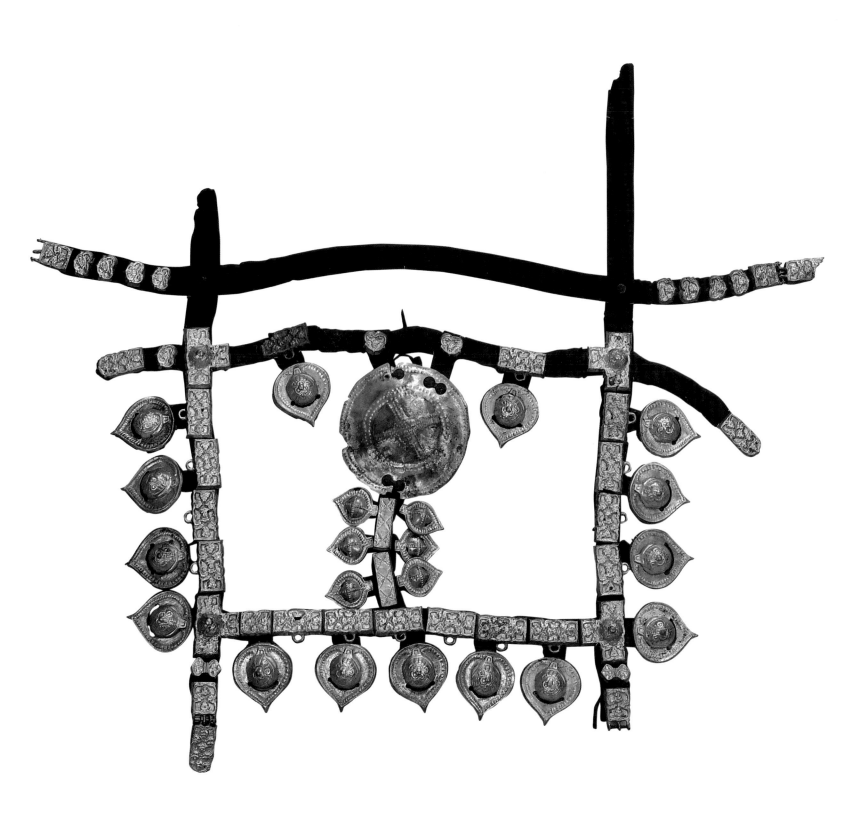

Shared horse culture, shared designs

Archaeological finds have confirmed the importance and sophistication of horse culture among the lands of the pastoral nomads since ancient times.[62] Later examples of horse equipment have been found in the burial grounds at Tuyetas in East Kazakhstan, dating to the ninth to eleventh centuries and the rule of the Kimek khaganate, which emerged after the collapse of the First Türk khaganate.[63] A magnificent bridle from the burial of a high-ranking Kimek warrior speaks to the importance of luxury horse equipment as a symbol of status and tribal affiliations among pastoral nomads (fig. 3.25).[64] The bridle is decorated with metal plaques, mostly made of silver, with embossed motifs, including a rounded plaque on the browband with a cross that refers to the solar symbol of Tengrism.[65]

At another important archaeological site, Karakaba, located in a high valley surrounded by mountains in eastern Kazakhstan, excavations have revealed graves of people buried with horses, horse equipment – such as a saddle, stirrups (see figs 3.28–3.29) and a bridle – and a range of weapons.[66] These include items made from organic materials that are remarkably well preserved, such as a leather container for a bow dating to the eighth to ninth centuries, decorated with silver plaques, including, intriguingly, one with a cruciform shape, though its symbolism is yet undetermined (fig. 3.26).[67] A matching quiver valve, for closing the mouth of a quiver made of leather, similarly decorated with rows of silver plaques, was found in the same burial (fig. 3.27).[68] Interestingly, a musical instrument made of wood with a long neck and oblong body was also discovered in this burial.[69] It is one of three musical instruments of different designs excavated at Karakaba, revealing hitherto unknown cultural, perhaps religious, dimensions that co-existed with martial aspects of the Turkic tribes that populated the Kazakh Altai around the seventh to ninth centuries.

3.25 *opposite*

Horse bridle, 800–1100. Excavated at Tuyetas, East Kazakhstan. Gilt silver, iron and leather. H. 72 cm, L. 168 cm. National Museum of the Republic of Kazakhstan, Astana.

3.26 *above*

Bow case, 700–900. Excavated at Karakaba, East Kazakhstan. Leather and silver. L. 99. 5 cm, W. 20 cm. National Museum of the Republic of Kazakhstan, Astana.

3.27 *right*

Quiver valve, 700–900. Excavated at Karakaba, East Kazakhstan. Leather and silver. H. 11.5 cm, L. 26 cm, D. 8 cm. National Museum of the Republic of Kazakhstan, Astana.

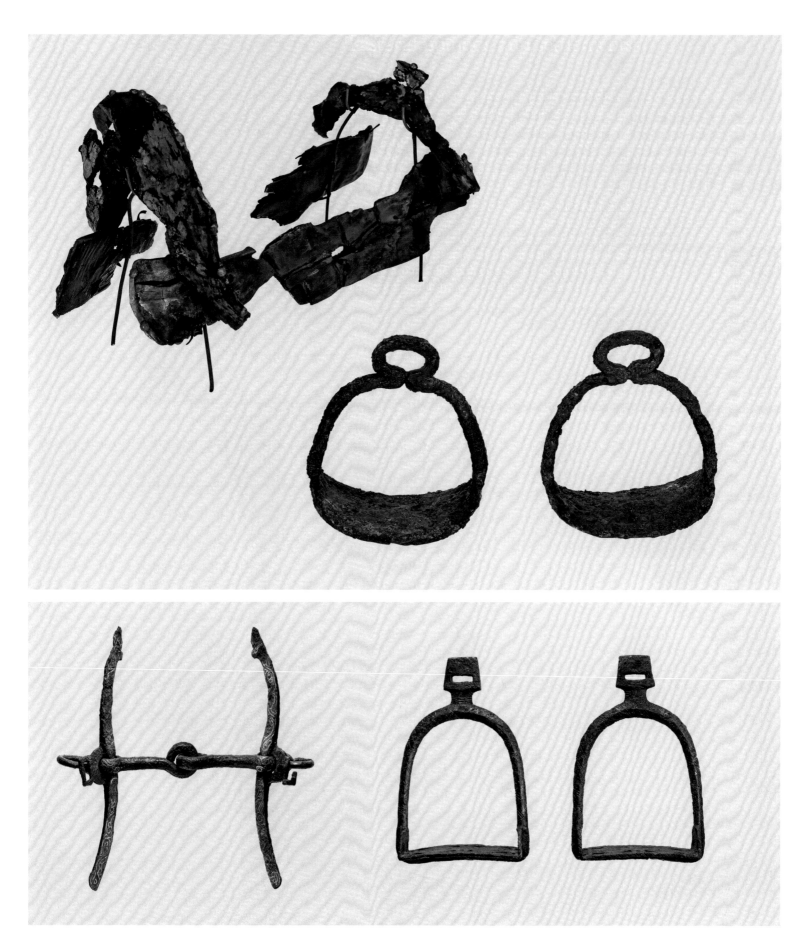

Saddles and stirrups

The Silk Roads acted as an important conduit for the transmission of horse equipment and military technology both east and west. Archaeological finds from across the steppe region demonstrate a variety of technological skills that were developed, adopted or adapted there. Excavations have enriched understanding of the developments in horse-riding equipment between 500 and 1000, building on practices that had existed for millennia along the steppe. A rare but informative survival is the wooden framework of a saddle, known today as a 'saddle tree', found at Tuyetas (fig. 3.28).[70] The rigid structure of solid saddle trees made of wood distributed the rider's weight evenly across the horse's back, protecting the animal's spine, particularly when the rider braced against the stirrups. Such rigid saddles developed among Turkic peoples no earlier than the first half of the sixth century, reproducing the semi-rigid saddles of previous periods.[71] This development is the precursor to all modern saddles with rigid frames.[72]

Another benefit of a rigid saddle is that it enables riders to make greater use of the stirrups to rise or stand in the saddle, which made cavalry attacks more effective.[73] Stirrups became popular around the fourth century onwards, coinciding with the development of tall saddlebows (the arched front part of a saddle), which made horse mounting more challenging.[74] The invention of tall saddlebows, preceding the Turkic saddletree, has been attributed to the Xianbei, another nomadic group based in the eastern Eurasian steppe.[75] This combination of saddle and stirrup became popular in East Asia in the fourth to sixth centuries. From there, the paired stirrup spread westward, primarily via the nomadic peoples of Central Eurasia, reaching Europe by the seventh or eighth century. Metal stirrups developed further following the invention of rigid saddles and became a standard part of horse equipment, perhaps the single most significant technological innovation in equestrianism around this time.[76] Examples of metal stirrups have been found at various sites, such as iron ones from Karakaba (fig. 3.29), while finer examples of a different shape, associated perhaps with the later semi-nomadic group known as Khazars based in the northern Caucasus (see p. 136), are made of iron inlaid with intricate silver ornamentation, a style also found on a bridle bit (figs 3.30–3.31).[77] These pieces of equipment, still so familiar to horse-riders today, had a significant impact on the development of horsemanship and mounted warfare, affording greater stability and control.[78]

Riding dress

Riding dress is another aspect of material culture related to horse riding that originated from the steppe and was later widely adopted. By the early first millennium BCE, pastoral nomads who roamed the steppe belt across Asia had invented sewn and fitted clothing that protected them from the region's harsh climate.[79] This type of clothing would subsequently develop into belted jackets and open unbelted coats that were worn, with variations, by people of different ethnic and cultural backgrounds from China to the Mediterranean and beyond by the sixth century.[80] The garments are known by a variety of different names that may overlap and are used interchangeably, such as coat, robe and kaftan. One suggested distinction between them is that coats open down the front, while kaftans are fastened to one side.[81] Examples of riding coats can be seen depicted on the ceramic tomb figures from Tang China (see fig. 1.36) and in actual garments excavated in Egypt (see fig. 5.17). They are referenced in the fashions of the Rus' in eastern Europe (see p. 140) and in a burial at Taplow, southeastern England (see p. 261). Trousers,

3.28
Saddle, 700–1000. Excavated at Tuyetas, eastern Kazakhstan. Wood and foil. H. 21 cm, W. 46 cm, D. 19 cm. National Museum of the Republic of Kazakhstan, Astana.

3.29
Stirrups, 600–900. Karakaba, eastern Kazakhstan. Iron. H. 13 cm, W. 12 cm. National Museum of the Republic of Kazakhstan, Astana.

3.30–3.31
Bridle and stirrups, 800–1000. Thought to be from near Perm, Russia. Iron inlaid with silver. W. 22.9 cm (bridle); H. 17.8 cm (stirrups). British Museum, London, 1878,0509.46–8.

typically worn with this outer garment, also seem to have originally developed as a form of clothing in connection to horseback riding and mounted warfare.[82]

While this kind of clothing was not new in the period 500 to 1000, there were notable developments during this time, including the adoption of steppe-style robes by the Tang court as official clothing (see p. 56). Such robes were also accepted as diplomatic gifts that were used to consolidate political relationships between imperial China and neighbouring lands.[83] Moreover, it has been suggested that this period saw greater cultural mixing in the making and design of steppe-style robes that combined motifs and techniques from different sources, together with silk and other textiles such as cotton and wool, a likely result of greater connectivity across Eurasia than before.[84]

Examples of this development may be found in the textiles excavated from tombs at Moshchevaya Balka in the mountains of the northwest Caucasus, near the Laba Pass that connected it to the Caspian and Black Sea regions.[85] The extraordinary finds from this site dating to the eighth to the ninth centuries include near-complete garments. Such textiles are seldom recovered from excavations in the region, where climatic conditions have led to the destruction of most perishable organic remains.[86] Notably, silks found at this site are thought to come from a variety of sources – Central Asia, Tang China, the Tarim Basin and the Mediterranean realm.[87]

One exquisite example of riding wear includes a kaftan and a pair of leggings, comparable to finds from Moshchevaya Balka (figs 3.32–3.33).[88] The kaftan, originally fur-lined, is made of finely woven linen with a decorative strip of silk sewn along the exterior and interior edges. These silk borders bear a pattern of rosettes and stylised animals in roundels, dyed in dark blue, yellow, red and white on a dark brown ground. The leggings are also made of silk and decorated with the distinctive roundels, while the parts covering the feet are made of linen. The pearl roundel pattern was widespread across Eurasia, from the eastern Mediterranean to Japan, particularly from the sixth to ninth centuries.[89]

It has been suggested that the robe and leggings could have belonged to a man from the Alan region in the Caucasus, then under Khazar domination.[90] The Khazars, a semi-nomadic Turkic group, emerged as an independent power after the break-up of the Western Türk khaganate in the seventh century. They created a powerful khaganate of their own that, over more than three centuries (c. 650–965), expanded into one of the foremost trading empires of the period, dominating a vast area from the Volga-Don steppes to the eastern Crimean Peninsula and into the northern Caucasus. For much of this time the Khazar khaganate served as a buffer between the Byzantine empire and the nomadic communities of the northern steppes, and was in contact with the Rus', a multiethnic group with a significant Scandinavian Viking element, who operated on and settled around the rivers of what is now Russia, Ukraine and eastern Europe (see pp. 138–45).[91]

Garments made to accommodate horse-riding highlight the significance of both this activity and horses – not only to the region but also to the Silk Roads more broadly, where travel and transportation underpinned human movement across varied terrains, some difficult and challenging. The discovery of such items in the Caucasus Mountains is also pertinent to the story of connections across continents. The region formed a pivotal link between Asia and Europe via its proximity both to the Black Sea, which offered routes to eastern and southern Europe, and the formidable Volga River, which flowed into the Baltic Sea, giving access to northern Europe. However, movement along such arteries was not one way. These routes also enabled peoples from northern Europe to travel south into steppe lands and make onward connections to West and Central Asia. The resulting exchanges, from the adoption of the kaftan to the trading of enslaved people for silver coins from the Islamic world, mark a fractious chapter in Silk Roads history – the activities of Scandinavian Vikings along the 'eastern way'.

3.32
Kaftan, 600s–800s. Caucasus region. Silk, linen and fur. H. 142 cm, L. 184 cm (shoulder line). The Metropolitan Museum of Art, New York, 1996.78.1. Harris Brisbane Dick Fund, 1996.

3.33
Leggings, 600s–800s. Caucasus region. Silk and linen. H. 81 cm (extant), W. 24 cm (extant heel to toe). The Metropolitan Museum of Art, New York, 1996.78.2a, b. Harris Brisbane Dick Fund, 1996.

Vikings on the *austrvegr*

Sue Brunning

The Eurasian steppe bordered a zone that was exploited by a group from more northern climes: Scandinavians, popularly known today as Vikings, whose homelands lay in present-day Norway, Denmark and Sweden. Their best-known activities, from the eighth to eleventh centuries, involved the raiding, conquest, settlement and exploration of lands further west and north, from Francia to Ireland, and Iceland to North America. Less well known are their travels southwards into the Mediterranean Sea, and eastwards to the Eurasian steppe and Islamic lands, at least as far as Khwarazm (in present-day Uzbekistan), where a Scandinavian named Slagvi met his end, according to a memorial raised by his father in Sweden (fig. 3.34). Overall, the Vikings' journeys covered some 8,000 kilometres, making them perhaps the most widely travelled people in this book.[1]

Scandinavia was linked to the east well before the Viking period, indicated by South Asian garnets in elite jewellery, as well as the Helgö Buddha, which opened this book (see p. 10). However, these contacts began to intensify and change in the late eighth century. Scandinavians themselves were increasingly crossing the Baltic Sea, heading for rivers that snaked into present-day Eastern Europe, Russia and Ukraine, providing access to lucrative markets in Byzantium, Islamic lands and even beyond, suggested by rare Swedish finds of Chinese silk and an Indian coin.[2] These riverine routes are known collectively in Old Norse as the *austrvegr*, or 'eastern way' (fig. 3.35). Its primary arteries were the Dnieper, leading to the Black Sea and Byzantium, and the Volga, for the Caspian Sea and beyond. The Vikings' shallow-draught ships could navigate these rivers far inland. Travellers also settled along the *austrvegr*, over time forging a network of trading and craft centres, waypoints and entrepôts that facilitated long-distance exchange to all compass points. Key sites, prominent at different times, included Staraya Ladoga and Gnezdovo in present-day Russia and Kyiv in Ukraine. Excavations show that *austrvegr* towns were home to multiethnic communities, drawn from the varied groups who lived and operated in the region. Alongside the many Scandinavians were Baltic, Finnic, Slav and various Turkic and steppe peoples, including women, indicating that families also took the eastern way. Most of the Scandinavians probably hailed from eastern Sweden, poised as it was on the Baltic Sea. Such was the origin of two crews buried in their boats on the tiny Estonian island of Saaremaa in the mid-eighth century. The early date hints that they were pioneers in the new, intensifying phase of eastern contacts, but did not survive the whole journey. Those who did operated across the region's overlapping cultural spheres, interacting most critically with the peoples of the steppe, and in eastern Islamic lands (see chapters 3 and 4).[3]

3.34
Rune stone commemorating Slagvi, *c.* 1010–50. Granite. H. 1.7 m, W. 1.9 m, D. 0.2 m. Stora Rytterne, Västmanland, L2003:7201 (Vs1).

3.35
Map of Scandinavia, the Baltic region and key routes on the *austrvegr*.

3.36
Artist's impression of a man wearing Rus' dress, including examples of objects found at Birka, Sweden. Drawing by Craig Williams.

Rus' identity: fashion and fighting

From the ninth century, a new cultural identity emerged along the eastern river routes. Known as Rus', it fused Scandinavian, Slav, Balto-Finnic and Turkic elements, with Scandinavians apparently always predominating. It also encompassed the distinctive *austrvegr* lifestyle, involving long-distance trade, mobility, craft production and warfare. The eclecticism of Rus' identity emerges in mixed burial customs, dress, artistic styles, war gear and more, traceable both archaeologically and in accounts by Arabic authors, some of whom encountered the Rus' in person.[4] These ideas flowed back to Scandinavia via its close ties with Rus' regions, with frequent travel occurring between the two spheres. For instance, excavations at Birka, a major centre in eastern Sweden, have revealed extensive eastern contacts during the tenth century.[5]

From head to toe, Rus' clothing blended Scandinavian and eastern trends, creating a cosmopolitan effect that conveyed prestigious connections (fig. 3.36). Silver fittings from a type of conical cap known from Moshchevaya Balka in the northern Caucasus have been found at Birka. One such fitting (fig. 3.37), speckled with fine granulation, echoes an example from Shestovitsa in present-day Ukraine, within the Rus' sphere. It contained a scrap of silk, hinting that such caps incorporated this valuable material, which was acquired from the Byzantine or Islamic worlds directly or via critical

intermediaries on the steppe, such as the powerful Khazars (see p. 136) and Volga Bulghars.[6]

Silks also enriched the upper body, either as whole garments lined with linen or wool, or as decorative panels and trims. A recent count identified silk in around sixty graves at Birka. An especially large fragment was excavated from grave Bj.735 (fig. 3.38). The patterned Byzantine fabric, perhaps from a tunic, is enhanced with Scandinavian-style tablet-woven bands that glitter with silver thread.[7] Rus' warriors also favoured the kaftan, popular on the steppe (see fig. 3.32) and in other eastern lands. Their bulbous buttons occur in Birka's garrison and several graves (fig. 3.39), some with fragile pieces of the original fabric.[8] The 'Abbasid ambassador Ahmad ibn Fadlan saw a gold-buttoned version on the body of a dead Rus' leader on the Volga in 922. The Birka buttons are copper alloy, which originally shone with a warm golden colour.[9] Around the waist, elaborate steppe-style belts, studded with engraved metal mounts, were popular with the Rus' (see fig. 3.3). Many are known from Birka, but their increasing appearance further west, including in Denmark and Norway, shows that ideas flowed far across the Norse sphere. Finally, Rus' legwear included voluminous trousers adapted perhaps from Persian and Arab fashions. These distinctive garments are described by the Arab geographer Ahmad ibn Rustah (d. 903) and appear on picture-stones on Gotland, a Baltic island that became a major *austrvegr* waypoint.[10]

As well as fashions, the Rus' adopted fighting gear from the east, including lamellar armour, axes, long knives and archery equipment associated with horse-riding warriors on the steppe (see chapter 3).

3.37 *below, right*
Cap mount, 900–1000. Found at Birka, Uppland, Sweden. Silver. Historiska Museet, Stockholm, 106830_HST (Bj.581). Acquired through the Swedish "kulturmiljölagen" program.

3.38 *below, left*
Fragment of an embroidered tunic, 900–1000. Found at Birka, Uppland, Sweden. Silk and silver thread. Historiska Museet, Stockholm, 617959_HST (Bj.735). Acquired through the Swedish "kulturmiljölagen" program.

3.39 *left*
Kaftan buttons, 900–1000. Found at Birka, Uppland, Sweden. Copper alloy. Diam. 0.8 cm, L. 1 cm (approx., each). Historiska Museet, Stockholm, 106508_HST and 181630_HST (Bj.1074). Acquired through the Swedish "kulturmiljölagen" program.

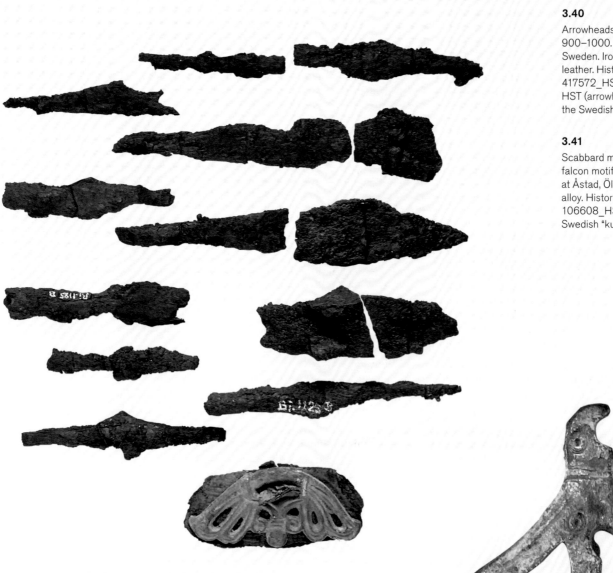

3.40

Arrowheads and quiver mount, 900–1000. Found at Birka, Uppland, Sweden. Iron, copper alloy and leather. Historiska Museet, Stockholm, 417572_HST (quiver mount), 581144_HST (arrowheads). Acquired through the Swedish "kulturmiljölagen" program.

3.41

Scabbard mount with swooping falcon motif, 800–1000. Found at Åstad, Öland, Sweden. Copper alloy. Historiska Museet, Stockholm, 106608_HST. Acquired through the Swedish "kulturmiljölagen" program.

These items all occur at Birka. Grave Bj.1125b contained a person wearing a kaftan and surrounded by eastern archery gear, including a cluster of arrowheads, a mount for a closed quiver and a loop from a bow case (fig. 3.40). The organic parts, made from leather, wood, horn, bark and bone, had decayed away. The quiver and bow case would have been attached to a belt and positioned for easy access from horseback. The eastern archer's *pièce de résistance*, the composite bow, was probably also buried in the grave, but did not survive. These formidable weapons combined wood, sinew and horn for exceptional flexibility and shock absorption, enabling eastern archers to fire faster, further and with deadlier power. Scandinavians who adopted these weapons were better able to compete against, or alongside, their eastern contacts, if the necessity arose. They also gained an edge against foes at home in Scandinavia since, as the arrowheads in grave Bj.1125b suggest, locally made projectiles could also be fired from composite bows.[11]

Eastern weapons did not replace Scandinavian gear, but instead comprised another cultural blend characteristic of the Rus'. An example appears in the eclectic late tenth-century 'Black Grave' at Chernihiv, a Rus' settlement now in Ukraine, where an individual was buried with a pair of typical Viking swords and a steppe-style sabre. Some Viking swords bore scabbard mounts that depicted a swooping falcon motif, which became deeply interwoven with Rus' identity (fig. 3.41). This symbol, stylised into a trident, adorns the Ukrainian coat of arms to this day. The Rus' falcon flew across the Norse sphere, roosting of course at Birka, but also reaching wider Scandinavia, Francia and England. Its transmission emphasises that there is no such thing as a 'western' and an 'eastern' Viking world. The networks they used conveyed people, objects and ideas across these regions without hindrance.[12]

Exchange with Islamic lands

Beyond the steppe, Scandinavia's eastern contacts extended into West and Central Asia, where Vikings forged a defining relationship with Islamic lands based on lucrative mutual interests. Steppe peoples remained key intermediaries, especially via hubs such as Itil, the Khazar capital, and Bulgar, of the Volga Bulghars, but Scandinavians also travelled to transact in person. The Arab geographer Ibn Khurradadhbih (d. 913) records them sailing the Caspian Sea and crossing deserts by camel to Baghdad, while runic inscriptions at home commemorate trips to Serkland, an unidentified place that probably included eastern Islamic lands.[13] Aside from silk, various objects of Central and West Asian origin reached Scandinavia during the Viking period, including copper alloy vessels, glassware, pottery and jewellery – primarily beads of glass, carnelian and crystal. In return, Scandinavia offered beeswax, honey, birds of prey, walrus ivory, and furs. The latter became hot property in elite Islamic circles for a time, fuelling intense exchange along a 'Fur Road' that linked the caliphate to regions rich in luxuriously pelted creatures, some from as far north as the Barents and White seas.[14]

Two particular commodities stand out in these exchanges. From the early ninth century, Islamic silver coins began to flow into the Baltic region, reaching Sweden and beyond. These dirhams arrived in two significant waves, the first in the ninth century involving coins from 'Abbasid West Asia, and the second in the tenth, with Samanid coins from Central Asian mints. Staggering volumes, estimated at more than 100 million coins, were involved, making dirhams the most common objects found across the Norse sphere. Many were recast into ingots and Scandinavian-style jewellery, identifiable by scientific analysis because their distinctive chemical signatures survived the crucible. The coins were also prized in their original form. Some were converted into necklace pendants, suggesting an intrinsic symbolic value encoded with the prestige that was conferred by contact with the powerful Islamic world. Islamic silver in all forms was hoarded across the Viking world, but most of all on Gotland, re-emphasising its critical position on the *austrvegr*. The largest silver hoard ever discovered, weighing some 67 kilograms, was unearthed on the island in 1999, at Spillings. Cut-up 'hacksilver' appears in all of these assemblages, demonstrating how this torrent of metal redefined the Baltic economy by becoming the basis of a payment-by-weight system. Furthermore, the silver was measured out against Islamic units of weight, on eastern-style collapsible scales, using Islamic weights or local copies that mimicked their distinctive shape and markings (fig. 3.42).[15]

The gleaming silver, however, carries a long shadow. The rhythm of its flow to Scandinavia during the ninth and tenth centuries coincided with an intense demand for labour in Islamic lands, suggesting that the two phenomena were intrinsically linked. It is now understood that each coin and cache was involved, at some stage, in the sale of enslaved people. The trade was big business, and the Silk Roads' overlapping networks were the arteries that kept it alive. While many different players, and places, were involved (see pp. 16–17), the trade between Scandinavians and the Rus', as suppliers, and the Islamic world, as customers, is considered the most lucrative. The sheer volume of silver recovered from the Viking world highlights its intensity and hints at its scale, estimated to have involved many thousands of people.[16]

Ibn Rustah and Ibn Fadlan record Rus' traders at Bulghar and Khazar markets exchanging captives for coins and beads. Indeed, the latter are second only to

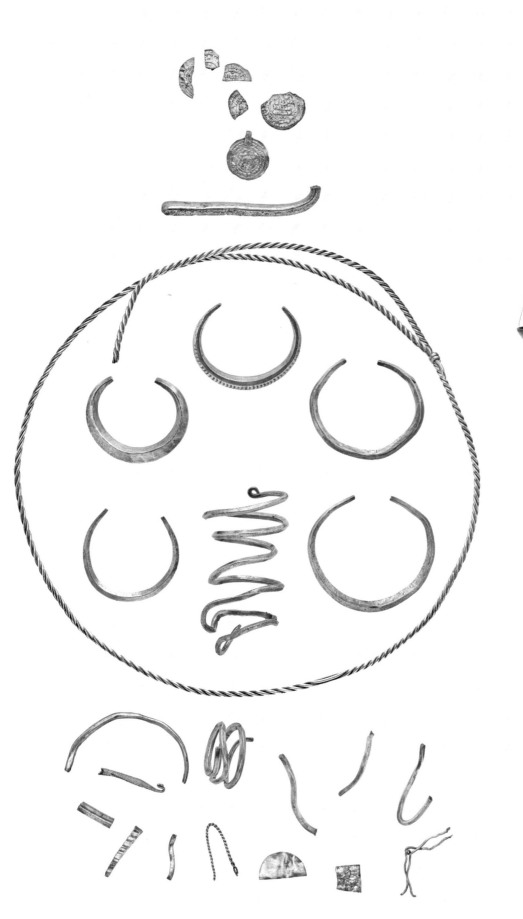

3.42

Dirham fragments, dirham pendant, ingot, neck and arm rings, hacksilver, and collapsible scales with travel case, 800–1100. Coins minted in Central or West Asia, all found on Gotland, Sweden. Copper alloy (scales and case); silver (other objects). H. 1.6–2.3 cm, Diam. 5.5–6.3 cm (scale pans and case); H. 4.4 cm, W. 10.1 cm (scale balance arm); H. 0.5–4.6 cm, W. 1–10 cm (dirhams, ingot and hacksilver, smallest to largest objects); H. 5.9–30.1 cm, W. 5.7–32.3 cm (arm and neck rings, smallest to largest objects). British Museum, London, 1921,1101.151, 306, 320–321, 341–350a, 350c–g, 351–353, 355, 357–360, 370. Purchased from Dr James Curle with a contribution from the Art Fund (as NACF).

3.43 *opposite top*

Stone fragment incised with a narrative scene, 800–900. Found at Inchmarnock, Buteshire, Scotland. Slate. H. 12 cm, W. 18 cm, D. 1.2 cm. Allocated via Treasure Trove to National Museums Scotland, Edinburgh and Bute Museum, Isle of Bute, X.2012.27.

dirhams in finds from Scandinavia and were another likely proxy for the trade.[17] Most of the enslaved were probably Slav peoples captured from Central and Eastern Europe, indicated by the Arabic term *saqaliba*, from the Latin *sclavus*, 'Slav', applied to them in written sources. Excavations in Slav regions have revealed possible evidence for raids to seize captives, including the destruction and fortification of settlements, mass graves, signals of depopulation, and cemeteries that are missing young people, the demographic particularly targeted by raiders.[18] Other lands within the Viking sphere also supplied human capital. Indeed, the term *saqaliba* was not limited to Slav captives. They were simply so ubiquitous in the trade that it became a horrifying catch-all term. A contemporary account relates the hair-raising experience of one captive in the Irish Sea region. Findan (d. 878), an Irish noble, was enslaved not once, but twice, by Vikings. After being freed once, he was recaptured and resold several times before being shipped towards Norway. During a stopover in Orkney, he took a desperate chance and fled his captors, hiding until they departed. A similar ordeal appears to be depicted on a slate from Inchmarnock in Buteshire, Scotland. The lightly incised scene shows a mail-coated figure leading a captive to a Viking-style longship (fig. 3.43).[19]

These sources offer a rare and important glimpse of the trade as experienced by its participants, both the Scandinavians doing the selling, and those whom they sold for Islamic silver. The trade is also powerfully encapsulated by an iron neck restraint, potentially used on a captive,[20] and a fine silver neck ring, probably cast from the proceeds of enslavement (figs 3.44–3.45). The startling resemblance between their forms is a viscerally powerful symbol of two anonymous human beings on opposite sides of the same trade, whose lives could scarcely have been more different.

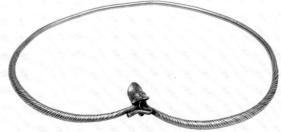

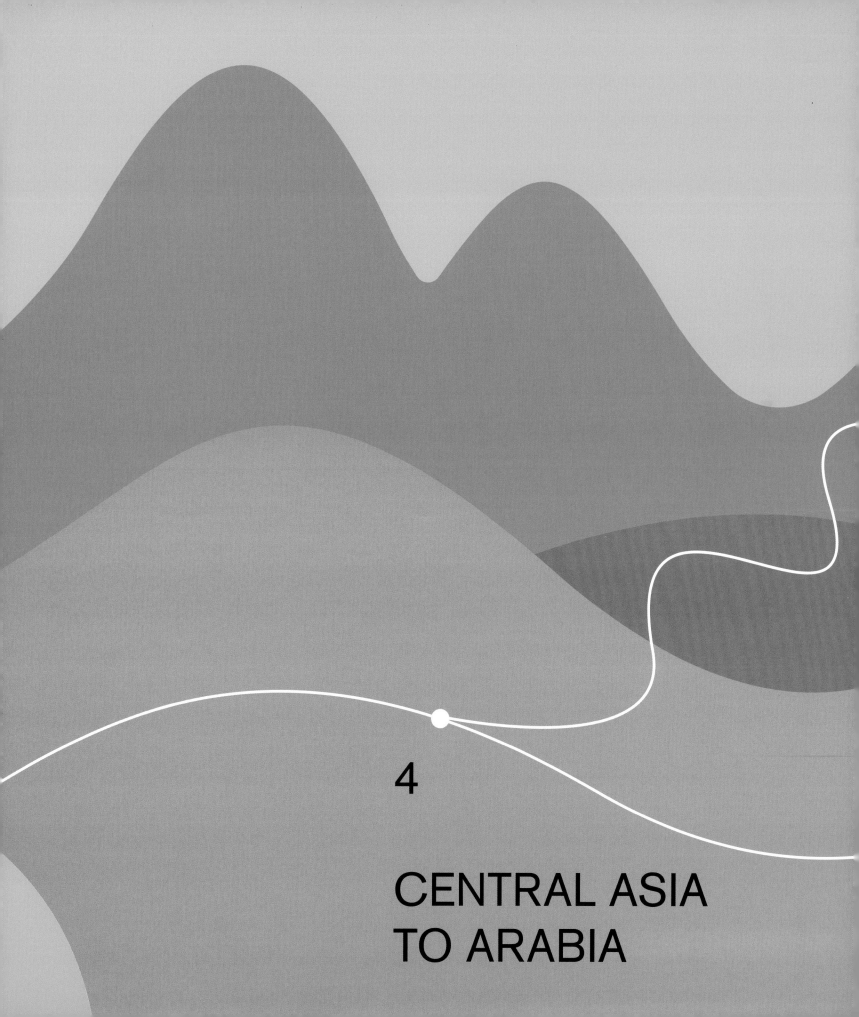

4

CENTRAL ASIA
TO ARABIA

Central Asia to Arabia

Tim Williams and Luk Yu-ping

The Vikings' eastern contacts bring the journey back to Central Asia and across to the various regions of West Asia.[1] During the sixth century and the first half of the seventh century, large parts of this area were dominated by the Sasanian empire (224–651 CE), based in Persia (fig. 4.1), and the Byzantine empire (330–1453 CE) in the Mediterranean (see fig. 5.2). Both played major roles in exchange along the Silk Roads, their varied activities bridging the continents of Asia, Africa and Europe. During the seventh century, a new power, the Islamic empire, emerged from Arabia, marking a new era in the history of connections across these regions.

According to the Muslim tradition, the word of God was revealed to the Prophet Muhammad (570–632), who was born in Mecca in present-day Saudi Arabia. By the time of his death, Muhammad had united many of the Arab tribes and most of the population of Arabia had become followers of Islam. Under his successors, known as caliphs, Islamic territories rapidly expanded into the Byzantine and Sasanian empires. By 714, the Umayyad caliphate (661–750), with its capital in Damascus, Syria, covered vast lands stretching from Sindh in present-day Pakistan to the Iberian Peninsula (fig. 4.2).[2]

During the 740s, the Umayyad dynasty faced increasing political discontent and internal disputes over succession. It was ultimately overthrown by a rival dynasty, the 'Abbasids, who began their revolution in Central Asia, at the eastern end of the empire. The new caliphate (750–1258) established its capital first in Kufa, in present-day Iraq, and then at the new city of Baghdad, founded in 762, which at its peak became the largest city in the world. By the later ninth century, however, the 'Abbasids' power had weakened, with dynasties under their suzerainty operating independently and rival caliphates challenging their authority, such as the Samanid dynasty (819–999) in the east, and the Fatimid caliphate (909–1171) in North Africa (see fig. 5.3).

The Arab conquests led to the establishment of a vast political and economic area under the banner of Islam, in which interregional and long-distance trade thrived.[3] People on the move following the empire's expansion included traders, pilgrims, artisans and scholars, whose travels facilitated the transmission and exchange of goods and ideas. The rulers of the new Islamic empire had to engage with a diverse population of different faiths, cultures and languages. Such interactions during this period gave rise to the adaptation of traditions and the development of distinctive identities.

4.1

Map of the Islamic conquest to c. 750 and the boundaries of the Sasanian and Byzantine empires c. 630.

4.2

Map of the 'Abbasid caliphate at its greatest extent and its subsequent fragmentation, including the Samanid dynasty.

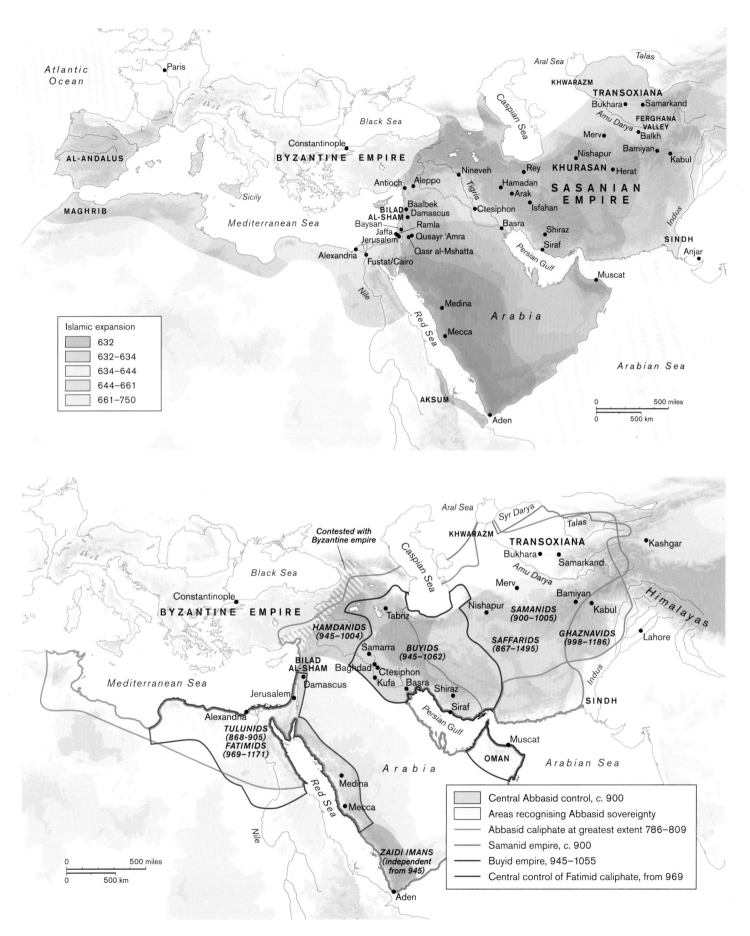

Map 1 (top)

Atlantic
Ocean

Paris

AL-ANDALUS

MAGHRIB

Sicily

Mediterranean Sea

BYZANTINE EMPIRE

Constantinople

Black Sea

Aral Sea

Talas

Caspian Sea

KHWARAZM

TRANSOXIANA

Bukhara • Samarkand

Amu Darya

FERGHANA VALLEY

Merv •

Balkh

Nishapur

Bamiyan

Kabul

KHURASAN

Rey

Herat

Nineveh

Hamadan

Arak

SASANIAN EMPIRE

Antioch

Aleppo

Baalbek
Damascus

BILAD
AL-SHAM

Ctesiphon

Isfahan

Tigris

Indus

Baysan

Ramla

Jaffa

Qusayr 'Amra

Jerusalem

Qasr al-Mshatta

Basra

Shiraz

Siraf

Persian Gulf

SINDH

Alexandria

Fustat/Cairo

Anjar

Muscat

Nile

Red Sea

Medina

Mecca

Arabia

Arabian Sea

Islamic expansion

- 632
- 632–634
- 634–644
- 644–661
- 661–750

AKSUM

Aden

0   500 miles
0   500 km

Map 2 (bottom)

Aral Sea

Syr Darya

Talas

Contested with
Byzantine empire

KHWARAZM

TRANSOXIANA

Kashgar

Caspian Sea

Bukhara •

Samarkand

Amu Darya

Black Sea

BYZANTINE EMPIRE

Constantinople

Merv •

Nishapur

SAMANIDS
(900–1005)

Bamiyan

Kabul

Himalayas

Tabriz

SAFFARIDS
(867–1495)

GHAZNAVIDS
(998–1186)

Lahore

HAMDANIDS
(945–1004)

Samarra

BUYIDS
(945–1062)

Baghdad

BILAD
AL-SHAM

Ctesiphon

Kufa

Basra

Shiraz

Damascus

Siraf

Indus

Mediterranean Sea

Jerusalem

Persian Gulf

SINDH

Alexandria

TULUNIDS
(868–905)
FATIMIDS
(969–1171)

Muscat

OMAN

Arabian Sea

Red Sea

Arabia

Nile

Medina

Mecca

ZAIDI IMANS
(independent
from 945)

Aden

0   500 miles
0   500 km

- Central Abbasid control, c. 900
- Areas recognising Abbasid sovereignty
- Abbasid caliphate at greatest extent 786–809
- Samanid empire, c. 900
- Buyid empire, 945–1055
- Central control of Fatimid caliphate, from 969

The Sasanian and Byzantine empires

In the early 600s, the Sasanian empire stretched from Alexandria in Egypt in the west, to Merv in present-day Turkmenistan in the east, and from the Red Sea and the Persian Gulf in the south, to the Caspian Sea in the north.[4] Its geographical span is evoked by a silver plate, which depicts a Sasanian king on a hunt, a metaphor for royal glory and good fortune (fig. 4.3). In fact, until its collapse in 651, the Sasanian empire was a bridge between Europe and Central Asia, supported by a powerful standing army equipped with quality, standardised equipment, as represented by a helmet discovered at Nineveh (fig. 4.4). The Sasanian conquest of southern Arabia in the sixth century CE gave the empire control of the trade in luxuries passing along land and sea routes between the Arabian Peninsula and the Byzantine empire to the west (see chapter 5).

Despite periodic conflict between the Sasanian and Byzantine empires, transregional trade continued to link eastern and western Eurasia across vast distances. For example, Sasanian glass vessels, dated to between the sixth and seventh centuries, have been found as far afield as the Japanese archipelago (see chapter 1).[5] Trade in silk and other luxury commodities generated tremendous wealth for the Sasanian state, enabling its capital Ctesiphon to become one of the largest and most cosmopolitan cities of the time.

Moreover, the Sasanian occupation of Yemen in the 570s put them in control of nearly all the ports on the South Arabian coast, while their shipping started to dominate maritime commerce in the western Indian Ocean.[6] The ports of southern Arabia controlled the arrival of ships on the north-east monsoon winds, from October to March, which led to markets being held there between January and March. One account notes that Persian traders waited at ports in India to purchase silk, preventing Aksumite traders from doing the same.[7] By the late sixth or early seventh century, maritime trade was integrated with overland trade across Arabia.

Neighbouring the Sasanian empire, the Byzantine empire reached its greatest extent during the reign (527–65) of Justinian I, controlling most of the Mediterranean. The early sixth century saw a flowering of Byzantine cities along the eastern edge of the empire, with significant investment of resources. Those such as Antioch and Apamea, in present-day Turkey and Syria respectively, were extensively rebuilt after earthquakes in the 520s, while widespread church building took place in the eastern Mediterranean region in the first half of the century.[8] Sasanian attacks during the 540s severely damaged many cities, including Antioch, but many were rebuilt after the enemy forces had been repelled. There is considerable debate, however, about how cities fared in the second half of the sixth century and into the seventh, before the Arab conquests. Growing archaeological evidence has challenged the traditional model of decline, suggesting a new interpretation in which cities were being transformed, with a rising urban merchant class, expanding markets and increasing industrial activities, alongside a changing rural landscape.[9] Together, this evidence implies that the trading connections within and beyond the region made communities resilient against turbulent politics and imperial struggles.

By the 630s, protracted warfare had exhausted both the Sasanian and the Byzantine empires. The Sasanians had depleted their treasury, leading to punitive taxation and political turmoil. Arab forces took advantage of their weakness. Under the command of Khalid ibn al-Walid (c. 592–642), they first occupied Byzantium's eastern provinces, before pushing into Sasanian heartlands. They captured Ctesiphon in 637, and in 642, under caliph 'Umar I (r. 634–44), they crushed the Sasanian army of King Yazdegerd III (r. 632–51) at the Battle of Nihavand (near

4.3

Plate showing a Sasanian lion hunt, 400–700. Silver with gilding. Diam. 27.6 cm, H. 6.5 cm. British Museum, London, 124092.

4.4

Helmet, 500–early 600s. Nineveh, northern Iraq. Iron, gold and copper alloy. H. 20 cm, W. 22 cm, D. 19 cm. British Museum, London, 22498.

present-day Hamadan, Iran).[10] Yazdegerd retreated eastwards and in 651, after unsuccessful diplomatic approaches to Tang China, he ended up at Merv at the edge of his empire, where he was killed – perhaps for his possessions, or perhaps at the instigation of the town governor.[11] However, his son and grandson managed to escape to Chang'an, the capital of Tang China, their flight highlighting the existence of long-distance diplomatic ties during this period (see chapter 1).

Contacts through conquest in Central Asia

Following Yazdegerd's death, Merv seems to have surrendered to Arab forces.[12] It became the base for the conquest of lands beyond the Amu Darya River. Armies led by the governor Qutayba ibn Muslim (705–15) undertook long sieges, eventually capturing Bukhara in 709, Afrasiab (Samarkand) in 711, and the rich oasis of Khwarazm at the southern end of the Aral Sea in 712. By 713 they had reached the fertile Ferghana Valley, and Sindh, encompassing the lower Indus Valley (see p. 77). Although revolts pushed them back at times, the Umayyad caliphate (661–750) went on to cover a huge 11.1 million square kilometres at its greatest extent.[13] Material culture from this early Islamic period in Central Asia, including pre-Islamic artefacts that were preserved, offers glimpses into the developments that followed.

Central Asia under early Islamic rule

The Sogdians from the city states of Sogdiana in Central Asia were active traders across Eurasia (see p. 105) before the region came under Islamic rule in the early eighth century. Like Merv, and many other places that Arab armies conquered, most cities in Sogdiana were spared from plunder and destruction, as local leaders negotiated terms of surrender.[14] In the case of Samarkand in 712, the agreement involved an immediate payment of two million dirhams and the provision of 2,000 enslaved people, along with an annual tribute payment.[15] This paints a picture of Sogdian wealth and highlights the extent of enslavement at the time.

The movement of luxury goods into Sogdiana apparently continued during the early Islamic period. This is suggested by the significant discovery of a group of seven elephant-ivory chess pieces from the Afrasiab site in Samarkand, thought to be among the earliest surviving chess pieces in the world (fig. 4.5). Among their ranks are two foot-soldiers, two mounted riders, an elephant with a rider, a figure with two horses, and another driving a three-horse chariot, probably representing divisions of an army.[16] The ivory used to make these pieces, or even the pieces themselves, probably came from India, where chess is believed to have originated around 500 CE.[17] Initially played among the nobility as a means of training in military tactics, it spread westwards to the Sasanian empire and later became popular across the Islamic world, before eventually reaching Europe.[18]

As Sogdian cities became integrated into the Islamic caliphate, their culture experienced a marked decline, and by the ninth century material traces of its distinctive features had largely disappeared in the region.[19] Recent scholarship argues that the reasons for this rapid change included the absence of an organised class of clerics among the Sogdians who could have ensured the continuation of religious practices, and the Arabs' dismantling of self-governing civic communities that had formed the foundation of the Sogdian city-states.[20]

A remarkable wall painting from the Bukhara Oasis (present-day Uzbekistan) offers possible insights into this period of change (fig. 4.6). It adorned the so-called 'Red Hall', a reception room named after its vivid background colour,

in the palace of Varakhsha, thought to have been constructed after Arab forces conquered the city in 709.[21] The building underwent further development during the years that followed, including the creation of this image, which covered an existing painting in the hall by the year 738.[22] The new work depicts a dramatic, continuous scene of figures riding elephants in battle with real and mythical creatures. Traces of a procession of animals can be seen above the main frieze, but only their legs are now preserved.

The wall painting from the 'Red Hall' is unique among extant examples from Sogdiana, which typically present a narrative rather than a repetition of similar compositions.[23] The identity of the elephant riders remains elusive: their *dhotis* (long loincloths), turbans and bare chests, as well as their animal mounts, bear resemblance to religious imagery from the Indian subcontinent, perhaps filtered through Tang China, where the elephant-riding bodhisattva Samantabhadra (Chinese: Puxian) was popular.[24] Alternatively, they could represent the supreme deity of the local form of Zoroastrianism, or even royalty fighting against invading troops, perhaps an allusion to Arab forces.[25] The wall painting has been attributed to the local ruler Tokespadhe (709–739), who was installed on the throne by the Arab commander and governor Qutayba ibn Muslim, and it may have been deliberately 'coded' to avoid censure.[26] This is plausible given what is known of Tokespadhe who, despite his position, tried to seek assistance from the Tang court to overthrow the Arabs.[27] After his assassination in Samarkand, his bones

4.5

Seven chess pieces, 700s. Excavated at Afrasiab (Samarkand). Ivory. H. 2.6–3.7 cm. Samarkand State Museum-Reserve, Uzbekistan, KP-3786/1.

were brought back to Bukhara, in accordance with the funerary practices of Zoroastrianism (see p. 108), suggesting he probably remained a follower.[28] The wall painting from the 'Red Hall' of Varakhsha is an intriguing work that speaks to the diverse sources that shaped Sogdian painting, and how it may have been adapted for a new world.

The rapid demise of Sogdian culture is considered unusual in the history of the early expansion of the Islamic caliphate.[29] Scholars have observed that, in other conquered lands, changes to everyday life were slow to take place and the process of Islamisation was more gradual and uneven.[30] This may be observed in Bamiyan, a site south of Sogdiana, in a mountainous region of present-day Afghanistan. Bamiyan was an important link between India and Central Asia, as its valley offered a natural corridor for travellers crossing the Hindu Kush mountain range.[31] The region grew into a major Buddhist centre by the second half of the sixth century, and Buddhist worship and artistic patronage continued to flourish there into the ninth century and even the tenth century after the arrival of Islam.[32] It seems to have come under the rule of the 'Abbasid caliphate in stages. One account records that, in the latter half of the eighth century, the local ruler of Bamiyan was already receiving orders from Baghdad.[33] Later, armies of the Saffarid dynasty (861–1002) and the Ghaznavid dynasty (977–1186) captured the region and fully integrated it into the Islamic realm.[34]

4.6
Section of wall painting from the Palace at Varakhsha, c. 730. Painted plaster. H. 176 cm, W. 250 cm. State Museum of Arts of Uzbekistan, Tashkent, 1618.

4.7

Seated Buddha, 500s. Cave 5,
Bamiyan, Afghanistan. Unbaked
clay. H. 49 cm, W. 45 cm, D. 23 cm.
Musée Guimet, Paris, MG 17943.
Délégation Archéologique Française
en Afghanistan (DAFA) excavations by
Joseph Hackin, 1929–30.

The continuation of Buddhist worship and patronage may seem to contradict what Bamiyan is perhaps most widely known for today: the destruction of two colossal rock-cut Buddha sculptures from the sixth and early seventh century by the Taliban, an Islamic fundamentalist group, in 2001.[35] At 38 and 55 metres in height respectively, the sculptures were part of a wider Buddhist complex in the valley, which included more than 700 cave temples containing sculptures and paintings. A seated Buddha figure from the same period was found inside a collapsed cave on the same cliff face to the east of the colossal Buddhas (fig. 4.7).[36] The modelling of its torso and drapery reflects the artistry of Buddhist sculpture of the time. Between the tenth and thirteenth centuries, after the site stopped being actively patronised, Muslims who encountered the colossal Buddha sculptures in their painted niches at Bamiyan referred to them in Arabic and Persian writings as marvels and wonders that demonstrated the creative power of God.[37]

Economic factors played a role in the complex processes underlying the spread of Islam, including its coexistence with other religions in both the Afghanistan region and the wider caliphate. A poll tax (*jizya*) was imposed upon all non-Muslim adult males under Islamic rule as a demonstration of their submission, in return for state protection and freedom to practice their religion.[38] Consideration for social status and commercial advantage over the non-Muslim population may help to explain the gradual, rather than sudden, decline of Buddhist and other religious establishments in conquered lands such as Bamiyan.[39]

In the 680s, ferocious fighting erupted among tribal groups in the province of Khurasan, the historical name for the region that includes parts of present-day Afghanistan, Merv in Turkmenistan and Nishapur in Iran.[40] The victor in this struggle, 'Abd Allah ibn Khazim (d. 692), subsequently ruled there almost independently of the caliphate.[41] Coins modelled on Sasanian designs were minted in his name, bearing inscriptions in Arabic, Bactrian (the language of Bactria in present-day northern Afghanistan) and Pahlavi, a form of Middle Persian.[42] Some examples exhibit a counterstamp, a small secondary mark used to revalidate coins in circulation. On one such coin (fig. 4.8), the stamp is visible on the upper right quarter of the obverse and may have been applied by the Hephthalites, a tribal confederation in Central Asia who later allied with 'Abd Allah ibn Khazim against the Umayyad caliphate.[43] Although small, these coins are important evidence for the complex multicultural and multilingual environment of this region.

The Samanids of Samarkand and Bukhara

The rebellion in Khurasan triggered the downfall of the Umayyad caliphate, which culminated in its defeat by the 'Abbasid dynasty in 750. However, within a century, the newly established 'Abbasid empire itself began to break apart. By 819, the Samanid dynasty had seized control of lower Central Asia (historically known as Transoxiana) and the Khurasan region. The Samanids probably originated from the Balkh area in present-day Afghanistan and converted to Islam after the Arab conquest of the region. While they nominally recognised the authority of the 'Abbasids, in practice they ruled largely independently. They established their capital at Afrasiab (Samarkand), until Ismail Samani (r. 892–907) made Bukhara his capital in 892. A mausoleum in Bukhara (fig. 4.9), decorated with complex brickwork, is thought by some scholars to have been commissioned by Ismail, perhaps for his father.[44] Today, it is one of the surviving masterpieces of Central Asian architecture. As the Samanid dynasty expanded across Central Asia to Iran, its territories emerged as a major hub for trade and exchange. They also promoted a new Muslim-Persian identity, highlighting again the cultural interactions that shaped life along the Silk Roads in the Islamic world.[45]

The Samanids derived much of their wealth from silver mines in Afghanistan, and the trade in enslaved people from northern Eurasia and

4.8

Coin of 'Abd Allah ibn Khazim, copying Sasanian issues of Khusraw II, 668. Minted in Khurasan (?). Silver. Diam. 3.2 cm, weight 3.8 g. British Museum, London, 1845, EIC.34. Donated by the East India Company.

4.9

The Samanid Mausoleum, probably commissioned by Ismail Samani, in Bukhara, Uzbekistan.

4.10
Panel decorated with medallions,
800–1000. Afrasiab (Samarkand).
Stucco. H. 102 cm, W. 282 cm.
Samarkand State Museum-Reserve,
Uzbekistan, A-94-9.

4.11
Bottle, 900–1000. Excavated at
Sultanabad, Iran. Glass. H. 20 cm,
Diam. 9 cm. British Museum, London,
1913,1009.1. Given by Stephen
Salisbury Bagge.

the steppe (see p. 143).[46] Turkic pastoral nomads and Slavs from eastern Europe, captured in warfare and raids, constituted the primary groups of people sold by the Samanids to the 'Abbasid caliphs, who relied on these captives for the military and domestic work.[47] It proved a lucrative business, and they even established schools to train captives in preparation for service.[48] In addition, the Samanids exchanged silver coins and luxury metalware for fur from Scandinavia, Russia and eastern Europe.[49] The extensive connections that thrived in the tenth century between Central and West Asia and northeastern Europe have been called the 'Fur Road' (see p. 143).[50]

By the Samanid period, abstract, geometric designs derived from vegetal motifs had become a distinctive feature of Islamic visual and material culture. This can be observed, for instance, in the decorated plaster panels that adorned buildings. Similarities in the basic compositions and visual repertoires of these panels found at many sites across the 'Abbasid caliphate dating to between the eighth and mid-ninth centuries suggest that artisans, probably carrying model designs, were commissioned to work at different sites.[51] Over time, regional differences and diversification appeared. An example from Samanid Afrasiab is more ornate and shows greater flexibility in its composition compared to the earlier plaster designs (fig. 4.10).[52] Abstract decorative styles extended beyond architecture to objects made of other materials, including glass. For example, a glass bottle excavated from Sultanabad (Arak), Iran, also from the Samanid period, has linear-cut decoration on its globular body (fig. 4.11). Such glassware has been identified at

4.12
Bowl with kufic inscription, 900s. Nishapur, Iran. Glazed pottery. H. 6.3 cm, Diam. 19.6 cm. British Museum, London, 1948,1009.1. Purchased from Mme Mousa through A. Haskell.

sites from Egypt to Iran, dating from between the eighth or ninth centuries to the eleventh, suggesting further transmission of skills and designs.[53]

In addition to visual motifs, the spread of the Arabic language in the Islamic world inspired new developments in material culture, including a new type of ceramic known as 'epigraphic wares', associated with Afrasiab and Nishapur under the Samanids.[54] Vessels of this type are characterised by written decoration, typically using dark slip or a clay solution applied onto a white slip-covered earthenware surface, and further covered in a transparent lead glaze before firing.[55] The result is a bold composition consisting of a strong contrast of black or brown text against a white background. The inscriptions on these ceramics include Arabic proverbs and blessings, as well as encouragements to eat and drink. One example from Nishapur reads 'Livelihood is distributed by God among the people', arranged in a radial layout (fig. 4.12). In the centre of this bowl is the word 'Ahmad', perhaps the name of the craftsman or part of another saying.[56] The text is written in kufic script, which was often used on monuments and for copying the Qur'an (see p. 170), but with additional wedge-shaped protrusions that enhance its artistic quality. While the intended audience for these wares is not known, it is likely that they were used in social settings and were designed to draw attention to their owner's and audience's knowledge of Arabic, as well as moral virtues and sayings in that language.[57] The population in Samanid territories predominantly spoke forms of the Iranian language, but Arabic was used in higher-level administration and in Islamic theology. This prompted a need among those with career aspirations to learn Arabic, which may also have helped to inspire an interest in epigraphic wares.[58]

The interplay of languages across diverse cultures and geographies is a notable consequence of expanding Silk Roads connections. In the case of the Samanid dynasty, although Arabic was adopted in some contexts and its importance was acknowledged, rulers also embarked on a policy to promote Persian language and culture. They integrated this into their identity, for example, by claiming descent from the rebel Sasanian army commander Bahram Chobin (r. 590–1).[59] The mausoleum in Bukhara, mentioned earlier, incorporated features derived from royal Sasanian architectural models blended with local elements.[60] Notably, an early form of New Persian was adopted, containing numerous Arabic and Sogdian loan-words and written in Arabic script rather than the Aramaic-derived Pahlavi script that was used in the Sasanian empire.[61] Samanid rulers sponsored literary works and the translation of important scholarship written in Arabic into this new form of Persian.[62] The most famous outcome of these patronage activities is the epic poem *Shahnama* ('Book of Kings'), compiled by the poet Abu'l Qasim Firdawsi (d. 1025), which narrates the tales of semi-mythical kings and heroes in ancient Persia (fig. 4.13).[63] Firdawsi began work on the *Shahnama* around 977 and completed it in 1010 after the Samanid dynasty had ended.[64] As a young man, he was patronised by a Samanid prince who enabled him to complete the first version of the text in 994.[65] Firdawsi drew inspiration from existing stories and legends that were already circulating widely by his lifetime. A ninth-century fragment of a Sogdian manuscript, recounting a story about the hero Rustam defeating demons, was discovered in Cave 17, Mogao Caves, Dunhuang (see chapter 2), far away from Firdawsi's homeland in Iran (fig. 4.14).[66] Narratives about Rustam are also depicted in the wall paintings of Penjikent in Sogdiana. Similarly, an illustrated page from a fourteenth-century manuscript produced in Shiraz, Iran, has a caption identifying the scene as Rustam's father Zal making him a paladin.[67] It is one of many later manuscripts reflecting the legacy and enduring popularity of the *Shahnama*.

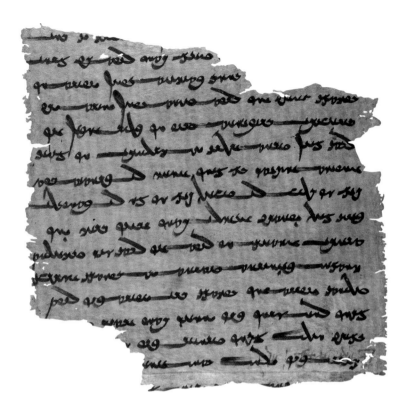

Towards Bilad al-Sham

To the west of Central Asia, beyond the Iranian Plateau, are present-day Iraq and the lands north of Arabia in what is now Bilad al-Sham, also known as the Levant or Greater Syria, where the capitals of the Umayyad and 'Abbasid caliphates were located (see fig. 4.2).[68] These lands were also home to Ctesiphon, the former capital of the Sasanian empire, as well as the eastern edge of the Byzantine empire. The material and visual culture of this region, from tiny coins to palaces and large-scale cities, offer further glimpses into the transition from the Sasanian and Byzantine empires to the early caliphates.

Adapting Sasanian and Byzantine motifs

Coins are among the most telling traces of this process. Early caliphs experimented with their visual identity by borrowing from past traditions. Their coins imitated and adapted those of the Byzantine and Sasanian empires, indicating continuities in administrative and economic life.[69] However, Arabic script professing the Muslim faith was added to their designs, as seen in the example minted in the name of the governor of Khurasan (see fig. 4.8). Arab-Byzantine coins imitated gold examples minted by the emperor Heraclius (fig. 4.15), but on the obverse, the Christian crosses on the diadems of the Byzantine emperor and his sons were omitted, while the cross motif on the reverse has lost its crossbar, leaving a pillar that may allude to the caliph's position as the axis of his peoples (fig. 4.16).[70] In 695/6, the caliph 'Abd al-Malik (r. 685–705) experimented with figural representation on his coins by inserting an image of himself holding a sword, known as the 'standing caliph' motif (fig. 4.17). This brief period of experimentation ended in 696/7 when he issued purely epigraphic coins,

inscribed with Arabic text including the Islamic profession of faith, 'There is no god but God, and Muhammad is the Messenger of God' (fig. 4.18).[71] These coins were lighter than their Byzantine models, and would become the new standard unit of trade in this part of the world.[72] Their inscriptions comprise the earliest examples of the use of an angular kufic style of script that was later seen on Samanid epigraphic ceramic wares (discussed above).[73]

In other areas of material and visual culture, the legacy of the Sasanian empire persisted into the 'Abbasid dynasty, for instance through motifs and the shape of objects. An example of this is a brass ewer showing relief decoration including a composite beast within a medallion (fig. 4.19).[74] The pear-shaped form of the ewer, along with its leaf-shaped thumb-rest, can be traced ultimately to classical antiquity, but was also found in the Sasanian period.[75] The fantastical creature depicted in the medallion, with what appears to be a dog's head, lion's legs and a peacock's tail, has traditionally been identified as the mythical *senmurv* (or *simorgh*), a bird-like beast from Iranian traditions. However, recent scholarship argues that it may instead represent a zoomorphised image of the concept of 'Divine Glory' (*xwarrah*) rooted in ancient Iranian culture, which was adopted in late Sasanian art.[76] The same creature appears on a fragment of a woven silk textile produced in either Iran or Central Asia (fig. 4.20). Muslim rulers inherited government-controlled silk weaving workshops of the Sasanian empire, and continued to enjoy motifs and techniques from the earlier period.[77] This piece of textile survived in Europe, where it is said to have been found in a reliquary once kept in the church of St Leu in Paris, which may have been brought there by Crusaders in the eleventh to thirteenth centuries.[78]

Umayyad palaces and cities

In 661 the Umayyads established their capital in Damascus, present-day Syria. Subsequently, the caliphs and the new Muslim elites constructed over thirty so-called 'desert castles' primarily in Bilad al-Sham.[79] They were wide compounds that contained a principal residence, often accompanied by a mosque, a bathhouse, other residential and service buildings, hydraulic systems and areas for agricultural production. Despite the common name 'desert castle', translated from the Arabic *qasr* (plural *qusur*), these structures were not military fortifications. Instead, they may have served a variety of functions, for example as aristocratic residences or retreats, and as political centres beyond the capital that connected the caliph with regional tribal powers, illustrating the peripatetic nature of the Umayyad court.[80] Notably, many of these complexes were positioned along major routes, so they may also have been part of the caliphate's transport and communication network, perhaps providing support and respite to travellers.[81]

Undoubtedly, these 'desert castles' would have been impressive presences along the Silk Roads. One of the largest (about 114 metres long on each side) and most magnificent examples is Qasr al-Mshatta, an Umayyad winter palace located 30 kilometres south of Amman, Jordan. It is thought to have been commissioned by the caliph al-Walid II (r. 743–4) and was left incomplete following his assassination. Mshatta is renowned for its ornate stone façade carved with animals and vegetation. It also displayed statuary, such as an expressive stone sculpture of a lion, which was found in the throne room (fig. 4.21).[82] A fragment of another lion's paw, discovered in the same location, suggests that two almost life-size lion sculptures may once have flanked the caliph's throne. This evokes the established association between lions and rulership as symbols of authority in the Sasanian and wider Late Antique worlds. Moreover, statues representing naked men and women once stood in the audience hall of the palace, which demonstrates a possible link with mythological representations in the Greek and Roman

4.17 *top*
Coin of Abd al-Malik showing the 'standing caliph' motif, 695. Probably minted in Damascus. Gold. Diam. 2 cm, weight 4 g. British Museum, London, 1954,1011.2. Donated by Prof. Philip Grierson.

4.18 *bottom*
Coin of 'Abd al Malik with Arabic inscriptions, 696–7. Minted in Damascus, Syria. Gold. Diam. 1.9 cm, weight 4.3 g. British Museum, London, 1874,0706.1.

4.19 *above*

 Ewer with composite beast decoration, 800s. Found in Iran. Brass. H. 28.5 cm, W. 16.4 cm, D. 13.5 cm. British Museum, London, 1959,1023.1. Purchased from Mrs Khalil Rabenou, funded by the Brooke Sewell Permanent Fund.

4.20 *top, right*

Textile with composite beast in a pearl roundel, 600–900. Made in Iran or Central Asia, said to be found in the church of St Leu in Paris. Woven silk. W. 54.3 cm. Victoria and Albert Museum, London, 8579-1863. Purchased from Baron M. Stanislas.

4.21 *right*

Sculpture of a lion on a thin rectangular plinth, 743–4. Qasr al-Mshatta, Jordan. Limestone. H. 72 cm, W. 122 cm, D. 42 cm. Museum für Islamische Kunst, Staatliche Museen zu Berlin, I. 6171. Gifted from the Ottoman Sultan to Kaiser Wilhelm II.

4.22
Mosaic (flooring), early 700s. Qusayr
'Amra, Jordan. Glass and stone.
H. 46 cm, W. 107 cm, D. 5 cm. Museum
für Islamische Kunst, Staatliche Museen
zu Berlin, I.1265. Purchased from
painter Alphons Leopold Mielich.

4.23
Ruins of the *cardo* (main street) of Anjar,
Lebanon, city founded during 705–15.

traditions, as well as an interest in figural representation in secular environments
during the early Islamic period.[83]

Naked figures are also strikingly represented in another 'desert castle', Qusayr
'Amra (small *qasr* of 'Amra), which, in contrast to the imposing Mshatta, is a small
complex located in the Jordanian desert.[84] Built during 723–43 as a site for royal
entertainment for al-Walid II before he became caliph, its audience hall and
bathhouse display a rich variety of wall paintings that celebrated earthly pleasures.
In addition, rooms in Qusayr 'Amra were decorated with mosaics, including a
colourful floor mosaic with a geometric design formed from stone pieces, as well
as red and green glass tesserae (fig. 4.22). Such mosaics in early Islamic art and
architecture relate to the Byzantine tradition, in which they were commonly
used in Christian churches. Indeed, mosaics adorning buildings in Damascus
and Medina were said to have been completed with the support of the Byzantine
emperor.[85] Being small and portable, tesserae that formed the mosaics could be
removed from Byzantine churches and other sites, transported and reused on
Islamic structures (see p. 173).[86]

In addition to the newly built 'desert castles', many cities in Greater Syria
flourished under Islamic rule, benefiting from regional as well as long-distance trade.
During late antiquity, they had already developed increased market facilities and a
growing merchant class, forming a foundation for further prosperity. Their resilience
can be observed in examples such as Baysan, which survived damaging earthquakes
in the seventh and eighth centuries.[87] Additionally, new cities were developed to
control specific areas and routes, among which perhaps the most spectacular was the
short-lived Umayyad city of Anjar, in the Beqaa Valley (around Baalbek), present-
day Lebanon.[88] Built in the early eighth century, it was a rectangular planned town
measuring 385 by 350 metres, following Roman and Byzantine town layouts, with
two main colonnaded streets lined with numerous shops, dividing the city into
four quarters (fig. 4.23). The grand palace of the caliph and a mosque occupied
the southeast quarter, while smaller palaces and great baths were located in the
northeast quarter. The other two quarters contained residential areas and markets.

Jerusalem under Islam

Jerusalem, a holy city for Judaism, Christianity and Islam, provides a meaningful lens through which to consider the early relationship between these faiths, through their co-existence there. Arab armies seized Jerusalem from the Byzantine empire by the year 638.[89] It is said that the patriarch Sophronius personally welcomed 'Umar I when he arrived at the city that year.[90] In return for submission and the payment of the poll tax mentioned earlier, Christians were allowed to continue worshipping in their churches, and Jewish people, who had been barred from the city under Byzantine rule, were permitted to return.[91] There is evidence that Christian and Jewish people welcomed their new Muslim rulers, and there was awareness of common ground between the three Abrahamic, monotheistic faiths.[92] The Umayyad caliphs invested considerably in the city, constructing the al-Aqsa Mosque, which became the main congregational mosque, and the Dome of the Rock, which was built on the site of a Jewish temple destroyed by the Romans in 70 CE.[93]

Commissioned by the caliph 'Abd al-Malik, completed around 692 and later renovated, the Dome of the Rock, with its shimmering gold dome, remains a spectacular landmark on Jerusalem's skyline, visible from across the city (fig. 4.24). Built as a shrine rather than a mosque, in features of its design, such as its octagonal shape and dome, the building recalls sacred structures in the Judaeo-Christian traditions, while its circumambulatory walkways echo the Ka'ba of Mecca, the holiest shrine in Islam.[94] This impressive structure would therefore have resonated with Christian, Jewish and Muslim worshippers alike, while at the same time projecting the glory of the Umayyad caliph and the transformation of Jerusalem into a holy Muslim site.[95]

Elaborate mosaics preserved at the Dome of the Rock show the use of vegetal and geometric scrolls and other designs that were developed from the Late Antique repertoire. Comparable motifs and exuberance in ornamentation

4.24
The Dome of the Rock, Jerusalem, first built 688–92, expanded 820s, restored 1020s and later.

4.25
Tray, possibly depicting the Dome of the Rock, 600–800. Syria, Jordan or Iran. Brass. H. 10 cm, Diam. 64.8 cm. Museum für Islamische Kunst, Staatliche Museen zu Berlin, I.5624. Purchased from Jacob Hirsch.

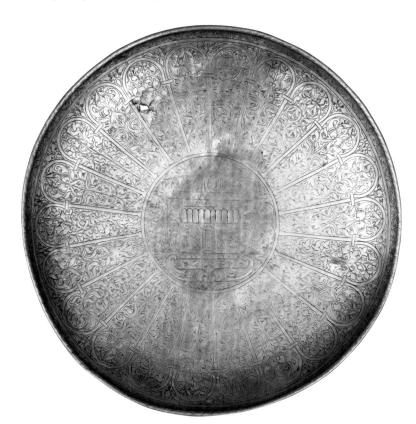

can be observed in a large brass tray dating to the seventh and eighth centuries (fig. 4.25).[96] Interestingly, the centre of the tray depicts a domed building with a row of arches, as well as a single pillar that appears under an archway, resembling designs on one of the coins issued by ʿAbd al-Malik that modified Byzantine prototypes (mentioned earlier). These features have led to speculation over whether the building depicted on the tray is a reference to the Dome of the Rock.[97]

Jerusalem attracted growing numbers of Muslim pilgrims who, according to records of complaints, also visited Christian pilgrimage sites in the city.[98] Their increasing presence encouraged the production of objects that catered to them.[99] Among these were small glass flasks of a type normally made for Christian and Jewish travellers, possibly to carry away earth, oil and sanctified water from the Holy Sepulchre and other shrines. Such flasks were adapted for the new Muslim pilgrims. One example incorporates a motif that resembles the 'standing caliph' design (fig. 4.26), as found on the early coinage of ʿAbd al-Malik (see fig. 4.17).[100] It has been suggested that Muslims may have collected ointments in these vessels, used to anoint the rock beneath the Dome of the Rock.[101]

The transformation of Jerusalem into a holy city of the Islamic caliphate is also expressed in a marble milestone, found on an important but difficult mountain road from Jerusalem to the new city of Ramla, founded by ʿAbd al-Malik to the northwest (fig. 4.27).[102] The milestone's inscription records that he ordered the construction of this road and the stone, which marks 'eight *mils*' (roughly 18 kilometres) from Jerusalem.[103] Ramla sat at an intersection between the holy city and the Mediterranean port of Jaffa, and on a route connecting Cairo to Damascus, the Umayyad capital. The use of distance markers and measurements to appropriate space recalls the imperial actions of Roman emperors.[104] The inscription also refers to Jerusalem as Iliya, the Arabic transcription of Aelia, a Roman name for the city, while the unit *mils* also roughly follows the Roman equivalent *mille*.[105] However, the inscription's Arabic kufic script clearly broadcasts

4.26
Juglet with hexagonal body, with image of the standing caliph, late 600s– early 700s. Probably from the southern Levant region. Glass. H. 13.5 cm, W. 6 cm, D. 8 cm. Ashmolean Museum, University of Oxford, 1949.144.a.

4.27
Milestone with kufic inscription, *c.* 685– 705. Jerusalem. White limestone. H. 39.5 cm, W. 57.5 cm, D. 8.5 cm. Musée du Louvre, Paris, AO 4087.

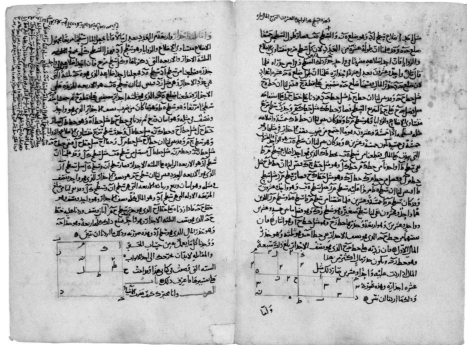

4.28

Yahya al-Wasiti, illustration of al-Hariri's *Maqamat* depicting scholars at an 'Abbasid library, 1236–7. Ink and colours on paper. H. 37 cm, W. 28 cm. Bibliothèque nationale de France, Paris, Ms Arabe 5847, fol. 5v.

4.29

Al-Khwarizmi, *al-Kitab al-mukhtasar fi hisab al-jabr wa'l-muqabala* (*The Compendium on Calculation by Completion and Balancing*), 1342, original around 830. Ink and colours on paper. H. 25 cm, W. 35 cm (approx.). The Bodleian Libraries, University of Oxford, MS. Huntington 214, fols 4b–5a. Purchased from Robert Huntington in 1693.

to all passers-by that the Umayyad caliph was the new ruler of this sacred land, and the successor to its imperial past.

Movement of scholars, pilgrims and ideas

Baghdad, the wealthy and cultured 'Abbasid capital, emerged as a major centre of intellectual activity. Its renowned House of Wisdom (Bayt al-Hikmah), with its grand library, became a pinnacle of scholarship under the patronage of caliph al-Ma'mun (r. 754–75).[106] Learning in a wide range of disciplines flourished in the cities of the Islamic caliphates and dynasties (fig. 4.28), and was actively fostered by wealthy patrons. The introduction of papermaking technology from Tang China, although not immediately replacing parchment, was to facilitate the dissemination of knowledge, at a time when literary works in Greek, Sanskrit and Persian were translated into Arabic.[107] Early Greek science, particularly the teachings of Aristotle (384–322 BCE), spread from Alexandria to Baghdad.[108] Many of the leading thinkers and writers of this time came from Central Asia, travelling in search of courtly sponsorship and writing their treatises in Arabic.[109]

Flourishing of learning

The thinkers and writers of this era were so numerous, and their contributions so wide-ranging, that only a few examples can be highlighted here. The polymath Muhammad ibn Musa al-Khwarizmi (*c.* 780–850), from Khwarazm in Central Asia, was appointed astronomer and head of the library at Baghdad's House of Wisdom in 820. His work included the preparation of star tables, which provided tools to pinpoint the position of the sun, moon and five planets in order to tell the time. These tables, which were used for centuries thereafter, spread along the Silk

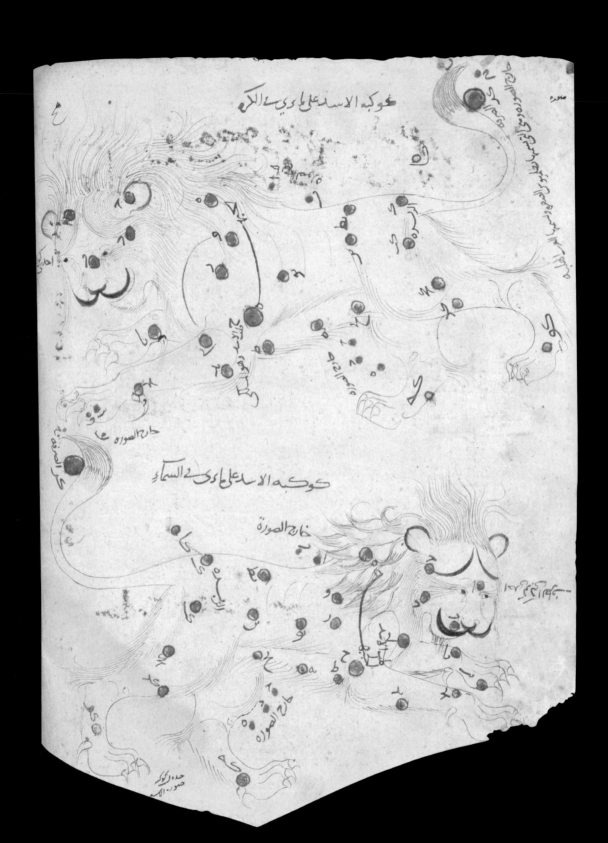

كوكبه الاسد على رأى الكره

كوكبه الاسد على رأى السماء

Roads as far as Europe, where they proved influential. Al-Khwarizmi's brilliance in mathematics is reflected in another of his works, *al-Kitab al-mukhtasar fi hisab al-jabr wa'l-muqabala* (*The Compendium on Calculation by Completion and Balancing*), which introduced the term 'algebra' (from *al-jabr* in the title) and established it as a mathematical discipline.[110] Pages from a later copy, produced around 1342, show geometrical solutions to two quadratic equations (fig. 4.29). The term 'algorithm', the steps for solving mathematical problems, evolved from al-Khwarizmi's Latinised name, Algorithmus.[111]

The astronomer 'Abd al-Rahman al-Sufi (903–986), from Rey in western Iran, worked at the court in Isfahan in central Iran, where he wrote the *Kitab suwar al-kawakib al-thabitah* (*Book of the Fixed Stars*) in Arabic in 964 (fig. 4.30). This monumental work drew on the earlier mathematical and astronomical treatise *Almagest* by Ptolemy (85–165 CE), who was based in Alexandria. It describes forty-eight constellations, including each star's longitudinal and latitudinal coordinates, as well as its magnitude, facilitating more precise calculations for navigation. Al-Sufi also compared the constellations known in pre-Islamic Arabia with their ancient Greek equivalents. His work exemplifies the interest among scholars of the Islamic world in ancient Mediterranean learning, which was accessible to Arabic readers through translations. For instance, large-scale translation projects were patronised by the politically powerful and wealthy Barmakid family, who were originally Buddhists from Balkh, Afghanistan.[112] They relocated to Baghdad to serve the 'Abbasid caliph, where they became major patrons of scholarship and the sciences.

Interest in, and the study of, mathematics and astronomy led to improvements in practical navigational tools. The mathematician Muhammad ibn Ibrahim

al-Fazari (746–806) is credited with being the first person in the Islamic world to build an astrolabe, an instrument consisting of rotating discs that can be used for telling the time and measuring the altitude of heavenly bodies above the horizon (fig. 4.31).[113] These complex objects were usually produced for elites at the court by highly specialised instrument makers. By the later ninth century the astrolabe was in use throughout the Islamic world, reaching al-Andalus on the Iberian Peninsula by the tenth. By around 1000 it had reached Christian Europe, although it does not appear to have been widely used there for some time (see p. 241). It was, however, to have a significant impact upon navigation, along both overland and maritime routes.

Scholars in the Islamic world also made significant contributions to medicine. A notable figure in this area was Ibn Bakhtishu (d. 1058), the last in an illustrious line of physicians who were followers of the Church of the East and were associated with a school of medicine at Gondeshapur, Iran.[114] They served several 'Abbasid caliphs, beginning with al-Mansur (r. 754–75), reflecting multicultural dimensions

4.33

Map of the world from *Nuzhat al-mushtaq fi ikhtiraq al-afaq* (*Book of Pleasant Journeys into Faraway Lands*, also known as the 'Book of Roger'), 1553 copy of original by al-Idrisi *c*. 1152. Possibly Cairo. Ink and colours on paper. H. 30 cm, W. 50 cm (approx.). The Bodleian Libraries, University of Oxford, MS.Pococke 375, fols 3b–4a.

at the court in Baghdad.[115] One of Ibn Bakhtishu's recorded works is a book on the characteristics of animals, their properties and usefulness of their organs. Passages from it may be preserved in a later treatise titled *Kitab na't al-hayawan* (*Book of the Characteristics of Animals*), dating to the thirteenth century. An illustration from it appears to show the physician in discussion with a pupil (fig. 4.32).[116]

Cartography was another area in which advancements were made. A tradition of atlases representing the 'Realm of Islam' developed in the tenth century.[117] It included world maps that indicate a spherical world encompassing Asia, Europe and Africa surrounded by a ring of water.[118] These maps are typically orientated southwards to bring attention to Arabia and Mecca, Islam's holiest city.[119] Al-Idrisi (active 1154), a Muslim scholar from al-Andalus, followed this tradition with a circular world map that he produced for a treatise completed in 1154, under the sponsorship of the Christian king of Sicily, Roger II (r. 1130–54) (fig. 4.33). The map shows Arabia as part of the wider world of Afro-Eurasia, with the Mediterranean coastline extending west to the Iberian Peninsula, and east across the Indian Ocean and reaching China. His wider treatise describes each part of the known world in detail, synthesising first-hand observations and the established scholarship available to him.[120] Although produced later than the year 1000, al-Idrisi's treatise reflects the perception of a connected world that already existed before this date.[121]

Transmission of the Qur'an and pilgrimage

The Qur'an is believed to contain the words of God as revealed to the Prophet Muhammad through the Archangel Gabriel. In addition to being transmitted orally, these revelations were also written down. By the time of the third caliph Uthman (r. 644–56), a standardised written holy book was compiled, which formed the basis of all subsequent Qur'ans.[122] An important factor in the Qur'an's transmission, as well as that of secular knowledge, was the spread of papermaking technology from China to the Islamic world. According to legend, Chinese prisoners captured after the Battle of Talas, which took place in 751 between the

4.34
Qur'an written in *al-ma'il* script, 700s. Probably Mecca or Medina. Ink on vellum. H. 31.5 cm, W. 21.5 cm. The British Library, London, Or.2165. Purchased by the British Museum from Rev. Greville John Chester.

4.35
Fragments of the Qur'an written in kufic script, 800s. Possibly Egypt. Ink and gold on vellum. H. 25 cm; W. 64 cm (each page, approx.). The Bodleian Libraries, University of Oxford, MS. Marsh 178. Bequeathed by Narcissus Marsh.

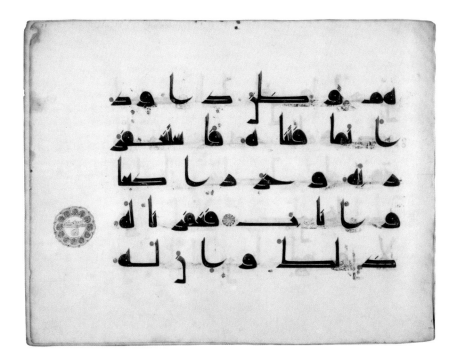

Tang and 'Abbasid armies, brought knowledge of papermaking to Samarkand, from where it spread to wider central Islamic lands.[123] More recent scholarship has demonstrated that paper was already in use in Samarkand decades before this. Although the precise process of transmission is not known, papermaking was undoubtedly introduced to West Asia through Central Asia by the eighth century, when the first papermill was established by the Barmakid family in Baghdad in 794–5.[124] This important development greatly expanded the scale of writing and transcriptions in the Islamic world.

Early Qur'ans were mainly written on parchment (animal skin) and less commonly papyrus. An eighth-century Qur'an written in *al-ma'il* script (fig. 4.34), exceptional for its portrait format, is written on a fine type of parchment known as vellum.[125] Other earlier examples are written in kufic in a landscape format, which was more suited to the elongated strokes of the script (fig. 4.35). These Qur'ans are large codices kept within a stiff binding and were labour intensive to produce. Paper was eventually adopted for use in this traditional domain by the late tenth century.[126] This change coincided with the acceptance of new scripts for copying the holy text. More cursive in style, these scripts developed from everyday writing used for secular documents on paper. Among them was *naskh* script, which was most easily legible to ordinary readers.[127] Eventually a new type of paper Qur'an, smaller in size and featuring a portrait book format, emerged, offering greater portability as it could be handheld (fig. 4.36). These changes, brought about by the spread of papermaking, helped to make the holy book more accessible to a wider Muslim audience.

4.36

Qur'an written in *naskh* script, copied by Abu l-Qasim Sa'id ibn Ibrahim ibn 'Ali, 1036. Probably Iraq or Iran. Ink and gold on paper. H. 18.5 cm, W. 14 cm (each page). The British Library, London, Add. Ms 7214. Purchased by the British Museum from Mary Mackintosh Rich.

4.37

Qur'an written in kufic script with Persian commentary in *naskh* script, 1000–1200, commentary possibly slightly later. Iran or Iraq. Ink on paper. H. 35.5 cm, W. 26.7 cm (each page). The British Library, London, Or.6573. Purchased from Mirza Sarkin Ayrazaoff.

4.38

The spiral minaret of the Great Mosque of Samarra, built 848–52.

As the Islamic world expanded, followers of the religion increasingly included those who were not familiar with Arabic. Debates emerged over whether the Qur'an, being a revelation from God, could and should be translated from Arabic into other languages.[128] It was believed that other languages could not accurately convey the nuances of the holy book of Islam. Commentaries, or translations considered a kind of commentary, provided a practical solution to this dilemma.[129] In an example from the eleventh or twelfth century, passages of the Qur'an in Arabic are accompanied by Persian annotations below (fig. 4.37). Qur'ans with Persian explanations seem to have been produced from around the later tenth century in the Samanid empire. For instance, Amir Mansur ibn Nuh (r. 961–76) is said to have commissioned the translation of forty volumes of al-Tabari's commentary (*Tarjama-ye tafsir-e Tabari*) into Persian when he found he had difficulty understanding the Arabic text.[130]

The revelations of the Qur'an and the teachings of the Prophet Muhammad united the diverse populations of the Islamic world. Followers were also physically brought together by pilgrimage to Mecca, the centre of the world in al-Idrisi's map (see fig. 4.33). Known as the Hajj, pilgrimage to Mecca is one of the pillars of Islam as attested in the Qur'an. All Muslims must go at least once in their lifetime, if they are able.[131] Many undertook the arduous journey to Mecca from across the expanding Islamic world, officially starting from 632 – the year when the Prophet Muhammad conducted the Hajj for the last time, known as his Farewell Pilgrimage.[132] Subsequently, caliphs saw it as their duty and expression of rulership to organise and care for pilgrims, and even sometimes led the Hajj themselves.[133] Their responsibilities included the improvement of roads leading to Mecca and the provision of supplies, especially water, which was vital across desert areas. During the 'Abbasid era, the Darb Zubayda, the route that connected cities in Iraq to Mecca, was the focus of an impressive feat of engineering, aimed at providing pilgrims with supplies and facilities at regular intervals to ease their journey across the desert of Arabia.[134] Other travellers besides pilgrims, such as traders, also used these routes.

Imports and innovations

As the Islamic caliphate gained control of Arabia and the important ports along the Persian Gulf and Red Sea, maritime trade flourished. From the late eighth century and the ninth, significantly greater numbers of ships than before brought a diverse array of goods by sea, which were then transported overland or along rivers to cities inland.[135] Chinese ceramics were particularly abundant and highly sought after. Local potters were inspired by the influx of these imports, which led to experimentation and innovations in production techniques.

Samarra

Archaeological finds on sites across Islamic lands reveal evidence of interregional and long-distance movement of objects during this period. One of these sites is Samarra in present-day Iraq, which temporarily replaced Baghdad as the capital of the 'Abbasid caliphate between 836 and 892. Because the city was not redeveloped in later times, Samarra's architectural remains have survived remarkably well, with a vast network of planned streets, houses, palaces and mosques still clearly visible or intact today (fig. 4.38). The 'Abbasid caliph is said to have summoned artisans from every town to develop the new capital, including from Egypt and the Basra region in southern Iraq.[136] Located on the

banks of the Tigris, Samarra was supplied by riverway and overland routes with access to imported goods.

The city's buildings were once richly decorated.[137] Painted, carved or moulded plaster panels were extensively used, along with wooden structures and decorations. One wooden horizontal panel has a carved abstract design in the 'bevelled' style, featuring a variation on vegetal forms (fig. 4.39). Recent scientific analysis of a piece of wood with similar carvings, excavated from the reception complex of the main palace of Dar al-Khilafa in Samarra, identified it as teak.[138] This timber, specifically the Tectona species, was native to South and Southeast Asia, and it seems probable that wooden panels in the 'bevelled' style were made of teak imported to Samarra.

While the architectural structures at Samarra have survived well, there are far fewer traces of the expensive decorative materials that originally adorned them, since most would have been removed after the city was largely abandoned following political turmoil, when the capital returned to Baghdad.[139] Some of the small archaeological finds from Samarra include glass tesserae in rough cube forms that may have been used for mosaics at the congregational mosque and palaces. These came in several colours, including gold, created by laying gold leaf onto cast panes of glass that were then cut into small pieces (fig. 4.40).[140] Scientific analyses have revealed that the glass tesserae, except for those with the gold leaf, have compositions that are consistent with the Roman or the eastern Mediterranean tradition, suggesting that they may have been imported to Samarra. One theory is that the tesserae were made from recycled glass taken from earlier Byzantine or Umayyad buildings to the west of Samarra.[141]

Small, fragmentary cobalt blue flasks, some with their stoppers intact, have also been discovered in the throne room of the Dar al-Khilafa palace (fig. 4.41). Again, scientific analysis of one of these indicated that it was made in the eastern Mediterranean, and probably held perfume that was exported along with its container.[142] At the same time, Samarra had its own glass and pottery production sites that produced objects including glass perfume bottles, which were in turn exported from the city (fig. 4.42). Samarra glass has been scientifically identified in large quantities at many sites across the Islamic world, such as Nishapur, Fustat (Old Cairo), and in Syria.[143]

Sherds of Tang Chinese ceramics, too, have been excavated at Dar al-Khilafa, including part of a whiteware bowl made in the Gongxian kilns in Henan province (fig. 4.43). Gongxian wares tended to be more heavily potted, made with

4.39 above
Frieze with stylised palmettes, 800s. Found in Samarra. Probably teak wood. H. 17.5 cm, L. 74 cm. British Museum, London, 1944,0513.3. Purchased from Sir Sydney Burney through Art Fund (as NACF).

4.40
Green, transparent and blue-black tesserae, 900s. Excavated at Samarra, Iraq. Glass and gold leaf. H. 1 cm, W. 1 cm, D. 1 cm (each, approx.). British Museum, London, OA+.12180. Given by H.M. Government.

4.41
Flask fragments, 800–1000. Excavated at Dar al-Khilafa, Samarra. Glass, cotton and papyrus. H. 3.3–5.5 cm. British Museum, London, OA+.13590.1–80. Given by H.M. Government.

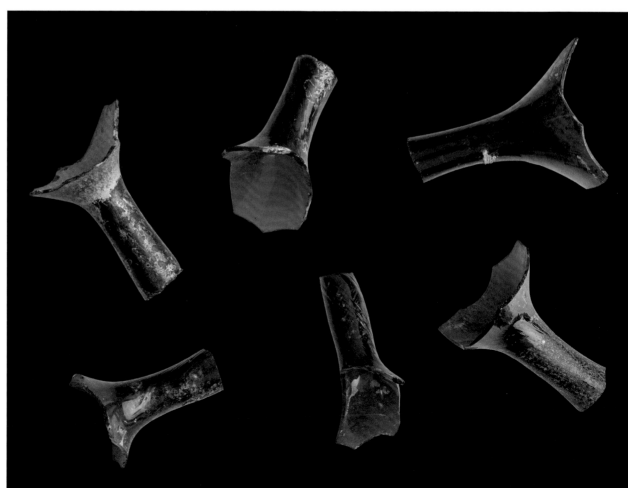

less pure clay covered with a white slip and a transparent glaze with a faint yellow tinge.[144] The coarser-grained clay is visible in the cross-section of the excavated sherd. Gongxian wares were among the ceramics found in the *Belitung* shipwreck and were also supplied to the domestic market in China, even the Tang court (see p. 68).[145] Although the Gongxian kilns did not produce the finest whitewares in China during this period (those would be from the Xing or Ding kilns further north), their material quality is still considered finer than the ceramics produced in West Asia.[146] The difference can be seen by comparing the Gongxian sherd with a fragment from the same site imitating Tang Chinese green-splashed ceramics, which has an earthenware body fired at a lower temperature (fig. 4.44).[147] These finds demonstrate that ceramics imported from Tang China co-existed with local imitation wares at the palaces of Samarra.

A particularly rare survival from Samarra is a linen fragment with silk embroidered inscription (fig. 4.45). It was made in Egypt, a major centre for producing flax and linen during this time, and was found in the palace of Jawsaq, where the private quarters of the caliph were located.[148] During the ʿAbbasid period, the number of government-controlled weaving workshops, known as Dar al-Tiraz, increased, catering to the court and the wider market. Many of the workshops were found in the fertile Nile Delta.[149] Given the findspot of this linen fragment, it was probably produced in one of these weaving workshops that made textiles for the caliph and his court. The inscription on the linen fragment, embroidered on a band also known as a *tiraz*, carries the name Al-Muʿtamid (r. 870–92), a caliph who was once imprisoned by his brother in Samarra. It was shortly before Al-Muʿtamid's reign in 868 that the ʿAbbasid dynasty lost direct control of Egypt, adding an intriguing historical layer to this textile fragment.

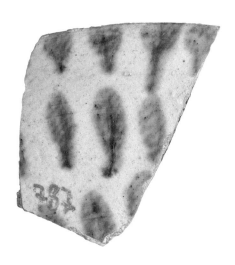

Although fragmentary, these modest archaeological finds from Samarra provide an impression of the range of imported goods that reached the city from multiple sources, stretching from Tang China to the Byzantine world.

4.42 *opposite top*

Bottles, probably for perfume, 800s. Excavated at Samarra, Iraq. Glass. H. 5.9 cm, Diam. 3.7 cm; H. 7.1 cm, Diam 3.9 cm; H. 5.6 cm, Diam. 3.4 cm. British Museum, London, OA+.13758, OA+.13746, OA+.13744.

4.43 *opposite middle*

Sherd, 618–907. Made at the Gongxian kilns, Henan province, China, excavated at Dar al-Khilafa, Samarra, Iraq. Stoneware. H. 6.2 cm, W. 8.5 cm, D. 10.7 cm. British Museum, London, OA+.900.1. Professor Ernst Herzfeld collection.

4.44 *opposite bottom*

Sherd imitating Tang Chinese green-splashed ceramics, 800s. Excavated at Dar al-Khilafa, Samarra, Iraq. Glazed earthenware. H. 7 cm, W. 7.3 cm, D. 1.7 cm. British Museum, London, OA+.2154. Professor Ernst Herzfeld collection.

4.45 *right*

Textile fragment, 870–92. Made in Egypt. Excavated at the palace of Jawsaq al-Khaqani in Samarra, Iraq. Flax and silk embroidery. H. 18 cm, W. 12 cm. Museum für Islamische Kunst, Staatliche Museen zu Berlin, I.8275.

Exchanges in Tang Chinese and Islamic ceramics

The discovery of the *Belitung* shipwreck off the coast of Indonesia (see p. 63) highlights the enormous scale of the transport of ceramics and other goods from Tang China to the ʿAbbasid caliphate across the Indian Ocean. This is further corroborated by sherds found at sites in ports along the Arabian Peninsula and Persian Gulf. The appeal of Chinese ceramics to audiences in West Asia lay in their aesthetic, and in their special materials and production techniques that differed from local potteries. Potters in China had access to fine raw materials, such as kaolin and petuntse for making porcelain fired at high temperatures, which was admired for its whiteness and translucency.[150] Potters in the early Islamic period, by contrast, produced coarser, low-fired earthenware.

As large quantities of Chinese ceramics reached the Islamic world, potters in West Asia started to imitate the imported wares. They masked their earthenware with a glaze that had been made opaque and white by the addition of tin oxide.[151] The result was a fine white ground on ceramics that could be fired at a relatively low temperature. Islamic potters also imitated the shapes of Chinese ceramics. They closely followed a type of bowl commonly known as the 'Samarra type' because it has been found in large quantities in that city (fig. 4.46).[152] Ceramics of this type are plain white wares with a rolled lip, ribbed body and broad flat foot.

The opaque white ground created using a tin glaze resulted in a surface that was suitable for decoration. Potters in the Islamic world, such as those working at Basra, Iraq, started using cobalt blue pigment, probably sourced from present-day Iran, to create a variety of patterns and sometimes inscriptions on the newly developed white surface.[153] One example is painted with a geometric decoration in dark blue (fig. 4.47). In addition to the glaze, the shape of the bowl, with its flared rim, suggests that the potters were referencing Chinese ceramics.

Interestingly, around the same time, potters at the Gongxian kilns in China started to experiment with using cobalt on stoneware, when previously it had only been used on low-fired pottery.[154] The cobalt in China was probably also imported from Iran, while the patterns they applied took inspiration from West Asian decorative traditions. The resulting wares seem to have been made for export to West Asia (see fig. 1.55). However, their production was apparently limited, as very little Tang-dynasty stoneware with cobalt-blue painted decoration has been identified outside China. For instance, only three examples were found on the *Belitung* shipwreck, while a single sherd from Gongxian has been found at Siraf, a trading port on the Persian Gulf.[155]

Splashed wares are another type of ceramic from the Islamic world that has an intriguing possible connection with wares from China. Made from earthenware, they are covered with a white slip to which splashes of glaze usually in green, brown and yellow were applied with a thin coating of transparent lead glaze to finish (on the use of lead glaze in the ceramics of al-Andalus, see p. 240).[156] The colours were allowed to run and create haphazard streaks during the firing. Some also bear incised decoration created in a technique known as sgraffito (fig. 4.48). The visual similarity between these wares and 'three-coloured' (*sancai*) wares from Tang China is striking (see figs 1.19 and 1.44). However, examples of *sancai* wares have so far not been discovered in West Asia.[157] There are, for instance, no *sancai* wares in the *Belitung* cargo. Instead, Tang whitewares with green dots or splashes were exported to, and clearly imitated by, Islamic potters (see figs 1.54 and 4.44). Therefore the question remains whether the multicoloured splashed decoration with a lead glaze was inspired by Chinese models, or if the visual similarities are merely a coincidence.

In the ninth century, potters in Iraq adapted a type of painted decoration on glass and applied it to the newly developed tin glaze on ceramics. Known as lustre

4.46

'Samarra type' bowl, 618–907. Probably Xing kilns, Hebei province, China. Stoneware ceramic. H. 4.4 cm, Diam. 15.2 cm. British Museum, London, 1956,1210.22.

4.47

Bowl with palmette design, 800–900. Iraq, probably Basra. Glazed earthenware. H. 7.5 cm, Diam. 24.5 cm. Victoria and Albert Museum, London, CIRC.122-1929.

painting, the technique involved the application of silver and copper oxides, mixed with a little vinegar, to the tin-glazed ware after it had been fired once.[158] The decorated pieces would then be fired again in a kiln environment with low oxygen, resulting in a metallic sheen (fig. 4.49). Requiring great skill to produce, these wares would have been more expensive than other Islamic pottery and may be described as luxury items.[159] Lustreware was later perfected under the Fatimid caliphate based in Egypt, and eventually spread to Europe (see chapter 5).

During the period 500 to 1000, the diverse region stretching from Central Asia to Arabia experienced the waning of Sasanian and Byzantine dominance and the rapid expansion of the Islamic empire. Yet, instead of a sudden and dramatic break from the past after military conquest, material culture reveals that changes to daily life in many parts of the empire were gradual. Muslim rulers sought to adapt elements familiar to their subjects while developing new, distinctive identities, as evident in archaeological finds such as the milestone that is carved in Arabic kufic script but uses Roman references (see fig. 4.27). Knowledge of different traditions was synthesised and built upon, and interregional and long-distance exchange that connected the Islamic realm with the wider world flourished. The next section moves across the Red Sea to introduce the Christian Kingdom of Aksum and the port city of Adulis around the 500s, when it was a hub for overseas trade in northeast Africa.

4.48

Bowl, 900s. Nishapur, Iran. Glazed earthenware. H. 7.1 cm, Diam. 24.1 cm. British Museum, London, 1951,1009.2.

4.49

Bowl with geometric decoration, 800–900. Basra, Iraq. Lustreware. H. 8 cm, Diam. 28.5 cm. British Museum, London, 1968,1015.1.

μαρμαρω δια · τὸν δὲ ναῦλον, θεμελιῶ · ὅτι αὐτοῦ
τῶ τιθούμενου τοῦ λόγου. δι μοσω δίφρος και τὸ
μάρμαρον, ἅμα οὕτωσ και αὐτοῦ ὁ πτολεμαῖοσ :

ὁ Δος δια τουσα απο αλου εἰσ α ζωνην :

εἰσι δὲ και τα γεγραμμένα ἐν τῆ εικονι, ταῦτα :—
βασιλεὸ μεγας πτολεμαῖοσ · ινϊ πτιασ ταξεωσ πτολεμαῖου ·

Aksumites and their port city, Adulis

Elisabeth R. O'Connell

Around 524 an anonymous Christian merchant from Alexandria, who was later known as Cosmas Indicopleustes, travelled to the Aksumite port city of Adulis on the Red Sea coast of Africa. Cosmas was in the city to buy elephant ivory, but the governor of Adulis invited him to copy Greek monumental inscriptions for the king of Aksum, Kaleb (r. *c.* 510–40), a fellow Christian, as Kaleb prepared to invade the Jewish Himyarite kingdom in South Arabia.[1] Cosmas was a trader and, at Adulis, an accidental diplomat.

The original monumental inscriptions are lost but, from Cosmas' record, modern scholars have been able to distinguish two extraordinary texts carved about 500 years apart. They are depicted in a remarkable drawing of Adulis (fig. 4.50) preserved in all three of the surviving manuscript copies of Cosmas' treatise, *Christian Topography*. Each inscription extols the vast territories under one of two different rulers' control. The earlier inscription, carved on a tall black stone stela with a triangular top, commemorates the elephant-hunting expeditions of the Macedonian king of Egypt Ptolemy III (r. 246–221 BCE), and his conquests using war elephants, so the text declares, all the way to Bactria in Central Asia.[2] The later inscription was carved on a white marble votive throne at the end of the second or in the early third century CE and celebrates the successes of the Aksumite king at the height of the empire's territorial expansion, stretching from the northern Horn of Africa across the Red Sea to the southwest Arabian Peninsula.[3] When Kaleb launched his military expedition in 525 it was nominally to redress the persecution of fellow Christians, but his claim to rule southwest Arabia was validated by historical claims bolstered by the inscriptions.[4] Kaleb and his army set sail from Adulis to fight against the Jewish Himyarite king Joseph, who was supported by the Zoroastrian Sasanian empire (fig. 4.51).[5] Arguably, Kaleb's expansionist intentions were inseparable from contemporary perceptions of religious rivalry and destiny.[6]

International conflict and diplomacy in the sixth century

The invasion of 525 followed several attacks on Christians settled in Zafar and Najran in South Arabia. Aksum had invaded the southwest tip of the Arabian Peninsula in 518 and brought a Christian Himyarite to power there (fig. 4.52). A few years later, a Jewish Himyarite king, Joseph, assumed power and undertook a series of violent persecutions, killing monks and laymen and burning churches or converting them to synagogues.[7] That the massacre in 523 was an international incident is demonstrated by the multilingual corpus of evidence that can be pieced together from inscriptions and

4.50

Monuments of Adulis illustrated in the *Christian Topography*, 1000s copy of *c.* 500s original. Ink and pigments on parchment. H. 22.5 cm, W. 18.6 cm. Biblioteca Medicea Laurenziana, Florence, Laur.Plut. IX.28, fol. 38r. In Medici family collection by 1495.

4.51

King Kaleb and his army sailing from Adulis in the *Life of Zamikaʾel Aragawi*, 1700–50. Ethiopia. Ink and pigments on paper. H. 32.4 cm, W. 29 cm. The Bodleian Libraries, University of Oxford, MS Aeth. d. 23, fol. 28r. Donated by Dr Bent Juel-Jensen.

4.52

Map showing Aksum with places discussed in this case study.

accounts embedded in literary texts. At a conference in Ramla, held under the auspices of an Arab sheikh, a client of the Sasanians, a letter was read in which Joseph himself reported on his persecution of Christians. The meeting brought together both Byzantine and Sasanian interests, as well as their respective regional Arab allies.[8] Hoards discovered in Yemen, comprised of Byzantine and Aksumite coins, probably belong to this context of the region's sixth-century political upheavals (figs 4.53–4.55).[9] Most spectacularly, a group of 868 Aksumite and 326 Byzantine coins were found in a pot some 70 kilometres west of Aden.[10] Once the Aksumites defeated the Himyarite king, direct rule was brief. The Aksumite general Abraha established autonomous rule for a period (*c.* 532–60), but disenfranchised Himyarites appealed to the Sasanian king, who sent an invading force.[11] With the support of the Sasanian empire, the Himyarites reportedly slaughtered many of the Aksumites, even killing pregnant women, and enslaved others.[12] Shortly after, in the 570s, the Sasanians established their rule in South Arabia until the Arab conquest some decades later (see chapter 4).

The Aksumite empire

Aksum was an international power, connected diplomatically, economically and culturally to the contemporary known world. By the mid-third century CE, the prophet Mani in Persia regarded Aksum as one of the four most important kingdoms of the ancient world, alongside Rome, Persia and 'Sileos' (probably China). Aksum occupied the highlands of what is today northeast Ethiopia and Eritrea from the first century CE to the eighth.[13] From the outset, its Red Sea port, Adulis, was a hub for international trade, connecting the Indian Ocean and the Mediterranean. Items traded included luxury materials from Africa, foremost ivory, but also rhinoceros horn and tortoise shell; Mediterranean wine, olive oil, textiles and glass; and Indian Ocean spices, iron and crucible steel – the latter had been developed in India in the mid-first millennium BCE.[14] A sixth–seventh-century CE shipwreck discovered off the coast of Adulis had a cargo of amphorae probably loaded at the northern Red Sea port of Aila (in modern Jordan).[15] The extent of Aksumite exchange networks in the east is shown by a hoard of 105 gold Kushan coins minted in Central Asia in the second–third century CE and found at Dabra Dammo, thousands of beads from South Asia found in a tomb at Aksum, and a fourth–sixth-century Gupta figure from India found at Adulis.[16] Aksumite pottery, coins and their imitations have been found in India.[17] The sixth-century Byzantine emperor Justinian is said to have sought the intervention of the Aksumites in the silk trade in order to undermine Sasanian interests.[18] Aksum's reputation

4.53–4.55

Aksumite coin (top), Aksumite imitation of a Byzantine coin (middle) and Byzantine coin (bottom), 450–500, *c.* mid-300–400s, 324–361 (respectively). Minted in Aksum (top), Aksum (middle) and Arles (bottom), found in Yemen. Gold. Diam. 1.7 cm, weight 1.58 g (top), Diam. 2 cm, weight 3.7 g (middle), Diam. 2 cm, weight 3.7 g (bottom). British Museum, London, 1904,0404.1–3. Donated by Ali Farah.

persisted after its decline at the end of the sixth century or the beginning of the seventh.[19] Even as late as the eighth century, the king of Aksum was depicted as among the rulers of the world in the wall-painting programme of the future Muslim caliph of the Umayyad empire, al-Walid II, at Qusayr ʿAmra (see fig. 0.12), the complex built in the Jordanian desert around 723–43.

An early Christian state

With the Aksumite rulers' adoption of Christianity in the mid-fourth century CE, the kingdom has claim to be one of the earliest officially Christian states. When the Byzantine emperor Constantius II (r. 337–61 CE) wrote to the rulers of Aksum, Ezanas and his brother Sazana, he asked them to send their bishop back to Alexandria to confer with its new archbishop. Perhaps as early as 340 CE, the charismatic archbishop Athanasius of Alexandria had appointed the Syrian monk Frumentius as bishop of Aksum, and Constantius II, who exiled Athanasius twice, sought to ensure that Aksum adhered to the theological position of his replacement in Alexandria.[20] Such evidence

4.56–4.57

Coins showing King Ezanas adopting Christianity, c. 300–40 (top), c. 340–60s (bottom). Minted in Aksum, Ethiopia. Gold. Diam. 1.5 cm, weight 1.8 g (top), Diam. 1.7 cm, weight 1.5 g (bottom). British Museum, London, 1989,0518.41, purchased from Roger Brereton (top), 1915,0108.81, purchased from Lt. A.R. Prideaux from the collection of the late Col. W.F. Prideaux (bottom). The first coin shows Ezanas with a disc and crescent above him, while the second shows a cross.

illustrates both the interconnectedness of the world at this time and the shared devotion to Christianity, to which the leaders of Byzantium and Aksum had only recently converted. This is the international context for the adoption of Christianity on the Horn of Africa.

Maritime trade may already have facilitated the establishment of expatriate communities of Christians in Aksum.[21] Nevertheless, with the exception of a recently discovered church at Beta Samati, there is little non-royal material evidence before the sixth century.[22] Instead, the adoption of Christianity can be traced through inscriptions erected and coinage issued by Ezanas.[23] In earlier inscriptions he calls himself 'the son of Mahrem', whose equivalent is given as Ares in Greek, while in later inscriptions he becomes a 'servant of Christ'. Pre-Christian coins show Ezanas surmounted by a disc and crescent. After his adoption of Christianity, a cross replaces these symbols (figs 4.56–4.57).

Languages and scripts

The Aksumite empire's engagement with the world beyond its borders is shown by the languages and scripts it employed on its coins and inscriptions. From its earliest appearance, Classical Ethiopic, or Geʽez, was written in a script derived from South Arabia. Towards the end of the third century CE, the kings of Aksum inaugurated a coinage of gold, silver and bronze.[24] The earliest coins issued by the state used Greek, the lingua franca of the period, increasingly alongside Geʽez. For their inscriptions, Aksumite rulers also employed combinations of Greek and Geʽez, both written from left to right, and often Geʽez written in the South Arabian Sabaic script, written from right to left.

Some of the earliest and most important luxury illustrated manuscripts to survive from the Christian world are in Geʽez. The so-called Garima Gospels, named after the monastery where they are preserved, contain three copies of the four gospels, translated from Greek into Geʽez. Each copy is preceded by ornately framed concordances of shared gospel passages known as canon tables (fig. 4.58), a system popularised by the bishop and Church historian Eusebius of Caesarea (d. c. 339 CE). Radiocarbon analysis confirms that manuscript III, dating to around 450–650, may be the oldest set of gospel books with portraits of the four evangelists. While the form of the gospel tables and other features are international, much of the visual content, for example local flora and fauna, is distinctively African. Contrary to some earlier scholarship, new research confirms that the Garima Gospels were copied by scribes and illustrated by painters on the Horn of Africa.[25]

In addition to original works, the Ethiopian manuscript tradition preserves copies of some texts that do not otherwise survive. Lost Greek patristic, canonical and liturgical texts, assembled around 450–550 and translated into Ge'ez before around 700, are found in an extraordinary manuscript dating to the thirteenth century and now known as the *Aksumite Collection*.[26] So too, the world history of John, Bishop of Nikiu, an eyewitness to both the Sasanian and Arab conquests of the seventh century, survives only in Ge'ez.[27] Originally written in Coptic with the use of Greek sources, John of Nikiu's *Chronicle* was translated into Arabic, then later into Ge'ez as part of the translation efforts of the Ethiopian court in 1602.[28] The Ge'ez manuscript tradition illustrates the region's cosmopolitan horizons.

Cosmas' Adulis

Written about twenty-five years after he transcribed the Greek inscriptions at Adulis, Cosmas' treatise in ten books entitled the *Christian Topography*, aimed to disprove the assertion that earth and heaven are spherical, promoting instead a cosmos comprised of a flat, rectangular earth surmounted by a firmament.[29] Thanks to his many digressions, Cosmas provides precious information based on his own travels, including his experience at Adulis recounted above. As the geographical setting for the two monumental inscriptions, the illustration of Adulis shows the royal city of Aksum (upper left) with travellers on the road between the two places (see fig. 4.50).[30] When Cosmas visited in the first quarter of the sixth century, he found 'countless churches'.[31]

At least three churches have been excavated at the port city of Adulis, providing material evidence for Christianity's flourishing there.[32] These churches share construction techniques with Aksumite churches elsewhere. They are built on high-stepped monumental platforms and have courses in alternating materials. Their interior spaces are, nevertheless, similarly configured to churches elsewhere in the eastern Mediterranean, Egypt and the Levant, in particular.[33] Their interiors demonstrate long-distance transportation of imported marbles originating from both the eastern and western Mediterranean. Petrographic analysis has shown that Proconnesian marble from the quarries around Constantinople, the capital of the Byzantine empire, furnished the interior chancel screen of the largest church in Adulis (figs 4.59–4.60).[34] In contrast with the Proconnesian marble 'church kits' that were sent by ship to Mediterranean cities in the sixth century, as evidenced by shipwrecks,[35] the imported marbles at Adulis are restricted to lighter architectural elements such as chancel screens, claddings and mouldings.[36] The fullest extent of the Adulis trade with the Mediterranean world is shown by fragments of black-and-white marble quarried in the

4.58
Canon table in Abba Garima III, *c.* 450–650. Ethiopia. Ink and pigments on parchment. H. 33.2 cm, W. 25.4 cm (page). Abba Garima Monastery, AG II, fol. 257r.

Pyrenees and green serpentine from the Peloponnese.[37] From the east, alabaster from South Arabia was also used to decorate the largest of the churches (fig. 4.61).[38] The size of the church, together with the presence of a baptistry and imported marble architectural elements, suggests that it was the cathedral of the port.

Cosmas' works shaped nineteenth-century views of Ethiopia in British antiquarian circles. When the British Museum sent Richard Rivington Holmes, an Assistant in the Department of Manuscripts, as a member of the 1868 British Expedition to Abyssinia launched against Tewodros II, the emperor of Ethiopia, the possibility of finding the Greek inscriptions transcribed by Cosmas at Adulis was one of the Museum's motivating factors. Holmes was unable to locate them, and they have never been rediscovered.[39] Under his watch, the Royal Engineers excavated the church at Adulis now thought to be its cathedral (fig. 4.62), and architectural fragments were sent to the British Museum (see figs 4.59–4.61).[40]

By the end of the sixth century, Aksumite hegemony over the Red Sea had ended. Having taken control of South Arabia, the Sasanians were now in the dominant position, but not for much longer.[41] The birth of the Prophet Muhammad around 570 is known as the Year of the Elephant, when Arabic sources recall the Aksumite Christian Abraha marched against Mecca. His lead war elephant is said to have stopped and refused to enter. Arabic sources also remember Aksum as a place of refuge for the early followers of Muhammad. Others report conflict. Around the same time, the production of Aksumite coins and inscriptions ceased, and the populations of both Aksum and Adulis declined. The centres of power had shifted.[42]

4.59–4.60 *opposite and above*
Fragments of Proconnesian marble chancel screen panels, *c.* 500–600. Quarried near Constantinople, found at excavated church at Adulis, Eritrea. Marble. H. 72 cm, W. 47 cm, D. 7.2 cm; H. 27.7, W. 25.9 cm, D. 4.5 cm. British Museum, London, OA.11008, 1868,1005.15. Donated by Sir Stafford Henry Northcote, 1st Earl of Iddesleigh.

4.61 *above left*
Fragment of alabaster panel, *c.* 500–600. Probably quarried in South Arabia, found at excavated church at Adulis, Eritrea. Alabaster. H. 13.1 cm, W. 14 cm, D. 3.8 cm. British Museum, London, 1868,1005.16. Donated by Sir Stafford Henry Northcote, 1st Earl of Iddesleigh.

4.62 *left*
Richard Rivington Holmes, View of excavated church at Adulis, 1867–8. Brown wash drawing on paper, H. 20.5 cm, W. 35.6 cm. British Museum, London, 1972,U.566. Donated by Sir Richard Rivington Holmes.

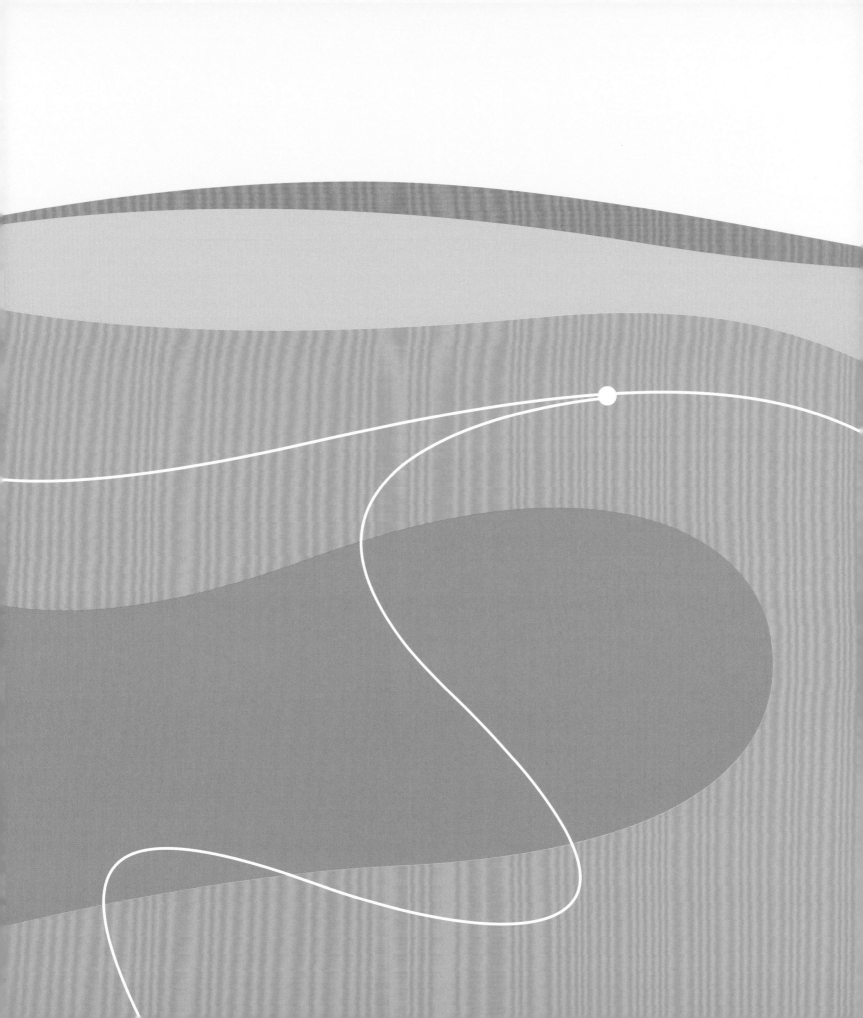

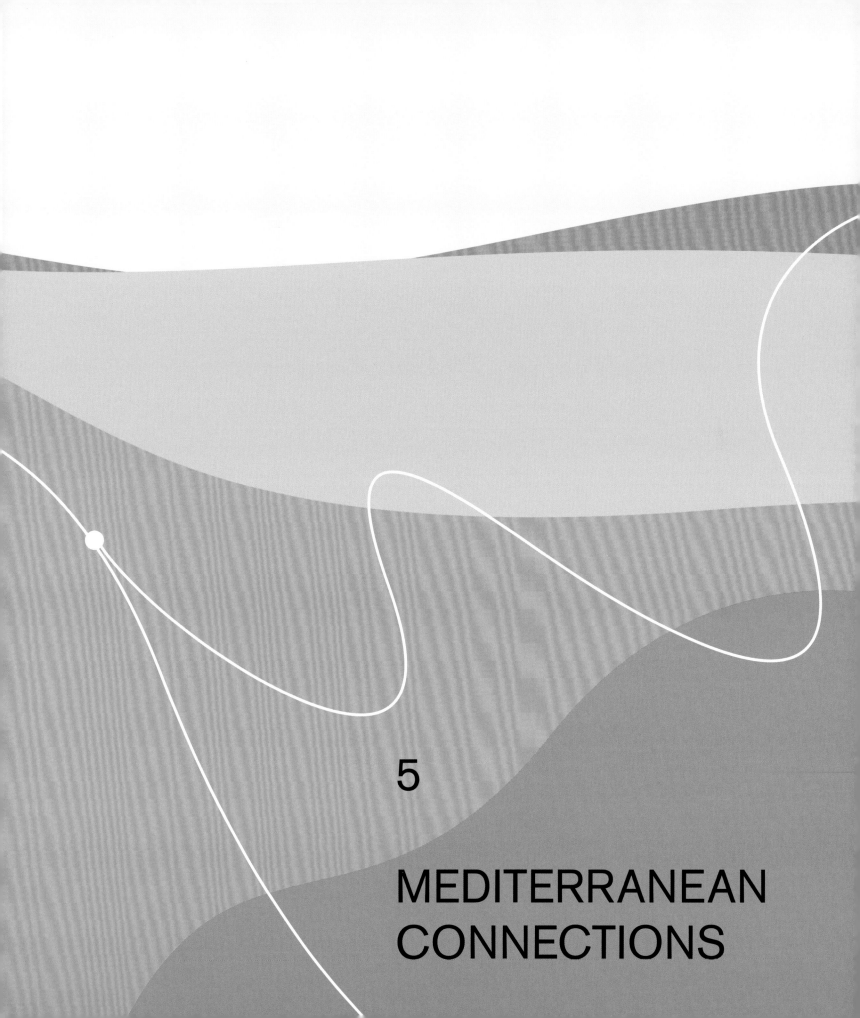

5

MEDITERRANEAN
CONNECTIONS

Mediterranean connections

Elisabeth R. O'Connell

Reached via overland, riverine and maritime routes, the Mediterranean Sea facilitated connections between Eurasia and Africa.[1] In the sixth century, Byzantium ruled most of the Mediterranean basin under the emperor Justinian (527–565).[2] As the direct continuation of the Roman empire, it was a Greek-speaking, Christian Roman empire; the word 'Byzantium', which is used today, was coined by a German in 1557 precisely in order to delegitimise the state's Roman inheritance.[3] The Byzantine empire was a successful, multiethnic state, which met migrating people with combinations of warfare, diplomacy and intermarriage.[4] Located at the 'hinge' of Eurasia, connecting east and west, Byzantium's capital, 'New Rome' or Constantinople (present-day Istanbul), occupied a strategic position from which it dominated the maritime empire that linked it to the known world (fig. 5.1).[5]

Byzantium's sixth-century dominance of the Mediterranean did not last (fig. 5.2). In the seventh century, the Sasanian and then Arab conquests challenged Byzantine hegemony temporarily and then definitively (see chapter 4). In the western Mediterranean, the rise of other Christian kingdoms left Byzantium with only parts of Italy.[6] Byzantium's recovery of territory into the reign of Basil II (976–1025), however, witnessed the maintenance of its heartland (western Turkey and Greece) and the conquests of central and eastern Anatolia (Turkey) and of the Bulgarian empire (the latter completed in 1018). Byzantine stability was reinforced by a treaty with the Fatimid caliphate (988, renewed 1001) and a marriage alliance with the Kyivan Rus' followed by their adoption of Christianity (988) (see p. 197). Many of Basil II's gains were longer-lasting, but only a generation after his death Byzantium was under attack by the Seljuks to the east and by the Normans to the west. Developments in the west led to the Crusades, initiated in 1095, and culminated in the sack of Constantinople in 1204.[7]

Byzantine rule in the southern Mediterranean was replaced by several Muslim states (see fig 4.2), until, by the end of the tenth century, the Fatimid empire controlled much of North Africa, the Levant and Hijaz (fig. 5.3). By 641, the general 'Amr ibn al-'As had seized control of Egypt, swiftly establishing a new capital, Fustat (now part of modern Cairo), just outside the walls of the Byzantine fortress at the apex of the Nile Delta. The strategic location of Egypt and its agricultural wealth supported and fuelled the westward expansion of Muslim rule. Several polities emerged in North Africa in the eighth and ninth centuries, each with different relationships to the dominant 'Abbasids of Baghdad (750–1258) and Umayyads in al-Andalus (756–1031). Control of trans-Saharan exchange routes was one key to success. In 909, the Fatimids boldly declared the creation of a new caliphate and, in 969, conquered Egypt, where they established their capital, Cairo, just north of Fustat. The significance of these twin cities, especially in day-to-day Mediterranean activities, is manifest in the survival of over 400,000 documents deposited by medieval Jewish communities in the *geniza* (storeroom)

5.1

Necklace with Aphrodite Anadyomene pendant, *c.* 600–700. Eastern Mediterranean. Gold, lapis lazuli, garnet (?) and rock crystal. L. 83 cm (chain), H. 4.5 cm (pendant without short chains). Dumbarton Oaks, Washington DC, BZ.1928.6. Gifted to Harvard University, 1940. The pendant combines a subject from Classical mythology with materials from beyond the Mediterranean, notably lapis lazuli from Afghanistan and rock crystal from Madagascar.

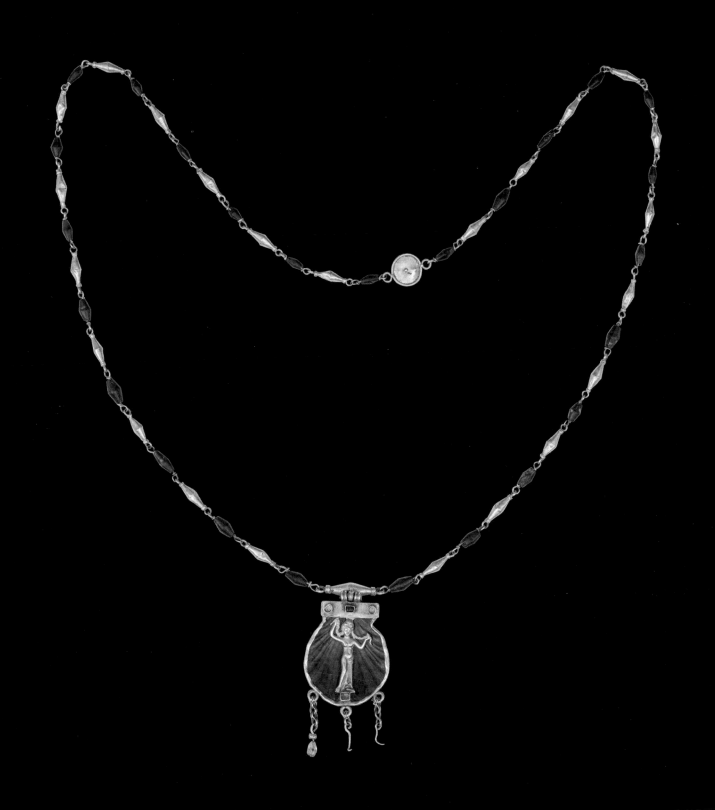

5.2

Map of the Byzantine empire, *c.* 555, showing places discussed in this chapter.

5.3

Map of Fatimid empire, *c.* 1000, showing places discussed in this chapter.

of the Ben Ezra Synagogue, today known as the 'Cairo geniza'. Religious texts were stored in this repository, but also everyday documents such as decrees, letters, contracts, petitions, accounts and tax receipts. These bring the Fatimid capital to life as a bustling hub with international connections from India to al-Andalus.

Justinian's Mediterranean

Under the emperor Justinian (r. 527–65), the Byzantine empire reached its greatest extent.[8] His treaty with the Sasanian empire in 532 allowed him to turn his attention to reclaiming Mediterranean territories taken by Germanic-speaking peoples in the previous century, particularly Goths and Vandals.[9] After swiftly retaking the Vandal capital at Carthage, Justinian's forces regained Rome's former African provinces and turned towards Italy, where his erstwhile allies, the Ostrogoths, ruled. Almost immediately, his Sasanian rival Khusruw I (r. 531–79) marched on the eastern territories (declaring war in 540), so that Byzantium now had to fight on two fronts, greatly stretching its resources. Then plague struck (see p. 17). Byzantine sources record what is now thought to be bubonic plague in the Egyptian port of Pelusium in 541 and in Constantinople in 542, where it reportedly decimated the population, and thereafter it is recorded throughout the Mediterranean and Europe, reaching Ireland in 544.[10] Outbreaks continued over the course of the following two centuries. Connectivity had its perils as well as its profits. But the Byzantines held off the Sasanians and completed the conquest of Italy by 555, also extending their rule westwards to the Iberian coast.

The Mediterranean was a region of social as well as political connectivity, with coastal communities from Iberia to the Black Sea bound together by similar rhythms of life.[11] In the sixth century the Byzantine navy dominated the Mediterranean, and this was integral to the identity of Byzantium as a maritime empire.[12] The glittering capital of Constantinople was at a key point on the Silk Roads, enabling the Byzantines to manage movement by policing maritime routes and harbour activities, extracting customs revenues, and controlling postal and military communication to Mediterranean hinterlands.[13] Byzantium was a Christian polity, but the visual legacy of Classical mythology remained compatible with the lived Christianity of the empire long after the temples of the old gods closed, and even after Justinian shut the school of philosophy at Athens in 529. A necklace with a pendant depicting the goddess Aphrodite Anadyomene (Aphrodite Rising-from-the-Sea) encapsulates the extent of exchange networks by land and sea, in its combination of a subject from Classical mythology with materials from distant places, above all lapis lazuli from Afghanistan and rock crystal from Madagascar (see fig. 5.1). The lapis lazuli beads were probably reused, showing the continuing value of imported materials and their refashioning over time.[14]

Objects and materials on the move

Luxury materials and consumables arrived in the Mediterranean over land and by sea as regional bulk trade networks intersected and further extended existing routes.[15] The Indo-Roman trade, well established by the first–second century, periodically flourished, with networks extending east via the Red Sea to the Indian Ocean.[16] In both his *Christian Topography* and a separate work transmitted together with it, the *Description of Animals and Trees of India and of the Island Taprobane*, Cosmas Indicopleustes (see pp. 76, 179) describes the variety of materials originating from, or trans-shipped through, India and Sri Lanka to the Mediterranean. From ports in India came pepper, copper, sesame wood and cloth, as well as musk and the aromatic oil spikenard, among other commodities. Sri Lanka was an entrepôt for ships to and from China, India, Persia and Aksum.[17] The island was itself a source of the gemstone hyacinth, and its merchants re-exported silk, aloe, cloves, clovewood and sandalwood from further east.[18] Byzantine jewellery, heavy with pearls and gemstones, is testament to this maritime trade.[19] Contemporary images

5.4
Necklace and earrings, *c.* 500–600. Probably found at or near Asyut, Egypt. Gold, pearl, sapphire and emerald. H. 8 cm, W. 7.1 cm, D. 0.7 (pendant), L. 101 cm (chain), H. 12.5 cm, W. 4.2 cm. D. 1 cm (earrings). British Museum, London, 1916,0704.2-4. Donated by Mrs Burns.

5.5

Palimpsest diptych bearing Latin and Greek texts, *c.* 430, reused up until *c.* 662. Acquired in Luxor, Egypt. Ivory and copper alloy. H. 25.5 cm, W. 11.9 cm, (left leaf); W. 6.5 cm (right leaf), D. 0.8 cm. British Museum, London, 1920,1214.1. Purchased from Durlacher Bros.

5.6 *opposite left*

Panels from the Maskell Passion casket, *c.* 420–30. Rome. Ivory. H. 7.6 cm, W. 10.1 cm, D. 1.6 cm (each approx). British Museum, London, 1856,0623.4–7. Purchased from Rev. William Maskell.

5.7 *opposite right*

Detail of the Incredulity of Thomas, Maskell Passion casket, *c.* 420–30. British Museum, London, 1856,0623.7. Digital microscope image by A.P. Simpson.

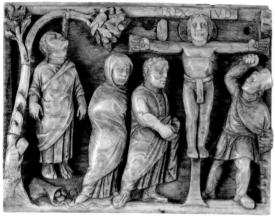

of imperial women – such as that of Justinian's wife, the empress Theodora (d. 548), in the Basilica of San Vitale, Ravenna (see fig. 5.22) – show how necklaces, bracelets, earrings and finger rings were worn. Reminiscent of such depictions is an exquisitely crafted sixth- or seventh-century gold necklace and pair of earrings, mixing pearls, sapphires and emeralds, which were perhaps an imperial commission (fig. 5.4).[20] Transported along with heavier or bulkier cargo, such small and portable luxuries were easily trans-shipped from port to port, potentially passing through many pairs of hands.

Smooth, lustrous and brilliant white, elephant ivory was a material of choice in Byzantium, where the carver's craft flourished. After the extinction of the North African elephant (200s CE), suppliers turned to India and Aksum. The mass production of some items suggests the great quantity of elephant ivory available. It also seems to have been relatively affordable. In an earlier source, the 'Edict on Maximum Prices' issued by the Roman emperor Diocletian (r. 284–305 CE), its cost per pound was one fortieth of the equivalent weight in silver.[21] Letters of appointment to high office by the emperor, on two leaves of wooden writing tablets joined by a hinge to make a diptych (literally, 'folded-in-two'), seem to have been the inspiration for 'appointative diptychs' on ivory, which were produced in large numbers (fig. 5.5).[22] The latter in turn inspired the fashion of presentation diptychs, such as those given as gifts upon the annual appointment of consuls. These finely carved works often show the appointee (see fig. 5.21), the emperor under whom he served, or games that he funded, which sometimes depicted animals imported from Africa and elsewhere. By comparison, Justinian's own diptych from his first consulship of 521 is remarkably plain, with only his monogram.[23]

Other ivory objects depict figures from Classical and Christian narratives. Ivory ateliers achieved astonishing results, with carvers displaying virtuoso skills. The four panels of a small casket portray seven events from the Passion of Christ (fig. 5.6). The narrative unfolds as the bearer turns the box, from Christ's condemnation by Pontius Pilate and death to his resurrection, where he stands surrounded by his disciples. One exquisite detail shows the apostle Thomas poised to insert his finger into Christ's wound to verify the story (fig. 5.7).[24]

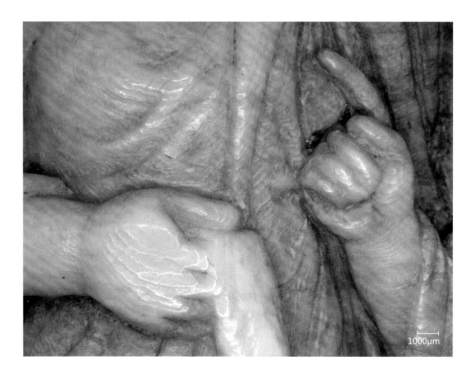

5.8

Diptych leaf, *c.* 525–50. Made in Constantinople. Ivory. H. 41.6 cm, W. 14.3 cm, D. 1.9 cm. British Museum, London, OA.9999. Acquired prior to 1856.

5.9 *opposite top*

Pyxis, 400–525. Probably made in Syria or Egypt. Ivory. H. 7.5 cm, W. 10 cm, D. 10.5 cm. British Museum, London, 1877,0706.3. Donated by Sir Augustus Wollaston Franks.

5.10 *opposite bottom*

Pyxis, 500–600. Probably made in Egypt, found at San Paolo fuori le Mura, Rome, Italy. Ivory. H. 8 cm, W. 11.6 cm, D. 12.3 cm. British Museum, London, 1879,1220.1. Purchased from Alexander Nesbitt.

Makers chose their materials carefully. African elephants are much larger than Indian ones, with their tusks growing up to 3.5 metres in length. At over 40 centimetres in height, the sheer size of one of two surviving leaves of a diptych depicting an archangel shows that it must have come from an African rather than Indian elephant. The curve in its left-hand edge traces the limit of the tusk's exploitable surface (fig. 5.8). Similarly, pyxides (cylindrical containers) made from elephant ivory show another way in which carvers could use the natural constraints of the material and shape of the tusk to their advantage (fig. 5.9). One sixth-century pyxis found at the Basilica of San Paolo fuori le Mura, Rome, narrates the martyrdom of Saint Menas, a soldier in Egypt (fig. 5.10).[25] Just as the story unfolds on the small ivory casket described above, so too the narrative of Menas' martyrdom is revealed as the container is turned. It begins with a Roman official ordering the execution of Menas, with a soldier behind holding a writing diptych, then another soldier raising his sword to kill Menas – an angel waits with covered hands to receive his soul – and culminates in Menas standing before his saint's shrine between two camels with male and female supplicants approaching him.[26]

Offcuts could be used for more everyday objects. The networks of exchange reached early medieval Britain, where bag rings of East African ivory have been identified in burials from the fifth to seventh centuries.[27] When routes were disrupted in the sixth and seventh centuries, ivory ceased to be imported in such high quantities; for the next centuries, existing objects were recarved or repurposed.[28] For example, what was once probably an appointative diptych was reused several times before its final function as a liturgical diptych that was read in church services (see fig. 5.5).[29] The production of ivories seems today to be fundamental to Byzantine elite identity, but it was the ability to import vast quantities of ivory via maritime routes that was essential to their initial manufacture.

Other materials were transported to Byzantium by both land and sea. In the sixth century, Cosmas Indicopleustes explained how silk was best transported over land, with the distance from China to Persia being much shorter than the maritime route.[30] Sea transport was essential for bulk goods, but high-value goods could profitably be transported by land, and after the seventh century this became more important, for the Byzantines had lost control of Egypt, their main avenue to the Indian Ocean. Silk was highly valued for its smoothness, strength, elasticity, durability, drape and dye receptivity.[31] It was first imported from the east as a finished product and later supplied as raw material to be woven in Byzantine workshops.[32] Silk was an imperial attribute and emblematic of rank for local officials, and its use was therefore restricted through manufacturing and sumptuary laws. Its distribution in the provinces is shown in a papyrus document from 325 CE in which a plaintiff seeks remuneration for 150 gold-embroidered silk garments made for regional officials.[33] A fifth-century Chinese compiler noted that the Sasanians blocked Byzantine access to silk,[34] and Justinian sought to bypass their monopoly via steppe and Red Sea routes.[35] Sericulture arrived in Byzantium in the sixth century. The Byzantine authors Procopius and Theophanes relate how two monks introduced sericulture after smuggling silk moth eggs from the east. This story perhaps says more about how Byzantines thought of themselves than the actuality of technology transmission – for knowledge, not just eggs, was needed to turn silkworms into silk, and the transmission route for this technology continues to be debated. Byzantine weavers turned their hands to both Christian subjects and traditional Roman ones, such as riders vanquishing enemies or hunting (fig. 5.11). Even as sericulture flourished around the Mediterranean, silk imports were still required to match Byzantine demand into the tenth century.[36]

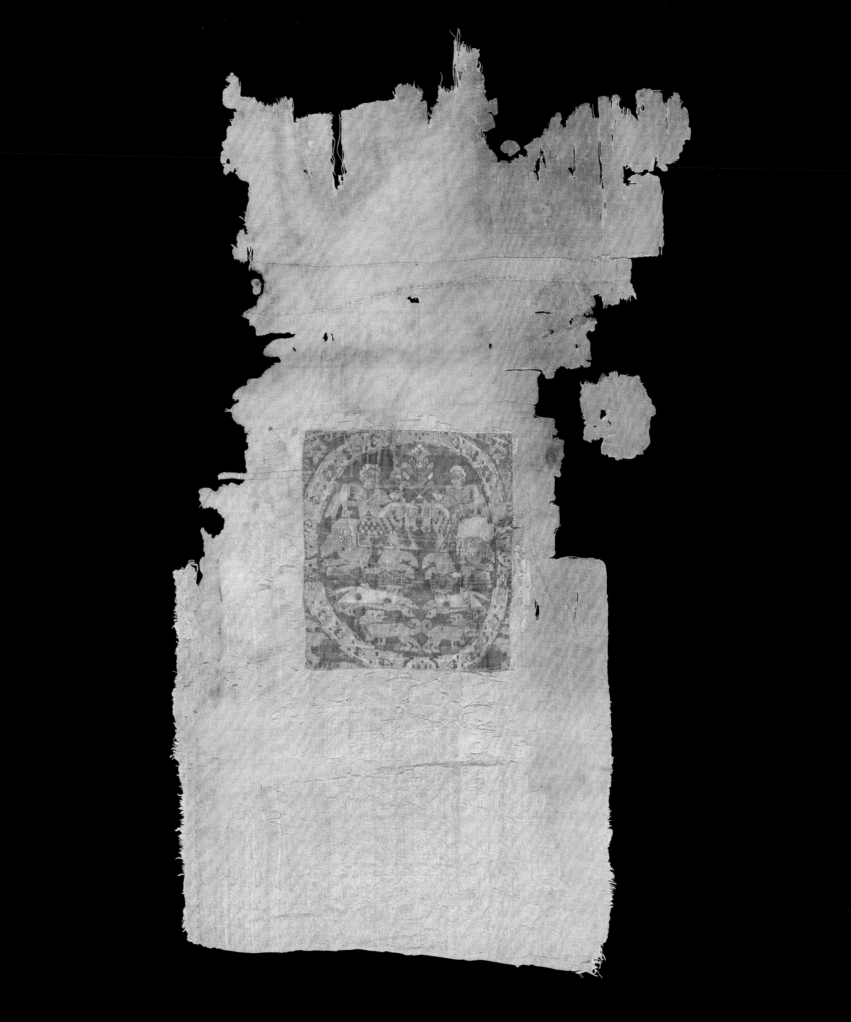

Like silk, purple dye from marine molluscs (known collectively as *murex*), found across the Mediterranean from Jerba in Tunisia to the Gulf of Corinth in Greece and beyond, was regulated and restricted for imperial use. Its production was labour-intensive, with 12,000 snails producing only 1.4 grams of pure dye.[37] The colour of this 'imperial purple' was imitated widely in other dyes (see figs 5.15–5.16). When Byzantium lost its Levantine and North African territories in the seventh century, it also lost access to many of its resources, not only many of the sources of purple, but also glass. The reduction of the latter's availability may be traced in the Byzantine use of glass for weights. While metal weights were used throughout Byzantine history, glass weights were only used briefly, from around the end of the fifth century until the mid-seventh century, when Byzantium lost control of Syria and Egypt, its sources of production for natron, a mineral used in glassmaking.[38] Later, Byzantium's formal trade agreements with the Fatimids in Cairo, made at the expense of the 'Abbasids in Baghdad, reoriented trade away from east–west overland routes and again towards Red Sea and Indian Ocean maritime routes.

Trade and other forms of exchange were multidirectional, neither one-way nor primarily east–west. While valuable imports are most associated with eastern trade, Byzantium received timber, fur, honey and Baltic amber from the north, as well as enslaved people. After the conversion of Khan Volodymir (958–1015) in 988, the newly Christian Kyivan Rus' received icons, liturgical silver and mosaic tesserae from Byzantium, as well as glass, wine and oil.[39] Byzantine painters and mosaicists travelled to work in Kyiv, as Volodymir and his successors commissioned great Christian churches commensurate with their status, such as St Sophia (where mosaics date to *c*. 1037–46).

People on the move

As across Afro-Eurasia, involuntary migration in the Mediterranean was precipitated by natural disaster, war and state coercion.[40] People also travelled voluntarily as diplomats, merchants, artists, teachers, students and pilgrims. Whether or not they moved of their own volition, they usually travelled with their possessions, for example their own clothing and accessories, consumables, table- and kitchenwares, as well as with their cultural attitudes. Chinese sources document up to eight overland embassies from Byzantium to China in the mid-fifth to mid-eighth centuries.[41] Individuals rarely travelled long distances, but people formed links in long chains transmitting information about distant lands. Cosmas Indicopleustes certainly visited Aksum, but may not have travelled as far as India and Sri Lanka; he was nevertheless familiar with information about these places. From the fourth century CE, Christian pilgrimage brought people from the far reaches of Christendom to Jerusalem and other locations described in the Bible. In the 380s, a pilgrim named Egeria travelled from somewhere in present-day Spain or France via Constantinople to Jerusalem, with excursions to Mount Sinai and Egypt, among other places. She described her journeys in an account addressed to a group of women at home. Networks of saints' shrines, established upon the sites of martyrs' tombs or miracles, extended the spiritual topography of early Christianity to the limits of the Byzantine empire and beyond.[42]

Prisoners of war, including the populations of entire cities, were captured and enslaved.[43] Other sources of enslaved people were victims of kidnapping (including citizens), abandoned children and the children of the already enslaved.[44] As under the Roman empire, slavery in Byzantium was imperially legislated.[45] In two letters dating to 427/8 CE, Augustine, the bishop of Hippo (in modern Algeria), appealing precisely on the grounds of the illegality of the capture and sale overseas of free Roman citizens, sought imperial intervention in North Africa, just before the Vandal conquest.[46] A hundred years later, during the codification of older

5.11

Fragment of a tunic, 700–800. Silk tunic with reused linen lining produced in Egypt, reused silk tabula produced in the eastern Mediterranean; acquired in Egypt. Linen and silk. H. 95 cm, W. 54 cm. British Museum, London, EA 17173 (1886,0723.3). Donated by Rev. William MacGregor.

Roman law and his own legislation in the 520s and 530s, Justinian increased and streamlined ways of freeing enslaved people, in keeping with Christian piety.[47] In time, treaties with Byzantium's neighbours ensured that prisoners of war were not automatically enslaved.

Prisoner exchanges with rival Muslim states became so prevalent that neither side became a major source of enslaved people for the other, and later Byzantium and the Rus' agreed to ransom one another's citizens if found at slave markets. Each state's prohibitions on the enslavement of co-religionists – Christians for the Byzantines, and Muslims for the caliphates – theoretically implied that each relied on sources of enslaved people from beyond their borders. In reality, such state-mandated prohibitions could be ignored, for example, by those Augustine described or by pirates, the threat of whom sometimes required the evacuation of whole towns. Forbidding the enslavement of those sharing the same faith nevertheless required the targeting of populations further afield, foremost in northern and Central Europe, the Caucasus, the Eurasian steppe and sub-Saharan Africa.[48] This religious dimension to medieval slavery, once developed, contributed to human trafficking across distances previously unknown.[49]

Ideas on the move

Constantinople was the pre-eminent source of Christian authority in the eastern Mediterranean, but the popes at Rome sought to define their own city as the legitimate heir to the Roman empire. By allying with the Franks and consecrating Charlemagne as Roman emperor in 800, the pope found a way to assert papal authority beyond the city (see chapter 6). Although many Christians migrated to Byzantine lands following the Arab conquest, many more stayed and made up the majority population of Muslim territories for centuries.[50] Christian material culture travelled regardless of precise confessional allegiances, so that, for example, pilgrims' flasks from the shrine of Saint Menas near Alexandria are found all the way from Britain to Uzbekistan (fig. 5.12).[51] Monasteries increasingly developed around saints' shrines and served as nodes on local and international pilgrimage routes, with Jerusalem and other places associated with the life of Jesus as the primary destination.

Although Greek and, decreasingly, Latin were the language of administration and the Church, vernaculars too gained status, both on the edges of the empire and outside it. Greek texts were translated into Coptic, Syriac, Armenian, Georgian, Ethiopic and Arabic.[52] Religious, philosophical, scientific and medical works were translated, adapted and extended, but so were stories about, for example, Alexander the Great.[53] Conversely, Indian, Persian and Arabic literature was transmitted into Greek and from there entered the manuscript traditions of medieval Europe.[54] By the end of the first millennium CE, Christians had recast Siddhartha Gautama, who became the Buddha, as an Indian prince, Joasaph, who adopted Christianity under the instruction of the ascetic saint Barlaam in the *Life of Barlaam and Joasaph* (or Josaphat) (fig. 5.13).[55] The story existed in Persian and Arabic before entering the Georgian Christian tradition, and the abbot and scholar Euthymios Hagioreites (d. 1028) translated the story into Greek. The survival of around 140 Greek manuscripts containing the story is indicative of its popularity, and, once retranslated into Latin, it took on a new life in medieval western Europe.

Byzantium and Persia

On the eastern frontier of Byzantium's territory, the Sasanian empire, its greatest rival in the sixth century, exerted sustained pressure, which periodically erupted into open conflict. The two empires also engaged in proxy and trade wars.[56]

5.12

Pilgrim's flask, c. 480–560. Made near Alexandria, Egypt, found in Kent, England. Ceramic. H. 9.2 cm, W. 7.4 cm, D. 2.2 cm. British Museum, London, 1929,0108.1. Donated by Thomas G. Barnett.

5.13 *opposite*

The *Life of Barlaam and Joasaph*, copied c. 1050–1150. Probably copied in Cyprus. Ink and pigments on parchment. H. 27.5 cm, W. 20.4 cm (page). Cambridge University Library, Cambridge, MS Add. 4491, fol. 3v. Purchased in 1909 from the Scrivener collection.

οἱ αὐτὸ ὁ πὸν μιλαο εἰ ἔθω τα ἐπ ὸ βασιλικει λοῦ · ὁ ιαδεὶο
μαχαι ρ ιερα τα ειτωρ δὲ ὁ ιρειμ ορ κει · ιεια ευ ὁ ὀφ
μει αὐτο ὀ θη ὅλ ὁ λι μο ὑπ λ ἡ ὁ ὁρ ἡ μελη · πᾶσα
ὑε ρι ωυ ὑτε ῥοὶ · τω λι τα ἀπ ὀ μα ρα εἰ τα ι τῶν
φε ωχ μι ασ ὀ μενα · ου γα ρ μι μο ο ὑλ ἰερ ν ἐπ ὀ
λη βθη σ τ λι ὀ σι μεφ ὀ ρα ὡ παρα μι θι ου μεν α ε
ὡ οι ὁ ι τα ὁ θεμ ὁι δ ασ ὁ θ ὁρ μεθα ·

✝ οἱ ι ερεῖς τοῦ βα
σιλέως ·
παρεκά
λεσαν τ
θευ δ αν
τὸν ὐ πελ
θεῖ ν πρὸ
τὸν βασι
χ΄ κὰ βο
η βησ ιαμ
τοῖς τοῦ
πιλά η κ
θύ ει ν τοῖς
εἰ δώ λοις ·

ε καρα π α μ ἐ τοι μι ν ὁ θε ελ α ο μεθ αι τ λι ὁ σι ρμα τα
ρ οἱ ον ο αε τ ὁ σα ολν ικ ος ὁ ρα π τα ο · ιεια ι εα ι
τω μ π ιλο α ε ρι θ εί α ο ὁ τα ρι ζε τ α ι · ιτ ο ρμα τ ε ων
π ο ε μ ρ α υ π τα ρ μι εα ε τ ον · α ο τα ρ ος τ α φα ι με α
ο υ μ ε ι α φμ ο ι δε π τα ρ ο θ ι ρε σ ο · ιεια ο ι τ θ κε ι μο οι α ε ι

In 540 Khusruw I invaded Byzantium and reached the Mediterranean (see p. 191), but fortunes changed over the course of the century. A few decades later, his grandson, Khusruw II (r. 590–628), fled to Constantinople after an internal revolt. He sought refuge at the court of the Byzantine emperor Maurice (r. 582–602), regaining his throne in 591. When Maurice was murdered and usurped by one of his generals, Khusruw II seized the moment and took, in quick succession, Edessa, Damascus, Antioch and Jerusalem. He captured Alexandria in around 619, and thereafter Byzantium's most precious asset, Egypt, which he ruled for a decade before it was briefly reclaimed by Byzantium, shortly before the Arab conquest beginning in 639/40.

Persian culture was influential in Byzantium in various ways. Despite the old criticism of 'luxurious' eastern fashions, in time they were adopted by the imperial household, court and other registers of society.[57] Persian costume had long been used in the Roman empire to depict people from the east, as for example in the eastern dress comprised of peaked caps, flared shirts and leggings in the portrayal the Roman deity Mithras and characters from the Bible, such as the three magi presenting gifts to the baby Jesus as narrated in the Gospel of Matthew.[58] A sixth- or seventh-century wall painting from south of Lykopolis (Asyut) in Egypt depicts a story from the Book of Daniel, in which three Hebrews are thrown into the fiery furnace for refusing to bow to a golden image erected by King Nebuchadnezzar II (r. 605–562 BCE) of Babylon. The three Hebrews in the central panel are shown in a style of Parthian Persian dress that would have been obsolete when the wall was painted (fig. 5.14).[59] Framing the central panel, in a different style and probably executed by a different artisan, are Christian martyrs labelled in Greek as Cosmas

5.14
Wall painting, c. 500–700. Excavated 25 km south of Asyut, Egypt. Stucco. H. 86.3 cm, W. 147.3 cm, D. 6.3 cm. British Museum, London, EA 73139 (1919,0505.1). Donated by the Byzantine Research Fund.

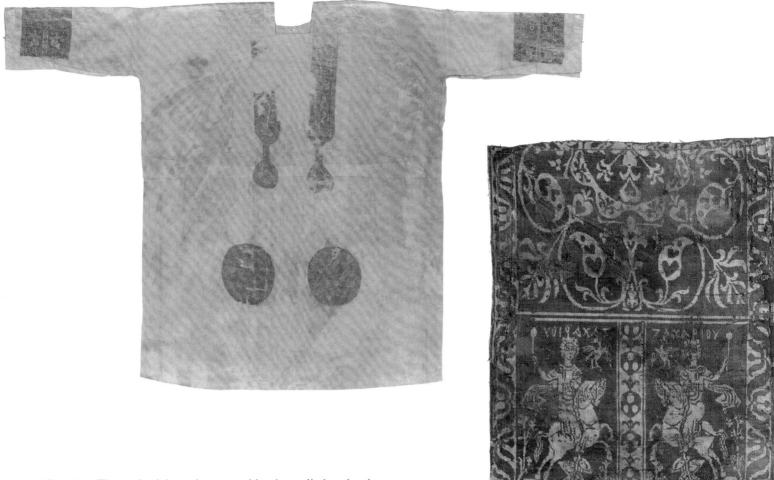

and Damian. These physician saints are said to have died under the emperor Diocletian, martyred along with their three brothers, named in labels, and shown at a smaller scale below. In contrast to the three Hebrews, the five brothers are shown wearing Byzantine dress.

As part of the Mediterranean dress tradition, Byzantine garments typically comprised tunics and cloaks for men and women alike (fig. 5.15). From around the second or third century CE, tunics were usually either woven to shape from a single piece of linen or wool or stitched together from three pieces.[60] Decorative elements were woven as part of the fabric or, after the sixth century, also stitched onto it, and included sets of bands (*clavi*), roundels (*orbiculi*), squares (*tabulae*), and trimmings around the neck opening, ends of the sleeves and skirt (fig. 5.16).[61] On rare occasions, costlier fabrics such as silk were used for tunics. Elements were often reused when garments fell into disrepair; for example, the linen lining of a yellow silk tunic was repurposed from an earlier tunic (see fig. 5.11).[62] Belts could be used to shape garments on the body and brooches to fasten cloaks.

By contrast, riding costumes originating from the Eurasian steppe and worn in Persia were tailored (see fig. 3.32). Flared shirts and crossover coats worn with gaiters were seen as suitable for riding.[63] Coats had overlong sleeves that could be worn over the hands or bunched up on the forearms, or indeed hang free over the shoulders with slits at the underarms, allowing the arms to pass through and remain unencumbered.[64] In Persian depictions dating to the third century CE, courtiers wear the coat sleeves over their hands as a sign of respect.[65] On a relief from the obelisk base of the emperor Theodosius (r. 379–95) at the Hippodrome of Constantinople, tribute-bearers' hands are covered by long coat sleeves and they wear peaked caps.

5.15

Tunic with silk panels, *c.* 600–800. Probably found at Akhmim, Egypt. Linen and silk. H. 137.2 cm, W. 210.5 cm (incl. sleeves); W. 110 cm (hem). Victoria and Albert Museum, London, inv. 820-1903. Purchased from L. Paul Philip.

5.16

Fragment of silk sleeve panel, *c.* 600–900. Probably found at Akhmim, Egypt. Silk. H. 30.6 cm, W. 23 cm. British Museum, London, 1904,0706.41. Purchased from Henry Wallis.

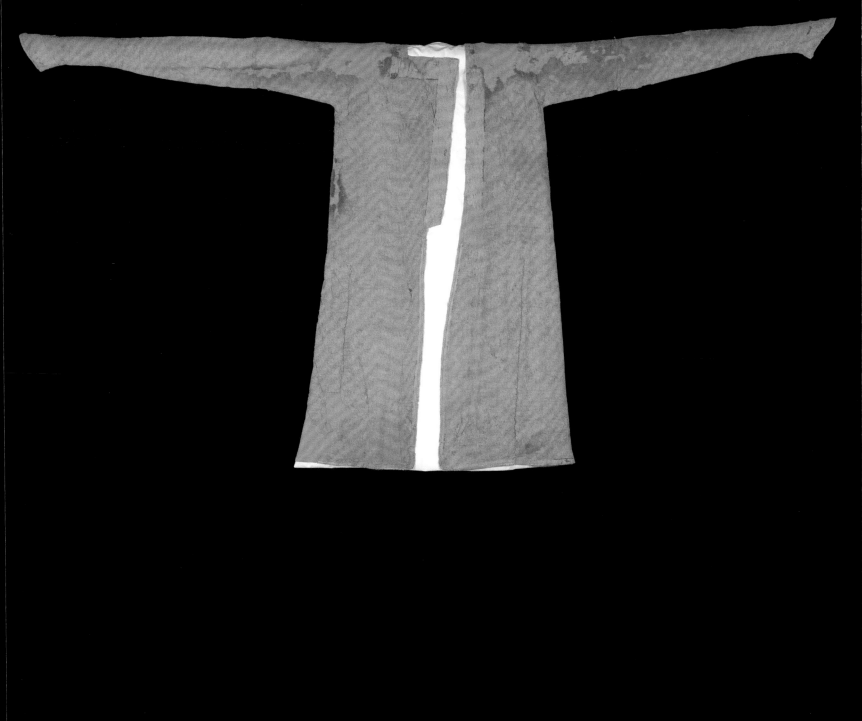

5.17 *opposite*

Riding coat, 450–550. Excavated at
Sheikh Ibada, Egypt. Cashmere and
sheep's wool fabric with fragments
of silk trimmings (now largely lost).
H. 123 cm, W. 238 cm. Berlin, Bode-
Museum, Museum für Byzantinische
Kunst, inv. 9923. Acquired through Carl
Schmidt, 1897.

5.18

Gaiters, 400–700. Excavated at
Sheikh Ibada, Egypt. Wool, silk and
linen. H. 73 cm, W. 23 cm, D. 20 cm.
Berlin, Bode-Museum, Museum
für Byzantinische Kunst, inv. 9926.
Acquired through Carl Schmidt, 1897.

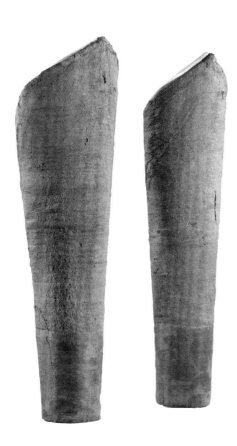

The remarkable survival of costume in Egypt demonstrates the range of
fashions, materials and dyestuffs from across the Eurasian world.[66] From male
burials at the Byzantine provincial capital Antinoopolis (Sheikh Ibada) come
more than a dozen examples of riding coats or fragments excavated at the end of
the nineteenth and early twentieth centuries.[67] Fashioned from wool and even silk
dyed in vibrant blue-green or red,[68] the coats were either ready-made imports or
created in a local Antinoopolis workshop making use of imported raw materials or
bales of fabric.[69] One man's blue-green riding coat, radiocarbon-dated to around
450 to 550, was woven from the finest blend of sheep's wool and cashmere (the
underfur of goats from the Kashmir region of the Himalayas) and trimmed with
silk (fig. 5.17).[70] The cashmere blend was dyed with indigo.[71] Worn under such
coats were flared shirts and gaiters, which were slipped over the legs and secured
to a belt with ties. In another burial, a man wore a flared tunic with the threads
twisted counterclockwise (or z-spun) rather than clockwise (or s-spun), indicative of
an eastern origin, together with gaiters with silk patterned trim (fig. 5.18), undyed
linen stockings with green wool heel reinforcements and tall leather boots.[72] Over
his shoulders was a green-blue coat, with the finest tablet-woven wool trimmings
rather than silk, and radiocarbon-dated to the mid-fifth to mid-seventh century.[73]
The question remains whether or not these riding coats from Middle Egypt are
imitations of eastern fashion or represent the importation of complete garments, but
both are possibilities, and one does not necessarily exclude the other. Another key
question relates to timescale. Who were the men buried in eastern riding costume?
They could have been Persians posted there during the occupation of Egypt
(*c.* 619–29). Radiocarbon-dated riding coats cluster earlier, in the mid-fifth to early-
seventh century, and do not exclude the possibility that their wearers were Persians
in Egypt before or after its conquest or others wearing imports or imitations.[74]
Additional scientific analysis, such as isotopic or DNA analysis of human remains,
may provide further clarity in the future.[75] Either way, the coats are so luxurious
that they must have belonged to members of the upper echelons of society.

Byzantium and Italy

From the fourth century CE, the westward push of the Huns across the Volga
and into Europe forced Germanic-speaking groups, such as the Goths previously
settled along the Danube frontier, into the empire, sparking what is sometimes
termed the 'Great Migration' or 'Migration period'.[76] From the perspective of
Greek and Latin writers, these 'barbarians' appear as unified groups such as
Goths, Vandals and Lombards, but they were more likely people of various origins
allied to dominant cultural groups.[77] Although sources often describe them as
'barbarian', it is important to remember that most Germanic-speaking people
had long-standing cultural contacts with Rome and Byzantium, including service
in imperial armies (see chapter 6).[78] For decades, the Huns harried the Romans,
periodically establishing treaties entailing trading rights and tribute comprised
of everything from precious metals to textiles. After the death of Attila in 453 CE,
one of the groups of Goths subjugated by the Huns, the Ostrogoths, re-emerged
in the Balkans. The fifth-century Byzantine emperor, Zeno (r. 474–5, 476–91 CE),
supported their leader, Theodoric (454–526), elevating him to consul in 484 CE
and sending him to Italy in 489 CE to overthrow a former ally, Odoacer, who had
deposed the emperor in Rome in the previous decade. Like Odoacer, Theodoric
governed on behalf of the emperor, but he ruled Italy as king in his own right, with
his capital at Ravenna.

Theodoric had been raised at court in Constantinople as a diplomatic
child-hostage and his prestige derived in part from his education there, his
familiarity with courtly life and his ability to deploy the visual apparatus of power.

5.19

Medallion, copy made before 1911 of *c*. 493–536 original. Original medallion, minted in Rome, Italy, found Senigallia, Italy. Electrotype. Diam. 3.3 cm, 8.8 g. British Museum, London, B.11479.

5.20 *opposite*

Selection of ornaments, *c*. 450–550. Found at Lagucci Farm, San Marino. Gold, glass, garnet and pearl. Clockwise, L. 14.1 cm (pin), H. 8.3 cm (earring), Diam. 3.3 cm (finger ring), H. 4.5 cm (each pendant). British Museum, London, 1933,0405.3-5 (pendants), 1933,0405.6 (earring), 1933,0405.7 (finger ring), 1933,0405.10 (pin). Purchased from Magyar Nemzeti Múzeum, funded by Art Fund (as NACF).

Like the Visigoths and Vandals, the Ostrogoths minted coins in the name of the Byzantine emperor. In one surviving instance, however, a gold medallion of Theodoric worth three solidi does not make reference to the emperor. Probably produced to celebrate a special occasion in his reign, it shows him wearing a characteristic Gothic hairstyle and moustache, but with all the trappings of Byzantine imperial power (fig. 5.19). Theodoric operated in a trilingual milieu, with the Latin and Greek of the Byzantine ruling elite and their subjects, together with the Gothic language to address his own people.[79] As a ruler, he utilised the Romano-Byzantine legal system but the Gothic military mode of operation. He developed major building projects, including his best-known today, his palace church of Christ the Redeemer, later dedicated to Saint Apollinaris (now known as Sant'Apollinare Nuovo) and a spectacular mausoleum. He and the Ostrogoths were, like other Gothic groups, Arian Christians, and so they were distinguished by their religion from the orthodoxy of the ruling Byzantine elite.[80] Theodoric actively engaged in marriage diplomacy, building a far-reaching family network. He himself married the sister of the Frankish king Clovis, his own sister married the king of the Vandals, and three of his daughters married, respectively, a Burgundian king, a Visigothic king and a Visigothic nobleman, the latter of whom, until his untimely death, was a potential successor for Theodoric himself. Such marriage unions were a diplomatic tool which served to strengthen political and social interests.[81]

A set of cloisonné garnet personal ornaments discovered in 1893 near Domagnano (now in the Republic of San Marino) show the adaptation of techniques in Italy (fig. 5.20, see p. 262). All made by the same workshop and possibly the same maker, probably at nearby Ravenna, the assemblage belongs to the fashions worn further east by peoples of the Danube region.[82] The circumstances of deposition are unknown, but one reconstruction suggests that most of the ornaments could have been worn by a woman dressed in east Germanic style with two pins holding a veil, and two brooches worn at the shoulders linked by the pendants.[83] The high quality suggests a royal client,[84] and the combination of eastern regional style and western production would have suited female family members of the Gothic kings of Ravenna.

Following Theodoric's death in 526, his widowed daughter Amalasuntha (495–535) ruled as regent for her son Athalaric (516–534) until he too died prematurely, and she briefly became queen. Praised by some contemporaries for her education and wisdom, Amalasuntha was an ally of the emperor Justinian, and her murder in 535 was among his reasons for going to war with the Ostrogothic kingdom. The Gothic War lasted almost twenty years (535–54) and destroyed much of the infrastructure of Italy.[85] The precarious balance of power between Byzantium and the Ostrogoths that preceded the war is evident in the diptych of Rufius Gennadius Probus Orestes, western consul in 530 (fig. 5.21). It is one of the last extant ivory consular diptychs prior to the abolition of the consulate by Justinian in 541/2.[86] Seated between personifications of the cities of Rome and Constantinople, Orestes holds the *mappa*, a white handkerchief that formed a badge of senatorial authority, and a sceptre. Above him are portrait medallions of Amalasuntha and Athalaric. Orestes' plight highlights the perils of the shifting political situation. Captured by the Ostrogothic army, he reportedly became a refugee and was later freed and sent to Sicily, but he was killed by the Ostrogoths alongside other senators in 552 in retribution for their king's death at the hands of Justinian's forces.

The Byzantines regained control of Ravenna in 540. Ravenna's transition from relative autonomy to an imperial possession is commemorated by the famous mosaics in the apse of San Vitale.[87] Started by the bishop Ecclesius (d. 532), who had himself portrayed in the apse, construction of the church was continued under the bishop Victor (d. 644), whose monograms decorate the Proconnesian marble columns and capitals of the ambulatory.[88] The mosaic programme for which the church is most famous was completed under Maximian (d. 556), who was appointed archbishop of Ravenna by Justinian and consecrated by the pope in 546. An extraordinary ivory panelled throne was probably sent from Justinian to Maximian as a precious gift that simultaneously asserted Constantinople's imperial power in Italy.

Although they never visited Ravenna, it is the emperor Justinian and the empress Theodora who are most closely associated with San Vitale (fig. 5.22). Unusually, two large panels high above both sides of the altar show secular figures, foremost Justinian and Theodora, each bearing gifts in a liturgical procession. Justinan is depicted flanked by generals, soldiers and clerics. Maximian is labelled on the mosaic. Theodora is shown with her ladies-in-waiting and unbearded officials, perhaps eunuchs, one of whom holds a curtain open for the empress. They all wear sumptuous silks, and the women spectacular jewellery. The full-length portraits of the rulers with their entourages record the imperial victory over the Ostrogoths and the effective victory of Catholic over Arian Christianity in Ravenna.[89] The bishops commissioned the mosaics for local audiences. When Charlemagne and his successors visited San Vitale in the late eighth and ninth centuries they took the message of building a round church to mark victory back with them to Aachen, where it resonates in the palace chapel (see p. 249).

In 568 the Lombards migrated to Italy from Pannonia, a province directly to the east. While the Byzantines controlled most of the coast and islands over the next decades, the Lombards held the inland areas and gradually eroded Byzantine territory so that even Ravenna was under Lombard control by 751.[90] Like other Germanic-speaking groups, the Lombards assumed Byzantine infrastructure, basing a capital at Pavia in imitation of Constantinople and Ravenna. Cemeteries reveal a mix of traditional Lombard and Byzantine grave goods. For example, one woman's grave contained a cobalt-blue glass drinking horn with white glass trail decoration (fig. 5.23), combining both traditions in a single object. Its form originates in northern Europe, but its material is Mediterranean glass.[91]

5.21 *opposite*

Consular diptych of Rufius Gennadius Probus Orestes, 530. Probably made in Rome or Ravenna, Italy. Ivory. H. 34 cm, W. 11.6 cm, D. 0.8 cm. Victoria and Albert Museum, London, 139-1866. Purchased from John Webb 1866.

5.22

Two mosaic panels showing Justinian (top) and Theodora (bottom) in liturgical procession, in the apse of San Vitale, Ravenna. Basilica of San Vitale, Ravenna.

While the Byzantines consolidated control of Sicily in the eighth century, Rome, Naples and Venice were effectively independent. From the ninth century onwards, Sicily was eventually taken by Arab, then Norman forces. Rome formed its own city-state by 800, allied with the kingdom of Francia. Much later, the rise of commercial Italian cities such as Amalfi, Genoa, Pisa and Venice diminished Byzantine interests in the eastern Mediterranean and, after the Crusaders' sack of Constantinople in 1204, weakened the once formidable empire, which eventually came to an end centuries later in 1453, following the Ottoman conquest.

The arrival of Islam

After the rapid success of Muslim armies further east (see chapter 4), the general 'Amr ibn al-'As entered Egypt in 639/40 and soon established a new capital at Fustat, just outside the walls of the Byzantine fortress at the apex of the Nile Delta.[92] Egypt was soon firmly under Muslim rule as a province of the caliphate. In the following centuries, strong governors with Persian–Turkic origins established de facto autonomous dynastic states in Egypt under 'Abbasid imperial and caliphal authority, namely the Tulunids (868–905) and the Ikshidids (935–69). Further west, several Muslim states emerged in North Africa in the eighth and ninth centuries, each with different relationships to the dominant Umayyads in al-Andalus (756–1031) and the 'Abbasids of Baghdad (750–1258), before the Fatimids' bold declaration of an independent Shi'i caliphate in Ifriqiya (central North Africa) in 909 (ruling from Egypt 969–1171).[93] Many of these western Mediterranean dynasties also had eastern origins, but their longevity and endurance required the alignment of 'Arab' interests with those of various indigenous populations.[94] These states faced both the Mediterranean and Africa at the same time.[95] The Fatimids capitalised on the success of western Mediterranean Muslim powers and the reinvigoration of trans-Saharan routes to build an empire that encompassed North Africa, the Levant and Hijaz (see fig. 5.3), with its relative stability facilitating large-scale exchange networks.

Fustat and Cairo: cosmopolitan twin cities

After conquering Egypt in 969, the Fatimids founded a new city just north of Fustat. The Fatimids called their new capital al-Qahira, 'the Victorious', which gave its name to modern Cairo. Within twenty years, a Syrian geographer of Iranian origin wrote that the city had surpassed Baghdad as Islam's greatest glory.[96] For the first time in a millennium, Egypt's wealth was not exported to capitals abroad such as Rome, Constantinople or Baghdad, but formed the basis of an extraordinarily wealthy empire, for extended periods controlling both Mecca and Medina. Cairo grew to become the largest city in the medieval Mediterranean. With its high-yield agricultural production and booming international trade, Egypt had the most diverse economy in the medieval Mediterranean until the disruptions of the Black Death in the fourteenth century.[97] The Fatimid navy dominated the sea, and the Red Sea ports were major conduits for Indian Ocean commerce. Rock crystal, sourced in Madagascar, was carved by artisans who reached impressive levels of precision and detail on thin-walled vessels and other objects (fig. 5.24).[98] Fatimid wealth was spectacular. Their gifts, both secular and religious, were displays of costly imports from across the known world. Upon the establishment of Cairo, the Fatimids sent a *shamsa* (ornament) to the Ka'ba shrine in Mecca; it was decorated with gold, pearls, emeralds and other stones, and filled with powdered musk. Later, the caliph al-Zahir (r. 1021–36) gave to one of his governors gifts from as far away as Khurasan, India and China.[99]

5.23
Drinking horn, 550–600. Excavated at the Via dei Condotti, Sutri, Lazio, Italy. Glass. H. 18.4 cm, W. 15.3 cm, D. 7.4 cm. British Museum, London, 1887,0108.2. Purchased through Rollin & Feuardent.

As a result of Fatimid stability, Cairo attracted migrants at the expense of 'Abbasid Baghdad.[100]

Under the Fatimids, Cairo became a centre of learning and a destination for scholars. The anonymous author of the eleventh-century *Book of Curiosities and of the Sciences and Marvels for the Eye* drew on earlier Greek, Coptic, Persian and Indian scholarship, combining it with direct knowledge of Fatimid naval military records and Shi'i missionary networks.[101] Among the many maps, its world map shows Egypt at the centre of the world (fig. 5.25). The author cites Ptolemy's second-century *Geography* as a source, as well as works by scholars commissioned in about 830 by the 'Abbasid caliph al-Ma'mun (r. 813–33). The map is upside-down to most modern viewers, with north at the bottom, the Atlantic coasts of West Africa and the Iberian Peninsula on the right and Arabia, India and China on the left. Egypt's Nile Delta is nearly in the centre, with the southern sources of the Nile at the top of the map.[102] It is the earliest known map showing a calibrated scale bar representing distance.

Before and after the foundation of Cairo as a capital of empire, Fustat was an economic powerhouse. Located at the apex of the Nile Delta, far from the coast, it

5.24

Ewer, 1000–50. Probably made in Cairo, Egypt. Rock crystal. H. 19.5 cm, Diam. 9 cm (base). Victoria and Albert Museum, London, 7904-1862. Purchased in 1862.

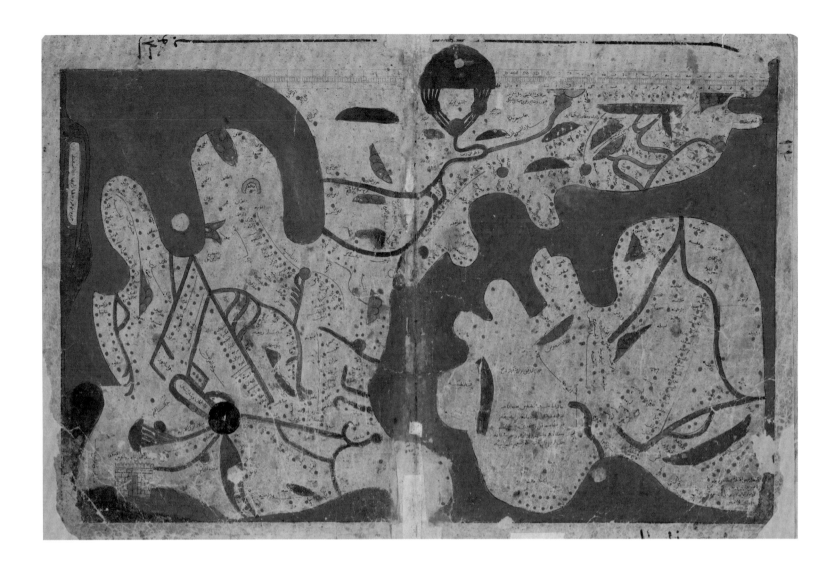

was safe from rival navies and pirates. Fustat benefited from the tax revenue of its population and soon became one of the most prosperous cities in the contemporary world. It was a production point for pottery and a major entrepôt for Egyptian agriculture, products and materials, including ivory in large quantities.[103] It also functioned as a trans-shipment point for high-value goods from across the Indian Ocean, which were routed from the Red Sea coast ports through the Eastern Desert to the Nile, and from there to Fustat and potentially onwards. Excavations of Fustat's homes and rubbish heaps have unearthed a wealth of imported objects. Fragments of Indian resist-dyed cotton textiles reveal links to the subcontinent's west coast. Although the trade in Indian textiles flourished especially in later centuries, radiocarbon dating has demonstrated that the earliest examples were produced in the late tenth and eleventh centuries.[104] One fragment of cotton textile depicting elephants and horses, dated to around 950–1000, was block-printed with resist and dyed light blue, then block-printed again with resist and dyed dark blue (fig. 5.26).[105] The success of the Indian Ocean trade is demonstrated, above all, by the hundreds of thousands of Chinese pottery sherds excavated at Fustat.[106] The earliest belong to the late Tang dynasty in the ninth century, prior to the ascendance of the Fatimids, but imports flourished under their rule and peaked in the twelfth to fourteenth centuries (fig. 5.27).[107] The quantity of Chinese pottery

5.25

World map from the *Book of Curiosities*, *c.* 1190–1210, copy of a *c.* 1020–50 work. Made in Egypt. Ink and pigments on paper. H. 32.4 cm, W. 24.5 cm (each page). Bodleian Libraries, University of Oxford, MS. Arab. c. 90, fols 23b–24a. The acquisition was made possible by a grant from the Heritage Lottery Fund and generous donations from the National Arts Collections Fund, the Friends of the Bodleian, Saudi Aramco, several Oxford colleges, and private individuals.

5.26 *opposite top*

Fragment of textile from India, 950–1000. Made in Gujarat, India, probably found at Fustat, Egypt. Cotton textile block-printed with resist. L. 33 cm, W. 8.5 cm. Ashmolean Museum, University of Oxford, EA1990.250. Presented by Professor Percy Newberry in 1941.

was so great that the excavators of a Fustat housing complex with relatively few Chinese sherds described it as comparatively 'proletarian'.[108]

Materials and finished products travelled from all points of the compass to Fustat, and so did enslaved people. At Fustat, the governor of Egypt, Ahmad ibn Tulun (835–884) established a slave market in one of the city's most densely populated quarters, just to the east of the Mosque of 'Amr ibn al-'As and easily accessed by four streets leading to the square. Archaeologists have discovered a ledger there recording the market's transactions.[109] Other documents on papyrus, parchment and paper survive in Egypt, providing evidence for the buying and selling of enslaved people from many different regions.[110] The production of such bills of sale was common practice elsewhere across Afro-Eurasia (see chapter 2), but the survival of significant bodies of documents is relatively rare outside of Egypt.[111] Arabic bills of sale record the names of the buyers, sellers, the enslaved people purchased and their prices. Such documents are formulaic and instrumental, produced in case of any future legal disputes. They nevertheless illustrate some of the mechanics of how the trade functioned and, crucially, provide rare and precious details of individuals and even families who were bought and sold. For example, documents detailing the sale of a Nubian woman, her daughter and grandchild tell us that they were sold in 994 for 40 dinars and resold a few days later for 49 dinars.[112] The enslaved individuals have names, but whether they were their own or given to them by their previous owners is not known. When places of origin are stated we learn that people came from beyond the *dar al-Islam* (Realm of Islam) or, less frequently, were born of enslaved parents.[113] According to Muslim jurists, neither Muslims nor non-Muslims living under their jurisdiction (*dhimmi* communities) could be enslaved; they had to be acquired from beyond the Realm of Islam, which created an ongoing demand for people from northern Europe and south of the Sahara. In Egypt, the people described in documents are most commonly Nubians (from the south) and Garamantes (from the Sahara), but people of Slavic, Byzantine (Arabic: Rum) and sub-Saharan Africa are also mentioned (see pp. 143, 145).[114] In a deed recording the acquisition of a Nubian

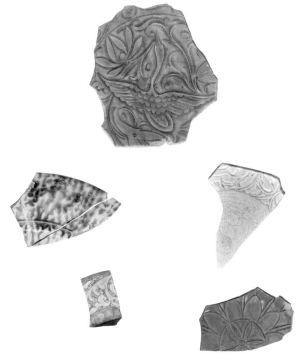

5.27
Chinese ceramic sherds, 700–800 (far left), 960–1279 (all other sherds). Found or probably found at Fustat, Egypt. Clockwise from top: H. 16.7 cm, W. 17.8 cm, D. 4.5 cm; H. 13.8 cm, W. 10 cm, D. 3.8 cm; H. 7.4 cm, W. 13 cm, D. 2.4 cm; H. 6.2 cm, W. 5 cm, D. 4.3 cm; H. 9 cm, W. 13.5 cm, D. 2 cm. British Museum, London, 1923,1112.1, 1927,0420.12, 1927,0420.2, donated by Sir John Home; OA+.903, donated by George Davis Hornblower; 1932,0613.1, donated by the Islamic Museum, Cairo.

woman, written on parchment in 983, the notary was careful to state she was 'non-Arab' and 'neither the product of pillage nor theft'.[115] In another document from the ʿAbbasid period, a Nubian woman named Shuʻla was sold by Ashʻath ibn Muhammad to Muhammad ibn Khalid (fig. 5.28). She was described in formulaic language testifying to her fitness and that she was not insane, night-blind or the object of a legal claim,[116] but personal physical characteristics recorded for the purposes of identification, including scars on her ear and abdomen, indicate Shuʻla's plight and everyday reality. Most medieval enslaved populations are otherwise nameless, having died in historical obscurity, making these documents all the more valuable.[117]

Egypt before and after the arrival of Islam

In the centuries both before and after the arrival of ʿAmr ibn al-ʿAs, people in Egypt of relatively modest means had access to imports, even if they lived far from the bustling ports on the Red Sea or the international trading hub of Alexandria and, later, Fustat/Cairo. Christian cemeteries in Middle Egypt demonstrate the connectedness of even the most provincial citizens.[118] Some were buried with objects originating from regions as distant as the Baltic, Aksum and present-day Indonesia. Beads were by far the most common. As durable items, they circulated sometimes for centuries after their production. Passed down through families, especially to brides upon marriage, heirloom items provide an intimate view of the lives of women and girls in particular. Imported beads conferred status and prestige, and they were more likely than locally produced ones to become valued heirlooms.[119] One young girl was buried with dozens of items of jewellery, earrings and finger rings, bracelets and bangles, necklaces and a torc, a string with two lead crosses, shells and masses of beads, all suggestive of her status within her family.[120] Due to the survival of organic materials as a result of Egypt's arid climate, the threads on which the beads were strung have often remained intact or were at least recorded by archaeologists so that they could later be restrung in modern museum collections.

Several female burials in cemeteries in Middle Egypt have yielded graduated angular amber-bead necklaces.[121] Baltic amber was valued for its rich colour, resinous smell, smooth feel and its electrostatic quality, meaning it becomes warm when rubbed. It was traded across maritime and river system routes and has been found in contexts stretching from early medieval Britain and Ireland to Tang dynasty (618–907) and especially Liao dynasty (907–1125) sites in China.[122] In the context of the late Roman and early Byzantine world, amber was part of a suite of material culture associated with Germanic-speaking groups, which became fashionable in the same way that Persian styles had (see p. 201).[123] In Egypt, components from complete necklaces of graduated amber beads originally dating to the fifth century were later dispersed and reused in new necklaces and bracelets (fig. 5.29).[124] That these angular amber beads appear in assemblages dating to the sixth–seventh and even the seventh–eighth centuries is testament to the fact that they were carefully curated over multiple generations.[125] One string found on the wrist of a child shows the ways in which assemblages came together across long chronological as well as geographical spans before reaching their final deposition with individuals in their graves.[126] The string is made up of locally produced 'date-palm' beads, ubiquitous in Egypt in the first to sixth centuries, tubular glass beads, broken amber beads (possibly fifth-century), a bone cross pendant dating to no earlier than the sixth or seventh century, and a Roman-period faience Bes amulet pendant (fig. 5.30). Therefore, the final deposition of the string post-dates the sixth or seventh century, but it contains much earlier elements. Bes was an ancient Egyptian deity whose domain was especially the protection of pregnant women

5.31

Strings of cloves, 400–600. Excavated
at Qaw el-Kebir, Egypt. Cloves.
L. 13.2 cm (left); L. 11.3 cm (right).
British Museum, London, OA 882.
Donated by the British School of
Archaeology, Egypt.

5.32

Beads and shell discs, 300–600.
Excavated at Qaw el-Kebir, Egypt.
Glass and shell. Diam. 0.5–1 cm (each
bead). Petrie Museum of Egyptian
Archaeology, London, UC 74134.
Donated by the British School of
Archaeology, Egypt.

and children. By the sixth century he was remembered in Christian monastic literature as the 'demon Bes', but in other areas, above all the household, ancient methods of protection were passed down because they were deemed effective.[127] The combination of all these transported materials and objects of different dates and origins on the wrist of a dead child, probably buried in the sixth or seventh century, now resonates poignantly.

From across the Red Sea and Indian Ocean, the cemeteries in Middle Egypt were supplied with Aksumite coins, Persian and Indo-Pacific beads and even a string of cloves originating from the Maluku Islands (Moluccas), in modern eastern Indonesia (fig. 5.31).[128] Indo-Pacific glass beads are found at least as far as Francia and probably also early medieval Britain.[129] They have been discovered in especially high numbers in the interior of northeast Africa and the Red Sea ports.[130] These distinctive green beads, formed of heat-rounded sections of cylindrically drawn tubes, are often found together with tiny shell discs, betraying the beads' maritime provenance (fig. 5.32). Scientific analysis has established their place of origin as South India or Sri Lanka.[131] At the port site of Berenike, they account for 40 per cent of the fourth–sixth-century bead assemblage.[132] Beads discovered at sites in Middle Egypt, such as Antaeopolis (Qaw el-Kebir), show how imports were distributed widely from the Red Sea coast and into the Nile Valley.[133]

The cemeteries of Middle Egypt also yield impressive imports after the Arab conquest. Some of the earliest datable examples of *tiraz* textiles have been excavated at Akhmim (Panopolis) among other sites. Originally produced by caliphal workshops, '*tiraz*' refers to high-quality silk fabrics with an edge typically embroidered with the date and place of manufacture, and often the name of the ruling caliph. The earliest dated *tiraz* is from Akhmim and names Marwan, probably Marwan II (r. 744–50). Its pattern and technical characteristics indicate it was woven in the east, perhaps in Central Asia, before it was embroidered in Ifriqiya, then transported to Egypt, where it ended up in a burial (fig. 5.33).[134] Silks had long been produced in Egypt, which was a renowned textile centre. By the eighth century, documents show that Muslims too were actively engaged in the production and trade of silk at a local level.[135]

Trans-Saharan exchange networks

By the time political control of Vandal North Africa was regained by Justinian's Byzantine forces, around 533, the Garamantian state in the Sahara had

diminished. From the third century BCE to the fifth century CE, the Garamantes were a key exchange partner with both the Roman-dominated Mediterranean and inland to the Sahara, where they established a prosperous urban network supported by agriculture on the desert fringe.[136] While the study of trade with the Mediterranean has been prioritised by modern scholars, new research suggests that commodities, such as cotton grown in Nubia and the desert oases of Libya and Egypt, circulated within northern Africa in parallel with cotton originating in India.[137] The widespread adoption of the camel in the first millennium CE revolutionised trans-Saharan exchange.[138] Mass-produced mould-made terracotta figures of camels from Egypt, such as one found at Akhmim pierced for suspension (fig. 5.34), wear saddles with reins and other details picked out in paint. The reinvigorating of trans-Saharan routes from the eighth or ninth century occurred alongside the development of North African Islamic states, and their competition for gold drove the explosion of trade in the tenth century. Investment in trans-Saharan routes guaranteed the wealth and stability of their economies, with the gold supplied from West African states such as Ghana and Gao (see pp. 8–9).

Interregional trade within West Africa flourished prior to, and independently from, trans-Saharan networks.[139] A major impetus for trade between the communities in the Sahara and others further south was the exchange of high-quality rock salt from Saharan sites like Taghaza for agricultural products, since salt in West Africa is a limited and precious commodity, essential for the human diet. Critically, these networks also facilitated the movement of high-quality alluvial gold from the headwaters of the Niger and Senegal rivers.[140] Once well-established, these routes conveyed other materials, including those from much further afield. Over 150,000 glass and carnelian beads were discovered at the site of Igbo Ukwu, which is located at the apex of the Niger River Delta (modern Nigeria) and flourished around 800 to 1300.[141] In order to arrive at Igbo Ukwu, beads and other commodities must have traversed the Sahara from multiple directions. Elemental and lead isotope analyses have shown that there were glass beads originating from Mediterranean, Levantine, Arabian and Indian sources[142] among other locally produced beads, including the earliest examples of West African glass production.[143] Elaborate bronze vessels and regalia excavated at Igbo Ukwu show that bronze-casting techniques developed using local ore and independently from Islamic traditions (fig. 5.35).[144] A knotted manilla-shaped wrist-ornament from Igbo Ukwu (fig. 5.36) is not only a striking example of the local casting tradition; it also relates to a wider material culture of ingot production and distribution in West Africa, and prefigures the manilla forms which became a major import to West Africa in exchange for enslaved people much later on, in the early modern period.

5.33

Three fragments of *tiraz*, probably reign of Marwan II, 744–50. Eastern Mediterranean or Central Asia, inscribed in Ifriqiya (Tunisia), probably found at Akhmim. Silk. Left to right: H. 30.3 cm, W. 50.7 cm; H. 5.5 cm, W. 45 cm; H. 15.2 cm, W. 21.5 cm. Victoria and Albert Museum, London, inv. 1314-1888, 1385-1888, T.13-1960. Purchased from Reverend Grenville John Chester in 1888 (inv. 1314-1888, 1385-1888); given by the Whitworth Art Gallery Manchester (T.13-1960).

5.34

Model of a camel, 500–700. Probably found at Akhmim, Egypt. Ceramic. H. 11 cm, W. 14.6 cm, D. 3.7 cm. British Museum, London, 1890,0530.28. Purchased from Rev. Grenville John Chester.

Crescent-shaped bowl and coiled wrist
ornament, 800–1000. Excavated at
Igbo Ukwu, Nigeria. Leaded bronze.
H. 6.5 cm, W. 16.4 cm, D. 8.7 cm (bowl);
H. 6.5 cm, W. 12.3 cm, D. 9.2 cm
(ornament). British Museum, London,
Af1956,15.3–4. Donated by Frank
W. Carpenter.

Historians and geographers writing in Arabic were quick to recognise the abundance and purity of the gold sourced from south of the Sahara.[145] Caravans arrived at the desert fringes of northern Africa, the Nile Valley, Ifriqiya and Maghrib. By the end of the ninth century, the traveller and historian al-Yaqubi (d. 897) reported Ghana to be the 'land of gold'.[146] Flourishing around 500 to 1 050, the Kingdom of Ghana (in modern southeast Mauritania and western Mali) controlled trade from the Sahara to the Senegal and Niger rivers (fig. 5.37), which yielded gold with a purity of up to 98–99 per cent.[147] The wealth was astonishing. The tenth-century Arab geographer Ibn Hawqal (d. 988) reported a huge credit note for 42,000 dinars written in Awdaghost (in modern Mauritania) for a merchant in Sijilmasa (modern Morocco). It was the largest he had ever seen; as he told people in Iraq, Fars and Khurasan, 'Nowhere in the East have I seen or heard of anything like it.'[148] By 1050, Ghana had assumed control of the trans-Saharan market town of Awdaghost, said to have been a fifty-day walk from Sijilmasa.[149] Excavations at the ruins of Awdaghost, today known as Tegdaoust, have revealed rich evidence of trans-Saharan connections, including gold ingots and inscribed Fatimid glass weights dating to the tenth century.[150] While there is some disagreement regarding the location of the ruins of Ghana's capital and the possibility that there may have been multiple capitals over time, the Andalusi traveller al-Bakri (d. 1094) reported that the capital of Ghana comprised two settlements, the king's town and a nearby Muslim town with at least twelve mosques.[151] In the following decade the Sunni Almoravids took both towns, eventually uniting the trans-Saharan network from Awdaghost to Sijilmasa and their newly founded capital, Marrakesh (established c. 1070), and, in 1090, across the strait of Gibraltar to al-Andalus.[152]

A separate trans-Saharan network linked the West African kingdom of Gao to Ifriqiya via the market town of Essouk-Tadmekka.[153] From the tenth century, Essouk-Tadmekka was known as a major site of the gold trade with a significant Ibadi Muslim presence.[154] While other Muslim dynasties are much better known through textual sources, archaeology shows that the Rustamid state helped establish early

5.37

Map page showing the Kingdom of Ghana, by al-Idrisi (d. 1166), 1300–1500 copy. Ink and pigments on paper. H. *c* .31 cm. Bodleian Libraries, University of Oxford, Bodleian MS Greaves 42, fols 9b–10a. Purchased from the estate of John and Thomas Greaves in 1678.

trans-Saharan routes that endured long after they lost political control of the region. Like the Isma'ili Fatimids, the Ibadi had emerged in what is now Iraq following the dynastic conflicts of early Islam. 'Abd al-Rahman ibn Rustam, of Persian descent, was the founder of the Rustamid Ibadi state (776–909). Following their defeat by the Fatimids in 909, they were driven from Tiaret and established their capital at Sedrata (both in modern Algeria).[155] The elaborate plaster decorations of interior spaces in that city are part of the common architectural vocabulary of the contemporary Muslim world, from Samarkand to al-Andalus (fig. 5.38).[156]

Local identities are also conveyed through Arabic language and script. A series of Arabic inscriptions in a West African kufic script at Essouk-Tadmekka (beginning from 1010) are the earliest known internally dated writing in West Africa.[157] Based on earlier sources, al-Bakri reported that Tadmekka (meaning 'Mecca-like') compared favourably to the city of Mecca itself, and was better built than Ghana or Gao.[158] The town of Tadmekka – the ruins of which are today called 'Essouk' – was situated within the territory of a regional Saharan Berber authority, a nomadic cultural group that would also have provided protection for caravans. Although they are in Arabic, the personal names in inscriptions from the site show an Indigenous

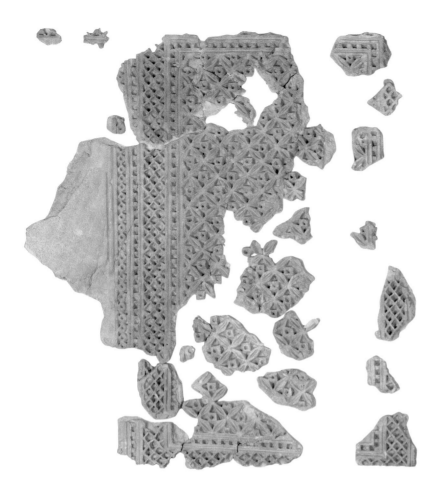

5.38

Architectural panel, 1100–1200.
Excavated at Sedrata, Algeria. Plaster.
H. 83 cm, W. 90.2 cm, D. 9 cm. Musée
du Louvre, Paris, MAO 346. Donated by
the General Government of Algeria.

Saharan Berber identity rather than a primarily Arab one.[159] As recent excavations have discovered, the town was not only an entrepôt for gold but also a centre for gold-processing, with moulds for coin blank production uncovered, a remarkable link with al-Bakri's description of 'unstamped coins of pure gold' at Tadmekka.[160] Trace elements consistent with gold from Essouk-Tadmekka have been found in gold dinars minted in Kairouan in Ifriqiya and Palermo in Sicily, while the gold itself was probably either from the region to the south of Gao on the Middle Niger or from the mines controlled by Ghana. Significant quantities of pottery at Essouk-Tadmekka from the Niger River region attest to the range of commodities that moved alongside gold. Archaeological evidence for the production of crucible steel at the site is otherwise only known from Central Asia at this date. In later periods at Essouk-Tadmekka, the global connections of this region are evidenced by a fragment of silk, possibly from Central Asia or China, a sherd of Chinese Qingbai porcelain pottery and cowrie shells from the Indian Ocean.[161]

Whichever state controlled the trans-Saharan trade was able to maintain a stable and reliable gold coinage. In turn, this supported both internal and Mediterranean trade.[162] In 909 the Fatimids challenged Sunni hegemony in North Africa, establishing a new caliphate in Ifriqiya and not only defeating the ruling Aghlabids but also driving the Rustamid Ibadi from their capital. The Fatimids swiftly minted their own coins, first at Kairouan from 912, then at their capital of Mahdia from 922 (both cities in modern Tunisia) and also, later, at Sijilmasa, where the percentage of gold in the coinage is exceptionally high.[163] When the Fatimids conquered Egypt and moved their capital to Cairo, they began minting coins there and in other eastern territories, with gold from Nile Valley sources.[164] Other commodities travelled along trans-Saharan routes, among them elephant ivory.[165] A Fatimid ivory casket made in Ifriqiya (fig. 5.39) features an inscription suggesting al-Mansuriyya as a production place and a date during the reign of Caliph al-Muʿizz li-Din Allah (r. 952–75) before he moved the capital to Egypt. The maker's surname is 'al-Khurasani', which suggests that his or his family's origin was in Khurasan. The casket eventually made its way to the monastery of San Zoilo in Carrión de los Condes on the Iberian Peninsula, where it was found in excavations in 1869.[166]

The unity of the Fatimid empire facilitated and strengthened internal connectivity. Trade intensified, with Sicily sending timber and wine to Ifriqiya in exchange for gold, olive oil and ceramics.[167] Egypt imported cloth (including silk) and cheese from Sicily and olive oil, soap and linen from Ifriqiya, and both sent hides and metals. In exchange, Egypt exported flax and sugar and commodities from the Indian Ocean trade, such as pepper.[168] At the end of the ninth century, paper production reached Egypt on its long journey from further east. Under the Fatimids, it became the prestige writing material, swiftly replacing papyrus.[169] Egypt had long exported papyrus for writing, but it disappeared within a century, with the first surviving dated paper document in Egypt belonging to 878 and the last papyrus one to the end of the tenth century. Within the same period, papyrus cultivation was replaced by flax to produce linen, but also paper, its by-product. Flax and finished linen cloth became Egypt's major export, along with sugar and the dye-fixer alum.[170] This internal connectivity strengthened the ability of traders to reach beyond the empire's borders. The day-to-day activities of traders across the Mediterranean and down the Red Sea to the Indian Ocean are visible in the dossiers reconstructed from the 'Cairo geniza' (see p. 224).

5.39
Casket, 950–75. Produced in al-Mansuriyya, Tunisia, excavated at the monastery of San Zoilo in Carrión de los Condes, Spain, in 1869. Ivory. H. 20 cm, W. 42 cm, D. 24 cm. Museo Arqueológico Nacional, Madrid, inv. 50887. Purchased from Mariano Pérez Mínguez in 1872.

Multilingualism and knowledge transmission

The adoption of Arabic overlapped but was not coterminous with conversion to Islam. Like many other Muslim territories (see p. 233), Egypt's population remained largely Christian for centuries, with a significant Jewish minority. While both groups in Egypt were sometimes persecuted, most notably under the Fatimid caliph al-Hakim (r. 996–1021), they periodically flourished. Evidence from Christian cemeteries shows remarkable deployments of traditional Mediterranean iconography on garments produced towards the end of the first millennium CE. The rare survival of a green silk tunic is a case in point. Its decorative panels depict Tyches (goddesses personifying cities), nereids and hunting youths from the Classical Mediterranean repertoire (fig. 5.40). Radiocarbon dates suggest that the tunic was made between the end of the eighth and the end of the ninth century.[171] Into the eleventh century, Muslims were still a minority in rural regions, only becoming a majority at some point before the thirteenth century.[172] When the Isma'ili Shi'i Fatimids moved their capital to the newly founded city of Cairo in 969, they ruled a largely Christian and Sunni Muslim population. Under their rule both Christian and Jewish communities achieved status in the administration of the empire.[173] Ceramic lustreware production, pioneered in the east, reached new heights under the Fatimids, with one spectacular example taking as its subject a Christian priest (fig. 5.41).

Under successive caliphates, the Greek language used to administer the Byzantine empire was replaced by Arabic at the uppermost levels.[174] In Egypt during the first centuries of Muslim rule, Coptic, the Egyptian language written in a mostly Greek script, was increasingly used for legal documents once the Byzantine legal restrictions to Greek for such documents were removed.[175] In specialist genres such as alchemy, novel concepts and methods known from Persian sources could circulate swiftly. For example, a corpus of ninth–tenth-century Coptic alchemical texts from Middle Egypt was translated from Arabic.[176] Multilingualism is well-documented in everyday texts, with Coptic often paired with the old or new administrative languages, Greek and Arabic.[177] In one private letter on papyrus (late 600s–900), the writer even begins in Latin and, when his language shifts to Arabic, continues to write in Latin script.[178] In their letters, Jewish communities living in Egypt wrote in Arabic using Hebrew script (see p. 226), often dropping in Hebrew and Aramaic words and sentences. Under the Fatimids, Arabic became a language of prestige, learning and social mobility among Christians. In the eleventh century the Coptic Church adopted Arabic as its sole language for correspondence, with Coptic then soon becoming primarily a liturgical language.[179]

Christian monasteries periodically flourished under Muslim rule, providing hubs for pilgrimage and knowledge transmission. Monastic centres produced important corpora of Coptic manuscripts into the tenth and eleventh centuries.[180] In addition to Coptic Christian monastic communities, Egypt was home to an important Syriac-speaking community, based in the Wadi Natrun alongside Coptic monasteries. Syriac Christian communities thrived in the east (see p. 54).[181] Egypt was particularly welcoming, however, because Christological controversies of the sixth century had often set the theology of Alexandria and Antioch against Constantinople and Rome.[182] Due to its dry climate, Egypt has preserved significant corpora of Syriac manuscripts and other evidence of Syriac-speaking communities, which do not otherwise survive in West Asia where the communities originated. A seventh-century palimpsest wooden board bearing an extract of the Gospel of John in Syriac, with a figure of the Tyche of Constantinople painted over the text, was excavated in the Upper Egyptian town of Edfu (Apollonopolis magna) (fig. 5.42).

5.40

Fragments of a tunic, 775–900. Akhmim, Egypt. Silk. H. 140 cm, W. 90 cm. Berlin, Bode-Museum, Museum für Byzantinische Kunst, inv. 9270. Purchased through Josef Strzygowski from D. Fouquet in 1900/01.

After monks in Egypt were ordered to pay a new tax, Moses of Nisibis, the
abbot of the Monastery of the Syrians in the Wadi Natrun, travelled to Baghdad in
926/7 to appeal to the caliph himself on their behalf. He was ultimately successful,
and not only in this endeavour. While in and around Baghdad, the abbot acquired,
through both gifts and purchases, some 250 books for his monastery.[183] These
are among the most spectacular Syriac manuscripts dating to the period before
1000. As might be expected, the monastery library housed biblical, liturgical and
theological works.[184] It also, however, contained historical and scientific writings.
One such work was a pharmacological treatise by Galen of Pergamon (129–217 CE),
the Roman period's most famous physician. The manuscript contains Syriac
translations by the physician and priest Sergius of Reshaina (d. 536) of the sixth,
seventh and eighth books of Galen's Greek *On the Powers and Mixtures of Simple
Drugs* (fig. 5.43).[185] The title page for the seventh book gives Sergius' introduction
followed by the table of contents, which lists the Greek names of plants followed
by the Syriac equivalent, including, in line 5, 'Cannabis which is cannabis' (giving
the Greek term in Syriac script, Qanabis, followed by the Syriac Qenapha),
attesting the medicinal use of the plant.[186] It was through Sergius' Syriac versions

5.41
Priest bowl, 1050–1100. Said to
have been found near Luxor, Egypt.
Lustreware. H. 10.4 cm, Diam. 23.5 cm
(mouth), Diam. 10.2 cm (foot). Victoria
and Albert Museum, London, inv. C.49-
1952. Purchased with Art Fund support
and the Bryan Bequest.

5.42 *left*

Palimpsest panel with Tyche of Constantinople painted over a Syriac extract from the Gospel of John, 600–50. Excavated at Edfu, Egypt. Spruce wood, ink and pigments. H. 37 cm, W. 18.6 cm, D. 0.7 cm. Musée du Louvre, Paris, AF 10878, AF 10879.

5.43 *below*

Sergius of Reshaina's Syriac translation of Galen, 550–650. Monastery of the Syrians, Wadi Natrun, Egypt. Parchment. H. 17 cm, W. 14.5 cm, D. 26 cm (each page, approx). The British Library, London, Add MS 14661, 31v–32r. Acquired through Henry Tatum from the monastery in 1843.

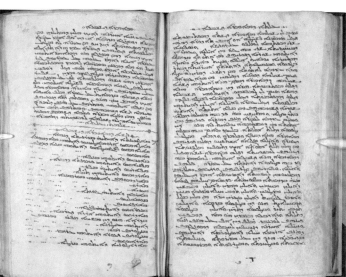

that Galen's works were later translated into Arabic.[187] Together with the Syriac manuscripts from St Catherine's Monastery in Sinai, those from the Monastery of the Syrians form the vast majority of the canon of Syriac literature that scholars study today.[188] Just as most documented examples of Byzantine silk now survive in the church treasuries of western Europe, so manuscripts representing eastern points of origin have often been best preserved far from their places of production.

The Cairo geniza: a Mediterranean society in the synagogue

The 'Cairo geniza' is a treasure trove for the history of the medieval Mediterranean and its Silk Roads connections far beyond. For hundreds of years, one of the Jewish communities of Cairo's earlier twin city, Fustat, not wishing to destroy any text that contained the name of God, placed their old books and documents in a storeroom, or *geniza*, of what later became known as Ben Ezra Synagogue (for Fustat/Cairo, see p. 188). Every synagogue may have had its geniza, but Ben Ezra's texts, unlike others, were never disposed of.[189] The manuscripts and related items first came to the attention of antiquarians towards the end of the nineteenth century and were largely dispersed to European and American libraries (figs 5.44–5.45). Today, the corpus attributed to the Cairo geniza numbers an estimated 400,000 items, with the period *c.* 1000–1250 best represented.[190] The social historian S.D. Goitein named his magisterial survey of its documents *A Mediterranean Society: The Jewish Communities of the Arab World as Portrayed in the Documents of the Cairo Geniza* (1967–93).[191] The documents' keyhole views provide extraordinarily vivid perspectives on a bustling centre and its international connections.

The synagogue belonged to the Jerusalemite or Shami community of Fustat, which was one of three Jewish communities together with the Iraqi and Qaraite.[192] As one would expect in a synagogue, its geniza was filled with all manner of religious texts. These include a wealth of biblical, liturgical and rabbinic manuscripts, some of which would have otherwise been lost to modern scholarship.[193] There are tens of thousands more fragments of biblical manuscripts, some of which travelled long distances. One of the oldest medieval Hebrew Bible fragments belonged to a parchment codex with a colophon that states its date (903/4) and location of

5.44

Hebrew inscription from over a doorway, 1000–1200 (?). From Ben Ezra Synagogue, Old Cairo, Egypt. Wood (walnut). H. 23.5 cm, W. 136 cm, D. 4.5 cm. The British Library, London, Or.6302. Acquired in 1897. The inscription contains parts of Deuteronomy 6:5 and Psalms 5:8, and mentions the name of a synagogue benefactor.

production in Gunbad-i-Mallgan in modern Dogonbadan, Iran.[194] Unsurprisingly, the Cairo geniza is still vital to biblical and rabbinic scholarship, and such fragments also illustrate the extent of religious communities' connections from Central Asia to Africa to the Iberian Peninsula.

Less expected are texts from other traditions that the Jewish community may have copied and/or read. There are, for example, extracts from the Qur'an written in Hebrew script. Distant textual traditions are represented by multiple manuscripts, such as Indian animal fables retold in Arabic. *Kalila wa Dimna* is the Arabic title for animal fables originating in Sanskrit around 300 BCE, passing through Middle Persian (Pahlavi) around 550, then Syriac by the end of the sixth century, and later translated into Arabic around 750. From the Arabic version, the fables were translated into Greek, Latin and Hebrew and back into Modern Persian.[195] An entertaining work transmitting ethics and practical philosophy, *Kalila wa Dimna* was read in royal courts and schoolrooms, and the survival of multiple copies in the Cairo geniza shows that it was also appreciated by the Jewish community there (fig. 5.46).

The Cairo geniza held so much more. In addition to literary texts, documents give insights into the daily life of Jewish communities under Islamic rule, and more generally of Jewish, Christian and Muslim communities in Egypt and far beyond.[196] The geniza contained all manner of private letters, legal contracts, official petitions, accounts and tax receipts. It has been described as an 'anti-

5.45 *left*
The scholar Solomon Schechter at work in Cambridge among c. 200,000 fragmentary documents he acquired in Cairo, 1898. Cambridge University Library, Cambridge.

5.46 *above*
Kalila wa Dimna in Arabic, 1000–1200. Found in Ben Ezra Synagogue, Old Cairo, Egypt. Ink and pigments on paper. H. 12 cm, W. 10 cm (page fragment). Cambridge University Library, Taylor-Schechter Genizah Collection, Cambridge, T-S Ar.40.9. Donated by Dr Solomon Schechter and his patron Dr Charles Taylor.

archive' or a 'counter-archive', because the assemblage is not what was kept, but what was discarded.[197] The manuscripts reveal a thriving Jewish community with international social and economic links from al-Andalus to India and even to Southeast Asia.[198] In addition to the Hebrew, Aramaic and Arabic documents, most letter writers used Judaeo-Arabic, in other words the Arabic language spoken as part of everyday life, written in the Hebrew script that they learned as part of their religious education (see fig. 2.40). Smaller quantities of texts in a dozen other languages, such as Coptic, Syriac and Persian, also survive. Documents are found on traditional Mediterranean writing media, papyrus and parchment, but especially the new writing material from the east, paper,[199] and even textiles, which seem to have been used by Jewish traders in India in the absence of paper.[200] The Cairo geniza's richness and variety of languages, scripts and materials parallel the find at the Library Cave at Dunhuang (see chapter 2).

Remarkably, the contents of the synagogue's geniza contain Fatimid court business too.[201] Official documents from the Fatimid caliphs' chancellery ended up in the geniza indirectly as a result of the regular trade in used paper, with the versos and wide margins of original Arabic documents exploited as writing material. As a result, the synagogue's geniza sheds light on fleeting and sometimes deliberately obscured moments in Fatimid history, such as the brief rule of Sitt al-Mulk (r. c. 1021–3), the sister of caliph al-Hakim, which is revealed by Arabic petitions addressed to her, later reused by a Jewish writer for biblical passages in Hebrew and Aramaic. In other cases, the medium is as illuminating as the messages. A surprising number of Fatimid state decrees – originally written to impress on impractically long vertical rolls, half a metre wide and 8 metres or more long, bearing large, calligraphic Arabic script with wide line spaces – were cut into sheets and reused (fig. 5.47).[202] The writing materials of the Cairo geniza can be as revealing as their contents, languages and scripts.

Medieval mobility

The Cairo geniza vividly demonstrates the extent of medieval mobility. People travelled as scholars and brides, refugees and captives, traders and traded. Some gained extraordinary wealth and prestige. The Jewish Tustari family emigrated from Persia via Ifriqiya and maintained links with al-Andalus and, to a lesser extent, the Levant. Becoming courtiers within the Fatimid palace brought the family status, but also enormous risk, most strikingly exemplified by the execution in 1047 of Abu Sa'd al-Tustari, who was advisor to the mother of the caliph.[203] Later, in the twelfth century, famous Andalusi scholars such as Judah ha-Levi (1075–1141) and Maimonides (1135–1204) left al-Andalus for Egypt, the former on his way to Jerusalem, the latter to settle permanently, but earlier intellectuals in search of knowledge also regularly travelled long distances.[204] Leading Jewish scholars criss-crossed the Mediterranean to take up positions as the heads of schools in places such as Kairouan and the academies at Jerusalem and Baghdad. Less eminent teachers as well as cantors also travelled for the purposes of work. The relative ease of travel is shown by one illustrious judge from Palermo who travelled to Egypt, where he traded Sicilian silk before leaving for the Baghdad Academy to study with its leader, Hai Gaon (d. 1038). Their scholarly networks were not exclusively Jewish. Hai Gaon sent the judge from Sicily to the head of the Syrian Christian community for advice on an obscure biblical phrase. Among Hai Gaon's students were not only Jewish pupils from Muslim lands, but also from Christian Italy. The Sicilian judge's intellectual and physical journey came full circle when, probably during his visit to the Andalusi city of Granada, he dedicated his biography of Hai Gaon to the Jewish vizier of the city's Berber king.

5.47
The Fatimid state, decree in Arabic, 1131–40; letter from one brother to another in Judaeo-Arabic, 1140. Ben Ezra Synagogue, Old Cairo, Egypt. Ink on paper. H. 39 cm, W. 20.8 cm. Cambridge University Library, Taylor-Schechter Genizah Collection, Cambridge, T-S 20.80. Donated by Dr Solomon Schechter and his patron Dr Charles Taylor.

5.48

Letter requesting charity in Hebrew, *c*. 950. Found in Ben Ezra Synagogue, Old Cairo, Egypt. Ink on parchment. H. 22.5 cm, W. 14.4 cm. Cambridge University Library, Taylor-Schechter Genizah Collection, Cambridge, T-S 12.122. Donated by Dr Solomon Schechter and his patron Dr Charles Taylor.

The Cairo geniza documents show that diplomatic marriages between families served to strengthen international ties within and across the global Jewish community. Daughters and sons in Fustat married their Jewish counterparts in al-Andalus, Ifriqiya and the Levant. For example, in 1037 the daughter of a chief judge from Sijilmasa married a leader of the Iraqi community in Fustat.[205] Marriage contracts provide a wealth of information, sometimes describing the contents of the bride's dowry, with all manner of imported items or their imitations indicating the high status of the family.[206] When Sarwa bat Sedaqa ben Jarir married Hezekiah ben Benjamin in Jerusalem in 1028, several of the dowry items were specified according to their origin: clothes from Sicily and Byzantium, a bucket from Baghdad, a pot from Damascus, and Tabari and Buziyon couches, from what are probably the Caspian coast of Iran and Afghanistan, respectively.[207]

The Jewish community in Cairo was considered one of the wealthiest in the known world, and distant and less fortunate individuals and communities often sought its assistance.[208] Hebrew literacy among Jewish communities from Asia to al-Andalus allowed requests to be made, understood and fulfilled, regardless of the petitioner's vernacular. When a man from Khurasan sought assistance in Jerusalem, he was attacked and robbed on his way, leaving him injured and bereft of everything, including his letters of introduction. In correspondence dated 1034/5, the head of the Academy in Jerusalem narrates his plight to his colleague in Fustat in an appeal for him to organise assistance to return the man home.[209] The source of another letter apparently in Kyiv is more unusual than its content. Written in Hebrew, the letter is on parchment and scored and folded in a way familiar from the Byzantine world (fig. 5.48). In it, a Jewish community introduces a man named Jacob, who must repay his brother's non-Jewish creditors after he was murdered and robbed. The community had paid enough to have him released from prison, but still sought to raise the remainder from the wealthy community in Cairo. Among the signatories of the letter are men with typical Hebrew names, but there are others too – these were all once interpreted as Turkic and used as evidence for Khazar converts to Judaism, but many are now thought to be Slavic.[210] Judah ha-Levi transmitted the tale of the Khazar king who invited a rabbi to instruct him so that he could choose between Christianity, Islam and Judaism. Whether or not the conversion account of the Khazars has more basis in legend than fact, the story was important to Jewish self-conceptualisation. The survival of copies of ha-Levi's *Khuzari*, and even school texts showing a student practising his penmanship with lines from it, underscore the text's importance to the Jewish community in Fustat.[211] Among the more than fifty letters concerning ha-Levi's visit to Egypt on his way to Jerusalem are some of his own handwritten correspondence.[212]

Traders

Under the Fatimids, networks of Jewish merchants extended west to Sicily, Ifriqiya and al-Andalus, and east to ports on the Arabian Peninsula, India and beyond.[213] Within the Mediterranean, textiles, above all linen but also silk, accounted for the largest share of trade. Merchants traded extensively in raw materials, including fibres, dyes and fixatives such as alum; semi-processed materials like silk and flax; and finished products such as garments and soft furnishings. They also traded in oil and wine in large quantities, as well as nuts, fruit and cheese. High-value gems, dyes and spices – culinary, but also medicinal and cosmetic – were exchanged, alongside household goods such as soap and wax, as well as books and paper.[214] By contrast, Indian Ocean commodities were higher in value and had smaller markets. These included spices, foremost among them pepper, but also cinnamon, cardamom and cloves; gemstones and pearls; tortoiseshell and musk; and dyes such as brazilwood, crimson and Indian indigo. Only copper and iron were important bulk goods.[215] The absence of key categories such as grain, timber, weapons and enslaved people, has been interpreted as indicative of the government's proprietary interests in them.[216]

The movement of things was the main topic of the mercantile correspondence in the Cairo geniza.[217] Often, the Jewish traders of Fustat/Cairo did not own the means of transport, such as the ships, camels and donkeys, that conveyed their goods.[218] To move a single bale, a trader might have to purchase canvas and rope, label the contents of the sections within the bale, engage baggage animals and drivers, rent warehouse space at points of loading and unloading, hire packers and porters, visit and negotiate with shipping agents and customs officials, and accompany the cargo or arrange for its supervision on board.[219]

Travel away from home, long-distance or otherwise, could be dangerous, and traders might be targeted as commodities for sale themselves. Nahray ben Nissim (c. 1025–1098) was a medium-scale trader of flax and linen, a banker, scholar and respected member of the Jewish community. An emigrant from Ifriqiya, he settled in Fustat and dealt in commodities from and between Ifriqiya, Sicily, Egypt and the Levant, as well as in-transit goods from the Red Sea and beyond, including pearls and lapis lazuli, tortoiseshell and musk, frankincense and betel leaves, pepper and cloves.[220] Nahray's business is attested by a corpus of around 330 documents in the Cairo geniza.[221] One of these letters illustrates some of the dangers of the trade. When three Jewish merchants were taken captive by Byzantine soldiers, who had almost beaten them to death before Italian merchants acquired them, an official in Alexandria appealed to Nahray ben Nissim to seek the funds to free them. The urgency to redeem captives was paramount, as failure to ransom them condemned them to enslavement. The price was typically 33⅓ dinars.[222]

At the end of the eleventh century there is a discernible pivot from the Mediterranean to the Indian Ocean in the Cairo geniza traders' correspondence.[223] The shift may mirror larger political change, with the expansion of the Fatimid empire, or it could be an accident of the documents that survive, or a combination of both.[224] Journeys eastwards were undertaken in stages, with stops of longer or shorter duration along the way. Travellers first went up the Nile, across the Eastern Desert, to one of the Red Sea ports; then sailed south to other nodes of trade such as the Dahlak islands opposite ancient Adulis (see p. 179), and on to Aden, where the local ruling dynasty was also Isma'ili Shi'i and allied with the Fatimids, and from there to India.[225] Traders' luggage comprised most of the things they would need on their journeys, not least drinking water, food and condiments, kitchen- and tableware, clothes and soap, and paper and ink to maintain business correspondence.[226] Traders dependent on the twice-yearly monsoons could stay away for years, leaving families behind, starting new ones, or possibly both.[227] Many did not return. Travellers faced storms which could result in shipwreck.[228] Maimonides, for example, lost his beloved brother David in a shipwreck en route to India. They also faced exposure, malnutrition and, above all, dehydration.[229] Other more mundane losses were a regular part of the business. For example, one set of eleventh-century documents pertains to a legal dispute between two Jewish traders, the travelling merchant Joseph al-Lebdi and his colleague, a Cairo businessman. Among the documents is one that concerns a shipwreck from which a single bale was rescued.[230] Writing via a scribe to the representative of the merchants in Aden, al-Lebdi mentions that he has bypassed Aden, where he was meant to collect what they were owed but instead travelled to Mirbat, also on the coast of South Arabia, and directly on to Dahlak. That al-Lebdi did not settle up in Aden exacerbated the dispute, which went on for years.

שהדותא דהות באנפנא אנן שהדי . דחתמי' לתחתא בטור זביני י...
ביננא צ טצבי דהוא חיעשה יושלין בירה בסלגו שנת אלפא ואר...
ושרין שנין למני אנא דרגישנא ביה בעיר אל לאזרה דאמירא לפסטואל
מצריס רעלגלניל נהרא מותביה חזרת אלנא סתאל אקלא בתמולו ור
יוסף הכיף ס איצתתיה עלי יהווה בר עלס ס ט ולאלת אלא אנסה ידן
עלי ואקנו לי מני מעטשין וכתבו וחתמו עלאי צבלנשאני לרפואארנא
והבולה לסתאלמנא בתנתא ני אלמנעניה דמרנווודבנא נהלאי הרב
המ ן צהרך זל מחמת דצאטן לפשי כדלא באונס קא מוריטא ל דמיכן
דעסיתת וצילת תמינה עשר דינרי דדהבא טבצי מעלי . תק ...
וזצעני ללק צרן אמתא דהותל אלעביה דמיקריא לנס צבינ ... מורין
חתיכין חלקא שריר וקיימי יהיבין ומשלמין לה לסרת אלמלא ...
ועילתה צתרה יג יומא לן נלטל ולא אישתאר לי בודרא אמתא שוס...
בעלמא משני פרוטה ולעילא ומלכתה סתאלמנא דא לקידא אמתא וולפאסא...
גמיריא וקנתה קנין גמור ושלוטה תרא ס תאלמוש ערא עלהזאיה אמתא דזבינא
לה עמיקשא ולאקנ ענאה ולאזרותי עלאחסנא ולמצונש ולחלפא ולאיש...
ושחרורה ולמיהב יאה צמיתנה לעל מא רתע צצי ואנש פה ימחי צ...
ירתה צתרה מקוצא דן ולעלם ואחריות זבינ איל עלאי אנא סת...
ירתא יצתראי צבלמא ד ליתצ ויטעון וייערער עלסת אלמלא דאאן עלירתה
בתרה אקוס או א סתאלאקרא דרוטאי צתראי ונפצי וצרי ונפצי ...
ושייצ ונצפל את צצי אילא וולים יתק ציד פתאלמנא דא עצ...
לעלם לא מאסמכנא ולא צטופסי דשטרי אלא כחומר עצטטרי מחזקי ...
דינא וכלכתב צבל כתב ולא ריפק ל מירעט ולצטלא ית זבינ איל צטילן ...
מעטשין קדמיכון וחטיצי צחספא צנוקא עלת ציה מעמא ולפ צי...
לעבלין ליוא מנהון וכלמווערי ותנאי ...
דל צטי לג לצינוק יעעטשיו ל ר מיכון צבלנשאני לאמור רצל צצ...
ותלצי ואמנצא דצ מוצ צקת לאמהן ופצירה וצטירה ... מן חבנרי ומן ...
עדרי מלצא ומלבתנ ורוצם דאנש ל אייתלל ומנ יליה ...
דשפיק ועד אחר דעצתק ועצנש מסת אל אקלא ...
עלצל מלדעתיצ ומפרש לעילא צמנצ דצטר למיק ...
יי יהוורה צד עלס פ ל צמצי דעצצצ אינתתיה סתאלאקרא ...
עלאי וקנ ומנ מעטשין לי נתר צי צ צמירתה לאמתה לעי ס ...
לנפשי צ צצי ד. כלוס ולא יתל ווערת וקנינאמ ...
קצ אמ לא לטולתה דא קצא אלצע אלצ עבהדיה אל...
לעילא צמ ל אצ צר למיקנפ צ ציה ושהדותף ...
לה לסת אל מלא למייהו ציצה ל כנ ולרא ...

The traded

Alongside the evidence from Arabic papyri from earlier periods, the Cairo geniza documents also offer further compelling and detailed information about the trade in enslaved people. The enslaved are sometimes mentioned in letters, but quantifiable evidence can be gathered from legal texts such as bills of sale and release.[231] Such documents provide price, name, gender, geographic origin and, less commonly, age and physical or distinguishing characteristics, giving at least some precious impressions of their presence and individuality. Women and girls far outnumber men and boys. In the Fatimid period, their origins are stated as Byzantine, Persian, Nubian and even Indian, showing the sheer distances people could be transported.[232] Like the earlier 'Abbasid corpus of Arabic documents (see p. 212), the most common indication of origin is Nubian, given that Muslims and non-Muslims living under their jurisdiction were theoretically ineligible to be enslaved.[233] The Jewish merchants of Fustat appear not to have engaged in the large-scale trade in people, but they did buy and sell individuals. For example, when they wanted to purchase or transport enslaved individuals, Nahray ben Nissim's colleagues sometimes turned to him for advice.[234] After Nahray's death, his widow Sitt al-Muna purchased a Nubian woman named Na'im from another Jewish woman in November 1108 for 20 dinars, the standard price in the period (fig. 5.49). Such bills of sale found in the Cairo geniza are usually written in Judaeo-Arabic. This one, however, is largely in Aramaic and follows a model given by Hai Gaon, the same head of the Baghdad Academy with whom the distinguished judge from Palermo studied (see p. 226). On the reverse of the same bill of sale appears another one, this time in Arabic script. It records the sale of Na'im for the same amount, 20 dinars, seven years later (1115) to a Christian man who was a known associate of Nahray ben Nissim.[235] The description of her is formulaic and gives a minimum of information. Nevertheless, among the nameless and forgotten masses exchanged across the medieval Silk Roads, there is Na'im.

From empires to individuals, this chapter has shown the range of networks that bound the Mediterranean basin to the Silk Roads and the wider world beyond, not only east and west, but also north and south. Those who plied such routes, whether voluntarily or involuntarily, brought with them both ideas and objects. Despite the high visibility of imperial power throughout the Mediterranean during this period, time and again it is the most everyday objects that tell the biggest stories – vividly encapsulated by beads of Baltic amber or Indo-Pacific glass circulating across continents. Egypt's arid climate ensures its central place in discussions of the Mediterranean, preserving as it does a range and abundance of organic material that does not survive elsewhere. The documents found here offer rare glimpses of everyday people who lived, worked, travelled and died in the Mediterranean, the most precious being details of enslaved individuals whose lives are otherwise largely invisible (see pp. 88, 143). While only a relatively small proportion of people travelled, the communities through which they passed were transformed in lasting and distinct ways. Such developments can be traced, too, further westwards and across the strait of Gibraltar, to the Iberian Peninsula.

5.49

Bills of sale for an enslaved woman named Na'im in Aramaic, 1108 (front) and Arabic, 1115 (back). Found in Ben Ezra Synagogue, Old Cairo, Egypt. Ink on paper. H. 32.5 cm, W. 21.2 cm. Cambridge University Library, Taylor-Schechter Genizah Collection, Cambridge, T-S 18J1.17r. Donated by Dr Solomon Schechter and his patron Dr Charles Taylor.

Peoples of al-Andalus

Sue Brunning

In 711 Muslim North African and Arab forces crossed the Gibraltar Strait to the Iberian Peninsula (present-day Portugal and Spain: fig. 5.50), seeking to expand the territory controlled by the Umayyad dynasty based in Damascus (see p. 160). Their arrival brought Islam to the west of the European continent. The peninsula, formerly Roman Hispania, had been ruled by the Christian Visigoths since the fifth century but, by the early eighth, political and religious infighting made it an easy target. The invading forces rapidly seized power centres, defeated Visigothic armies, and killed their king, Roderic (r. 710–11). By 718 much of Iberia was under Muslim control. The region, named al-Andalus soon after the conquest, was governed as a western province until Umayyads fleeing an ʿAbbasid coup in Syria made it an independent emirate under ʿAbd al-Rahman I (r. 756–88), the caliph's grandson. In 929 his descendant, ʿAbd al-Rahman III (r. 929–61), proclaimed al-Andalus a caliphate, rivalling the ʿAbbasid east and Fatimid south. It endured beyond the chronology of this book, eventually replaced by multiple kingdoms known as *taifas* following civil war in 1031.[1]

Al-Andalus's rulers were respected international players, cultivating relationships as well as occasional conflicts with neighbours and competitors. The Christian poet–dramatist Hrosvitha (d. 973) praised Córdoba, its vibrant capital, as the 'shining glory of the world'.[2] Here, the Umayyad court developed a lavish culture, using its worldly connections to acquire foreign luxuries for people and palaces, including Arabian aromatics, Egyptian kohl and Chinese porcelain vessels, as well as materials for courtly workshops, notably African elephant ivory, which was skilfully carved into sumptuous containers. Indeed, arts, culture and learning flourished to a height that, by the mid-tenth century, matched the great Islamic and Byzantine centres. The catalyst for this cultural flowering was, in part, the unique blend of cultures, faiths and peoples, including Muslim, Christian, Jewish, North African, Visigothic, Roman, Byzantine and more, all of whom met on the peninsula. What began in 711 as military conflict led, in time, to the emergence of a new Andalusi identity, which can still be experienced in southern Spain today.[3]

Cultures in communication

Islamic rule triggered social, cultural and religious change as the new and existing populations began to live together. It touched many realms of life, from domestic layouts to eating habits. Ceramics are remarkably informative about these developments. New eastern pottery types like portable bread ovens (*tannurs*) herald new cooking methods, Islamic oil lamps evoke a different domestic feel, and the adaptation of Visigothic

FRANCIA

Cantabrian Mountains

Pyrenees

León •

San Millán de
la Cogolla •

• Pamplona

CHRISTIAN

KINGDOMS

Duero

Ebro

Sierra Guadarrama

• Madrid

Tagus

• Toledo

AL-ANDALUS

Júcar

Guadiana

Balearic Islands

Madinat al-Zahra •
Guadalquivir •• Córdoba

Mediterranean
Sea

Sierra Nevada

Atlantic
Ocean

	Northern border of al-Andalus
0	100 miles
0	100 km

5.50

Map of the Iberian Peninsula under
Umayyad rule, 900s.

pottery, such as the application of Islamic-style painted
ornament, reflects cultural syncretism. By the later tenth
century, this long and regionally varied process had
forged an Islamised society in which al-Andalus's diverse
communities lived by Islamic traditions, even if they
practised different faiths and spoke different languages.[4]

Communication was a critical issue immediately
after the conquest, since the existing population spoke
vernacular Visigothic and Latin, while their new rulers
spoke Arabic. The spread of Arabic apparently followed
a faster trajectory than other developments, becoming
predominant by around the late ninth century. Gold
coins minted by early Andalusi governors evoke this
rapidity, progressing in ten short years from Latin-
inscribed solidi (711/12), via bilingual Latin-Arabic dinars
(716/17) to dirhams bearing fully Arabic legends (721/2)
(fig. 5.51). These changes may have symbolic undertones

too, hinting that an initial concern to accommodate non-Arabic speakers gave way to an expectation of Arabic literacy, the coins emphasising that Iberia was now an Arabic-speaking realm.[5]

Animal bones inscribed with the Arabic alphabet provide a glimpse of how people learned the language (fig. 5.52). They were probably used as practice pieces, mnemonics or models. Several examples excavated from a Córdoban suburb where Islamic scholars worked suggest that language teaching occurred there. Eventually, some people became fully bilingual. Analysis of a late ninth-century Bible fragment produced in al-Andalus has shown that its parallel columns of Latin and Arabic were written by the same scribe (fig. 5.53). Visigothic twists to the Arabic suggest that the person was a Latin speaker who was so comfortable with their second language as to have developed a personal way of expressing it. The same fragment illustrates an Andalusi contribution to the wider Arabic-speaking world. The scribe wrote in a style of writing known as Maghribi round script, which developed in al-Andalus and, from the tenth century, spread throughout the western Islamic world, where it formed the basis for a vigorous calligraphic tradition that equalled its eastern counterpart.[6]

The arrival of Islam to a predominantly Christian region prompted religious change, but also coexistence and collaboration between faiths. As practitioners of fellow Abrahamic religions, Christian and Jewish people were to some degree protected in Islamic lands. In al-Andalus, they experienced relative religious freedom, albeit with certain limitations such as special taxes. Positive interfaith relations supported intellectual, cultural and artistic exchange. Non-Muslims were not excluded from political office or other trusted positions. 'Abd al-Rahman III,

5.51 *above*

Coins with Latin, bilingual and Arabic inscriptions, 711–23. Minted in al-Andalus. Gold. Diam. 1.5–2.4 cm, weight 3.6–4.2 g. Museo Arqueológico Nacional, Madrid, 2004/117/1, 2004/117/14 and 104279. Purchased from D. Antonio Vives y Escudero.

5.52 *right*

Cow scapula with Arabic text, *c.* late 900s. Found in Madrid, Spain. Animal bone. H. 6.5 cm, L. 20.6 cm. Museo Arqueológico Nacional, Madrid, 1986/60/V-4. From the 1984 excavation campaign of the wall of Madrid, Calle Angosta de los Mancebos, 3.

for instance, had a Jewish physician, Hasdai ibn Shaprut (*c.* 915–970), and a Christian secretary, Recemundus (d. 961). Nevertheless, by the tenth century, Islam had become the dominant faith on the Iberian Peninsula. Its progress can be traced archaeologically. Burials evoke a shift from Christian to Muslim funerary rites. Animal bone waste indicates a move from pork, prohibited in the halal diet, to sheep, goat and chicken consumption in certain places. Mosques emerged, whether newly built or repurposed from existing buildings. Córdoba's Great Mosque (see p. 232), one of al-Andalus's most iconic structures, came into being when the Muslim community outgrew the Visigothic Basilica of San Vicente, which it had been sharing with local Christians.[7]

Christianity endured in al-Andalus, even as its practitioners adopted other Islamic customs. There is little trace of the widespread church destruction reported in some written sources, although tensions occasionally arose, illustrated by the so-called martyrs of Córdoba, who were executed in the mid-ninth century for publicly condemning Islam.[8] Christian kingdoms on al-Andalus's northern border fostered political and marital alliances with their Muslim neighbours, forging familial ties

between rulers. Such interactions could explain the presence of a spectacular ivory processional cross at the monastery of San Millán de la Cogolla, northern Spain (fig. 5.54). Its three preserved arms,[9] each just under 40 centimetres long and 2 centimetres thick, are exquisitely carved with furling plants inhabited by four-legged and feathered beasts. Only al-Andalus possessed the ivory, and the ivory-working skill, to produce such a piece, so an Islamic link is certain, but its nature is not. Traditionally, the cross has been seen as a product of Christian artisans with close knowledge of Islamic artistic traditions acquired from the south, but its stylistic blend of motifs paralleled both in Christian illuminated manuscripts and mid-tenth-century Córdoban court ivories do not exclude the possibility of an Andalusi maker, perhaps even in the caliphal workshop. For instance, an open-work lidded vessel (pyxis) commissioned for caliph al-Hakam II (r. 961–76) shares the cross's splayed bird motif and distinctive scaled border.[10] Recent research speculates that the cross moved north either as a diplomatic gift from ʿAbd al-Rahman III to his aunt, Queen Toda of Pamplona (d. 959), or as a commission by her from his workshop, intended for San Millán de la

Cogolla's consecration in 959. In either reading, the cross is a rich evocation of religious relations in al-Andalus: an iconic Christian symbol, made by an artisan working in or drawing upon an Islamic artistic context, for use in Christian sacred rituals.[11]

Al-Andalus's Jewish community is not well represented archaeologically, but literary sources depict Jewish people participating widely in political, commercial and intellectual life. Key to the latter was Hasdai, the aforementioned physician, who used his influence to help stimulate Hebrew scholarship. A proportion of Jewish people probably converted to Islam or adopted other Islamic ways while continuing to practise their own faith. Indeed, al-Andalus's tolerant atmosphere offered them a calmer life, following persecution under Visigothic rulership. They appear to have lived in most Andalusi towns and some rural areas, with large communities recorded at places like Lucena, near Córdoba, in the mid-ninth century. Córdoba's own Jewish community is evidenced by a rare archaeological find, comprising a marble gravestone dedicated to Yehudah bar Akon, who died in the ninth century (fig. 5.55). Its findspot, in the Zumbacón neighbourhood outside the city walls, signals a Jewish cemetery there.

5.53 *opposite*
Fragment of Saint Paul's Epistle to the Galatians, in Latin and Arabic, *c.* late 800s–early 900s. Produced in al-Andalus. Parchment, paper and wood. H. 39 cm, W. 26.7 cm, D. 4.5 cm (manuscript). Biblioteca Apostolica Vaticana, Vatican City, Vat. Lat. 12900, fol. IIr. Transferred from Sigüenza Cathedral.

5.54 *right*
Processional cross, late 900s. From the monastery of San Millán de la Cogolla, La Rioja, Spain. Ivory and gold. H. 37 cm, W. 14 cm, D. 1.7–1.8 cm (max., each arm). **Upper and lower arms** Musée du Louvre, Paris, OA 5944–5, donated by Félix Dostau. **Left arm (as pictured)** Museo Arqueológico Nacional, Madrid, 63935, purchased from Asunción Gurruchaga.

The gravestone's date and text are in Hebrew, suggesting that Jewish traditions were upheld in the community, at least by those who buried him.[12]

Adoption, adaptation, innovation

Al-Andalus's cultural blend stimulated the adoption and adaptation of styles, ideas and technologies from all available sources, past and present, east and west, resulting in innovations with a characteristic Andalusi flavour.

Architecture offers a monumental expression of this, epitomised by 'Abd al-Rahman III's palace complex at Madinat al-Zahra (see fig. 0.16), built from 936, and the Great Mosque of Córdoba, particularly caliph al-Hakam II's lavish extension in the later tenth century. Both buildings incorporated Visigothic horseshoe arches, modified with Syrian Umayyad red-and-white striped bands, which became a typical Andalusi architectural element.[13] The arches were supported by columns bearing marble capitals. The earliest were reused Roman and Visigothic examples, Corinthian in style with verdant acanthus. Local copies followed, virtually indistinguishable from their models and, by the mid-tenth century, an Andalusi version had evolved, blending the leafy Roman outline with deeply carved, Islamic-style abstract foliage. An example from Córdoba (fig. 5.56) combines such foliage with Roman 'bead and reel' and a kufic inscription, which links it to al-Hakam II's building works. The capital's maker was clearly versed in al-Andalus's dynamic stylistic blend. His name, Safar, is carved into the flat top of the capital.[14]

Islamic palaces and elite rural estates were often surrounded by gardens that reflect al-Andalus's blended traditions. These spaces drew upon older Roman practices on the Iberian Peninsula and contemporary Islamic examples at sites such as al-Rusafa in Syria, which were rooted partly in Persian gardening traditions. Arabic literature evokes the multisensory atmosphere of Andalusi gardens, combining fine buildings with lush plantings, running water, shaded corners and fragrant fruit trees, some imported from afar. A colourful tale links Spain's first pomegranate trees to fruits conveyed from Syria by an ambassador to 'Abd al-Rahman I

in the eighth century. Successful cultivation at the emir's al-Rusafa estate, named after the Syrian palace, sparked their proliferation throughout al-Andalus. Date palm trees may also have arrived at this time. A poem attributed to 'Abd al-Rahman I himself addresses a palm at al-Rusafa, which, like him, is now far from its eastern home. Archaeological evidence is scarce, but plum, pear, fig and apple have emerged from Córdoba's botanical record, along with various other plants.[15]

Madinat al-Zahra's spectacular terraced remains include two levels of gardens, furnished with lawns, aromatic plants, a fish pool and the ubiquitous fruit trees. Menageries and aviaries are also recorded there, again very likely drawing from eastern Islamic spaces described in texts. The gardens' verdancy spilled into the palace buildings, whose walls bore limestone panels carved with vegetation, including elegant palm leaves (fig. 5.57), and whose aspect offered views of the greenery outside, creating a panorama of lushness.[16] Marble fountains made from repurposed Roman sarcophagi have been found, along with metal animal-shaped spouts. One, in the form of a deer, received water through a pipe in its base, which was propelled through its hollow legs and body, before cascading from a hole in its mouth (fig. 5.58). This refined piece, delicately engraved and gilded, offers an impression of the twelve bejewelled gold fountainheads which 'Abd al-Rahman III is said to have commissioned for a green marble basin gifted by the Byzantine emperor. Several marble fountain basins, carved with foliage, felines and gazelles, have been unearthed at al-Rummaniyya, a nearby villa (*munya*) which offered similarly sweeping views over its terraced gardens (fig. 5.59). Such spaces were not mere ornamentation. They symbolised the caliph's power and connections, while evoking the Islamic idea that his generosity made the natural world flourish.[17]

The gardens were watered by hydraulic technologies that combined existing and imported methods. Old Roman infrastructure was refurbished to working order, including a first-century CE aqueduct that supplied Madinat al-Zahra. Underground channels, known as *qanats*, and water-lifting machines, including Syrian-style waterwheels, were introduced. One type, which

5.55 *opposite top*

Grave marker of Yehudah bar Akon, mid-800s. Found in Córdoba, Spain. Marble. H. 23 cm, W. 33.3 cm, D. 3 cm. Museo Arqueológico y Etnográfico de Córdoba, Córdoba, DJ033334. Entered the museum after emergency excavation in 2008.

5.56 *opposite middle*

Capital with Arabic inscriptions, 964–5. Found in Córdoba, Spain. Marble. H. 29.5 cm, W. 32 cm, D. 32 cm. Museo Arqueológico y Etnográfico de Córdoba, Córdoba, CE003469. Deposited by the Provincial Monuments Commission in 1923.

5.57 *opposite bottom*

Architectural panel with palm leaf carving, c. 950–60. Probably from Madinat al-Zahra, Spain. Limestone. H. 32 cm, W. 16.5 cm, D. 6.5 cm. Victoria and Albert Museum, London, A.106-1919. Given by Dr W.L. Hildburgh, F.S.A.

paired an upright and a horizontal wheel driven by animals or humans, was fitted with ceramic buckets that raised water from a well below (fig. 5.60). These water supply methods had applications beyond the garden wall, such as irrigation, which involved the collection and redistribution of water to support the cultivation of plants, trees and crops in drier areas. Though not a new technology, it appears to have been practised and developed further by peasant farmers working al-Andalus's lands.[18]

Recent scientific analysis of ceramic artefacts used in elite spaces has revealed a remarkable innovation born from al-Andalus's cultural blend. Glazing technology had declined on the peninsula after the Roman period, but re-emerged in certain urban centres, including Córdoba, during the mid-ninth century. The phenomenon was initially explained as a knowledge transfer from eastern Islamic lands, where glazing was an established and distinctive cultural element (see p. 176). However, the Andalusi glazes were found to have a high lead composition similar to local glass, indicating a different production method, in which this glass was crushed, applied to ceramics, and fired to make the glaze. Apparently, a taste for fine glazed eastern wares among the Andalusi elite drove technological innovation at home, to meet the demand. The artisans' ingenuity was to turn to lead, an abundant, affordable local resource with reserves near Córdoba itself. Their products were fine enough to compete with the very imports that most likely inspired their development (fig. 5.61).[19]

Sharing knowledge

Al-Andalus's worldly connections contributed to a vibrant intellectual culture, which, in turn, disseminated knowledge to wider Europe. The fruits of such exchange mostly ripened after 1000 but, in some areas, the process may have begun as early as the tenth century. Astronomical learning had long been flowing into al-Andalus from eastern Islamic lands, which themselves had drawn from Greek and Indo-Persian traditions. Conduits included travelling scholars and books from

5.58 *top*
Fountain spout, c. 950–1000. From Madinat al-Zahra, Spain. Copper alloy. H. 61.6 cm. Museo Arqueológico y Etnográfico de Córdoba, Córdoba, CE000500.

5.59 *right*
Fountain basin, mid-900s. Found at al-Rummaniyya, near Madinat al-Zahra, Spain. Marble. H. 12.5 cm, W. 62.6 cm, W. 47.5 cm. Museo Arqueológico y Etnográfico de Córdoba, Córdoba, CE009387. Donated by D. Manuel Gómez-Moreno y Martínez in 1946.

centres such as Baghdad, which the scientifically interested al-Hakam II collected into an enormous Córdoban library. Andalusi scholars further developed, refined and expanded this scientific knowledge.[20]

Early signs of transmission to Europe emerged in Catalonia, northern Iberia, which geographically and politically bridged the Muslim south and Christian north. Late tenth-century Latin texts reflect discussions of Arabic treatises and scientific instruments, with the earliest translations of Arabic astrological texts ascribed to one Gerbert of Aurillac (d. 1000), who himself may have helped to spread knowledge north. Educated in Iberia, perhaps under some Muslim scholars, he became a teacher and religious leader in various European centres before being elected as pope. Other pathways for knowledge included diplomatic exchange between Córdoba and Christian courts in western Europe, and links between intellectual centres on either side of the Pyrenees, including monasteries such as Santa María de Ripoll, which has been viewed as especially influential. The result of these exchanges resounds within Latin texts like the *Alchandrea*, a tenth-century astrological work that bears the fingerprints of Arabic learning.[21]

Knowledge of the astrolabe also reached Europe from al-Andalus. These instruments, developed in Greek antiquity and familiar in eastern Islamic lands from

5.60 *top*

Waterwheel bucket, *c.* 900–1000. Found in Spain. Ceramic. H. 14.5 cm. Museo Arqueológico Nacional, Madrid, 50955.

5.61 *left*

Glazed serving bowl, *c.* 900–1000. Found at Madinat al-Zahra, Spain. Ceramic. H. 5 cm, Diam. 21 cm. Museo Arqueológico Nacional, Madrid, 63049. Deposited by the Commission for the Excavations of Madinat al-Zahra, 1943.

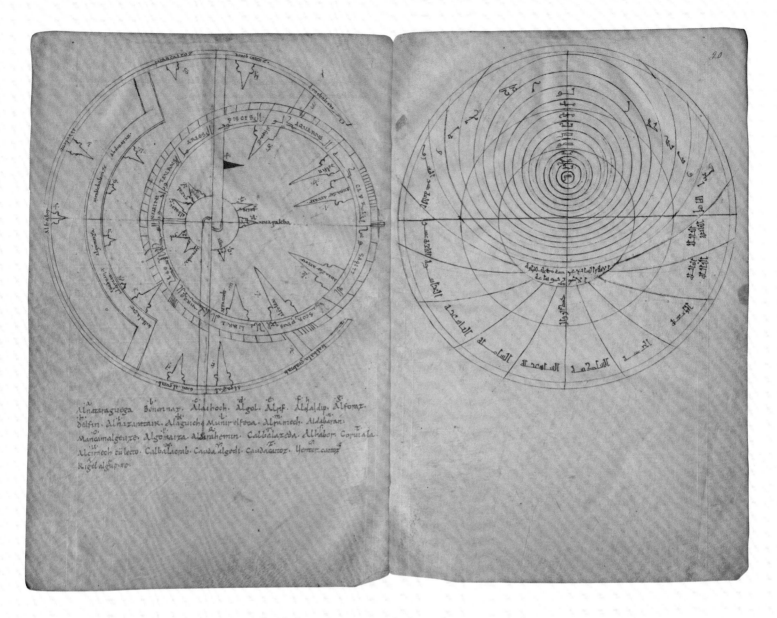

the ninth century, were calculators for astronomical time and handheld models of the universe.[22] The oldest surviving Andalusi example was made in Córdoba in 1026–7 by Muhammad ibn al-Saffar (fig. 5.62), whose brother Ahmad wrote an astrolabe treatise that was translated into both Latin and Hebrew, and circulated in Europe into the fifteenth century. Signs that astrolabes had reached Europe by 1000 emerge from the earliest known Latin manuscript about them. Its illustrations of an astrolabe signed by Andalusi astronomer Khalaf ibn al-Mu'adh are accurate enough to have been drawn from life (fig. 5.63). The instrument's Arabic inscriptions are rendered faithfully in kufic script, with the star names transliterated into Latin. Therefore, the manuscript not only evokes familiarity with Arabic and Islamic scientific concepts, but also a concern to illustrate an Andalusi object for a Latin reader, embodying the transmission of knowledge across cultural and linguistic borders.[23]

5.62 *opposite*

Astrolabe, 1026–7. Made in Córdoba, Spain. Brass. Diam. 15.5 cm. National Museums Scotland, Edinburgh, T.1959.62. Given by James H. Farr.

5.63

Manuscript containing illustrations of an Andalusi astrolabe, late 900s–early 1000s. Probably made in Catalonia, Spain. Parchment, ink, wood. H. 25 cm, W. 17.5 cm, D. 4.2 cm. Bibliothèque nationale de France, Latin 7412, fol. 20r–20v.

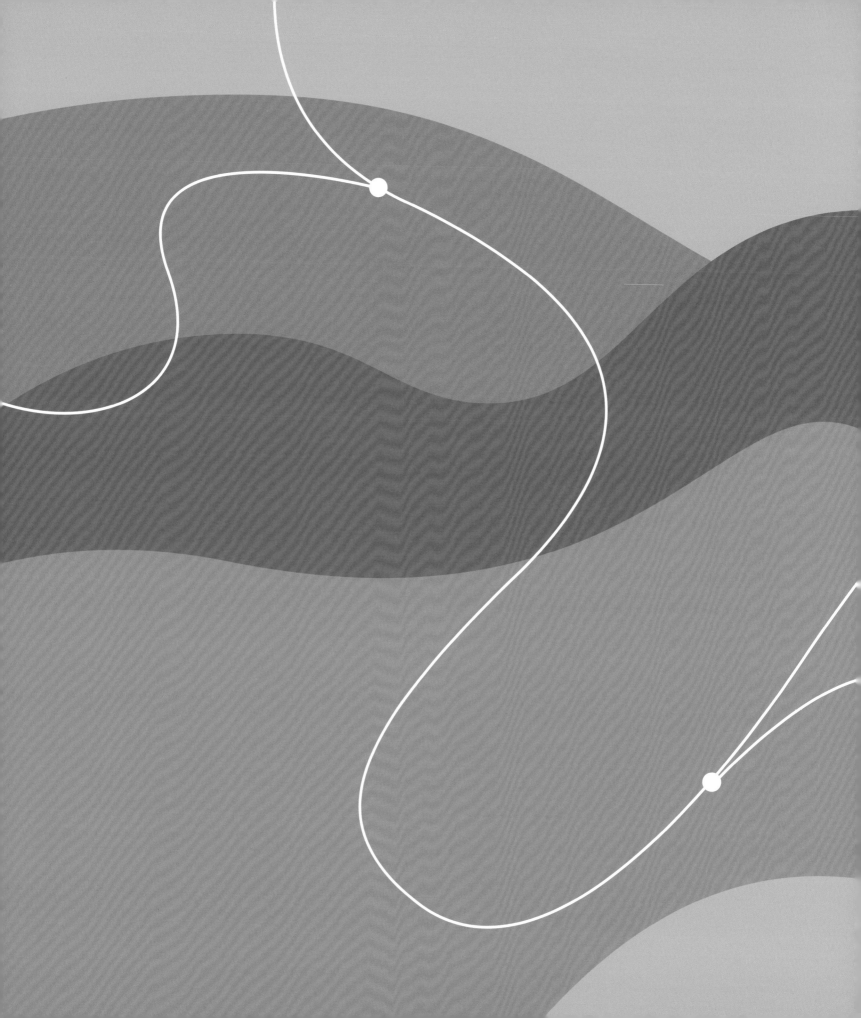

6

NORTHWEST
EUROPE

Northwest Europe

Sue Brunning

From al-Andalus, routes through the Pyrenees linked the Iberian Peninsula to northwest Europe, defined here as the region of present-day France, Germany, the Low Countries, Britain and Ireland (fig. 6.1). This zone rarely features in discussions of the Silk Roads between 500 and 1000, despite growing evidence for contacts with the wider world, including the rest of Europe, the Mediterranean, parts of Africa, West, Central and South Asia and beyond.[1] Northwest Europe was connected by land routes over the Alps to Italy, through Central Europe and the Balkans to the Byzantine empire, along river systems such as the Rhône, Rhine and Danube, and via sea lanes that linked the Baltic and North seas with the Atlantic Ocean and the Mediterranean.[2] Its largely lowland landscape, criss-crossed by waterways and, in places, old Roman roads, was easier to navigate than some Silk Roads networks. Dense forest, marshlands and rushing rivers presented a stiffer challenge, as did the Alps and Pyrenees, which formed soaring, though not impenetrable, barriers to the south. Wintry weather was no impediment, however. Thick snow and ice transformed wild rivers and heavy bogs into navigable routes, indicated by the remains of sledges, skis, bone skates and iron crampons.[3]

The dramatic history of northwest Europe from around 500 to 1000 shaped its connectedness in complex and lasting ways.[4] The end of the Western Roman empire in the late fifth century disrupted ancient links across Continental Europe and around the Mediterranean into Asia. It also fuelled economic, commercial and demographic flux, worsened by climate cooling and bubonic plague, which, in Britain alone, may have killed half the population.[5] The impact was once considered catastrophic, transforming northwest Europe into a backwater. Now, it is understood to have varied regionally. Connectivity fluctuated as routes opened, closed and switched between roads, rivers, seas and back again; but even at the height of its turmoil, the region was never isolated. After the empire, new cultural and ethnic groups migrated into Rome's former lands, some, like the Avars, hailing from far away (see p. 253). The arrival of different languages, practices and material cultures fostered continuity and change, as rulers adopted and adapted existing ways and innovated by blending available ideas.[6]

The late seventh and eighth centuries witnessed economic recovery. Dynamic growth and improving connectivity followed, supported by advances in travel technology and infrastructure. One feature was the development of emporia on North Sea coastal sites such as Ipswich in eastern England, Quentovic in northern France, Dorestad in the Netherlands, and Ribe in Denmark. These busy settlements became hubs for production, exchange, minting and distribution, frequented by merchants operating both regionally and long-distance. Emporia represent an early stage in urbanisation and commercial intensification. They were eclipsed by larger towns from the later ninth century, partly fuelled by Viking activity that boosted overseas links via the *austrvegr* (see pp. 138–45).[7]

6.1

Map of northwest Europe,
c. 500s–800s, showing key locations
discussed in the text.

Most exchange in northwest Europe was local, in bulk and utilitarian. Long-distance exchange, involving small amounts of exotic luxuries travelling by relay, was relatively marginal.[8] However, access to long-distance routes had a wider effect on the region's culture, wealth and social life. Imported goods entered graves, royal and church treasuries, artisanal workshops, monastic scriptoria, medical kits and pantries. South Asian gemstones festooned brooches, buckles and book covers; Byzantine silk wrapped elite bodies in life and death; African elephant ivory was carved into devotional plaques; Afghan lapis and other minerals, such as golden Mediterranean orpiment and Egyptian blue, brightened manuscripts and wall paintings; and Indian peppercorns seasoned meat at royal feasts, its spicy qualities so familiar that they formed the basis of an Old English riddle (see p. 268).[9] Eastern visual culture, fashion and architecture became sources of inspiration. People on the move in northwest Europe included merchants and migrants as well as the enslaved, whose sale boosted northwest Europe's economy at this time (see pp. 16–17).[10] Journeys of pilgrims, scholars, diplomats and mercenaries can be traced in texts and material culture, while bioarchaeology is revealing stories of more ordinary folk who died in Europe but were born far away, such as a girl with West African ancestry at Updown in Kent, eastern Mediterranean individuals in Wales, and North Africans buried with Muslim rites in Nîmes, France. In years to come scientific techniques will continue to reveal the diversity of northwest Europe's demographic, uncovering tales that would otherwise not be told.[11]

Charlemagne's empire

Francia was the most powerful polity to emerge on the lands of the former Western Roman empire. Comprising most of present-day France, the Low Countries and Germany, it was ruled by successive dynasties of Franks, whose power was enhanced by contacts beyond their territorial borders. The Merovingians (c. 481–751), for instance, interacted with their North Sea neighbours, the Byzantine empire to the east, and Visigothic and Islamic Iberia (al-Andalus) to the south. Ecclesiastical institutions and royal courts kept some of their legal records on Egyptian papyrus until around 700. South Asian garnets and foreign silks were popular in elite Merovingian dress, while those in the wider community were sometimes buried with imports, from vessels of Mediterranean glass to tiny beads that have been traced chemically to the Indo-Pacific.[12]

Under the succeeding Carolingian dynasty, Francia developed into the political and economic powerhouse of northwest Europe. Its most celebrated ruler, popularly known as Charlemagne (r. 768–814), forged an empire that stretched from the North Sea into present-day Hungary and Italy. In 800 he was crowned in Rome as emperor, the first in the west since the mid-fifth century. Charlemagne's activities opened new lines of communication with the wider world, crucially the Islamic and Byzantine spheres. Francia's international markets swelled and drew merchants from Ireland, England, Frisia, Scandinavia, Spain, Italy and, as time progressed, from as far away as Iraq. The proceeds, combined with booty from military expansion, bankrolled a cultural and spiritual renaissance that absorbed and modified foreign ideas.[13]

Heirs to Rome

Charlemagne and his courtiers constructed a vision of the Franks as heirs to ancient Rome. They embraced, modified and deployed imperial symbolism from the Roman and Byzantine empires, departing significantly from Frankish traditions, not least in the acclamation of Charlemagne and his heirs as *imperator* (emperor) rather than *rex* (king). Despite his biographer Einhard's claim that Charlemagne shunned 'foreign' clothing for humbler Frankish dress, when he died he was shrouded in a Byzantine 'charioteer' silk and laid inside a carved antique marble sarcophagus.[14]

Charlemagne oversaw the building of palaces at Paderborn (776/7), Ingelheim (c. 787) and, most famously, Aachen (794), which echoed Mediterranean buildings, both outside and within. Entering their halls, visitors walked upon pavements made from mosaic or *opus signinum* (concrete containing crushed brick and ceramic) and encountered glazed windows, painted walls, Roman-style inscriptions and *opus sectile* friezes of coloured marble. The octagonal domed Palatine Chapel at Aachen echoes the plan of the Church of San Vitale at Ravenna in Italy (see p. 206) or the Church of the Holy Sepulchre in Jerusalem. Its outer walls were vibrant pink, clad in mortar mixed with brick dust. The emulation surpassed mere imitation. According to a surviving letter from Pope Hadrian I, Charlemagne's palaces incorporated genuine antique marble wall and flooring panels, statues and porphyry columns transported from sites in Italy. Other features were Frankish adaptations of Roman and Byzantine ideas. Aachen's mosaic flooring, for instance, blended Carolingian imitations with reused antique pieces. Casting-mould fragments indicate that the chapel's 4-metre-high bronze doors were local work, incorporating features such as lion-headed handles that copied Late Antique examples, as seen on surviving ivories.[15] Some ideas may have arrived via another

6.2 *opposite*
The Lothar Psalter, c. 840–55. Made probably in Aachen, Germany. Parchment, ink, gold, wood, leather, silk, velvet, silver and copper alloy. H. 23 cm, W. 19 cm (each page). The British Library, London, Add MS 37768, fol. 4r. Bequeathed by Sir Thomas Brooke in 1908.

6.3
Finger ring with Roman gem, c. 800–900. Silver, sard, gold and glass. H. 3 cm, W. 3 cm, D. 1.6 cm. British Museum, London, AF.495. Bequeathed by Sir Augustus Wollaston Franks.

conduit. The Islamic world was also building monumental palaces and religious structures at this time. It has been theorised that Aachen's extensive use of marble and striped arches drew from alternating dark-and-light stonework utilised in Islamic architecture. Charlemagne's interactions with the 'Abbasid caliphate (pp. 258–9) could have brought such ideas into his orbit.[16]

On a smaller scale, artisans linked to the court crafted fine objects which also blended Roman, Byzantine and Carolingian ideas. Illuminated manuscripts evoke Late Antique purple parchment and use metallic inks, their scribes writing both in Romanising capitals and Caroline Minuscule, a new script adapted from antique examples. Manuscript illuminators painted illusionistic portraits of evangelists in Roman clothing, writing with Roman-style tools between mottled porphyry columns.[17] A psalter made for Charlemagne's grandson, Lothar I (r. 817–55), written primarily in gold Caroline Minuscule, portrays him in the style of a Roman emperor, enthroned against purple and wearing a gem-encrusted cloak (fig. 6.2).

6.4
Diptych leaf remodelled as a book cover panel, made *c.* 500, modified *c.* 800–75. ***Left*** Carolingian carving. ***Right*** planed-down Byzantine carving. Ivory. H. 16.6 cm, W. 10.1 cm. British Museum, London, 1855,0730.2. Purchased from Amédée Bouvier.

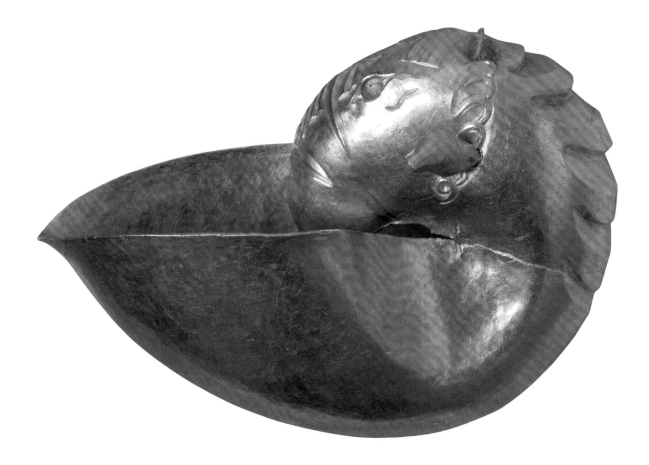

The garment combines blue sapphires, green emeralds and white pearls, favoured in Late Antique and Byzantine visual culture, with red garnets, popular in traditional elite Frankish accoutrements.[18] Coloured gems also adorned deluxe Carolingian metalwork. Again, as seen at Aachen, artisans sometimes incorporated genuine antiques into their productions. A fine example is a ninth-century silver-gilt finger ring, which shows Carolingian-style beasts clasping a Roman gem engraved with a muscular bull (fig. 6.3). Similarly, ivory diptychs were refashioned into new Carolingian plaques that evoked Roman and Byzantine models in their form and imagery (fig. 6.4; see p. 193). Such remodelling could simply reflect restricted access to new elephant ivory via Africa at this time, but it also correlates with the symbolic use of Mediterranean *spolia* in Carolingian contexts.

Charlemagne's treatment of Roman and Byzantine symbolism did not simply copy those cultures. It also projected imperial power, helping to portray him as an equal alongside his Byzantine and Islamic rivals to the east, while simultaneously promoting Carolingian culture by bringing local ideas into the cultural mix. His palace at Paderborn embodies these attitudes. Raised on Saxon territory beyond the old Roman frontier, it brought his brand of *Romanitas* to new lands.

6.5

Vessel in the shape of a nautilus shell, probably 700s. Found in Sânnicolau Mare (formerly Nagyszentmiklós), Romania. Gold. H. 10.6 cm, W. 15.8 cm. Antikensammlung, Kunsthistorisches Museum, Vienna, VIIb.5. Purchased from Kristóf Nákó (Nákó Sándor), landowner in Nagyszentmiklós, 1799.

Avars

In 791 Charlemagne's armies attacked the Avars, based in Central Europe but with a more distant origin. Originally nomadic, they migrated west from the northeast Asian steppe after conflicts with Turkic-speaking groups (see chapter 3), establishing themselves in the Carpathian Basin (present-day Hungary) by the later sixth century. They developed a powerful realm headed by a khagan, whose formidable horse-riding warriors agitated, with mixed success, against Constantinople. Early Avar wealth, fuelled by Byzantine loot and tribute, is displayed in elite burials containing precious metal belt-sets, weapons, composite bows, gold-wrapped staffs, and the remains of horses with fine trappings. Thousands more regular burials demonstrate a gradual coalescence from a multiethnic culture incorporating elements from Asia, the Black and Mediterranean seas, Slav lands and western Europe, into a more homogenous one, indicating assimilation between groups that coexisted in and around the Avar realm. By the time of Charlemagne's invasion, Avar culture was less military and more sedentary, but links with northeast Asia persisted. Archaeological and written evidence indicates continuity of traditions such as hair-braiding, fighting methods and the use of titles like 'khagan' in Avar social hierarchies.[19]

Avar wealth and connections are summed up by a dazzling treasure of twenty-three gold vessels found at Sânnicolau Mare (formerly Nagyszentmiklós) in Romania, probably made in the Carpathian Basin in the eighth century. One piece imitates an Indo-Pacific nautilus shell, its spiral part adapted into an animal's head (fig. 6.5). The vessel's naturalistic style hints that it was modelled on a real shell, perhaps obtained via trade that brought such items into Europe. Imagery on other items, such as winged felines, horned lions, griffins, frog-hunting birds, a backwards-turned rider and an apparent version of the Greek myth of Ganymede, indicate goldsmiths familiar with Mediterranean, Byzantine, Sasanian and steppe arts. One bowl highlights the complexity of such exchanges (fig. 6.6). A dramatic scene on its underside, showing a griffin seizing a goat, may have drawn on Byzantine silks illustrating the story of Bahram Gur, a fifth-century Sasanian king. The Byzantine fabrics themselves may have adapted ideas from early Islamic silks that, in turn, drew upon older Sasanian traditions. The wide popularity of animal fighting scenes from the East Asian steppe to the Roman empire makes it difficult to pinpoint the precise channels of inspiration. This is also true of the griffin, which was a common late Avar symbol with an ancient and dispersed iconographic past. Inside the bowl, a Byzantine-style open-work roundel depicting a cross is surrounded by an inscription apparently in a Turkic language but written in Greek script. The prominence of the cross inside the bowl, relegating the traditional animal scene to the back, is a tantalising clue that the Avars had been exposed to Christianity, probably via Constantinople, by this period.[20]

The Sânnicolau Mare/Nagyszentmiklós treasure also reflects a more violent cross-cultural exchange. Its vessels, fine enough for the khagan himself, evoke the colossal spoils which Charlemagne's forces seized from the Avar political centre, known as the Ring, in 796. The treasure probably escaped the same fate by being hidden before the attack. Charlemagne's plunder was so immense that it made the news in England, where annals written in York reported that fifteen four-ox wagons were required to shift it. This wealth boost came at a time when Charlemagne was cultivating his imperial vision for Francia. It enabled him to endow friends, rivals and religious institutions in the manner of an emperor distributing largesse, while also supporting his imperialising symbolism. The metallic inks that characterise fine manuscripts made after the conquest may have derived, in part, from molten Avar gold.[21]

6.6

Inscribed bowl, probably 700s. Found in Sânnicolau Mare (formerly Nagyszentmiklós), Romania. Gold. Diam. 12 cm, H. 3.2 cm. Antikensammlung, Kunsthistorisches Museum, Vienna, VIIb.34. Purchased from Kristóf Nákó (Nákó Sándor), landowner in Nagyszentmiklós, 1799.

Liturgical luxuries

Before the Avar conflict, Charlemagne's defeat of the Lombards in 774 brought control over parts of Italy and its valuable eastern connections through ports such as Ravenna and Venice. This helped to shrink the distance between the Carolingian, Byzantine and Islamic spheres, invigorating commercial exchange, as symbolised by a Carolingian penny and an Islamic dirham found fused together in Venice's Torcello market district.[22] Contemporary authors highlight Italy as a conduit for eastern wares that were exported north via the Alps, portraying its people as purveyors of imported aromatics, spices and fabrics. Along with the secular elite, the Carolingian Church consumed such imports, some of which were central to liturgy and ritual. Their cost and distant origin may have enhanced their sacredness, while also evoking prestigious links and patronage.[23]

One such commodity was balsam, an aromatic plant resin that was mixed with oil to make chrism, used in sacraments such as baptism. Originating in the eastern Mediterranean, Egypt or Arabia, it was strictly controlled by Islamic authorities, inspiring, in one documented case, somewhat creative procurement. Willibald, an extraordinarily well-travelled English monk, missionary and bishop in Francia,

6.7

Chrismatory, *c.* 700–800. Made in England or northern France. Copper alloy, silver, gold and wood. H. 15.6 cm, W. 12.6 cm, D. 5.8 cm. Wyvern Collection. Purchased from Sam Fogg in 2007.

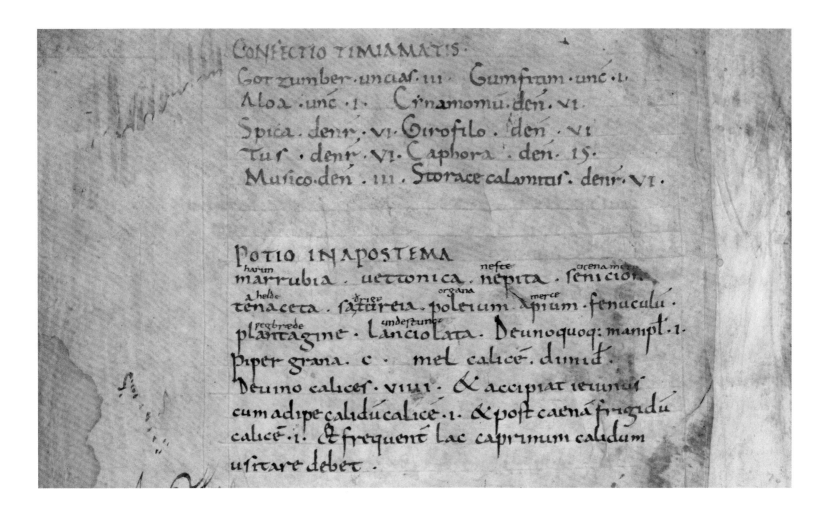

CONFECTIO TIMIAMATIS·

Cozumber·uncas·iii   Gumfram·unc·i·
Aloa·unc·i·   Cinamomu·den·vi·
Spica·denr·vi·Girofilo·den·vi
Tur·denr·vi·Caphora·den·15·
Musico·den·iii·Storace calamtis·denr·vi·

POTIO INAPOSTEMA
marrubia·   uettonica·   nepita·   senicion·
tenaceta·   satureia·poleium apium·fenuculu·
plantagine·   lanciolata·   Deunoquoq: mampl·i·
piper grana·c·   mel calice·dimid·
Deuino calice·viui·& accipiat ieunus
cum adipe caliducalice·i·&post caena frigidu
calice·i·& frequent lac caprinum calidum
usitare debet·

6.8

Detail of a manuscript with incense recipe (upper text), c. 800–1000. Made in Saint-Vaast, Arras, France. Ink on parchment. H. 25.2 cm, W. 35.5 cm (open). Corpus Christi College Library, Cambridge, MS 223, p. 2. Given by Daniel Rogers.

attempted to smuggle it through customs at Tyre (in present-day Lebanon) by pouring it into a dried gourd, covering it with a hollow reed and filling the rest with mineral oil. This petroleum-based substance masked the balsam's telltale aroma when officials performed a sniff test, enabling Willibald to escape with his precious cache, and his life, since the penalty for smuggling was death. Balsam's value is further evoked by a rare surviving chrismatory, a container for scented chrism. Made in England or Northern France, it was richly gilded and embellished over generations of use. Its Greek and Latin inscriptions are another reminder of Christendom's geographical scope (fig. 6.7).[24]

Incense was liturgically indispensable, burned on saintly altars and in censers to perfume religious structures, from small churches to soaring cathedrals. Recipes preserved in Carolingian manuscripts show the range of available ingredients. Some were local plants like fennel, but others had journeyed thousands of kilometres. One recipe, added to a manuscript made in Saint-Vaast, France, uses only imported substances, including aromatic cozumber and confitum from West Asia or East Africa, frankincense from Arabia, camphor, aloe wood and storax from Southeast Asia, cinnamon from South or Southeast Asia, musk and spikenard from the Himalayas, and cloves from eastern Indonesia (fig. 6.8). The absence of cozumber, confitum and camphor in earlier Greek and Roman recipes suggests that these aromatics were introduced to western Europe during the Carolingian period. While such commodities became increasingly available over time, they retained a special aura, evoked by their use as elite gifts across the Carolingian empire.[25]

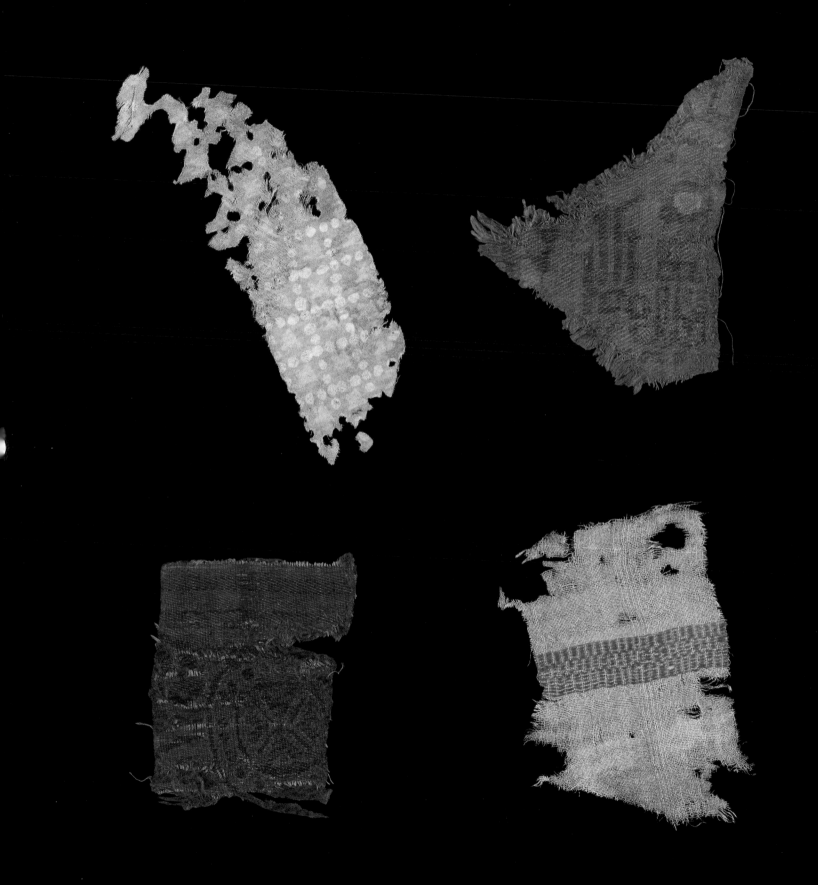

Of all imports consumed by the Carolingian Church, silk played the most
visible role. Its preservation in church treasuries offers a glimpse of Francia's
once-magnificent silken culture. Sumptuous fabrics, woven in the Byzantine
empire, Islamic lands and beyond, clothed living ecclesiastics and dead saints,
as well as manuscripts, altars, furniture and holy relics. Collections of relic
wrappings, though composed of tiny scraps, provide a panorama of the Church's
connections. Technical and scientific analysis of silk wrappings preserved in the
medieval reliquary of Saint Eustace of Basel, Switzerland, has suggested a range
of origins. One probably seventh-century fragment, decorated with a yellow-
and-white resist-dyed pattern, bears parallels with Chinese silks and is coloured
with dyes including sappanwood, native to India, Southeast Asia and most of
China. Another pink-ish piece dated between the mid-seventh and mid-eighth
centuries features a Central Asian-style bird-in-roundel motif (see p. 136), and
has an unusual dye combination indicating manufacture in Central or West
Asia. Two other early medieval fragments, one a rich blue and the other white
with a mauve stripe, were probably made closer to home in the Mediterranean,
signalled by the use of dyes such as madder, indigo and weld in the first piece,
and kermes with cochineal in the second (fig. 6.9).[26]

Remarkably, complete silk vestments also survive from early medieval Europe,
albeit after the Carolingian period. Outstanding among them is a chasuble (a
priest's sleeveless garment worn during Mass) associated with Saint Albuin, made
from rose-purple silk patterned with enormous black and gold eagles (fig. 6.10).
Dated to around 1000, it evokes the extravagant vestments worn by Frankish
bishops from the ninth century onwards, while again demonstrating elite
emulation of imperial Mediterranean culture. Its vivid colour, achieved with costly
Tyrian purple dye, along with the eagles, emblematic of emperors since antiquity,
epitomise the Byzantine court, where the fabric was undoubtedly woven. Having
reached Albuin as a gift from the Holy Roman emperor, who himself most likely
received it from the Byzantine emperor, the chasuble illustrates the way in which
prized foreign items arrived in Europe, hand to hand, via overlapping networks
that spanned vast distances.[27]

Relations with the Islamic world

During the eighth century, Carolingian and Islamic territorial expansion brought the two worlds more firmly into each other's orbit. The establishment of al-Andalus on the Iberian Peninsula created a border zone between them, fuelling periodic military incursions as well as trade, while Charlemagne's seizure of Lombard Italy improved links to the eastern caliphate. Diplomatic exchanges took place both before and after Charlemagne, but the most celebrated instances occurred between him and the ʿAbbasid caliph, Harun al-Rashid (r. 786–809), based in Baghdad, one of the most populous and cosmopolitan cities of the age. Carolingian sources record three embassies to Harun, in 797, 802 and 809, and at least two from Harun to Charlemagne, in 801 and 807. The objectives behind these meetings are unclear, but political, economic and military concerns may be assumed, especially given their common Byzantine rival. Historically, Charlemagne has been seen as the primary beneficiary, perceived as the more 'junior' power of the two, but recent research has recalibrated the relationship by viewing the embassies within each side's political context. For Charlemagne, the exchanges may have boosted his claim to imperial standing while, for Harun, they demonstrated his far-reaching influence at a time of domestic strife. Certainly, such long and arduous journeys would not have been embarked upon lightly, given that all but one of Charlemagne's envoys, a Jewish man named Isaac, died on the first round trip to Baghdad.[28]

According to Carolingian sources, the embassies exchanged gifts from each side's respective realms. Charlemagne offered horses, hunting dogs and prized red fabrics, while Harun sent silks, aromatics, ivory chess pieces, a multicoloured tent, a water clock and, most remarkably, an elephant named Abu al-ʿAbbas. The beast's origin, whether African or Indian, is debated, but he captured Frankish imaginations. The Irish monk Dicuil (active 825) wrote that many Franks had the opportunity to see the elephant, including perhaps an illuminator at the Abbey of Saint-Denis near Paris, who embellished an initial 'B' with a lifelike elephant's head.[29] The later emperor Otto III's gift of an elephant-patterned silk for Charlemagne's tomb around 1000 hints that memories of Abu lingered for centuries. Possibly, part of Abu himself survived, too. An ivory plaque depicting the Virgin Mary, which, unusually, was not recycled from an antique ivory, has a radiocarbon age estimated to the time of the elephant's death in 810. Intriguingly, only one Carolingian pyxis, a vessel of tusk-like cylindrical form, survives and has been attributed to an Aachen workshop at around the same date (fig. 6.11). Given the apparent dearth of fresh ivory at the time, it is tempting to speculate that Abu's tusks supplied the material for these pieces.[30]

Another object could be related, albeit cautiously, to the embassies. It is a Carolingian-style silver-gilt cross brooch dated to the late eighth or early ninth century, with a central setting that was custom-made for an Islamic glass seal (fig. 6.12). The seal's angular, wheel-cut Arabic inscription, reading *tubna lillah*, 'We have repented to God', finds its closest parallels in the eastern Islamic world, indicating a potential point of origin. Traditionally, the seal's arrival in Francia has been explained as the result of Viking exchange with Islamic lands, which peaked during the ninth and tenth centuries (see pp. 143–5).[31] However, the Carolingian–ʿAbbasid embassies around 800 offer an alternative scenario that aligns more closely with the brooch's date of manufacture. The seal, perhaps set into a finger ring, could have been carried to Charlemagne's court by a member of Harun's retinue, eventually entering Frankish hands through unknowable means, such as an accidental loss, or even as a gift between ambassadorial counterparts. The recipient may then have had it set into a bespoke brooch which, as an intercultural composite, symbolised and commemorated collaboration between individuals from different cultures and faiths.[32]

Unfortunately, the real story behind this remarkable object remains a tantalising mystery. However, an ambassadorial context offers a speculative challenge to another popular theory about the brooch. Its likeliest orientation sets the seal's inscription vertically rather than horizontally, fuelling the view that the brooch's maker and wearer were ignorant of Arabic. This seems less plausible if the seal was, indeed, acquired via direct interaction with Arabic speakers. While there is little evidence for Arabic literacy in Francia, growing contacts with Arabic-speaking communities may have increased familiarity with the language among those who were involved (directly or indirectly) in commerce and diplomacy, not only with the 'Abbasid east, but also with al-Andalus to the south.[33] Indeed, a silver-gilt Carolingian pyxis, made in the mid-ninth century and found in Spain, could relate to diplomacy between Charlemagne's grandson Charles the Bald (r. 843–77) and the Andalusi emir Muhammad I (852–86).[34] Arabic speakers may even have moved in the elite circles that produced the brooch. Among them could have been Isaac, the Jewish diplomat who led Charlemagne's first embassy to Baghdad, and the Iberian Theodulf, who became bishop of Orléans at around the same time (*c.* 798–818). Such exchanges between the Frankish and Islamic spheres do appear to have fostered cross-linguistic awareness on both sides. Theodulf, for instance, wrote that he could recognise Arabic writing on gold coins, while Ibn al-Nadim, who compiled the renowned bibliographic catalogue *Kitab al-fihrist* in tenth-century Baghdad, claims to have known Frankish writing from imported inscribed swords and a diplomatic letter sent by a Frankish queen to Caliph al-Muktafi (r. 902–8). In this light, the seal's orientation could be interpreted, very tentatively, as a sign not of ignorance, but of recognition that its text communicated in a language that was written and read differently from Latin and Frankish: right to left, rather than the opposite.

Britain and Ireland

Leaving Francia, maritime routes connected the European continent with Britain and Ireland. The perception of these islands as remote and seabound was discussed by early authors in Britain, such as Gildas (d. 570) and Bede (d. 735). Knowledge of distant lands inevitably diminished this far west, often relying upon fantastical depictions in texts like *The Marvels of the East*. Nonetheless, the surrounding seas were connective tissue, linking Britain and Ireland to networks that supported contact across the Silk Roads map.[35]

Imports and identity after Rome

Archaeology has helped to dispel the view that Britain was plunged into isolation after Roman rule ended in the early fifth century. The presence, in various contexts, of imports demonstrates that long-distance connections endured. Although it is not clear whether their origins were always understood, the ways in which foreign items were used suggest that they were prized, and played an active role in social dynamics, from expressions of identity to political relations.

In England between the fifth and late seventh centuries, this story is chiefly narrated through the dead, who were cremated or buried with objects. Some graves contained well-travelled items, such as vessels of eastern Mediterranean glass, Red Sea cowrie shells, African ivory pouch-rings, and beads of Egyptian glass, South Asian amethyst and Baltic amber. The geographical distribution of such items suggests a degree of controlled access, probably through local leaders. Their ownership and display, therefore, may have conveyed certain social and political affiliations.[36]

Far more unusual, however, are imports found in a small group of spectacular burials dating to the late sixth and early seventh centuries. Their extravagant contents and monumentality, incorporating wooden chambers, earth mounds and even ships, indicate occupants of the highest status, hence their popular categorisation as 'princely'. The exceptional imports placed in these burials are widely interpreted as gifts exchanged across networks that linked rulers from Britain to Byzantium.[37] A silver platter from the ship burial at Sutton Hoo in Suffolk, eastern England, offers a theoretical scenario. Control stamps, similar in function to modern hallmarks, indicate that it was crafted in Constantinople during the reign (491–518) of Emperor Anastasius I. The historian Gregory of Tours (d. 594) records that Anastasius made the Frankish king Clovis a consul in 508, investing him with Byzantine-coded gifts including a purple tunic, a *chlamys* (cloak) and perhaps other luxuries that were not explicitly mentioned, such as silverware. According to both Gregory and Bede, Clovis' great-granddaughter, Bertha, married King Æthelberht of Kent in *c.* 580, a transaction that also involved gifts. At this time, Kent had control of East Anglia, where Sutton Hoo is located. As part of this relationship, the East Anglian king, Rædwald, accepted Christianity along with presents to mark the occasion. These special tokens may have accompanied him back to East Anglia where, eventually, one or more may have been selected for burial in the Sutton Hoo ship. Though entirely conjectural, this hypothesis presents a feasible mechanism of elite exchange which could have conveyed objects, in stages and over time, from a Byzantine workshop to an East Anglian burial ground.[38]

Tantalisingly, recent research has proposed a more direct channel of acquisition for certain imports with a distinctly Syrian flavour. According to contemporary texts, in 575 the Byzantine empire recruited mercenaries from

6.13

Coat of mail armour, early 600s. Found at Sutton Hoo, Suffolk, England. Iron and copper. H. 7.9 cm, W. 60 cm, D. 30 cm. British Museum, London, 1939,1010.92. Donated by Mrs Edith M. Pretty.

6.14

Flagon, *c.* 500–600. Found in Prittlewell, Essex, England. Copper alloy. H. 21.9 cm, Diam. 13.3 cm. Southend Museums, Prittlewell, SOUMS:A2019.6.1. Transferred to Southend Museums, Southend City Council, post excavation.

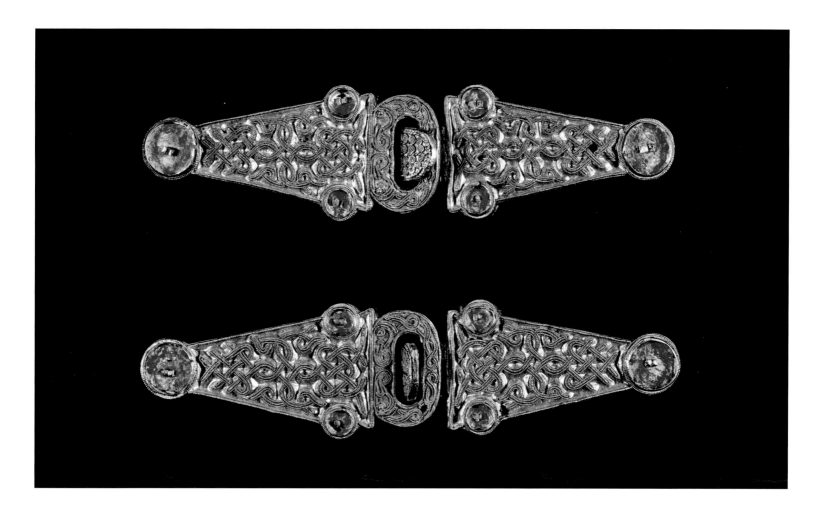

6.15

Clasps, c. late 500s–early 600s.
Found in Taplow, Buckinghamshire,
England. Copper alloy and gold.
H. 2.9 cm, D. 0.9 cm (loop); H. 3 cm,
D. 1.3 cm (hook); W. 11.7 cm (overall).
British Museum, London, 1883,1214.2–3.
Donated by Rev. Charles T.E. Whateley.

beyond the Alps for a war against the Sasanian empire (572–91; see pp. 198–200). Kitted out and paid in gold, these hired warriors campaigned into Syria, their movements suggested by finds of northwest European-style objects along the way. Some are inscribed with northern names, like that of 'Framarich', engraved on a silver chalice found in the Beqaa Valley in Lebanon. England's Byzantine links, evidenced increasingly at sites such as Rendlesham near Sutton Hoo, make it a plausible supplier of mercenary fighters to these campaigns. If so, the 'princely' burials, which occur at this time, may be those of soldiers who joined the cause and were buried with items collected during their eastern service.[39] At Sutton Hoo, such pieces include bitumen chunks chemically provenanced to Syria, perhaps acquired for curative qualities that were well known in traditional Persian medicine. There are also wool garments woven in a Syrian style, and a coat of mail armour (fig. 6.13), unique in England but common in the Byzantine army. Its iron rings are fixed with copper rivets, echoing a mid-third-century CE mail-armour fragment from Dura-Europos in Syria.[40]

At Prittlewell in Essex, eastern England, a copper-alloy flagon has a Syrian connection. It was customised with a bracelet showing the soldier–saint Sergius, whose shrines at Sergiopolis may have attracted mercenaries. The flagon was perhaps a pilgrim's vessel for water or holy oil, with its handle doubling as a loop for a saddle (fig. 6.14), summoning up the extraordinary image of a mounted northern soldier traversing the desert.[41] A burial at Taplow in Buckinghamshire, southeastern England, hints that ideas were also absorbed in the east. The deceased person was apparently buried in a red wool wrap-over garment similar to steppe-style riding coats (pp. 123, 135–6, 141 and 203, and figs 3.32 and 5.17) but modified locally with gold-embroidered borders. It was fastened with two clasps that may have adapted the form of eastern models, but were decorated with local-style animal motifs (fig. 6.15). This cut of coat appears on the iconic Sutton Hoo helmet, implying that such garments were favoured by northern European rulers at the time.[42] Ultimately, the mechanisms that brought these items to England are unknowable, although direct acquisition by mercenaries is an attractive and plausible scenario. Nevertheless, the deliberate placement of unusual, eastern-coded objects within the 'princely' burial group appears to signal a desire to convey a specific identity that was closely linked to the Byzantine world and beyond.

Another fashion of eastern origin became entwined with elite identity in England during this period. Garnet cloisonné metalwork, involving the setting of wafer-thin garnets into intricate gold cell-work, developed perhaps in the Black Sea, Caucasus or West Asia region in the early centuries CE. It became fashionable across Europe over the following centuries, as migrant and settled groups adopted and remodelled it to their tastes. The garnets, another foreign element, were sourced from as far away as South Asia. Garnet cloisonné's popularity with western and northern elites has been widely attributed to its Byzantine associations, although its earlier use by the wealthy, powerful Huns under Attila (d. 453 CE) is thought by some to be an overlooked source of inspiration.[43] The Sutton Hoo ship burial has yielded some of the finest surviving examples of garnet cloisonné. Recent scientific analysis has indicated, for the first time, the origin of garnets in some of its pieces, and how they were used to create a rich and intricate effect.

All but one of the analysed pieces combine different types of garnet linked to sources in India and Sri Lanka, in South Asia, and Bohemia (present-day Czechia), in Central Europe. Each type displays subtly different hues ranging from purple to orange. The makers exploited these colour contrasts in their designs. A cross motif on a sword-scabbard button is accentuated by setting orange Bohemian garnets against purple Indian stones (fig. 6.16). On a shoulder-clasp, the maker contrasted purple-red Indian stones in the bodies of two boars with tiny orange-red Bohemian and Sri Lankan 'bristles' along their backs (fig. 6.17).[44] This implies that the maker selected gems by colour rather than source. An imitation buckle from the same sword-scabbard (fig. 6.18) conveys a different impression. Analysis of its gems has indicated a source in Rajasthan, India, which purveyed large, high-quality, purple-red garnets. On the shoulder-clasp, stones of this origin appear to have been reserved for the largest cells, while orange-hued Bohemian and Sri Lankan garnets pick out tinier details. On the buckle, however, the

6.16
Sword-scabbard button, early 600s.
Found at Sutton Hoo, Suffolk, England.
Gold and garnet. H. 2 cm, Diam. 2.1 cm.
British Museum, London, 1939,1010.27.
Donated by Mrs Edith M. Pretty.

smallest stones have also been traced to the Indian source. In this case, their
orangey hue was probably achieved by cutting the stones more thinly. The
virtuoso gem-setting and flawless polishing, visible under microscopy, testify
that no effort was spared in creating this piece. Perhaps the maker chose to use
the same type of garnets throughout because of their superior quality, or simply
because of prestige attached to their Indian origin.[45]

    The cloisonné from Sutton Hoo represents an eye-catching adaptation of
foreign ideas, but such an approach was neither new nor exclusive to England.
Humbler-looking objects from a century earlier tell a similar story of international
connections. Fragments of ceramic tableware and amphorae from elite settlements
in southwest England, Wales, Ireland and Scotland show that, between the late

fifth and mid-sixth centuries, rulers were engaged in far-flung exchange. The amphorae shipped wine, oil and foodstuffs such as nuts, fruits, spices and grain thousands of kilometres from the eastern Mediterranean, through the Gibraltar Strait, via the Iberian and Frankish coasts, to Atlantic Britain and Ireland, where they were probably exchanged for Cornish tin, Irish iron, lead and precious metals. Their sherds occur from Tintagel in Cornwall to Rhynie in northeast Scotland, with many sites in between, such as Dinas Powys in Wales and Dalkey Island in Ireland. The largest haul derives from Tintagel, on the northern Cornish coast, but Rhynie, the most northerly findspot, lies 40 kilometres inland, signalling how far these coveted items could travel (figs 6.19–6.20). The correlation with high-status sites, such as hill forts, implies that such products were intrinsic to elite identity and lifestyle. Feasting upon Mediterranean food and drink in such settings enabled rulers to cast themselves in a cosmopolitan role, evoking the prestigious, powerful Byzantine empire and their connections to it.[46]

6.19 *opposite*

Amphora fragments, 500–600. Found at Tintagel Castle, Cornwall. Ceramic. H. 13.1 cm (largest piece). British Museum, London, 1949,0501.1-3, 18-19, 24, 27. Donated by Inspectorate of Ancient Monuments.

6.20

Amphora fragments, 500–600. Found in Rhynie, Aberdeenshire, Scotland. Ceramic. H. 15.5 cm, W. 9 cm (largest piece). University of Aberdeen, SF042, SF044, SF1822, SF161110, SF161153. Excavated by the Department of Archaeology, University of Aberdeen.

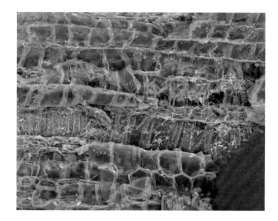

6.21

Top Psalter cover, late 700s. Found in Faddan More, County Tipperary, Ireland. Leather and papyrus. H. 31 cm, W. 25.5 cm, D. 4.7 cm. National Museum of Ireland, Dublin, 06E0786:13.
Bottom Variable pressure scanning electron microscopy (SEM) image of papyrus sample 4 from the psalter lining cover, 2010.

6.22 *opposite*

Window head, window glass, wall plaster and flooring fragments, *c.* 700s. Found in Jarrow, Tyne and Wear, England. Stone, glass, plaster and concrete. Window head: H. 30.5 cm, W. 56 cm, D. 21.5 cm; other fragments: L. 9.7 cm, W. 9 cm, D. 4.5 cm (largest piece). Jarrow Hall, Tyne and Wear, England. Transferred from the Archaeology Department at Durham University.

Britain and Ireland in Christendom

The adoption of Christianity in early medieval Britain and Ireland facilitated access to a Christian network that traversed the Continent, the Mediterranean and beyond. Gradually, the islands developed regionally diverse Christian cultures that adapted ideas from near and far, highlighting religion's leading role in cultural connections and exchange.

Christianity had been practised in Ireland and parts of Britain since the fifth century. The faith apparently declined in Britain's lowlands after the end of Roman rule, in tandem with the arrival of non-Christian Germanic-speaking groups from the Continent, but in Ireland it flourished. During the sixth and seventh centuries, a well-connected monastic culture developed there, which spread to Britain and overseas, with the foundation of Irish houses as far afield as Italy. Irish monks, pilgrims, missionaries and scholars travelled across the Continent, evangelising, establishing monastic scriptoria, attending Church councils and visiting holy sites, their efforts contributing to Christian culture and learning wherever they went.[47] A late eighth-century psalter, preserved in a bog at Faddan More, County Tipperary, has fuelled speculation that the eastern Mediterranean Church in places such as Syria and Egypt inspired aspects of Irish monastic practice, art and manuscript traditions.[48] The psalter's leather cover, a unique survival in western Europe, provokes tantalising questions about its origin. The wrap-around form, binding style and papyrus lining, identified scientifically (fig. 6.21), are best paralleled in Egypt, raising the possibility that the cover was imported, or acquired by travelling Irish clerics in a Christian hub, such as Rome. However, strikingly similar book covers are illustrated in broadly contemporary Irish Gospel books. This presents an alternative scenario, in which the cover was locally made but drew upon foreign ideas and materials such as the papyrus, available from Merovingian Francia or Rome. The manuscript found with the cover was certainly a local production, judging from its materials and script.[49] Notably, the cover does not fit the manuscript, indicating that the two components were made separately and brought together. The psalter therefore blends resources, technologies and ideas from cultures that, though geographically divided, were united by the Christian faith.

Mediterranean currents in England's early Church

Irish clerics played a key role in bringing Christianity to the kingdoms of early medieval England, but missionaries from Rome were also significant. Bede narrates their arrival in Kent in 597, headed by Augustine and laden with Mediterranean-style liturgical equipment, vestments and sacred books.[50] The ensuing blend of different Christian traditions across England gave its Church a hybrid quality from the start, visible in its nuanced architecture, material culture, scholarship and art.

An important witness to this phenomenon is Monkwearmouth-Jarrow, a twin monastery founded in the kingdom of Northumbria in 673 (Monkwearmouth) and 681 (Jarrow), respectively. According to Bede, its founder, Benedict Biscop (*c.* 628–689), inspired by visits to Rome, imported foreign stonemasons and glaziers to construct buildings in a style that had been absent from Britain since Roman rule. Excavations at Jarrow support Bede's account, uncovering, among other structures, a guest house with dressed stone window heads, multicoloured window glass, red-striped plaster and *opus signinum* flooring (fig. 6.22). The monastery's Mediterranean aspect was amplified by its contents, which Biscop imported or acquired overseas, including relics, vestments, sculptures, paintings, books, vessels and liturgical equipment. The latter may have included objects similar to a sixth-

or seventh-century Byzantine censer found at Glastonbury Abbey, which still contains the residue of an aromatic resin, probably myrrh or olibanum.[51]

Mediterranean ideas also shaped early Christian learning, conveyed for instance by scholars who travelled to England from afar. Around 669, the Pope despatched Abbot Hadrian (d. 709), born in North Africa, and Theodore (602–690), from Tarsus in Turkey, to reorganise England's nascent Church. These distinguished Greek-speaking scholars, who had trained in centres in North Africa, the eastern Mediterranean and Rome, established a school at Canterbury, Kent, which became an unparalleled intellectual centre. Bede's account of the school, together with the so-called *Canterbury Commentaries* comprising notes taken during teaching, evoke its astonishingly diverse curriculum, covering Greek, Latin, law, astronomy, medicine, music and computus, much of which was based on Hadrian and Theodore's knowledge of scholarship from Rome to Antioch. It was here that the scholar Aldhelm encountered the work of the Late Antique North African poet Symphosius, which inspired him to compose works that formed the basis of the Old English riddling tradition (fig. 6.23).[52]

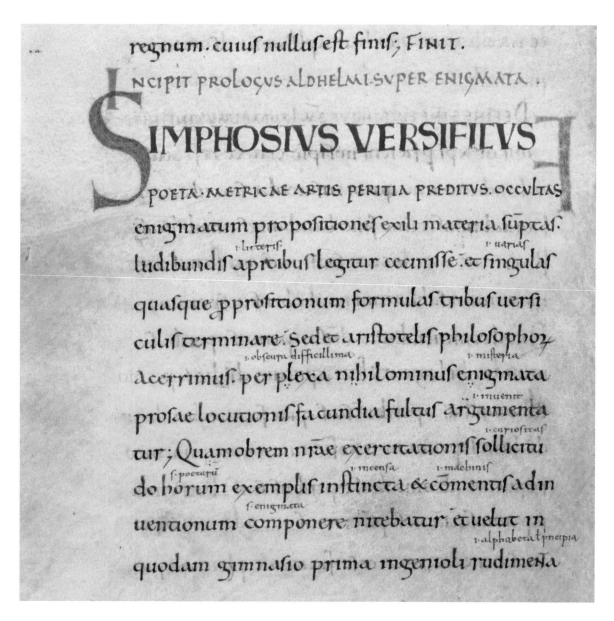

6.23

Detail of a manuscript containing Aldhelm's *Riddles*, *c.* 1000. Made at Christ Church, Canterbury, England. Parchment, ink, leather and gold. H. 26 cm, W. 19 cm (each page). The British Library, London, fol. 79v, Royal MS 12 C XXIII. Presented by George II in 1757.

6.24

Stone sculpture, *c.* 800. Found at Lichfield Cathedral, Lichfield, England. Limestone. H. 63.5 cm, W. 37 cm, D. 32.3 cm (separate pieces combined). Lichfield Cathedral, Lichfield, LCA 0923. Excavated at Lichfield Cathedral, 2003.

Christian art absorbed and adapted foreign ideas, too, traceable through illuminated manuscripts, ivory carvings and stone sculptures. A series of eastern-flavoured stone carvings was made for religious buildings in the kingdom of Mercia, central England, during the reign of Offa (757–96). The church at Breedon on the Hill, Leicestershire, rewarded visitors who climbed the hill with a spectacle of cavorting lions, peacocks, griffins, centaurs, eagles and *buraqs* (winged equines) drawn from eastern Mediterranean and Sasanian traditions.[53] The beasts are joined by religious figures, including the Virgin Mary and an angel, who raise their right hands in the Byzantine form of blessing with the thumb and ring finger touching. The finest sculpture of this period is another angel, excavated from within Lichfield Cathedral in 2003 (fig. 6.24). Its extraordinary preservation permits a full appreciation of its Late Antique and eastern Mediterranean features, expressed in the 'Insular' art style popular in Britain and Ireland. These include the elegantly draped clothing, delicate feathered wings and finely modelled hair. Particularly striking are the eyes, drilled for glass inserts that once made them glitter with life. This feature, also seen at Breedon, is thought to be a Byzantine effect that transferred westwards, perhaps via imported ivories and icons.[54]

West and Central Asian connections

Traditionally, early medieval Britain and Ireland are thought to have possessed limited information about the world beyond Byzantium into West and Central Asia, both before and during Islamic rule. However, artefacts reached northern Europe from and via West Asia, while letters between clerics in Continental Europe, Britain and Ireland during the eighth century signal awareness of Muslim expansion, at least in literate circles.[55] Some of the islands' inhabitants even possessed first-hand knowledge. Theodore and Hadrian probably fled the Mediterranean during Muslim expansion, and references in the *Canterbury Commentaries* to West Asian flora, fauna and material culture, as well as the term 'Saracens' (applied to Muslims in texts at this time) may derive from their eyewitness accounts. Pilgrims who visited eastern Christian sites now under Islamic rule returned not only with objects such as Willibald's balsam (see pp. 254–5), but also with information. The Irish abbot Adomnán of Iona (d. 704) recorded a supposedly first-hand account of Jerusalem from Arculf, a Frankish bishop whose homeward ship was blown off course to Britain. The tale crossed to Northumbria where Bede summarised it, lauding its value to those whose worldly knowledge came from reading rather than travel.[56]

Traces of Central Asian connections emerge from surviving objects, too. A mid-ninth-century Carolingian silver-gilt cup, buried with a hoard in North Yorkshire (fig. 6.25), displays aspects of form and decoration that echo metalwork made in the Sasanian tradition. Its animal-inhabited roundels, interspersed with plants, may adapt an influential motif that traversed different media (see p. 136). Such ideas could have journeyed west with artisans displaced by Islamic expansion, or via imported objects. Astonishingly, an example of the latter may have been discovered in Balmaghie in Dumfries and Galloway, Scotland: a similarly shaped and decorated cup, found wrapped in textiles and containing silk-wrapped objects (fig. 6.26). The cup's decorative roundels, revealed through the wrappings by 3D X-ray imaging, indicate an even closer affinity with Central Asia. Particularly suggestive is a pillar-like motif with a flaming top, which strongly resembles Zoroastrian fire-altars as depicted in Sasanian art (see p. 108). Metallurgical analysis has also indicated an eastern origin for the cup. Its niello inlay has been traced to a Sasanian silver mine, now located in present-day Iran.[57]

Those operating in rarefied, well-connected circles may have been able to acquire a nuanced understanding of the Islamic world. A gold coin minted by the Mercian king Offa so closely resembles a dinar of the 'Abbasid caliph al-Mansur (r. 754–75) that it must have been modelled on a real example, or an excellent copy. Both of its faces bear Arabic inscriptions with only minor errors (fig. 6.27). The obverse cites part of the *Shahadah*, the Islamic declaration of faith, while the reverse gives the model dinar's minting date (157 in the Muslim Hijri calendar, equivalent to 773–4) and refers to the Prophet Muhammad as the 'Apostle of God'. Along with Byzantine gold coins, Islamic gold dinars were high quality and the preferred currency for elite trade in the Mediterranean. Offa's imitation could therefore reflect his awareness of Islamic coinage's prestige and, by association, the caliph's power and wealth, all of which he may have wished to emulate.[58]

Offa's coin, however, includes an intriguing amendment. On the reverse, the minter inserted the Latin phrase *OFFA REX*, 'King Offa', between the lines of Arabic, and inverted in relation to them. This topsy-turvy blend of languages, along with the flawed inscriptions, has been attributed to an ignorance of Arabic, echoing the popular view of the vertically oriented Islamic seal in the Carolingian cross brooch discussed above (see pp. 258–9). However, might it also signal an awareness that Arabic and Latin were written in opposite directions? Tantalisingly, these two objects with unusually positioned Arabic texts were made

6.25 *opposite top*

Cup, mid-800s. Found near Harrogate in North Yorkshire, England. Silver, gold, niello. H. 9.2 cm, Diam, 12 cm. British Museum, London, 2009,8023.1. Jointly acquired with York Museums Trust through the Treasure Act, with contribution from the Art Fund, National Heritage Memorial Fund, British Museum Friends, York Museums Trust and the Wolfson Foundation.

6.26 *opposite bottom*

Lidded cup, probably *c.* 650–800. Found in Balmaghie, Dumfries and Galloway, Scotland. Silver, gold, niello, textile and silk. H. 10 cm. National Museums Scotland, Edinburgh, X.2018.12.71. Acquired with support from the National Heritage Memorial Fund and the Art Fund.

6.27

Dinar coin, *c.* 773–96. Found in Rome, Italy. Minted in the kingdom of Mercia (central England). Gold. Diam. 2 cm, weight 4.3 g. British Museum, London, 1913,1213.1. Purchased from the PWP Carlyon-Britton collection through Sotheby's.

6.28
The Franks Casket, *c.* 700. Probably
made in northern Britain, found in
Auzon, France. Whalebone. H. 13.3 cm,
W. 23.1 cm, D. 19.1 cm. British Museum,
London, 1867,0120.1. Donated by Sir
Augustus Wollaston Franks.

in neighbouring, closely connected realms. As powerful contemporaries, Offa in England and Charlemagne in Francia were in personal contact and occasionally exchanged gifts, recorded in surviving correspondence. These included prized foreign items such as silk cloaks and an Avar sword, which Charlemagne sent to Offa in 796. This channel of communication could certainly have been one means through which Offa acquired a gold dinar of al-Mansur, with whom Charlemagne's father had treated, and, along with it, intelligence about the Islamic world, its power, prestige and language.

Interwoven worlds

The myriad stories told by the surviving art, archaeology, literature and other sources from northwest Europe between *c.* 500 and 1000 belie the age-old paradigm that the region, after the Romans, became a benighted place whose inhabitants knew nothing of, and went nowhere in, the wider world. Instead, a vivid portrait emerges of an interconnected and outward-looking region, a focal point of constant, multidirectional motion, receptive and contributory to the transfer of people, objects and ideas across immense distances. By now, the presence of a South Asian Buddha figure on a small Swedish island (see p. 10) should not surprise. The reasons for, and details of, its epic journey remain uncertain, but the transfer itself is completely credible. Still too often, such out-of-place artefacts are branded as curios or exotica, based on an assumed unawareness of their origin, intended meaning, function and method of manufacture, given that they had travelled so far to get to Europe. Their perceived oddity in a European context is often thought to have granted them symbolic, amuletic or prestigious qualities that elevated them above more familiar, locally made artefacts. This compartmentalisation is easily challenged when imported objects are viewed in a wider geographical perspective.

If the Helgö Buddha embodies tangible exchanges across the Silk Roads, a final object from northwest Europe evokes the parallel, and equally valuable, transfer of intangible commodities such as knowledge, ideas and intellectual concepts. The Franks Casket, made in Northumbria around 700 and now named after its donor to the British Museum, is carved with stories from Jewish history, Christian tradition and Roman and northern mythology, narrated in Latin and Old English, written respectively in Roman and runic letters (fig. 6.28). The casket's form is also foreign-inflected, most likely drawing from Late Antique Mediterranean types. It was clearly made at an intellectual centre such as a monastery, and for an elite patron. Beyond this, it is a mystery. Perhaps it was a moral guide for good Christian rulership, or a kind of universal history lesson;[59] but it is important to eschew its riddling and to view it, too, in an international perspective. It is clear that the casket's iconographic programme was not random, but an artful syncretism of tales designed to convey a message. As such, it reflects a deep and comfortable knowledge of a world of stories and scholarship, which could be mined at will to make just the right point, whatever that may have been. The casket embodies connectedness, made in what many might consider to be an unexpected place and time. Aptly, its most prominent inscription, on the front panel, dedicates the casket not to a king or an archbishop, or even to God, but to the whale from whose bone it was carved: a whale that, until beached on the Northumbrian shore, swam the seas that linked these islands to the rest of the world.

Notes

Introduction

1 Bo Gyllensvärd et al., *Excavations at Helgö XVI: Exotic and Sacral Finds from Helgö* (Stockholm: Almqvist & Wiksell International, 2004); Eric Ramírez-Weaver, 'Islamic Silver for Carolingian Reforms and the Buddha-Image of Helgö: Rethinking Carolingian Connections with the East, 790–820', in *China and Beyond in the Mediaeval Period: Cultural Crossings and Inter-Regional Connections*, Dorothy C. Wong and Gustav Heldt (eds) (Amherst, New York: Cambrian Press, 2014), pp. 171–86.

2 Ramírez-Weaver 2014, p. 173.

3 Matthias Mertens, 'Did Richthofen Really Coin "The Silk Road"?', *The Silk Road*, vol. 17 (2019), pp. 1–9.

4 Ibid., p. 6.

5 On Richthofen's map, see Tamara Chin, 'The Invention of the Silk Road, 1877', *Critical Inquiry*, vol. 40, no. 1 (2013), pp. 194–219.

6 Mertens 2019, p. 6. On Richthofen's idea of the Silk Road, also see Chin 2013; Daniel C. Waugh, 'Richtofen's "Silk Roads": Toward the Archaeology of a Concept', University of Washington Faculty Web Server (2010), faculty.washington.edu/dwaugh/publications/waughrichthofen2010.pdf (accessed 2 April 2024), a revised version of an article in *The Silk Road*, vol. 5, no. 1 (2007), pp. 1–10.

7 Tim Winter, *Geocultural Power: China's Quest to Revive the Silk Roads for the Twenty-First Century* (Chicago, IL: University of Chicago Press, 2019).

8 Chin 2013, p. 196.

9 Peter Hopkirk, *Foreign Devils on the Silk Roads: The Search for the Lost Treasures of Central Asia* (London: John Murray, 2006); Justin Jacobs, *The Compensations of Plunder: How China Lost its Treasures* (Chicago, IL: University of Chicago Press, 2020).

10 Winter 2019, pp. 46-55. Examples of exhibitions include Susan Whitfield and Ursula Sims-Williams (eds), *The Silk Road: Trade, Travel, War and Faith* (London: The British Library, 2004); Arnoud Bijl and Birgit Boelens (eds), *Expedition Silk Road: Journey to the West: Treasures from the Hermitage* (Amsterdam: Museumshop Hermitage Amsterdam, 2014).

11 Susan Whitfield, 'The Expanding Silk Road: UNESCO and BRI', *Bulletin of the Museum of Far Eastern Antiquities*, vol. 81 (2020), pp. 23–42.

12 Winter 2019, p. 70.

13 Tansen Sen, 'Inventing the "Maritime Silk Road"', *Modern Asian Studies*, vol. 57, no. 4 (2023), pp. 1059–104.

14 The policies were initially announced in 2013 as the 'New Silk Road Economic Belt' and the '21st Century Maritime Silk Road'. There are many publications about the Belt and Road Initiative. See, for instance, Ye Min, *The Belt Road and Beyond: State-Mobilized Globalization in China: 1998–2018* (Cambridge: Cambridge University Press, 2020).

15 Winter 2019, pp. 101–32.

16 Susan Whitfield (ed.), *Silk Roads: Peoples, Cultures, Landscapes* (London: Thames & Hudson, 2019), pp. 8–9.

17 For instance, Khodadad Rezakhani, 'The Road that Never Was: The Silk Road and Trans-Eurasian Exchange', *Comparative Studies of South Asia, Africa and the Middle East*, vol. 30, no. 3 (2010), pp. 420–33; Ravi K. Mishra, 'The "Silk Road": Historical Perspectives and Modern Constructions', *Indian Historical Review*, vol. 47, no. 1 (2020), pp. 21–39.

18 On research from the perspective of Chinese sources, see Rong Xinjiang 荣新江, 丝绸之路与东西文化交流 (*The Silk Road and cultural exchanges between East and West*) (Beijing: Beijing daxue chubanshe, 2015); Rong Xinjiang, *The Silk Road and Cultural Exchanges between East and West*, ed. and trans. Sally K. Church et al. (Leiden: Brill, 2023).

19 For instance, James A. Millward, *The Silk Road: A Very Short Introduction* (Oxford: Oxford University Press, 2013), pp. 20–23, 25; Juping Yang, 'Alexander the Great and the Emergence of the Silk Road', *The Silk Road*, vol. 6, no. 2 (2009), pp. 15–22.

20 For instance, Whitfield and Sims-Williams (eds) 2004 focuses on the first millennium CE; Peter Frankopan, *The Silk Roads: A New History of the World* (London: Bloomsbury, 2015), continues to the 1800s, while he goes beyond that timeline in Peter Frankopan, *The New Silk Roads: The Present and Future of the World* (New York: Alfred A. Knopf, 2019).

21 Susan Whitfield, *Life along the Silk Road* (Berkeley, CA: University of California Press, 2015), p. 1; Susan Whitfield, 'Introduction', in Whitfield (ed.) 2019, pp. 14–19, at p. 15.

22 For a recent example focused on Europe, see Josephine Quinn, *How the World Made the West: A 4,000-Year History* (London: Bloomsbury Publishing, 2024).

23 See the global popularity of Frankopan 2015.

24 For instance, Valerie Hansen, *The Silk Road: A New History* (Oxford: Oxford University Press, 2015); Peter Brown, 'The Silk Road in Late Antiquity', in *Reconfiguring the Silk Road: New Research on East-West Exchange in Antiquity*, ed. Victor H. Mair and Jane Hickman (Philadelphia: University of Philadelphia Press, 2014), pp. 15–22; Ronit Yoeli-Tlalim, 'The Silk Roads as a Model for Exploring Eurasian Transmissions of Medical Knowledge: Views from the Tibetan Manuscripts of Dunhuang', in *Entangled Itineraries: Materials, Practices, and Knowledges across Eurasia*, ed. Pamela H. Smith (Pittsburgh, PA: University of Pittsburgh Press, 2019), pp. 47–62; Xin Wen, *The King's Road: Diplomacy and the Remaking of the Silk Road* (Princeton, NJ: Princeton University Press, 2023).

25 Whitfield (ed.) 2019; Frankopan 2015; Sara Ann Knutson, 'Archaeology and the Silk Road Model', *World Archaeology*, vol. 52, no. 4 (2020), pp. 619–38, at p. 619.

26 For instance, Marika Mägi, *In Austrvegr: The Role of the Eastern Baltic in Viking Age Communication across the Baltic Sea* (Leiden: Brill, 2018); Seth M.N. Priestman, *Ceramic Exchange and the Indian Ocean Economy (AD 400–1275)*, British Museum Research Publication 223 (London: The British Museum, 2021); Timothy Power, *The Red Sea from Byzantium to the Caliphate: AD 500–1000* (Cairo and New York: AUC Press, 2012).

27 Fedir Androshchuk, *Vikings in the East: Essays on Contacts along the Road to Byzantium* (Uppsala: Uppsala Universitetet, 2013); Pauline Asingh and Kristian Jensen (eds), *Rus: Vikings in the East* (Moesgaard: Moesgaard Museum, 2022); Charlotte Hedenstierna-Jonson, 'Archaeological Evidence of Contacts between Scandinavia and Central Asia in the Viking Age and the Tang Dynasty', *Bulletin of the Museum of Far Eastern Antiquities*, vol. 81 (2020), pp. 43–64.

28 On issues of mapping the Silk Roads as seen in UNESCO's strategy for the World Heritage list, see Tim Williams, 'Mapping the Silk Roads', in *The Silk Road: Interwoven History*, vol. 1: *Long-distance Trade, Culture, and Society*, ed. Mariko Namba Walta and James P. Ito-Adler (Cambridge: Cambridge Institutes Press, 2015), pp. 1–42.

29 Michael McCormick, *Origins of the European Economy: Communications and Commerce, AD 300–900* (Cambridge: Cambridge University Press, 2001), p. 694; Chris Wickham, *Framing the Early Middle Ages: Europe and the Mediterranean, 400–800* (Oxford: Oxford University Press, 2005), p. 695ff.; Hansen 2015, pp. 3–5; Chris Wickham, *The Donkey and the Boat: Reinterpreting the Mediterranean Economy, 950–1180* (Oxford and New York: Oxford University Press, 2023), pp. 15–16.

30 McCormick 2001, p. 501.

31 Kate Franklin, 'Moving Subjects, Situated Memory: Thinking and Seeing Medieval Travel on the Silk Road', *International Journal of Historical Archaeology*, vol. 24 (2020), pp. 852–76.

32 Williams 2015, p. 17.

33 Whitfield 2015, p. 1; Hansen 2015, pp. 3–6; Millward 2013, p. 6.

34 Whitfield (ed.) 2019, p. 18; Franklin 2020.

35 Victoria Amorós Ruiz and Sonia Gutiérrez Lloret, 'Ceramics in Transition from the First Islamic Period in the Western Mediterranean: The Example of al-Andalus', *Libyan Studies*, vol. 51 (2020), pp. 99–125; Wickham 2005 , p. 693ff.; Whitfield (ed.) 2019, pp. 18–19.

36 Gyllensvärd et al. 2004, p. 23; Ramírez-Weaver 2014, pp. 174–5; Neil Price, *The Children of Ash and Elm* (London: Penguin Books, 2022), p. 446.

37 Johannes Preiser-Kapeller, Lucian Reinfandt and Yannis Stouraitis (eds), *Migration Histories of the Medieval Afroeurasian Transition Zone: Aspects of Mobility between Africa, Asia and Europe, 300–1500 CE* (Leiden: Brill, 2020), pp. 4 - 5.

38 Ibid.; Claudia Rapp, 'Mobility and Migration in Byzantium: Who Gets to Tell the Story?', *Early Medieval Europe*, vol. 31 (2023), pp. 360–79; Claudia Rapp (ed.), *Mobility and Migration in Byzantium: A Sourcebook* (Göttingen: V&R Unipress, 2023); Leslie Brubaker, Rebecca Darley and Daniel Reynolds (eds), *Global Byzantium: Papers from the Fiftieth Spring Symposium of Byzantine Studies* (London and New York: Routledge, 2023); the research project 'EurAsian Transformation', involving the Austrian Academy of Sciences, University of Vienna, Central European University and the University of Innsbruck, 2023–8; Marek Jankowiak and Felix Biermann (eds), *The Archaeology of Slavery in Early Medieval Northern Europe: The Invisible Commodity* (Cham: Springer International Publishing, 2021); Jacek Gruszczyński, Jonathan Shepard and Marek Jankowiak (eds), *Viking-Age Trade: Silver, Slaves and Gotland* (London: Taylor & Francis, 2021); Alice Rio, *Slavery after Rome, 500–1100* (Oxford: Oxford University Press, 2017); Craig Perry et al. (eds), *The Cambridge World History of Slavery*, vol. 2 (Cambridge: Cambridge University Press, 2021); Johannes Preiser-Kapeller, 'Migration', in *A Companion to the Global Early Middle Ages*, ed. Erik Hermans (Leeds: ARC Humanities Press, 2020), pp. 477–509.

39 Susan Whitfield, *Silk, Slaves and Stupas: Material Culture of the Silk Road* (Oakland, CA: University of California Press, 2018), pp. 250–72.

40 McCormick 2001, pp. 733–77; Rio 2017; Janel M. Fontaine, 'Early Medieval Slave-Trading in the Archaeological Record: Comparative Methodologies', *Early Medieval Europe*, vol. 25 (2017), pp. 466–88.

41 Ben Raffield, 'The Slave Markets of the Viking World: Comparative Perspectives on an "Invisible Archaeology"', *Slavery & Abolition*, vol. 40, no. 4 (2019), pp. 682–705; Marek Jankowiak and Felix Biermann, 'Introduction: An "Invisible Commodity"?', in Jankowiak and Biermann (eds) 2021, p. 2; Marek Jankowiak, 'Tracing the Saqaliba: Slave Trade and the Archaeology of the Slavic Lands in the Tenth Century', in Jankowiak and Biermann (eds) 2021, pp. 161–82; Gruszczyński, Shepard and Jankowiak (eds) 2021; Matthew C. Delvaux, 'Transregional Slave Networks of the Northern Arc, 700–900 CE.', PhD thesis, Boston College, Morrissey College of Arts and Sciences Graduate School, 2019.

42 McCormick 2001, pp. 733–77; Michael McCormick, 'New Light on the "Dark Ages": How the Slave Trade Fuelled the Carolingian Economy', *Past & Present*, vol. 177 (2002), pp. 17–54; Jeff Fynn-Paul, 'Empire, Monotheism and Slavery in the Greater Mediterranean Region from Antiquity to the Early Modern Era', *Past & Present*, vol. 205 (2009), pp. 3–40; Youval Rotman, 'Migration and Enslavement: A Medieval Model', in Preiser-Kapeller, Reinfandt and Stouraitis (eds) 2020, p. 405; Jelle Bruning, 'Slave Trade Dynamics in Abbasid Egypt: The Papyrological Evidence', *Journal of the Economic and Social History of the Orient*, vol. 63, no. 5–6 (2020), pp. 682–742, at p. 684, pp. 690–1.

43 Peter Sarris, 'Climate and Disease', in Hermans (ed.) 2020, pp. 511–37, at p. 524.

44 John Haldon et al., 'Plagues, Climate Change, and the End of an Empire: A Response to Kyle Harper's *The Fate of Rome*', parts 1–3 ('Climate', 'Plagues and a Crisis of Empire', 'Disease, Agency and Collapse'), *History Compass*, vol. 16, no. 12 (2018); Marcel Keller et al., 'Ancient Yersinia pestis genomes from across Western Europe Reveal Early Diversification during the First Pandemic (541–750)', *P.N.A.S.*, vol. 116 (2019), e12363–12372; Sarris 2020; Peter Sarris, 'Viewpoint: New Approaches to the "Plague of Justinian"', *Past & Present*, vol. 254 (2022), pp. 315–46.

45 Jane Kershaw et al., 'The Scale of Dirham Imports to the Baltic in the Ninth Century: New Evidence from Archaeometric Analyses of Early Viking Age Silver', *Fornvännen*, vol. 116 (2021), pp. 185–204.

46 Abe Yoshinari et al., 'Did Ancient Glassware Travel the Silk Road? X-ray Fluorescence Analysis of a Sasanian Glass Vessel from Okinoshima Island, Japan', *Journal of Archaeological Science: Reports*, vol. 40, Part A (2021), pp. 1–8.

47 Duncan Sayer, Dominic Powlesland and Allison Stewart, 'Individual Encounters: Capturing Personal Stories with Ancient DNA', *Current Archaeology*, vol. 392 (2022).

48 Whitfield (ed.) 2019, p. 18; Quinn 2024.

49 For useful chronologies of most of the relevant regions during this period, see Preiser-Kapeller, Reinfandt and Stouraitis (eds) 2020; Timothy Venning, *A Chronology of Early Medieval Western Europe 450–1066* (Abingdon: Routledge, 2018); and Hansen 2015, p. xviii.

50 Frances Wood, *Did Marco Polo Go to China?* (New York: Routledge Taylor & Francis Group, 2018) has questioned the veracity of Marco Polo's journey.

51 Erik Hermans, 'Introduction', in Hermans (ed.) 2020, pp. 1–12, at pp. 4–5.

52 Jaś Elsner and Stefanie Lenk (eds), *Imagining the Divine: Art and the Rise of World Religions* (Oxford: Ashmolean, 2017); Jaś Elsner (ed.), *Empires of Faith in Late Antiquity: Histories of Art and Religion from India to Ireland* (Cambridge and New York: Cambridge University Press, 2020).

53 Valerie Hansen, *The Year 1000: When Explorers Connected the World – and Globalization Began* (London: Viking, 2020).

54 A recent project that also connects the extremities of Eurasia is the online exhibition *Nara to Norwich – Explore Arts and Beliefs at the Ends of the Silk Roads*, available at naratonorwich.org (accessed 3 April 2024).

55 For new work focusing on Central Asia see, for instance, the 'Central Asian Archaeological Landscapes' project (CAAL) at the UCL (University College London) Institute of Archaeology, available at uclcaal.org (accessed 2 April 2024).

Three capitals in East Asia

1 I would like to thank Rosina Buckland, Sang-ah Kim, Li Baoping and Hyun-tae Lee for their comments on drafts of this chapter.

2 For a concise introduction to these periods, see Brett L. Walker, *A Concise History of Japan* (Cambridge: Cambridge University Press, 2015).

3 For an overview of Silla Korea, see Soyoung Lee and Denise Patry Leidy (eds), *Silla: Korea's Golden Kingdom* (New York: The Metropolitan Museum of Art, 2013).

4 For an overview of Tang China, see Mark Edward Lewis, *China's Cosmopolitan Empire: The Tang Dynasty* (Cambridge, MA: Belknap Press of Harvard University Press, 2012).

5 Tineke D'Haeseleer, 'China', in *A Companion to the Global Early Middle Ages*, ed. Erik Hermans (Leeds: ARC Humanities Press, 2020), pp. 161–90, at p. 166.

6 For the reasons behind the campaign, see Shao-yun Yang, *Late Tang China and the World 750–907 CE* (Cambridge: Cambridge University Press, 2023a), pp. 39–45.

7 For an introduction to the Shōsōin and the Silk Roads, see, for instance, Hayashi Ryoichi, *The Silk Road and the Shoso-in*, vol. 6 (New York: Weatherhill, 1975); William E. Mierse, 'The Significance of the Central Asian Objects in the Shōsōin for Understanding the International Art Trade in the Seventh and Eighth Centuries', *Sino-Platonic Papers*, vol. 267 (2017), pp. 1–52; Jun Hu, 'Global Medieval at the "End of the Silk Road" circa 756 CE: The Shōsō-in Collection in Japan', *The Medieval Globe*, vol. 3, no. 2 (2017), pp. 177–202. See also resources on the Shōsōin official website: www.kunaicho.go.jp/e-about/shisetsu/shosoin1.html (accessed 3 January 2024).

8 Hayashi 1975, pp. 88–93, fig. 91, fig. 98; Seth Priestman, 'The Silk Road or the Sea? Sasanian and Islamic Exports to Japan', *Journal of Islamic Archaeology*, vol. 3, no. 1 (2016), pp. 1–35, at p. 10; Mierse 2017, pp. 11–12.

9 Priestman 2016, p. 10, citing St John Simpson, 'From San Marco to South Arabia: Observations on Sasanian Cut Glass', in *Facts and Artefact: Arts in the Islamic World: Festschrift for Jens Kröger on his 65th Birthday*, ed. A. Hagedorn and A. Shalem (Leiden: Brill, 2007), pp. 59–88, at pp. 64, 73.

10 Dorothy Wong, *Buddhist Pilgrim-Monks as Agents of Cultural and Artistic Transmission: The International Buddhist Art Style in East Asia ca. 645–770*, (Singapore: NUS Press, 2018), p. 237, fig. 6.9.

11 Hu 2017, p. 190.

12 Ellen Johnston Laing, 'A Report on Western Asian Glassware in the Far East', *Bulletin of the Asia Institute*, vol. 5 (1991), pp. 109–21, at p. 120; An Jiayao, 'The Art of Glass along the Silk Road', in Watt (ed.) 2004 *China: Dawn of a Golden Age, 200–750 AD*, ed. James C.Y. Watt (New York: The Metropolitan Museum of Art, 2004), pp. 57–66.

13 Priestman 2016.

14 Ibid., p. 10.

15 Ibid., p. 11.

16 Dr Andrew Meek, Scientific Research Department, British Museum, conducted the surface XRF analysis. I am grateful to him for sharing the results.

17 On the analysis of glass beads from various sites, see Laure Dussubieux and Heather Walder (eds), *The Elemental Analysis of Glass Beads: Technology, Chronology and Exchange* (Leuven: Leuven University Press, 2022).

18 Charlotte von Verschuer, *Across the Perilous Sea: Japanese Trade with China and Korea from the Seventh to the Sixteenth Centuries*, trans. Kristen Lee Hunter (Ithaca, NY: Cornell University, 2006), p. 2.

19 Ross Bender, 'Japan', in Hermans (ed.) 2020, pp. 111–32, at p. 114.

20 Ibid.

21 Verschuer 2006, p. 11.

22 Ibid., p. 5.

23 Charlotte von Verschuer, 'Japan's Foreign Relations 600 to 1200 AD: A Translation from Zenrin Kokuhōki', *Monumenta Nipponica*, vol. 54, no. 1 (1999), pp. 1–39, at p. 5.

24 Verschuer 2006, p. 11.

25 Bender 2020, p. 114; Verschuer 2006, p. 13.

26 Verschuer 2006, p. 12.

27 Verschuer 1999, p. 5.

28 Wang Zhenping, *Ambassadors from the Islands of Immortals: China–Japan Relations in the Han–Tang Period* (Honolulu, HI: University of Hawai'i Press, 2005), p. 16. For exhibitions on the missions, see for instance, Tokyo National Museum and Asahi Shimbun (eds), 遣唐使と唐の美術 (*Japanese envoys and Tang art*) (Tokyo: Asahi Shimbun, 2005); Nara National Museum (ed.), 大遣唐展覧:平城遷都 1300 年記念 (*Imperial envoys to Tang China: Commemorating the 1300th anniversary of the move of the capital to Heijō-kyō*) (Nara: Nara National Museum, 2010).

29 Wong 2018, p. 98.

30 Ibid.

31 Wang 2005, pp. 78–9.

32 Ibid., p. 60. On a history of shipbuilding in East Asia, see Jun Kimura, *Archaeology of East Asian Shipbuilding* (Gainesville, FL: University Press of Florida, 2016).

33 Ibid., pp. 101–2.

34 Wong 2018, p. 98.

35 Tokyo National Museum and Asahi Shimbun (eds) 2005, p. 29, cat. no. 2.

36 Wong 2018, p. 99.

37 *Epitaphs of Ancient Japan*, exh. cat. no. 10, Nara National Research Institute for Cultural Properties website, www.nabunken.go.jp/english/e-catalogue/3.html (accessed 3 January 2024).

38 Wang 2005, p. 68.

39 Verschuer 2006, p. 15.

40 Wang 2005, p. 196.

41 Verschuer 2006, pp. 16–17.

42 Wang 2005, p. 231.

43 Ibid., p. 232.

44 Ibid., pp. 204–15.

45 On Ganjin/Jianzhen's journey see ibid., pp. 207–15; see also Wong 2018, pp. 221–50.

46 Rong Xinjiang 荣新江, 丝绸之路与东西文化交流 (*The Silk Road and cultural exchanges between East and West*) (Beijing: Beijing daxue chubanshe, 2015), p. 138.

47 See colbase.nich.go.jp/collection_items/nabunken/6AAICJ59000021?locale=ja (accessed 9 December 2023).

48 For instance, the monk Enchin (814–891). See Yiwen Li, *Networks of Faith and Profit: Monks, Merchants, and Exchanges between China and Japan, 839–1403 CE* (Cambridge: Cambridge University Press, 2023), pp. 27–8.

49 Bender 2020, p. 119.

50 William Coaldrake, 'City Planning and Palace Architecture in the Creation of the Nara Political Order', *East Asian History*, vol. 1 (1991), pp. 37–54, at p. 40.

51 William Wayne Farris, 'Trade, Money, and Merchants in Nara Japan', *Monumenta Nipponica*, vol. 53, no. 3 (1995), pp. 303–34, at p. 303.

52 On the architectural style, see Coaldrake 1991, pp. 46–50.

53 Ibid., pp. 48–50.

54 Ibid., p. 50.

55 Ibid., pp. 50–1; Bender 2020, pp. 116–19.

56 Charles Holcombe, *A History of East Asia: From the Origins of Civilization to the Twenty-First Century* (Cambridge: Cambridge University Press, 2017), pp. 120–2.

57 John S. Brownlee, *Political Thought in Japanese Historical Writing: From Kojiki (712) to Tokushi Yoron (1712)* (Waterloo, Canada: Wilfrid Laurier University Press, 1991), pp. 8–40.

58 Holcombe 2017, p. 122.

59 Ibid.

60 William E. Deal and Brian Douglas Ruppert, *A Cultural History of Japanese Buddhism* (West Sussex, UK: Wiley, Blackwell, 2015), p. 30; Bender 2020, p. 115; Walker 2015, p. 31.

61 Patricia Buckley Ebrey and Anne Walthall, *Pre-Modern East Asia to 1800: A Cultural, Social, and Political History* (Boston, MA: Wadsworth, Cengage Learning, 2013), p. 123.

62 Melody Rod-ari, 'Death, Disease, and Buddhist Patronage in Japan: The Great Smallpox Epidemic of 735', in *Teaching about Asia in a Time of Pandemic*, ed. David Kenley (Association for Asian Studies, 2020), pp. 41–8, at p. 41; William Wayne Farris, *Population, Disease and Land in Early Japan, 645–900* (Cambridge, MA: Harvard University, 1985), p. 66.

63 Rod-ari 2020.

64 Donald F. McCallum, 'The Earliest Buddhist Statues in Japan', *Artibus Asiae*, vol. 61, no. 2 (2001), pp. 149–88.

65 Junghee Lee, 'The Origins and Development of the Pensive Bodhisattva Images of Asia', *Artibus Asiae*, vol. 53, no. 3/4 (1993), pp. 311–57, at pp. 349–52.

66 National Museum of Korea, Quarterly Magazine, vol. 47, issuu.com/museumofkorea/docs/nmk_v47/s/12254335 (accessed 7 June 2024).

67 Wong 2018.

68 On this, see Peter Kornicki, 'The Hyakumantō Darani and the Origins of Printing in Eighth-century Japan', *International Journal of Asian Studies*, vol. 9, no. 1 (2012), pp. 43–70, and 'Empress Shōtoku as a Sponsor of Printing', in Peter Kornicki, Hildegard Diemberger and Franz-Karl Ehrhard (eds), *Tibetan Printing: Comparison, Continuities, and Change* (Leiden: Brill, 2016); Wong 2018, pp. 218–19.

69 Hsueh-man Shen, 'Between One and Many: Multiples, Multiplication and the Huayan Metaphysics', *Proceedings of the British Academy*, vol. 181 (2012), pp. 205–58, at p. 238.

70 Lee and Leidy (eds) 2013; National Museum of Korea (ed.), *National Museum of Korea: The Permanent Exhibition* (Seoul: National Museum of Korea, 2017), p. 75.

71 Also called Daegyeong, Geumgyeong and other names. See Noh Choong Kook, 'The Royal Capital of Silla', *Journal of Korean Art & Archaeology*, vol. 13 (2019), pp. 25–47, at p. 25.

72 Soyoung Lee and Denise Patry Leidy 'Introduction', in Lee and Leidy (eds) 2013, pp. 3–11, at p. 9. On this type of ornament, see Jeffrey L. Richey, 'The Comma at the End of the Silk Road: *Magatama* and the Development of an Early Eastern Ornamental Motif', *Sino-Platonic Papers*, vol. 299 (March 2020), pp. 1–33.

73 Lee and Leidy 2013.

74 Ibid., p. 8.

75 On glass beads in the Korean Peninsula, see Insook Lee, 'Of Glass and Gold: Silla Tombs, the Silk Road, and the Steppes', in Lee and Leidy (eds) 2013, pp. 115–31, at pp. 115–19; Insook Lee, 'The Silk Road Treasures of Ancient Korea: Glass and Gold', in *The Eastern Silk Road Story, 2015 Conference Proceeding* (Paris, Bangkok: UNESCO, 2016), pp. 53–60, at pp. 53–5.

76 Gyeongju National Museum (ed.), *Gyeongju National Museum* (Seoul: Tongcheon Publishing Co., 2017), p. 79.

77 Lee 2016, p. 55. See also Yoon Sangdeok's forthcoming article in *Orientations* (Autumn 2024).

78 Date given in Ham Soon-seop, 'Gold Culture of the Silla Kingdom and Maripgan', in Lee and Leidy (eds) 2013, pp. 31–67, at p. 40.

79 Lee 2016, p. 56.

80 Hwang Eunsoon, 'Silla Kingdom: In Search of the Way from the Silk Road', *National Museum of Korea: Quarterly Magazine*, vol. 53 (2020), pp. 34–7, at p. 35.

81 Gyeongju National Museum (ed.) 2017, p. 70.

82 On this dagger, see Yoon Sangdeok 윤상덕, '계림로 14호묘의 축조연대와 피장자의 성격' ('The construction date and owners of Gyerim-ro Tomb no. 14') , 고고학지 (*Journal of the institute of Korean archaeology and art history*), vol. 17 (2011), pp. 345–67; Yoon Sang-deok, 'The Gyerim-ro Dagger and the Riddle of Silla's Foreign Trade', in Lee and Leidy (eds) 2013, pp. 133–140; and Yoon Sangdeok 윤상덕, '경주 계림로 보검으로 본 고대문물교류의 단면' ('The treasured dagger and scabbard from Gyerim-ro, Gyeongju, and a cross-section of ancient cultural exchange'), in 신라의 황금문화와 불교미술 (*Silla's gold culture and Buddhist art*) (Gyeongju: Gyeongju National Museum, 2015), pp. 214–21.

83 On the condition of the dagger, see Shin Yongbi 신용비 and Jeong Subin 정수빈, '경주 계림로 출토 보물 제635호 보검의 보존' ('Conservation of the dagger and scabbard (Treasure no. 635) excavated from Gyerim-ro, Gyeongju'), 박물관보존과학 (*Museum Conservation Science*), vol. 11 (2010), pp. 1–8.

84 Yoon 2013, p. 136.

85 Ibid.

86 Ibid., p. 139.

87 On the burial, see Yoon 2011.

88 Lee and Leidy 2013, p. 9. On the adoption of Buddhism in Silla, see Denise Patry Leidy with the assistance of Huh Hyeong Uk, 'Interconnections: Buddhism, Silla, and the Asian World', in Lee and Leidy (eds) 2013, pp. 143–88.

89 Gyeongju National Museum (ed.) 2017, p. 151; Maliya Aihaiti 马丽亚·艾海提, Jin Chengshi 金诚实 and Hao Chunyang 郝春阳, '丝绸之路上的中亚玻璃器 — 兼论中亚玻璃向中国、朝鲜半岛和日本之传播' ('Central Asian glass vessels along the Silk Roads – also, on the spread of Central Asian glass in China, the Korean Peninsula and Japan'), 考古与文物 (*Archaeology and cultural relics*), no. 6 (2017), pp. 104–10, at pp. 106–7.

90 Aihaiti, Jin and Hao 2017, p. 107; Gyeongju National Museum, 오색영롱: 한국 고대 유리와 신라 (*Colour and radiance: Glass treasures of Silla and ancient Korea*) (Gyeongju: Gyeongju National Museum, 2021), p. 254.

91 Noted on the National Museum of Korea website page: www.museum.go.kr/site/eng/relic/represent/view?relicId=2480 (accessed 27 January 2024).

92 Youn-mi Kim, 'Buddhist Architecture, Politics, and Gender in the Three Kingdoms and Unified Silla', in *A Companion to Korean Art*, ed. J.P. Park, Burglind Jungmann and Juhyung Rhi (Hoboken, NJ: John Wiley & Sons Inc., 2020), pp. 87–106, at p. 98.

93 National Museum of Korea, 'Sarira Reliquaries from East and West Stone Pagodas of Gameunsa Temple', *Smarthistory*, 30 January 2023, smarthistory.org/sarira-reliquaries-east-west-stone-pagodas-gameunsa-temple (accessed 27 January 2024).

94 Young-Ae Lim, 'Images of the Four Heavenly Kings in Unified Silla as the Symbol of National Defense', *Buddhist Studies Review*, vol. 32, no. 2 (2016), pp. 271–93, at p. 279.

95 Ibid., pp. 274–5.

96 Ibid.

97 Kurt A. Behrendt, *How to Read Buddhist Art* (New York: The Metropolitan Museum of Art, 2019), pp. 23–8.

98 Xinru Liu, *Silk and Religion: An Exploration of Material Life and the Thought of People, AD 600–1200* (Oxford: Oxford University Press, 2004), pp. 32–48; Tansen Sen, *Buddhism, Diplomacy, and Trade: The Realignment of India-China Relations, 600–1400* (Lanham, MD: Rowman & Littlefield, 2016), pp. 57–60.

99 Donald S. Lopez Jr, *Hyecho's Journey: The World of Buddhism* (Chicago, IL: University of Chicago Press, 2017), p. 64.

100 On Hyecho, see Lopez Jr 2017.

101 Wm Theodore de Bary (ed.), *Sources of East Asian Tradition* (New York: Columbia University Press, 2008), p. 518.

102 Juhyung Rhi, 'The Ancient City Gyeongju: Space and Monuments', in Lee and Leidy (eds) 2013, pp. 13–29, at p. 16.

103 Noh 2019, p. 27.

104 Ibid., pp. 31–2.

105 Rhi 2013, p. 16.

106 Ibid.

107 Sarah M. Nelson, *Gyeongju: The Capital of Golden Silla* (New York: Routledge, 2017), p. 9.

108 Lee and Leidy 2013, p. 9.

109 Richard D. McBride II, 'Korea', in Hermans (ed.) 2020, pp. 133–60, at p. 146.

110 Ibid., p. 146.

111 Ibid.

112 Ibid., pp. 146, 152.

113 Ibid., pp. 152–4.

114 Ibid., pp. 150–7.

115 Kim Han In-Sung, 'Islamic Material Culture in Medieval Korea and its Legacy', PhD dissertation, SOAS, University of London, 2016, pp. 62–4.

116 Denise Patry Leidy and Lee Soyoung, 'Silla, the Steppes, and Continental Culture', in Lee and Leidy (eds) 2013, pp. 87–113, at p. 92.

117 Gyeongju National Museum and Jeju National Museum (eds), 新羅 서 아시아를 만나다 (*Silla meets West Asia*) (Gyeongju and Jeju: Gyeongju National Museum, Jeju National Museum, 2008), p. 103.

118 Ibid.; Min Byung-hoon 민병훈, 실크로드와 경주 (*Silk Road and Gyeongju*) (Seoul: Tongcheon munhwasa, 2015), pp. 132–5; National Museum of Korea 2017, p. 91; Kim 2016, pp. 60–6.

119 Leidy and Lee 2013, p. 92.

120 Ibid., p. 97 identifies him as a foreigner of West Asian ethnicity. Also in Gyeongju National Museum and Jeju National Museum (eds) 2008, p. 105.

121 Gyeongju National Museum and Jeju National Museum (eds) 2008, p. 122.

122 Lee and Leidy 2013, p. 9.

123 Leidy and Lee 2013, pp. 101–2.

124 On *sancai* wares and their use, see Xie Mingliang 謝明良, 中國古代鉛釉陶的世界 (*The world of ancient Chinese lead-glazed pottery*) (Taipei: Shitou chubanshe, 2014), pp. 113–16.

125 Leidy and Lee 2013, pp. 102–3.

126 Ibid., p. 103.

127 Ibid.

128 Rong Xinjiang, 2015, p. 4.

129 Linda Rui Feng, *City of Marvel and Transformation: Chang'an and Narratives of Experience in Tang Dynasty China* (Honolulu, HI: University of Hawai'i Press, 2016), p. 4. On the layout of Chang'an, see Nancy Shatzman Steinhardt, *Chinese Imperial City Planning* (Honolulu, HI: University of Hawai'i Press, 1990), pp. 94–108.

130 Victor Cunrui Xiong, *Sui-Tang Chang'an: A Study in the Urban History of Medieval China* (Ann Arbor, MI: Center for Chinese Studies, University of Michigan, 2000), p. 198.

131 Susan Whitfield, 'Silkworms and Mulberry Trees: Silk Road Settlers', in *Silk Roads: Peoples, Cultures, Landscapes*, ed. Susan Whitfield (London: Thames & Hudson, 2019), pp. 310–15.

132 Ibid.

133 See table 2.1 in Ma Debin, 'The Great Silk Exchange: How the World was Connected and Developed', in *Textiles in the Pacific, 1500–1900* (London: Routledge, 2005).

134 Rong Xinjiang, 'The Silk Road is a Road of "Silk"', in *Silks from the Silk Road: Origin, Transmission and Exchange*, ed. Zhao Feng (Hangzhou: Zhejiang University Press, 2016), pp. 22–30, at p. 22.

135 Helen Wang, 'Textiles as Money on the Silk Road?', *Journal of the Royal Asiatic Society*, vol. 23, no. 2 (2013), pp. 165–74, at p. 167.

136 Angela Sheng, 'Determining the Value of Textiles in the Tang Dynasty: In Memory of Professor Denis Twitchett (1925–2006)', *Journal of the Royal Asiatic Society*, vol. 23, no. 2 (2013), pp. 175–95, at p. 183.

137 Valerie Hansen, *The Silk Road: A New History* (Oxford: Oxford University Press, 2015), p. 42.

138 Ibid., p. 107.

139 Valerie Hansen and Helen Wang, 'Introduction', *Journal of the Royal Asiatic Society*, vol. 23, no. 2 (2013), pp. 155–63, at p. 160.

140 Ibid.

141 Jonathan Karam Skaff, *Sui-Tang China and its Turko-Mongol Neighbors: Culture Power and Connections 580–800* (Oxford: Oxford University Press, 2012), p. 265.

142 Table 8.4 in ibid.

143 Ibid., p. 259.

144 Sun Ji 孙机, '唐代的马具与马饰' ('Horse harnesses and horse ornaments of the Tang dynasty'), 文物 (*Cultural relics*), no. 10 (1981), pp. 82–8 and 96, at p. 83.

145 James T.C. Liu, 'Polo and Cultural Change: From T'ang to Sung China', *Harvard Journal of Asiatic Studies*, vol. 45, no. 1 (1985), pp. 203–24.

146 Lewis 2012, p. 148; Shao-yun Yang, *Early Tang China and the World 618–750 CE* (Cambridge: Cambridge University Press, 2023b), p. 33.

147 Skaff 2012, pp. 105–6.

148 Edward H. Schafer, *The Golden Peaches of Samarkand: A Study of T'ang Exotics* (Berkeley and Los Angeles, CA: University of California Press, 1985), p. 29.

149 Bret Hinsch, *Women in Tang China* (Lanham, MD, and London: Rowman & Littlefield, 2020), pp. 7–8.

150 Holcombe 2017, pp. 102–4.

151 Xiong 2000, p. 170; Hansen 2015, p. 148.

152 Xiong 2000, p. 174.

153 Elfriede Regina Knauer, *The Camel's Load in Life and Death: Iconography and Ideology of Chinese Pottery Figurines from Han to Tang and their Relevance to Trade along the Silk Routes* (Kilchberg/Zürich: Akanthus, 2011), pp. 78–97.

154 Edwin G. Pulleyblank, 'Chinese-Iranian Relations i. In Pre-Islamic Times', *Encyclopaedia Iranica*, available at www.iranicaonline.org/articles/chinese-iranian-i (accessed 14 April 2024).

155 One interpretation is summarised in Tonia Ekfield, *Imperial Tombs in Tang China* (Hoboken, NJ: Taylor and Francis, 2005), p. 113.

156 Schafer 1985, pp. 84–5.

157 Johannes Preiser-Kapeller, 'Migration', in Hermans (ed.) 2020, pp. 477–519, at pp. 495–6.

158 Ibid., p. 496.

159 Hansen 2015, p. 149.

160 Skaff 2012, pp. 197–200.

161 Rong 2015, p. 65.

162 Ibid., pp. 65–6.

163 Yang 2023a, pp. 37–8; Hassan Rezāī Bāghbidi, 'New Light on the Middle Persian-Chinese Bilingual Inscription from Xī'ān', in *The Persian Language in History*, ed. Mauro Maggi and Paola Orsatti (Wiesbaden: Dr. Ludwig Reichert Verlag, 2011), pp. 105–15, at p. 111.

164 Yang 2023a, p. 37; Bāghbidi 2011, p. 111.

165 Yang 2023a, p. 38; Bāghbidi 2011, pp. 112–13.

166 Jessica Rawson, 'Inside Out: Creating the Exotic within Early Tang Dynasty China in the Seventh and Eighth Centuries', *World Art*, vol. 2, no. 1 (2012), pp. 25–45, at p. 40.

167 Liu Qi 刘琪, '唐三彩胡俑的时空演变探微' ('Exploring the temporal and spatial development of Tang three-coloured *hu* figurines'), 四川文物 (*Sichuan cultural relics*), vol. 211, no. 3 (2020), pp. 82–91, at p. 83. Also see Fan Yingfeng 樊英峰, 丝路胡人外来风：唐代胡俑展 (*Hu people from the Silk Road and styles from abroad: Exhibition on Tang dynasty* hu *figurines*) (Beijing: Wenwu chubanshe, 2008).

168 The term to denote foreign or non-Han Chinese in such cases is usually *hu*. Broadly defined, *hu* refers to all non-Han Chinese from the north and west of China. Narrowly defined, *hu* refers to peoples of West and Central Asia, and most specifically Sogdians. The term could also suggest 'barbarians', as opposed to the civilised Han Chinese, but this is not always the case. On the definition of *hu* in Tang China, see Rong Xinjiang 荣新江, '何谓胡人？—隋唐时期胡人族属的自认与他认' ('What is *huren*? – Ethnic selfhood and ethnic otherness of *hu* people during the Sui-Tang periods'), 乾陵文化研究 (*Qianling culture research*) (2008), pp. 3–9.

169 Zhou Weizhou 周伟洲, '唐代的昆仑奴与僧祇奴 —兼论出土文物中的昆仑奴形象' ('*Kunlun* slaves and *Sengqi* slaves of the Tang dynasty – Also on the *Kunlun* slave figure among excavated artefacts'), 乾陵文化研究 (*Qianling culture research*) (2008), pp. 93–100, at pp. 93–4; Don J. Wyatt, 'The Image of the Black in Chinese Art', in *The Image of the Black in African and Asian Art*, ed. David Bindman, Henry Louis Gates Jr and Suzanne Preston Blier (Cambridge: Cambridge University Press, 2018), pp. 299–300; Julie Wilensky, 'The Magical Kunlun and "Devil Slaves": Chinese Perceptions of Dark-Skinned People and Africa before 1500', *Sino-Platonic Papers*, vol. 122 (2002), pp. 1–51.

170 Zhou 2008, p. 94; Wilensky 2002, p. 6.

171 Zhou 2008, pp. 94–5.

172 Wyatt 2018, p. 305; Wilensky 2002, p. 7.

173 Wyatt 2018, pp. 300–6.

174 Yang Jin 杨瑾, 汉唐文物与中外文化交流 (*Han-Tang cultural relics and sino-foreign cultural exchange*) (Xi'an: Shaanxi renmin chubanshe, 2018), pp. 46–58, at p. 47.

175 Xiong 2000, p. 181.

176 Sun Ji 孙机, '唐代胡俑' ('Ceramic figurines of *hu* people from the Tang dynasty'), 乾陵文化研究 (*Qianling culture research*) (2008), pp. 106–9, at pp. 107–8.

177 Rong 2015, p. 335.

178 Lewis 2012, p. 93.

179 On Xuanzang, see, for instance, Benjamin Rose, *Xuanzang: China's Legendary Pilgrim and Translator* (Boulder, CO: Shambhala Publications, 2021).

180 Wong 2018, p. 25.

181 Ibid.

182 Ibid., p. 27. The structure was probably more of a tower stupa based on the model of the Kanishka stupa. I am grateful to Professor Susan Whitfield for this information.

183 Ibid., pp. 89, 92.

184 Ibid., p. 98.

185 On Amoghavajra, see Geoffrey C. Goble, *Chinese Esoteric Buddhism: Amoghavajra, the Ruling Elite, and the Emergence of a Tradition* (New York: Columbia University Press, 2019).

186 Xiong 2000, p. 239.

187 Ibid.

188 Rong Xinjiang 荣新江, '祆教初传中国年代考' ('The earliest date of Zoroastrianism's spread to China'), 国学研究 (*Studies in sinology*), no. 3 (1995), pp. 335–53.

189 Hansen 2015, pp. 146–7.

190 Judith A. Lerner, 'Aspects of Assimilation: The Funerary Practices and Furnishings of Central Asians in China', *Sino-Platonic Papers*, no. 168 (Dec 2005), pp. 1–65, at p. 8. Also Judith A. Lerner, 'Zoroastrian Funerary Beliefs and Practices Known from the Sino-Sogdian Tombs in China', *The Silk Road*, vol. 9 (2011), pp. 18–25.

191 On this object, see Patrick Wertmann, *Sogdians in China: Archaeological and Art Historical Analyses of Tombs and Texts from the 3rd to the 10th Century AD* (Darmstadt: Verlag Philipp von Zabern, 2015), pp. 124–5.

192 Rong 2015, p. 76. Hansen 2015, p. 145.

193 Rong 2015, p. 76; Xiong 2000, pp. 236–7.

194 Rong 2015, pp. 76–7.

195 Erica C.D. Hunter, 'The Persian Contribution to Christianity in China: Reflections in the Xian Fu Syriac Inscriptions', in *Hidden Treasures and Intercultural Encounters: Studies on East Syriac Christianity in Central Asia and China*, ed. Dietmar W. Winkler and Li Tang (Berlin and London: Lit and Global, 2009), pp. 71–86, at p. 72.

196 Max Deeg, 'The Brilliant Teaching: Iranian Christians in Tang China and their Identity', *Entangled Religions*, vol. 11, no. 6 (2020), pp. 1–13, at p. 5.

197 Matteo Nicolini-Zani, *The Luminous Way to the East: Texts and History of the First Encounter of Christianity with China*, trans. William Skudlarek (New York: Oxford University Press, 2022), p. 66.

198 Deeg 2020, p. 12. For other views, see Nicolini-Zani 2022, pp. 66–7; R. Todd Godwin, '*Da Qin*, *Tajiks*, and their Doctors: East Syrian Scientists across the Courts of Early Medieval Persia, China, and Tibet in *Artifact, Text, Context: Studies on Syriac Christianity in Medieval Central Asia and China*, ed. Li Tang and Dietmar W. Winkler (Zürich: Lit Verlag, 2020), pp. 43–60.

199 Rong 2015, pp. 335–6. There may have been a second church in Liquan Ward, which is referred to as a *Bosi* (Persian) church in textual sources. Xiong 2000, p. 237, says it is Zoroastrian because it was set up by the prince of the Sasanian dynasty; Rong 2015, pp. 76–7, thinks it is more likely Church of the East, established at the behest of Persian communities in the city.

200 Max Deeg, 'A Belligerent Priest: Yisi and his Political Context', in *From the Oxus River to the Chinese Shores: Studies on East Syriac Christianity in China and Central Asia*, ed. Li Tang and Dietmar W. Winkler (Zürich: LIT, 2013), pp. 107–21, at pp. 108–9; Deeg 2020, p. 5.

201 Deeg 2013, pp. 109–10.

202 Ibid., p. 117.

203 Ibid.

204 Zsusanna Gulácsi, 'Manichaeism: Its Flourishing and Demise', in Whitfield (ed.) 2019, pp. 356–63, at p. 361.

205 Kyoko Nomoto, 'Dressing as Horsemen: The Universalisation of Steppe Dress in the First Half of Tang Dynasty China (618–755)', PhD dissertation, University of Oxford, 2022, p. 23. I am grateful to Dr Nomoto for sharing her PhD dissertation with me.

206 Ibid., pp. 10–12.

207 Ibid., pp. 1–2.

208 Skaff 2012, p. 160; Nomoto 2022, pp. 137–56.

209 Schafer 1985, pp. 155–65.

210 Ibid., esp. p. 158.

211 Huang Bing, 'The Religious and Technological History of the Tang Dynasty Spherical Incense Burner', *Religions*, vol. 13, no. 6 (2022), doi.org/10.3390/rel13060482 (accessed 6 May 2024). See also Flavia Xi Fang's dissertation on 'Navigating the Smellscape in Medieval China' (University of Cambridge).

212 See Carol Michaelson, *Gilded Dragons: Buried Treasures from China's Golden Ages* (London: The British Museum Press, 1999), cat. no. 73, pp. 111–12 for a description of a similar one.

213 Huang 2022, p. 12.

214 Chuanming Rui, *On the Ancient History of the Silk Road* (Singapore: World Scientific Publishing, 2021), p. 184.

215 Zhang Qingjie, '*Hutengwu* and *Huxuanwu*: Sogdian Dances in the Northern, Sui and Tang Dynasties', in *Les Sogdiens en Chine*, ed. Étienne de la Vaissière and Éric Trombert (Paris: École française d'Extrême-Orient, 2005), pp. 93–106.

216 Watt (ed.) 2004, pp. 250–1, cat. no. 149.

217 John E. Myers, *The Way of the Pipa: Structure and Imagery in Chinese Lute Music* (Kent, OH: Kent State University Press, 1992), pp. 7–8.

218 Ibid., p. 14.

219 Liang Mian 梁勉, '从唐代壁画中的竖箜篌谈中西文化交流' ('A discussion of East-West cultural exchange through the depiction of the angular harp on Tang-dynasty wall paintings'), 文博 (*Relics and museology*), no. 5 (2008), pp. 15–18.

220 Kishibe Shigeo 岸邊成雄, 唐代音樂史的研究 (*Research on music history of the Tang dynasty*), trans. Liang Zaiping 梁在平 and Huang Zhijiong 黄志炯 (Taipei: Zhonghua shuju, 1973), pp. 6, 13, 16–18.

221 David R. Knechtges, 'Gradually Entering the Realm of Delight: Food and Drink in Early Medieval China', *Journal of the American Oriental Society*, vol. 117, no. 2 (1997), pp. 229–39, at p. 231.

222 See Schafer 1985, pp. 117–19 for peaches and pp. 146–7 for spinach.

223 Chen Yi, 'Platters with Teeth and Ewers Lifted from One Side: New Vessel Forms and Foodways in Tang China (618–907)', in *Visual, Material and Textual Cultures of Food and Drink in China, 200 BCE–1900 CE*, ed. Stacy Pearson (Cambridge: Cambridge Scholars Publishing, 2022), pp. 190–7. I am grateful to Dr Chen for sharing her article with me.

224 Rui 2021, pp. 180–3.

225 François Louis, 'The Hejiacun Rhyton and the Chinese Wine Horn (*Gong*): Intoxicating Rarities and their Antiquarian History', *Artibus Asiae*, vol. 67, no. 2 (2007), pp. 201–42.

226 Ibid., p. 205.

227 Qi Dongfang 齐东方, 唐代金银器研究 (*Studies on the gold and silver vessels of the Tang dynasty*) (Beijing: Zhongguo shehui kexue chubanshe, 1999), p. 42.

228 Jessica Rawson, 'Central Asian Silver and its Influence on Chinese Ceramics', *Bulletin of the Asia Institute*, vol. 5 (1991), pp. 139–51, at pp. 144–5. Tang silver vessels in the British Museum have been scientific analysed by Alessandro Armigliato with contributions from Laura Perucchetti, Janet Lang and Ruiliang Liu. For a summary of this work, see forthcoming article in *Orientations* (autumn 2024).

229 Ibid., p. 26.

230 Ibid., p. 27.

231 Chen 2022, p. 206.

232 Qi 1999, p. 102.

Seafarers in the Indian Ocean

1 I would like to thank Dr Li Baoping (School of Archaeology, University of Oxford, and School of Archaeology and Museology, Shanxi University) for his comments on a draft of this chapter.

2 Michael Flecker, 'A Ninth-Century AD Arab or Indian Shipwreck in Indonesia: First Evidence for Direct Trade with China', *World Archaeology*, vol. 32, no. 3 (2001), pp. 335–54, at p. 337. I am following Natali Pearson in calling the ship *Belitung*. See Natali Pearson, *Belitung: The Afterlives of a Shipwreck* (Honolulu, HI: University of Hawai'i Press, 2023).

3 Flecker 2001, pp. 345–8. Regina Krahl et al. (eds), *Shipwrecked: Tang Treasures and Monsoon Winds* (Washington, DC, and Singapore: Arthur M. Sackler Gallery, Smithsonian Institution/Singapore Tourism Board, 2011), p. 29.

4 Flecker 2001, pp. 347–8.

5 Pearson 2023, p. 41.

6 Ibid., pp. 41–2.

7 Alan Chong and Stephen A. Murphy (eds), *The Tang Shipwreck: Art and Exchange in the 9th Century* (Singapore: Asian Civilisations Museum, 2017), pp. 250–65.

8 Michael Flecker, 'The Origin of the Tang Shipwreck', in Chong and Murphy (eds) 2017, pp. 22–39, at p. 37.

9 Flecker 2017, pp. 37–8; Stephen A. Murphy, 'Asia in the Ninth Century: The Context of the Tang Shipwreck', in Chong and Murphy (eds) 2017, pp. 12–20, at p. 18.

10 Murphy, 'Asia in the Ninth Century', p. 13.

11 Chong and Murphy (eds) 2017, p. 261.

12 Ibid., pp. 256–9.

13 Murphy 2017, p. 18.

14 J. Keith Wilson and Michael Flecker, 'Dating the Belitung Shipwreck', in Krahl et al. (eds) 2011, pp. 35–7. Shen Hsueh-man 沈雪曼, 黑石号沉船与 9–10 世纪印度洋上的中国陶瓷贸易 ('The *Belitung* shipwreck and Chinese ceramic trade in the Indian Ocean during the ninth to tenth centuries'), in 大唐宝船：黑石号沉船所见9–10世纪的航海、贸易与艺术 (*The Tang treasure ship: Navigation, trade and art during the ninth and tenth centuries as seen in the* Belitung *shipwreck*), ed. Shanghai Museum (Shanghai: Shanghai shuhua chubanshe, 2020a), pp. 194–210, at pp. 194–5.

15 Murphy, 'Asia in the Ninth Century', p. 12.

16 For a summary of the views, see Chen Kelun 陈克伦, '印尼"黑石号"沉船出水瓷器与唐代陶瓷贸易' ('The *Belitung* shipwreck and the Tang-dynasty ceramics trade'), in 宝历风物：黑石号沉船出水珍品 (*The Baoli era: Treasures from the Tang shipwreck collection*), ed. Shanghai Museum (Shanghai: Shanghai shuhua chubanshe, 2020b), pp. 11–24, at pp. 21–2. Shen 2020, pp. 204–5. Another view is that the wares were assembled in Srivijaya in Southeast Asia.

17 Wang Zhenping, 'T'ang Maritime Trade Administration', *Asia Major*, vol. 4, no. 1 (1991), pp. 7–38, at pp. 7–11. John W. Chaffee, *The Muslim Merchants of Premodern China: The History of a Maritime Asian Trade Diaspora, 750–1400* (Cambridge: Cambridge University Press, 2018), p. 15.

18 John Guy, 'Rare and Strange Goods: International Trade in Ninth-Century Asia', in Krahl et al. (eds) 2011, pp. 19–27, at p. 20.

19 Chaffee 2018, pp. 12, 18.

20 Ibid., p. 18. Derek Heng, 'The Tang Shipwreck and the Nature of China's Maritime Trade during the Late Tang Period', in Chong and Murphy (eds) 2017, pp. 142–59, at p. 152.

21 Heng 2017, pp. 149, 152.

22 Flecker 2017, p. 37.

23 Xiang Kunpeng 项坤鹏, '管窥 9–10 世纪我国陶瓷贸易的域外中转港现象 — 以东南亚地区为焦点' ('A look into the phenomenon of foreign entrepôts of Chinese ceramic trade during the ninth to tenth centuries – with a focus on Southeast Asia'), in Shanghai Museum (ed.) 2020a, pp. 176–93.

24 Chaffee 2018, pp. 25–6.

25 Cited in Alain George, 'Direct Sea Trade Between Early Islamic Iraq and Tang China: From the Exchange of Goods to the Transmission of Ideas', *Journal of the Royal Asiatic Society*, vol. 25, no. 4 (2015), pp. 579–624, at p. 584.

26 On the reconstruction, see Tom Vosmer, 'The Jewel of Muscat: Reconstructing a Ninth-century Sewn-Plank Boat', in Krahl et al. (eds) 2011, pp. 121–35.

27 Heng 2017, pp. 143–6.

28 Ibid., p. 147.

29 On the issues surrounding the salvage of the *Belitung* shipwreck and its subsequent display, see Pearson 2023.

30 On the Changsha wares, see Liu Yang, 'Tang Dynasty Changsha Ceramics', in Krahl et al. (eds) 2011, pp. 145–59; Kan Shuyi, 'Ceramics from Changsha: A World Commodity', in Chong and Murphy (eds) 2017, pp. 44–60.

31 Guy 2011, p. 20.

32 Flecker 2017, p. 28.

33 Kan 2017, pp. 52–4.

34 The types of wares are summarised in the introduction to, and the relevant chapters on the categories of ceramics in, Krahl et al. (eds) 2011, and in Chong and Murphy (eds) 2017. For a summary of the recent attributions to the kiln sites, see Shen 2020, pp. 195–200.

35 For discussions on the blue-and-white ceramics of the Tang and Yuan dynasties, see Li Baoping, 'The Origins of Blue and White: Research Progress, Latest Finds and their Significance', *Oriental Ceramic Society Newsletter*, vol. 16 (2008), pp. 9–11; Nigel Wood and Seth Priestman, 'New Light on Chinese Tang Dynasty and Iraqi Blue and White in the Ninth Century: The Material from Siraf, Iran', *Bulletin of Chinese Ceramic Art and Archaeology*, no. 7 (2016), pp. 47–60; Weng Yanjun and Li Baoping, *New Finds of Yuan Dynasty Blue-and-White Porcelain from the Luomaqiao Kiln Site, Jingdezhen: An Archaeological Approach* (London: Unicorn, 2021).

36 Krahl et al. (eds) 2011, p. 211.

37 John Guy, 'Early Ninth-century Chinese Export Ceramics and the Persian Gulf Connection: The Belitung Shipwreck Evidence', in *Chine-Méditerranée: Routes et échanges de la céramique avant le XVIe siècle, Taoci*, vol. 4 (2005), pp. 9–20, at p. 16. For a summary of the different views, see Liu Chaohui 刘朝晖, '唐青花菱形花叶纹补说' ('Additional notes on the lozenge-shaped leaf pattern on Tang blue-and-white ceramics'), in Shanghai Museum (ed.) 2020a, pp. 338–51.

38 Shen 2020, p. 205.

39 Ibid.

40 Flecker 2001, p. 339.

41 Flecker 2017, p. 28.

42 Heng 2017, p. 157.

43 Geraldine Heng, 'An Ordinary Ship and its Stories of Early Globalism: World Travel, Mass Production, and Art in the Global Middle Ages', *Journal of Medieval Worlds*, vol. 1, no. 1 (2019), pp. 11–54, at p. 17.

44 On gold- and silverware, see François Louis, 'Metal Objects on the Belitung Shipwreck', in Krahl et al. (eds) 2011, pp. 85–91; Qi Dongfang, 'Gold and Silver on the Tang Shipwreck', in Chong and Murphy (eds) 2017, pp. 184–94.

45 Qi Dongfang 齐东方, 唐代金银器研究 (*Studies on the gold and silver vessels of the Tang dynasty*) (Beijing: Zhongguo shehui kexue chubanshe, 1999), pp. 356–8.

46 Ibid., p. 390.

47 François Louis, 'Metal Objects on the Tang Shipwreck', in Chong and Murphy (eds) 2017, pp. 204–19, at p. 210; Heng 2017, p. 154.

48 Qi 2017, p. 187.

49 Heng 2017, p. 153.

50 Qi 2017, p. 185.

51 Louis 2011, p. 91.

52 Ibid.; Heng 2017, p. 156.

53 On the two inscribed vessels and Tang court ceramics see Xiang Kunpeng 项坤鹏, '黑石号"沉船中"盈"、"进奉"款瓷器来源途径考 — 从唐代宫廷用瓷的几个问题谈起' ('The source of ceramics with "ying" and "jinfeng" marks from the Belitung shipwreck: A few questions on Tang-dynasty ceramics for court use'), 考古与文物 (*Archaeology and cultural relics*), no. 6 (2016), pp. 47–55; Lu Minghua 陆明华, '黑石号"沉船及出水陶瓷器的认识与思考' ('Knowledge and reflections on the Belitung shipwreck and its salvaged ceramics'), in Shanghai Museum (ed.) 2020b, pp. 25–49, at pp. 35–41; Xiang Kunpeng 项坤鹏, '唐代宫廷用瓷源流考' ('Research on the origin and development of Tang ceramics for court use'), 古代文明辑刊 (*Journal of ancient civilisations*), no. 15 (2021), pp. 251–7.

Southeast Asia to the Tarim Basin

1 I would like to thank Richard Blurton, Alexandra Green, Sureshkumar Muthukumaran, Lilla Russell-Smith and Diego Tamburini for their comments on draft sections of this chapter.

2 There are different views over the name of this polity. In English scholarship, 'Tibetan empire' is the standard term, and it is followed here for the sake of clarity. The name for this polity in Chinese historical sources is used in Chinese scholarship and is increasingly being adopted in English scholarship as well. There is much debate over whether this Chinese name should be pronounced 'Tubo', 'Tufan' or another variation. 'Tubo' is the current officially recognised romanisation.

3 For an introduction to Srivijaya, see Pierre-Yves Manguin, 'Kingdom of Srivijaya', in *The Encyclopedia of Empire*, vol. 4, ed. John M. MacKenzie et al. (Chichester: John Wiley & Sons, 2016), pp. 2011–16.

4 John Guy, 'Principal Kingdoms of Early Southeast Asia', in *Lost Kingdoms: Hindu-Buddhist Sculpture of Early Southeast Asia*, ed. John Guy (New York: The Metropolitan Museum of Art, 2014), pp. 14–21, at p. 21. For a brief introduction, see Alexandra Green, *Southeast Asia: A History in Objects* (London: Thames & Hudson/British Museum, 2023), pp. 40–1.

5 Pierre-Yves Manguin, 'Early Coastal States of Southeast Asia: Funan and Śrīvijaya', in Guy (ed.) 2014, pp. 111–15, at p. 114.

6 Guy 2014, p. 21. On Yijing's voyage see I-Tsing, *A Record of the Buddhist Religion as Practised in India and the Malay Archipelago (AD 671–695)*, trans. J. Takakusu (Oxford: Clarendon Press, 1896).

7 Guy 2014, p. 21.

8 See the Victoria and Albert Museum website: collections.vam.ac.uk/item/O40333/sculpture-figure-unknown (accessed 22 February 2024).

9 Guy (ed.) 2014, p. 250.

10 For an introduction to early Mataram, see Marijke J. Klokke, 'Central Javanese Empire (Early Mataram)', in *The Encyclopedia of Empire*, vol. 1, ed. John M. MacKenzie et al. (Chichester: John Wiley & Sons, 2016), pp. 450–5.

11 John K. Whitmore, 'Southeast Asia', in *A Companion to the Global Early Middle Ages*, ed. Erik Hermans (Leeds: ARC Humanities Press, 2020), pp. 65–93, at p. 78.

12 Kurt A. Behrendt, *How to Read Buddhist Art* (New York: The Metropolitan Museum of Art, 2019), p. 55.

13 Douglas Inglis, 'The Borobudur Vessels in Context', MA dissertation, Texas A & M University, 2014, available at core.ac.uk/download/pdf/147241786.pdf (accessed 22 February 2024), pp. 108–14.

14 Inglis 2014.

15 Guy 2014, p. 20. The original Chinese text for 'Persian' is *bosi*, although the description of the ship suggests it may have been an Austronesian or Indian ship. See Philippe Beaujard, *The Worlds of the Indian Ocean: A Global History*, vol. 1: *From the Fourth Millennium BCE to the Sixth Century CE* (Cambridge: Cambridge University Press, 2019), p. 515.

16 Guy 2014, p. 21.

17 Tansen Sen, 'Introduction: Buddhism in Asian History', in *Buddhism Across Asia: Network of Material, Intellectual and Cultural Exchange*, vol. 1, ed. Tansen Sen (Singapore: ISEAS Publishing, 2014), pp. xi–xxx, at p. xvii. On Xuanzang's travels see Xuanzang *Si-Yu-Ki: Buddhist Records of the Western World*, trans. Samuel Beal (London: K. Paul, Trench, Trübner, 1906); on Hyecho see Donald S. Lopez Jr et al., *Hyecho's Journey: The World of Buddhism* (Chicago, IL: University of Chicago Press, 2017).

18 Susan L. Huntington and John C. Huntington, *Leaves from the Bodhi Tree: The Art of Pāla India (8th–12th Centuries) and its International Legacy* (Dayton, OH: Dayton Art Institute/University of Washington Press, 1990), p. 76.

19 On Pala art, see Huntington and Huntington 1990. For a brief introduction, see Richard T. Blurton, *India: A History in Objects* (London: Thames & Hudson/British Museum, 2022), pp. 130–1.

20 Christine Chaillot, *The Assyrian Church of the East: History and Geography* (Oxford: Peter Lang, 2021), p. 43.

21 Ibid., p. 44.

22 Ibid.

23 Khaliq Ahmad Nizami, 'Early Arab Contact with South Asia', *Journal of Islamic Studies*, vol. 5, no. 1 (1994), pp. 52–69, at p. 54.

24 Ibid., pp. 57–8. On Muslim settlements and architecture in South India, see Mehrdad Shokoohy, *Muslim Architecture of South India: The Sultanate of Ma'bar and the Traditions of the Maritime Settlers on the Malabar and Coromandel Coasts (Tamil Nadu, Kerala and Goa)* (London and New York: Routledge, 2003).

25 Hugh Kennedy, *The Great Arab Conquests: How the Spread of Islam Changed the World We Live In* (Philadelphia, PA: Da Capo Press, 2007), p. 299.

26 Tansen Sen, *Buddhism, Diplomacy and Trade: The Realignment of India-China Relations 600–1400* (Honolulu, HI: Association for Asian Studies and University of Hawai'i Press, 2003), p. 16.

27 Ibid.

28 Ibid., pp. 38–9, 164. See also Xinru Liu, *Ancient India and Ancient China: Trade and Religious Exchanges AD 1–600* (Delhi: Oxford University Press, 1994); Xinru Liu, *Silk and Religion: An Exploration of Material Life and the Thought of People AD 600–1200* (Delhi: Oxford University Press, 1996).

29 Sen 2003, pp. 182–4.

30 For a history of Tibet, see Sam van Schaik, *Tibet: A History* (New Haven, CT: Yale University Press, 2013). For the Tibetan empire, see Christopher I. Beckwith, *The Tibetan Empire in Central Asia: A History of the Struggle for Great Power among Tibetans, Turks, Arabs, and Chinese during the Early Middle Ages* (Princeton, NJ: Princeton University Press, 1993). For an introduction in Chinese with a focus on art, see Wang Xudong 王旭东 and Tom Pritzker 汤姆·普利兹克 (eds), 丝绸之路上的文化交流: 吐蕃时期艺术珍品 (*Cultural exchange along the Silk Road: Masterpieces of the Tubo period*) (Beijing: Zhongguo Zangxue chubanshe, 2020).

31 Lewis Doney, 'Tibet', in Hermans (ed.) 2020, pp. 191–223, at p. 193.

32 Sen 2003, pp. 171–4.

33 Lily Xiao Hong Lee and Sue Wiles (eds), *Biographical Dictionary of Chinese Women: Tang through Ming 618–1644* (Armonk, NY: M.E. Sharpe 2015), pp. 194–6, 204–5.

34 The painting can be viewed on the Palace Museum, Beijing website, available at www.dpm.org.cn/collection/paint/234620 (accessed 27 March 2024).

35 Amy Heller, 'Tibetan Inscriptions on Ancient Silver and Gold Vessels and Artefacts', *Journal of the International Association for Bon Research*, vol. 1, no. 1 (2013), pp. 259–90, at p. 265; Wang and Pritzker (eds) 2020.

36 Heller 2013.

37 Amy Heller, *Early Himalayan Art* (Oxford: Ashmolean Museum, 2008), cat. no. 15, pp. 20, 74.

38 Doney 2020, p. 209.

39 Heather Stoddard, *Early Sino-Tibetan Art* (Warminster: Aris and Phillips, 1975), pp. 4–5.

40 Anya King, *Scent from the Garden of Paradise: Musk and the Medieval Islamic World* (Leiden: Brill, 2017), pp. 1, 272.

41 Ibid., p. 14.

42 Anya King, 'Tibetan Musk and Medieval Arab Perfumery', in *Islam and Tibet: Interactions along the Musk Routes*, ed. Anna Akasoy, Charles Burnett and Ronit Yoeli-Tlalim (Farnham: Ashgate, 2011), pp. 145–61, at p. 154.

43 See, for instance, Akasoy, Burnett and Yoeli-Tlalim (eds) 2011; King 2017.

44 For an introduction to the history of Dunhuang and Dunhuang studies, see Rong Xinjiang, *Eighteen Lectures on Dunhuang* (Leiden: Brill, 2013).

45 Imre Galambos, *Dunhuang Manuscript Culture: End of the First Millennium* (Berlin: De Gruyter, 2020), p. 6. The estimated number of Dunhuang manuscripts has grown over the years. The current number provided by the Dunhuang Academy is some 70,000.

46 Galambos 2020, p. 3.

47 For a summary of scholarly views on the reasons behind the sealing of the cave, see Sam van Schaik and Imre Galambos, *Manuscripts and Travellers: The Sino-Tibetan Documents of a Tenth-Century Buddhist Pilgrim* (Berlin: De Gruyter, 2012), pp. 18–28.

48 Rong Xinjiang, 'The Nature of the Dunhuang Library Cave and the Reasons for its Sealing', trans. Valerie Hansen, *Cahiers d'Extrême-Asie*, vol. 11 (1999), pp. 247–75.

49 Suggested by Marc Aurel Stein, *Serindia: Detailed Report of Explorations in Central Asia and Westernmost China*, 5 vols (Oxford: Clarendon Press, 1921), vol. 2, p. 820, and Paul Pelliot, 'Une bibliothèque médiévale retrouvée au Kan-sou', *Bulletin de l'École française d'Extrême-Orient*, vol. 8 (1908), pp. 500–29, at p. 506.

50 Schaik and Galambos 2012, pp. 18–28; Xin Wen, *The King's Road: Diplomacy and the Remaking of the Silk Road* (Princeton, NJ: Princeton University Press, 2023), pp. 19–25.

51 On Stein's expeditions, see for instance Helen Wang (ed.), *Sir Aurel Stein: Colleagues and Collections* (London: The British Museum Press, 2012); Susan Whitfield, *Aurel Stein on the Silk Road* (London: The British Museum Press, 2004); Justin Jacobs, *The Compensations of Plunder: How China Lost its Treasures* (Chicago, IL: University of Chicago Press, 2020).

52 On the Stein collection in the UK, see Helen Wang and John Perkins (eds), *Handbook to the Collections of Sir Aurel Stein in the UK*, British Museum Research Publication 129 (London: The British Museum, 1999).

53 Roderick Whitfield, *The Art of Central Asia: The Stein Collection in the British Museum*, vol. 3: *Textiles, Sculpture and Other Arts* (Tokyo and New York: Kodansha International Ltd, 1985), pl. 1, pp. 281–4; Neville Agnew, Marcia Reed and Tevvy Ball (eds), *Cave Temples of Dunhuang: Buddhist Art on China's Silk Road* (Los Angeles, CA: The Getty Conservation Institute, 2016), cat. no. 10, pp. 204–7.

54 Agnew, Reed and Ball (eds) 2016, p. 205.

55 Ma De 马德, '敦煌刺繡《灵鹫山说法图》的年代及相关问题' ('The date of the Dunhuang embroidery "Preaching on the Vulture Peak" and related issues'), 东南文化 (*Southeast culture*), no. 1 (2008), pp. 71–3, at p. 72.

56 Identified as Shakyamuni Preaching on the Vulture Peak in Whitfield 1985, vol. 3, pl. 1, pp. 281–4.

57 Wu Hung, 'Rethinking Liu Sahe: The Creation of a Buddhist Saint and the Invention of a "Miraculous Image"', *Orientations*, vol. 27, no. 10 (1996), pp. 32–43, at p. 39.

58 Roderick Whitfield, *The Art of Central Asia: The Stein Collection in the British Museum*, vol. 2: *Paintings from Dunhuang II* (Tokyo: Kodansha International Ltd, 1983), pl. 59, pp. 336–7; Agnew, Reed and Ball (eds) 2016, cat. no. 8, pp. 200–1; Haewon Kim, 'An Icon in Motion: Rethinking the Iconography of Itinerant Monk Paintings from Dunhuang', *Religions*, vol. 11, no. 9 (2020), p. 479.

59 In addition to sources already cited, see Xie Jisheng 谢继胜, '伏虎罗汉、行脚僧、寶胜如来与达摩多罗 — 11至13世纪中国多民族美术关系史个案分析' ('Arhat with a tiger, travelling monk, Ratnasambhava and Dharmatrata: A case study of the history of multi-ethnic art relations from the eleventh to the thirteenth centuries'), 故宫博物院院刊 (*Palace Museum journal*), vol. 141, no. 1 (2009), pp. 76–96.

60 For an introduction to Esoteric Buddhism in Dunhuang, see Henrik H. Sørensen, 'Esoteric Buddhism at the Crossroads: Religious Dynamics at Dunhuang, 9th–10th Centuries', in *Transfer of Buddhism across Central Asian Networks (7th to 13th Centuries)*, ed. Carmen Meinert (Leiden: Brill, 2016), pp. 250–84. On visual culture, see for instance Michelle C. Wang, *Mandalas in the Making: The Visual Culture of Esoteric Buddhism at Dunhuang* (Leiden: Brill, 2018).

61 Sørensen 2016, p. 253.

62 Sam van Schaik, 'Tibetan Buddhism in Central Asia: Geopolitics and Group Dynamics', in Meinert (ed.) 2016, pp. 57–81, at p. 67.

63 Susan Whitfield and Ursula Sims-Williams (eds), *The Silk Road: Trade, Travel, War and Faith* (London: The British Library, 2004), cat. no. 129, pp. 209–10.

64 Ibid.

65 From the abstract of a seminar given by Professor Zsuzsanna Gulácsi on 1 April 2024 at Princeton University. I am grateful to Professor Gulácsi for sharing this and a recording of her talk with me and to Dr Lilla Russell-Smith

for alerting me to this new interpretation.

66 Li Tang, 'Christian or Buddhist? An Exposition of a Silk Painting from Dunhuang, China, Now Kept in the British Museum', in *Artifact, Text, Context: Studies in Syriac Christianity in China and Central Asia*, ed. Li Tang and Dietmar W. Winkler (Zürich: Lit Verlag, 2020), pp. 233–43.

67 Ibid., p. 242.

68 Email correspondence with Professor Gulácsi, 14 February 2024. The argument is developed from her article, 'A Manichaean "Portrait of the Buddha Jesus": Identifying a Twelfth- or Thirteenth-century Chinese Painting from the Collection of Seiun-ji zen Temple', *Artibus Asiae*, vol. 69, no. 1 (2009), pp. 91–145; and from the Kara Totok banner painting in the Museum für Asiatische Kunst in Berlin discussed below.

69 Bibliothèque nationale de France, Paris, PT.1058; The British Library, London, Or.8210/S.6168; Berlin-Brandenburg Academy of Sciences and Humanities, Mainz 0725. See Ronit Yoeli-Tlalim, *ReOrienting Histories of Medicine: Encounters along the Silk Roads* (London: Bloomsbury Publishing, 2021), pp. 85–101.

70 Wladimir Zwalf (ed.), *Buddhism: Art and Faith* (London: The British Museum Press, 1985), pp. 82–3.

71 Ibid.

72 Whitfield 1983, vol. 2, pl. 75, pp. 344–5.

73 Galambos 2020, pp. 25–7.

74 Mauro Maggi, 'A Chinese–Khotanese excerpt from the Mahāsāhasrapramardanī', in *La Persia e l'Asia Centrale da Alessandro al X secolo* (Rome: Accademia nazionale dei Lincei, 1996), pp. 123–37, at p. 129. References to comparable demons have been identified in Chinese and Sanskrit texts. See pp. 124–5.

75 Maggi 1996.

76 Wang Fang 王芳, '敦煌唐五代旷野鬼夜叉图像小议' ('A discussion on Dunhuang Atavika images from the Tang to the Five dynasties'), 敦煌研究 (*Dunhuang research*), no. 6 (2016), pp. 58–70; Meng Sihui 孟嗣徽, '护诸童子十六女神像叶与于阗敦煌地区的护童子信仰' ('*Pothi* images of sixteen child-protecting female deities and the belief in protecting children in the Khotan and Dunhuang regions'), 艺术史研究 (*The study of art history*), no. 23 (2020), pp. 183–234.

77 Sam van Schaik, 'Phrasebooks for Silk Route Travellers', 2014, International Dunhuang Programme website, available at idpuk.blogspot.com/2014/05/phrasebooks-for-silk-route-travellers.html (accessed 18 Jan 2024). It is further expanded here: earlytibet.com (accessed 18 Jan 2024).

78 Wen 2023, pp. 192–5.

79 See F.W. Thomas and L. Giles, 'A Tibeto-Chinese Word-and-Phrase Book', *Bulletin of the School of Oriental and African Studies, University of London*, vol. 12, nos 3/4 (1948), pp. 753–69 for transcriptions and translations of the text.

80 Roderick Whitfield, *The Art of Central Asia: The Stein Collection in the British Museum*, vol. 1: *Paintings from Dunhuang I* (Tokyo and New York: Kodansha International Ltd, 1982), pl. 16, pp. 311–12; Stoddard 1975, pp. 9–13; Wang 2018, pp. 98–104.

81 Ibid.

82 Ibid.

83 Galambos 2020, p. 183.

84 Whitfield 1982, vol. 1, pls 46–8, pp. 333–4; Whitfield and Sims-Williams (eds) 2004, cat. no. 131, p. 210; Michelle Wang, Xin Wen and Susan Whitfield, 'Buddhism and Silk: Reassessing a Painted Banner from Medieval Central Asia in The Met', *Metropolitan Museum Journal*, vol. 55 (2020), pp. 8–25, at pp. 16–17. Wang Ruilei 王瑞雷, '敦煌藏经洞出土新样幡画与吐蕃、于阗及克什米尔之关系' ('A new type

of banner painting from the Library Cave, Dunhuang, and the artistic interactions between the Tibetan empire, Khotan and Kashmir)', 浙江大学学报(人文社会科学版) (*Journal of Zhejiang University (Humanities and Social Sciences)*), vol. 53, no. 3 (2023), pp. 5–15, summarises the literature on this.

85 For the connection to Kashmir, see Whitfield 1982, vol. 1, p. 334; Blurton, 2022, pp. 94–5.

86 Whitfield 1982, vol. 1, p. 334.

87 Ibid.

88 Wang, Wen and Whitfield 2020, p. 16. Whitfield 1982, vol. 1, pl. 48, p. 334; Whitfield and Sims-Williams (eds) 2004, cat. no. 131, p. 210.

89 Wang Ruilei (Wang 2023) thinks the painting was produced in Dunhuang during the Tibetan period by a Tibetan painter who was familiar with Kashmir and Swat (Pakistan) Buddhist styles.

90 Wen 2023.

91 Ibid., p. 61.

92 Ibid., p. 58.

93 Ibid.

94 Ibid., pp. 42–50.

95 Rong 2013, pp. 129, 327–8.

96 Whitfield 1983, vol. 2, pl. 56, pp. 333–4; Whitfield and Sims-Williams (eds) 2004, p. 129; Agnew, Reed and Ball (eds) 2016, no. 7, pp. 198–9; Wen 2023, pp. 82–3.

97 Reproduced in Whitfield and Sims-Williams (eds) 2004, p. 129.

98 Wen 2023, p. 78.

99 Ibid., pp. 79–80.

100 The side with writing can be viewed on the British Museum Collection Online, available at www.britishmuseum.org/collection/object/A_MAS-697 (accessed 22 February 2024).

101 Li Delong 李德龙, '敦煌遗书S.8444号研究 — 兼论唐末回鹘与唐的朝贡贸易' ('Research into Dunhuang manuscript S.8444: Also on the tribute trade between the late Tang Uyghurs and the Tang dynasty'), 中央民族大学学报 (*Journal of Minzu University of China*), no. 3 (1994), pp. 35–9, at pp. 37–8; Wen 2023, p. 206. See translation of the seal in Sun Weizu, *The History and Art of Chinese Seals* (Beijing: Foreign Language Press, 2010), p. 160.

102 Wen 2023, p. 207, table 8.2; Wang Le 王乐 and Zhao Feng 赵丰, '吐鲁番出土文书和面衣所见波斯锦' ('Persian brocades as seen in manuscripts and face covers excavated from Turpan'), 艺术设计研究 (*Art and design research*), no. 2 (2019), pp. 19–25. 'Persian' (*bosi*) textile may refer to its design rather than its place of production.

103 Valerie Hansen, 'The Tribute Trade with Khotan in Light of Materials Found at the Dunhuang Library Cave', *Bulletin of the Asia Institute*, vol. 19 (2005), pp. 37–46, at p. 39.

104 Whitfield and Sims-Williams (eds) 2004, cat. no. 42, pp. 147, 149.

105 Liu Cuilan, 'Law and Slavery on the Silk Roads: How did Buddhist Monks and Nuns Participate in the Slave Trade?', *Buddhist Road Paper*, vol. 3, no. 2 (2022).

106 Shi Pingting 施萍婷, '从一件奴婢买卖文书看唐代的阶级压迫' ('Class oppression in the Tang dynasty as seen in the contract for the sale of an enslaved person'), 文物 (*Cultural relics*), no. 12 (1972), pp. 68–71.

107 Pamela Crossley, 'Slavery in Early Modern China', in *The Cambridge World History of Slavery*, vol. 3, ed. David Eltis and Stanley L. Engerman (Cambridge: Cambridge University Press, 2011), pp. 186–214, at pp. 189–90.

108 Ibid., p. 190.

109 Rong Xinjiang 荣新江, '何谓胡人？ —隋唐时期胡人族属的自认与他认' ('What is *huren*? – Ethnic selfhood and ethnic otherness of *hu* people during the Sui-Tang periods'), 乾陵文化研究 (*Qianling culture research*) (2008), pp. 3–9.

110 Rong Xinjiang, 'Khotanese Felt and Sogdian Silver: Foreign Gifts to Buddhist Monasteries in Ninth- and Tenth-century Dunhuang', *Asia Major*, vol. 17, no. 1 (2004), pp. 15–34, at p. 24 this is translated as 'Iranian powder'.

111 For the Chinese text see Rong Xinjiang 荣新江, 丝绸之路与东西文化交流 (*The Silk Road and cultural exchanges between East and West*) (Beijing: Beijing daxue chubanshe, 2015), pp. 266–9, table 1.

112 In Rong 2004, p. 33, this is translated as 'glazed vase'. There are different views about the meaning of *liuli*. In Buddhist scriptures, *liuli* can also refer to gemstones. See discussion in Yu Xin, 'Liuli in Buddhist Rituals and Art in Medieval China', *Hualin International Journal of Buddhist Studies*, vol. 1, no. 2 (2018), pp. 231–68, at pp. 238–9.

113 Whitfield 1982, vol. 1, pl. 56, p. 337; Whitfield and Sims-Williams (eds) 2004, pp. 156–7; Yu 2018, p. 248.

114 Yu 2018, p. 236; Whitfield and Sims-Williams (eds) 2004, pp. 156–7.

115 For an introduction, see St John Simpson, 'Sasanian Glass: An Overview', in *Neighbours and Successors of Rome: Traditions of Glass Production and Use in Europe and the Middle East in the Later First Millennium AD*, ed. Daniel Keller, Jennifer Price and Caroline Jackson (Oxford: Oxbow Books, 2014), pp. 200–31.

116 Yu 2018, p. 248. Ma Yan suggests this is from the Chernyakhov culture in the northern Black Sea region in the fourth century CE. See Ma Yan 马艳, '大同出土北魏磨花玻璃碗源流' ('The origin of a facet-cut glass bowl of the Northern Wei period excavated from Datong'), 中原文物 (*Cultural relics of central China*), no. 1 (2014), pp. 96–100. See also Marta Żuchowska and Bartłomiej Sz. Szmoniewski, 'Glass along the Silk Road in the First Millennium AD', *Archaeologia Polona*, vol. 55 (2017), pp. 161–88, at fig. 6, p. 170.

117 MAS.697, dated to 400–600. See the British Museum Collection Online entry, available at www.britishmuseum.org/collection/object/A_MAS-697 (accessed 22 February 2024).

118 Whitfield 1982, vol. 1, p. 337.

119 Zhao Feng (ed.), *Textiles from Dunhuan in UK Collections* (Shanghai: Donghua University Press, 2007), p. 98.

120 The Musée Guimet example is numbered EO 1199. The Victoria and Albert Museum examples are numbered 763-1893 and 1746-1888. The Shroud of Saint Columba and Saint Lupus is reproduced in Mariachiara Gasparini, 'Sogdian Textiles along the Silk Road', *The Sogdians: Influencers on the Silk Roads*, Freer Gallery of Art Smithsonian Institution online exhibition, www.sogdians.si.edu/sidebars/sogdian-textiles-along-the-silk-road (accessed 25 January 2024). There is also another silk textile with the same type of pattern used as the shroud of Sts Innocents in Sens Cathedral. I am grateful to Kosuke Goto for this information.

121 Nicholas Sims-Williams and Geoffrey Khan, 'Zandaniji Misidentified', *Bulletin of the Asia Institute*, vol. 22 (2008), pp. 207–13, at p. 208.

122 Ibid., pp. 210, 211.

123 Diego Tamburini, 'Investigating Asian Colourants in Chinese Textiles from Dunhuang (7th–10th century AD) by High Performance Liquid Chromatography Tandem Mass Spectrometry: Towards the Creation of a Mass Spectra Database', *Dyes and Pigments*, vol. 163 (2019), pp. 454–74; Diego Tamburini and Joanne Dyer, 'Fibre optic reflectance spectroscopy and multispectral imaging for the non-invasive investigation of Asian colourants in Chinese textiles from Dunhuang (7th–10th century AD)', *Dyes and Pigments*, vol. 162 (2019), pp. 494–511; Diego Tamburini et al., 'An Investigation of the Dye Palette in Chinese Silk Embroidery from Dunhuang (Tang Dynasty)', *Archaeological and Anthropological Sciences*, vol. 11 (2019), pp. 1221–39; Diego Tamburini et al., 'Bordering on Asian Paintings: Dye Analysis of Textile Borders and Mount Elements to Complement Research on Asian Pictorial Art', *Heritage*, vol. 4, no. 4 (2021), pp. 4344–65.

124 Liu Jian et al., 'Profiling by HPLC-DAD-MSD reveals a 2500-year history of the use of natural dyes in Northwest China', *Dyes and Pigments*, vol. 187 (2021), pp. 109–43.

125 This work was led by Diego Tamburini (Scientist: Polymeric and Modern Organic Materials) with contributions from Joanne Dyer (Scientist: Colour Science), Caroline Cartwright (Scientist), Antony Simpson (Scientist), Laura Perucchetti (Scientist: Metals) at the Department of Scientific Research, British Museum. See Diego Tamburini et al. 'Reconstructing Archaeological Textiles from Dunhuang (China, 8th–10th century CE) – A Focus on Scientific Analysis', *Heritage Science* (forthcoming).

126 Diego Tamburini, 'Dyes along the Silk Roads', in *Textiles and Clothing along the Silk Roads*, ed. Zhao Feng and Marie-Louise Nosch (Paris and Hangzhou: UNESCO and China National Silk Museum, 2022), pp. 53–71, at p. 63.

127 The two other textiles are MAS.876 and 877 (same pattern produced with the clamp-resist dyeing technique) and MAS.857, an embroidery with gold-wrapped thread.

128 This work was led by Zhao Feng, Wang Shujuan, Liu Jian and Long Bo. The Dunhuang textile reconstruction project is a collaboration between the British Museum, the China National Silk Museum and Zhejiang University, China. For an overview of the reconstruction project, see Zhao Feng et al., 'Reconstructing Dunhuang textiles (TBC)', *Orientations* (autumn 2024) (forthcoming).

129 James A. Millward, *Eurasian Crossroads: A History of Xinjiang* (New York: Columbia University Press, 2021), p. 41.

130 Ibid., pp. 50–4.

131 Valerie Hansen, *The Silk Road: A New History* (Oxford: Oxford University Press, 2012), p. 285.

132 Hansen thinks they were probably not ethnically Chinese but embraced Chinese customs: ibid., pp. 90–1.

133 Zhu Lei 朱雷, '龙门石窟高昌张安题记与唐太宗对麴朝大族之政策' ('The inscription of Zhang An at the Longmen rock-cut caves and Tang Taizong's policy towards the major Qu clan'), 敦煌吐鲁番文书论丛 (*Collected essays on Dunhuang and Turpan manuscripts*) (2000), pp. 89–96.

134 Hansen 2012, p. 92.

135 Ibid.

136 Jonathan Skaff, 'Sasanian and Arab-Sasanian Silver Coins from Turfan: Their Relationship to International Trade and the Local Economy', *Asia Major*, vol. 11, no. 2 (1998), pp. 67–115, at p. 95.

137 Hansen 2012, pp. 99–102 and table 3.1; also Skaff 1998, pp. 90–2 and table 5.

138 Hansen 2012, p. 95.

139 Skaff 1998, p. 67, n. 1.

140 Ibid., pp. 79, 89.

141 Ibid., p. 103.

142 Helen Wang, *Money on the Silk Road: The Evidence from Eastern Central Asia to c. AD 800* (London: The British Museum Press, 2004); Helen Wang with Valerie Hansen (issue eds), 'Special Issue: Textiles as Money on the Silk Road', *Journal of the Royal Asiatic Society*, vol. 23, no. 2 (2013).

143 Wang 2004, p. xv.

144 Ibid.

145 Marc Aurel Stein, *Innermost Asia: Detailed Report of Explorations in Central Asia Kan-Su and Eastern Īrān Carried out and Described under the Orders of H.M. Indian Government by Sir Aurel Stein* (Oxford: Clarendon Press, 1928), p. 649.

146 Ibid.

147 Helen Wang, 'How Much for a Camel? A New Understanding of Money on the Silk Road Before AD 800', in Whitfield and Sims-Williams (eds) 2004, pp. 24–33, at p. 25. Stein 1928, p. 649.

148 Stein 1928, pp. 645–7.

149 Skaff 1998, p. 69.

150 Tao Chen et al., 'Archaeobotanical Study of Ancient Food and Cereal Remains at the Astana Cemeteries, Xinjiang, China', *PLOS ONE*, vol. 7, no. 9 (2012), e45137.

151 Robert N. Spengler, *Fruit from the Sands: The Silk Road Origins of the Food We Eat* (Oakland, CA: University of California Press, 2019), pp. 91–106, esp. p. 100.

152 Ibid., p. 106. Susan Whitfield, 'From Plov to Paella', *Index on Censorship*, vol. 34, no. 1 (2005), pp. 125–30.

153 Spengler 2019, p. 227.

154 Ibid., pp. 179, 180.

155 On grapes, see ibid., pp. 175–95.

156 Li Fang 李昉 et al., 太平御览 (*Imperial readings of the Taiping era*) (repr. Beijing: Zhonghua shuju, 1960), juan 844, p. 3733.

157 Whitfield 1985, vol. 3, p. 328; Anne Ewbank, 'How to Recreate 1,300-Year-Old Cookies', *Atlas Obscura*, 15 April 2021, www.atlasobscura.com/articles/how-to-make-ancient-cookies (accessed 21 January 2024).

158 Yiwen Gong et al., 'Investigation of Ancient Noodles, Cakes, and Millet at the Subeixi Site, Xinjiang, China', *Journal of Archaeological Science*, vol. 38, no. 2 (2011), pp. 470–9; Spengler 2019, p. 147.

159 Chen Yi, 'Platters with Teeth and Ewers Lifted from One Side: New Vessel Forms and Foodways in Tang China (618–907)', in *Visual, Material and Textual Cultures of Food and Drink in China, 200 BCE–1900 CE*, ed. Stacey Pierson (Newcastle upon Tyne: Cambridge Scholars Publishing, 2022), pp. 184–237. I am grateful to Dr Chen for sharing her article with me. One example with filling inside, found in Xinjiang, has been called a 'mooncake' (*yuebing*), linking it to mooncakes eaten by Chinese communities today at the Mid-Autumn Festival. See Sun Weiguo 孙维国, '漫谈阿斯塔那墓地出土的月饼及相关问题' ('Discussion on a mooncake excavated from the Astana Cemetery and related issues'), 文物天地 (*Cultural relics world*), no. 10 (2022), pp. 43–6.

160 Beshbaliq was the summer capital. See Millward 2021, p. 46; Michael Brose, 'The Medieval Uyghurs of the 8th through 14th Centuries', *Oxford Research Encyclopedia of Asian History* (June 2017), p. 8.

161 Zsuzsanna Gulácsi, 'The Manichaean Roots of a Pure Land Banner from Uygur Kocho (III 4524) in the Asian Art Museum, Berlin', in *Language, Society, and Religion in the World of the Turks: Festschrift for Larry Clark at Seventy-Five*, ed. Zsuzsanna Gulácsi (Turnhout: Brepols, 2018), pp. 337–76; also discussed in Chhaya Bhattacharya-Haesner, *Central Asian Temple Banners in the Turfan Collection of the Museum für Indische Kunst Berlin: Painted Textiles from the Northern Silk Route* (Berlin: Reimer, 2003), cat. no. 497, pp. 352–5. On cotton in Turpan, see Eric Trombert, 'The Demise of Silk on the Silk Road: Textiles as Money at Dunhuang from the Late Eighth Century to the Thirteenth Century', *Journal of the Royal Asiatic Society*, vol. 23, no. 2 (2013), pp. 327–47, at pp. 341–3.

162 Gulácsi 2018, p. 345.

163 Ibid., p. 344.

164 Ibid., p. 343.

165 Bhattacharya-Haesner 2003, pp. 352–5.

166 Gulácsi 2018.

167 Susan Whitfield (ed.), *Silk Roads: Peoples, Cultures, Landscapes* (London: Thames & Hudson, 2019), pp. 356–63; Samuel N.C. Lieu, *Manichaeism in the Later Roman Empire and Medieval China* (Tübingen: J.C.B. Mohr, 1992).

168 On Manichaeism, see for instance, Lieu 1992; Michael Tardieu, *Manichaeism*, trans. M.B. Devoise (Champaign, IL: University of Illinois Press, 2009). A short introduction is given in Li Tang, *A History of Uighur Religious Conversions: 5th–16th Centuries* (Singapore: Asia Research Institute, National University of Singapore, 2005), p. 16.

169 Yukiyo Kasai, 'Manichaeism and Buddhism in Contact: The Significance of the Uyghur History and its Literary Tradition', *Entangled Religions*, vol. 14, no. 2 (2023), pp. 1–20, at p. 2; Tang 2005, p. 19.

170 Yukiyo Kasai, 'Uyghur Legitimation and the Role of Buddhism', in *Buddhism in Central Asia*, vol. 1, ed. Carmen Meinert and Henrik Sørensen (Leiden: Brill, 2020), pp. 61–90. On a history of Uyghur Buddhism, see Johan Elverskog, *A History of Uyghur Buddhism* (New York: Columbia University Press, 2024).

171 Reproduced in Heuser Manfred and Hans-Joachim Klimkeit, *Studies in Manichaean Literature and Art* (Leiden: Brill, 1998), fig. 10. On architectural elements that survive from Kocho, see Lilla Russell-Smith et al., *The Ruins of Kocho: Traces of Wooden Architecture on the Ancient Silk Road* (Berlin: Museum für Asiatische Kunst, Staatliche Museen zu Berlin, 2016).

172 Lilla Russell-Smith, *Uygur Patronage in Dunhuang: Regional Art Centers on the Northern Silk Road in the Tenth and Eleventh Centuries* (Leiden: Brill, 2005), p. 49; Herbert Härtel and Marianne Yaldiz, *Along the Ancient Silk Routes: Central Asian Art from the West Berlin State Museums* (New York: The Metropolitan Museum of Art, 1982), p. 174.

173 Härtel and Yaldiz 1982, cat. no. 119, p. 181.

174 Zsuzsanna Gulácsi, 'Dating the "Persian" and Chinese Style Remains of Uygur Manichaean Art: A New Radiocarbon Date and its Implications for Central Asian Art History', *Arts Asiatiques*, vol. 58 (2003), pp. 5–33, fig. 10, p. 16.

175 Russell-Smith 2005, pp. 113–14.

176 Gulácsi 2003.

177 Kasai 2023, p. 2.

178 Gulácsi 2018.

179 Larger sections, probably from the front hall, are in the Hermitage, St Petersburg. Whitfield and Sims-Williams (eds) 2004, p. 316; Whitfield 1985, vol. 3, pp. 308–9; Roderick Whitfield and Anne Farrer, *Caves of the Thousand Buddhas: Chinese Art from the Silk Route* (London: The British Museum Press, 1990), p. 179. On the name of the temple complex, see Tian Lu 田璐, '焉耆七个星佛寺名称源流考' ('The origin and development of the name of the Shikshin Buddhist temple near Karasahr'), 美术大观 (*Art panorama*), no. 3 (2023), pp. 135–7. I am grateful to Tian Lu for sharing this article and the reference below with me.

180 Cui Zhonghui 崔中慧, '焉耆明屋锡格沁写经图再探' ('Revisiting the images of sutra copying at Ming-oi Shikshin, near Karasahr'), *Meishu daguan* 美术大观 (*Art panorama*), no. 3 (2023), pp. 32–5, at p. 32.

181 See discussion in Whitfield 1983, vol. 2, cat. no. 149, p. 179; Cui 2023, pp. 33–5.

182 Stein 1921, vol. 3, p. 1214. On the *pothi* format and Uyghur script see Yukiyo Kasai, 'Central Asian and Iranian Influence in Old Uyghur Buddhist Manuscripts: Book Forms and Donor Colophons', *The Syntax of Colophons: A Comparative Study across Pothi Manuscripts*, ed. Nalini Balbir and Giovanni Ciotti (Berlin: De Gruyter, 2022), pp. 373–98, at p. 376.

183 Whitfield and Farrer 1990, p. 170; Cui 2023, p. 34.

184 Whitfield 1982, vol. 1, dates it to the eighth and ninth centuries based on style, cat. no. 95, pp. 328–9; Russell-Smith 2005, p. 201 dates it to the tenth century.

185 Carol Michaelson, 'Jade and the Silk Road: Trade and Tribute in the First Millennium', in Whitfield and Sims-Williams (eds) 2004, pp. 43–9.

186 Whitfield and Sims-Williams (eds) 2004, p. 134.

187 Whitfield (ed.) 2019, p. 221.

188 For instance, a fragment of clamp-resist dyed silk from Balawaste (eastern Khotan) is in the Victoria and Albert Museum's collection (Loan: Stein.303).

189 Whitfield and Sims-Williams (eds) 2004, p. 128.

190 Zhang Zhan, 'Two Judaeo-Persian Letters from Eighth-Century Khotan', *Bulletin of the Asia Institute, vol.* 31 (2022–3), pp. 105–33, at pp. 106–8.

191 Zhang Zhan 张湛 and Shi Guang 时光, '一件新发现犹太波斯语信札的断代与释读' ('Dating and interpretation of a newly discovered Judaeo-Persian letter'), 敦煌吐鲁番研究 (*Studies in Dunhuang and Turpan manuscripts*) vol. 11 (2008), pp. 77–99; Yutaka Yoshida, 'Some New Interpretations of the two Judeo-Persian Letters from Khotan', in *A Thousand Judgements: Festschrift for Maria Macuch*, ed. A. Hintze, D. Durkin-Meisterernst and C. Neumann (Wiesbaden: Harrassowitz, 2019), pp. 385–94; Nima Asefi, 'An Old Letter from Khotan: A Review of an Early Judeo-Persian Letter Called Dandān-Uiliq II', *Persica Antiqua*, vol. 3, no. 4 (2023), pp. 49–60; Zhang 2022–3.

192 Whitfield (ed.) 2019, p. 252.

193 Yoshida 2019.

194 Whitfield (ed.) 2019, p. 252.

195 Joanna Williams, 'The Iconography of Khotanese Painting', *East and West*, vol. 23, no. 1/2 (1973), pp. 109–54, at pp. 150–2; Whitfield 1985, vol. 3, p. 326; Susan Whitfield, *Silk, Slaves, and Stupas: Material Culture of the Silk Road* (Oakland, CA: University of California Press, 2018), pp. 137–48.

196 Matteo Compareti, 'The Representation of Non-Buddhist Deities in Khotanese Paintings and Some Related Problems', in *Studies on the History and Culture along the Continental Silk Road*, ed. Li Xiao (Singapore: Springer, 2020), pp. 89–119, at pp. 101–8, 112–14.

197 Whitfield 1985, vol. 3, cat. no. 68, pp. 315–16; Whitfield and Sims-Williams (eds) 2004, cat. no. 26, p. 137.

198 Three from Dandan Uiliq and one from Khadaliq were collected by Aurel Stein. Four others purchased on the antique market are said to be from Dandan Uiliq. See Williams 1973.

199 Whitfield 1985, vol. 3, pl. 66, pp. 314–15.

200 Compareti 2020.

201 Whitfield 2018, p. 195.

202 Ibid.

203 Qing Duan and Helen Wang, 'Were Textiles Used as Money in Khotan in the Seventh and Eighth Centuries?', *Journal of the Royal Asiatic Society*, vol. 23, no. 2 (2013), pp. 307–25, at p. 308.

204 Whitfield 2018, p. 195, n. 18.

205 Lee and Wiles 2015, p. 195.

206 Ibid.

Sogdians from Central Asia

1 I would like to thank Zumrad Ilyasova for her comments on a draft of this chapter.

2 Pavel Lurje, 'Sogdiana', in *Expedition Silk Road: Journey to the West; Treasures from the Hermitage*, ed. Arnoud Bijl and Birgit Boelens (Amsterdam: Hermitage Amsterdam, 2014), p. 180.

3 Étienne de la Vaissière, *Sogdian Traders: A History*, trans. James Ward (Leiden and Boston, MA: Brill, 2005), p. 95. The early networks are notably recorded in the Sogdian 'Ancient Letters' (312/13 CE), found near Dunhuang, China: see Nicholas Sims-Williams, 'Ancient Letters' (and the references listed there), *The Sogdians: Influencers on the Silk Roads*, Freer Gallery of Art, Smithsonian Institution online exhibition, www.sogdians.si.edu/ancient-letters (n.d., accessed 20 May 2024).

4 Judith Lerner and Thomas Wide, 'Who Were the Sogdians, and Why Do They Matter?', *The Sogdians: Influencers on the Silk Roads*, www.sogdians.si.edu/introduction (accessed 20 January 2024). Yutaka Yoshida, 'Sogdian Language', *Encyclopaedia Iranica*, 2016 online edition, available at www.iranicaonline.org/articles/sogdian-language-01 (accessed 12 January 2024).

5 Lurje 2014, p. 180.

6 Vaissière 2005, pp. 204, 333.

7 Rong Xinjiang, 'Sogdian Merchants and Sogdian Culture on the Silk Road', in *Empires and Exchanges in Eurasian Late Antiquity: Rome, China, Iran, and the Steppe, ca. 250–750*, ed. Michael Maas and Nicola Di Cosmo (Cambridge: Cambridge University Press, 2018), pp. 84–95, at p. 85.

8 Rong 2018, pp. 85–6.

9 Vaissière 2005, p. 137.

10 Yutaka Yoshida thinks this may be the trademark of a Sogdian merchant: Yutaka Yoshida, 'On the Sogdian Brands', *Museum*, Tokyo National Museum (August 1987), p. 17.

11 Lurje 2014, p. 180.

12 Nicholas Sims-Williams, 'The Sogdian Merchants in China and India', in *Cina e Iran da Alessandro Magno alla Dinastia Tang*, ed. Alfredo Cadonna and Lionello Lanciotti (Florence: Leo S. Olschki, 1996), pp. 45–67, at pp. 52–6.

13 Vaissière 2005, ch. 3.

14 Ibid., p. 74; Stephen A. Murphy, 'Ports of Call in Ninth-Century Southeast Asia: The Route of the Tang Shipwreck', in *The Tang Shipwreck: Art and Exchange in the 9th Century*, ed. Alan Chong and Stephen A. Murphy (Singapore: Asian Civilisations Museum, 2017), pp. 234–49, at p. 242.

15 Lurje 2014, p. 180; Vaissière 2005, p. 197.

16 Judith A. Lerner, 'The Merchant Empire of the Sogdians', in *Monks and Merchants: Silk Road Treasures from Northwest China (Gansu and Ningxia 4th–7th Century)* ed. Judith Lerner and Annette Juliano (New York: Harry N. Abrams, 2001), pp. 220–9, at p. 223.

17 Cited in Alain George, 'Direct Sea Trade between Early Islamic Iraq and Tang China: From the Exchange of Goods to the Transmission of Ideas', *Journal of the Royal Asiatic Society*, vol. 25, no. 4 (2015), p. 598; also see Vaissière 2005, pp. 279–82.

18 Lerner 2001, p. 223.

19 Lerner and Wide n.d.

20 Yutaka Yoshida 吉田豊 and Takao Moriyasu 森安孝夫, Xinjiang Uighur Autonomous Museum, '麹氏高昌国時代ソグド文女奴隷売買文書' ('A Sogdian contract for the purchase of an enslaved woman from the kingdom of Gaochang during the rule of the Qu clan'), 内陸アジア言語の研究 (*Studies on the inner Asian languages*), vol. 4 (1988), pp. 1–50; Yutaka Yoshida, 'Translation of the Contract for the Purchase of a Slave Girl Found at Turfan and Dated 639', *T'oung Pao*, vol. 89, no. 1/3 (2003), pp. 159–61.

21 Yoshida 2003, p. 160.

22 Qi Dongfang 齐东方, 唐代金银器研究 (*Studies on the gold and silver vessels of the Tang dynasty*) (Beijing: Zhongguo shehui kexue chubanshe, 1999), pp. 306–7, 333–44. On Sogdian metalwork, see Boris I. Marschak (Marshak), *Silberschätze des Orients: Metallkunst des 3.–13. Jahrhunderts und ihre Kontinuität* (Leipzig: E.A. Seemann, 1986); Boris I. Marshak, 'A Sogdian Silver Bowl in the Freer Gallery of Art', *Ars Orientalis*, vol. 29 (1999), pp. 101–10.

23 Qi 1999, p. 340.

24 Frantz Grenet, 'La vaisselle en argent du 4e au 6e siècle', in *Splendeurs des oasis d'Ouzbékistan*, ed. Rocco Rante and Yannick Lintz (Paris: Musée du Louvre, 2022), pp. 108–9, at p. 108.

25 Qi 1999, pp. 306–15. See also Judith A. Lerner, 'Winged Camel Ewer', *The Sogdians: Influencers on the Silk Roads*, www.sogdians.si.edu/winged-camel-ewer (accessed 11 May 2024).

26 Grenet, 'La vaisselle', in Rante and Lintz (eds) 2022, p. 109.

27 Mariachiara Gasparini, 'Sogdian Textiles along the Silk Roads', *The Sogdians: Influencers on the Silk Roads*, www.sogdians.si.edu/sidebars/sogdian-textiles-along-the-silk-road (accessed 11 May 2024).

28 On these issues see Mariachiara Gasparini, *Transcending Patterns: Silk Road Cultural and Artistic Interactions through Central Asian Textile Images* (Honolulu, HI: University of Hawai'i Press, 2020); Regula Schorta, 'Le tissage de la soie', in Rante and Lintz (eds) 2022, pp. 116–18.

29 Nicholas Sims-Williams and Geoffrey Khan, 'Zandanījī Misidentified', *Bulletin of the Asia Institute*, vol. 22 (2008), pp. 207–13.

30 For instance, see Vaissière 2005, pp. 77–9.

31 Nicholas Sims-Williams, 'Sogdian Language and its Scripts', *The Sogdians: Influencers on the Silk Roads*, www.sogdians.si.edu/sidebars/sogdian-language (accessed 11 May 2024).

32 Ibid.

33 Markus Mode, 'Sogdiana iv. Sogdian Art', *Encyclopaedia Iranica*, online edition, 2016, available at www.iranicaonline.org/articles/sogdiana-vi-sogdian-art (accessed on 25 March 2024).

34 Tomoyuki Usami, Alisher Begmatov and Takao Uno, 'Archaeological Excavation and Documentation of Kafir Kala Fortress', *Studies in Digital Heritage*, vol. 1, no. 2 (2017), pp. 785–96.

35 Alisher Begmatov et al., 'New Discoveries from Kafir-Kala: Coins, Sealings, and Wooden Carvings (Introduction, and Drawings of Wooden Carvings)', *Acta Asiatica: Bulletin of the Institute of Eastern Culture*, vol. 119 (2020), pp. 1–20, at p. 2.

36 Frantz Grenet, 'The Wooden Panels from Kafir-kala: A Group Portrait of the Samarkand nāf (Civic Body)', *Acta Asiatica: Bulletin of the Institute of Eastern Culture*, vol. 119 (2020), pp. 21–42.

37 For a summary of the interpretation on this work, see Frantz Grenet, 'Kafir-kala : la porte en bois', in Rante and Lintz (eds) 2022, pp. 149–53.

38 See Judith Lerner, 'Believers, Proselytizers, Translators: Religion among the Sogdians', *The Sogdians: Influencers on the Silk Roads*, www.sogdians.si.edu/believers-proselytizers-translators (accessed 12 January 2024).

39 I am following Frantz Grenet in referring to this as Zoroastrianism rather than Mazdeism. See Frantz Grenet, 'La coexistence des religions : Le zoroastrisme', in Rante and Lintz (eds) 2022, pp. 83–5. On religions among the Sogdians see Lerner, 'Believers, Proselytizers, Translators', www.sogdians.si.edu/believers-proselytizers-translators (accessed 12 January 2024).

40 Frantz Grenet, 'Mullakurgan Ossuary', in *The Everlasting Flame: Zoroastrianism in History and Imagination*, ed. Sarah Stewart (London and New York: I.B. Tauris, 2013), pp. 100–1, cat. no. 36. Judith Lerner, 'Mulla Kurgan Ossuary', *The Sogdians: Influencers on the Silk Roads*, www.sogdians.si.edu/mulla-kurgan-ossuary (accessed 20 January 2024).

41 Pavel Lurje, 'La religion préislamique du Soghd, de la Bactriane et du Khorezm : Panthéon', trans. Julie Raewsky, in Rante and Lintz (eds) 2022, pp. 160–3. For more on the religion of the Sogdians see Shenkar, Michael, 'The Religion and the Pantheon of the Sogdians (5th–8th centuries CE) in Light of their Sociopolitical Structures', *Journal Asiatique*, no. 2 (2017), pp. 191–209.

42 Thomas Watters, *On Yuan Chwang's Travels in India 629–645 AD* (London: Royal Asiatic Society, 1904), p. 94.

43 On some of the more recent research on the 'Hall of the Ambassadors' wall paintings, see Matteo Compareti and Étienne de la Vaissière (eds), *Royal Nauruz in Samarkand: Proceedings on the Conference Held in Venice on the Pre-Islamic Paintings at Afrasiab* (Pisa: Istituti editoriali e poligrafici internazionali, 2006); Frantz Grenet, 'What was the Afrasiab Painting about?', *Rivista degli studi orientali*, vol. 78 (2006), pp. 43–58; Matteo Compareti, *Samarkand the Center of the World: Proposals for the Identification of the Afrāsyāb Paintings* (Costa Mesa, CA: Mazda Publishers, Inc., 2016); Frantz Grenet, 'À l'occasion de la restauration de la "Peinture des Ambassadeurs" (Samarkand, c. 660). Retour sur une œuvre majeure de la peinture Sogdienne', *Comptes-rendus des séances de l'Académie des Inscriptions et Belles-Lettres*, vol. 162 (2018), pp. 1849–72; Frantz Grenet, 'Afrasiab et la "Peinture des Ambassadeurs"', in Rante and Lintz (eds) 2022, pp. 125–31. Wang Jing 王静 and Shen Ruiwen 沈睿文, 大使厅壁画研究 (*Study on the murals of the Ambassadors Hall*) (Beijing: Wenwu chubanshe, 2022).

44 On the depiction of silks on this wall painting, see Zumrad Ilyasova, 'From Cocoons to Kaftans: Splendid Silks at the Sogdian Court in Samarkand', *Orientations* (Sept 2024) (forthcoming).

45 Grenet 2006, p. 53.

46 Ibid.

47 Grenet, 'Afrasiab', in Rante and Lintz (eds) 2022, p. 128.

48 Matteo Compareti and Simone Cristoforetti, 'Proposal for a New Interpretation of the Northern Wall of the "Hall of the Ambassadors" at Afrasyab, in Central Asia from the Achaemenians to the Timurids', *Archaeology, History, Ethnology, Culture. Materials of the International Conference Devoted to the Centenary of Aleksandr Markovič Belenickij*, ed. V.P. Nikonorov (St Petersburg: Institute of History of Material Culture (RAS), 2005), pp. 215–20; Grenet 2006.

49 Wang Pu 王溥, 唐会要 (*Institution history of the Tang*) (Shanghai: Shanghai shangwu yinshuguan, repr. 1935), *juan* 99, p. 1774; Gaozong had already recognised Varkhuman as governor between 650 and 655. See Ouyang Xiu 欧阳修, 新唐书 (*New book of Tang*) (Beijing: Zhonghua shuju, repr. 1975), *juan* 221, p. 6244.

50 Shao-yun Yang, *Late Tang China and the World, 750–907 CE* (Cambridge: Cambridge University Press, 2023), pp. 22–38, 41.

51 Vaissière 2005, p. 2.

Central Asia and the steppe

1 Luk Yu-ping would like to thank Sue Brunning for her comments and detailed edits of an earlier draft of this chapter. Thanks to Elisabeth O'Connell and St John Simpson for their comments and references, and to Saltanat Amirova and Valerii Kolchenko for information on artefacts from Kazakhstan and Kyrgyzstan, respectively.

2 Warwick Ball, *The Eurasian Steppe: People, Movement, Ideas* (Edinburgh: Edinburgh University Press, 2022), p. 38.

3 Michael D. Frachetti et al., 'Nomadic Ecology Shaped the Highland Geography of Asia's Silk Roads', *Nature*, vol. 543 (2017), pp. 193–8. See also David Christian, 'Silk Roads or Steppe Roads? The Silk Roads in World History', *Journal of World History*, vol. 11 (2000), pp. 1–26.

4 Michael R. Drompp, 'Inner Asia', in *A Companion to the Global Early Middle Ages*, ed. Erik Hermans (Leeds: Arc Humanities Press, 2020), pp. 225–52, at p. 225.

5 Peter Golden, 'The Turks: A Historical Overview', in *Turks: A Journey of a Thousand Years, 600–1600*, ed. David J. Roxburgh (London: Royal Academy of Arts, 2005), pp. 18–31, at p. 20.

6 These have been displayed, for example, in the exhibitions *Scythians: warriors of ancient Siberia* (British Museum, 2017–18) and *Gold of the Great Steppe* (Fitzwilliam Museum, 2021–22). On Turkic polities and the Silk Roads, see, for instance, Christopher I. Beckwith, *Empires of the Silk Road: A History of Central Eurasia from the Bronze Age to the Present* (Princeton: Princeton University Press, 2009), pp. 112–39; Christoph Baumer, *The History of Central Asia: The Age of the Silk Roads* (London: I.B. Tauris, 2014); Étienne de la Vaissière, *Asie centrale 300–850 : Des routes et des royaumes* (Paris: Les Belles Lettres, 2024).

7 Zainolla Samashev, Azat Aitkali and Yerlik Tolegenov, 'К вопросу о сакрализации образа кагана' ('On the question of the sacralisation of the image of the khagan'), in *Поволжская археология* (*The Volga River Region Archaeology*), vol. 2 (2022), pp. 21–34; Mehmet Kutlu, 'Preliminary Evaluation on the Kurgans of Turkic Period at Eleke Sazy Valley', in *Social and Humanities Science: Research, Theory*, ed. Şükrü Ünar and Senem Karagöz (Lyon: Livre de Lyon, 2021), pp. 107–18.

8 Samashev, Aitkali and Tolegenov 2022, p. 31.

9 Esther Jacobson-Tepfer, *Monumental Archaeology in the Mongolian Altai: Intention, Memory, Myth* (Leiden: Brill, 2023), pp. 201–25. *Balbal* can also mean small stones extending in a row to the east: see ibid., p. 198, n. 22.

10 Earlier examples of stone statues related to the Scythians are mentioned in St John Simpson and Svetlana Pankova (eds), *Scythians: Warriors of Ancient Siberia* (London: Thames & Hudson/The British Museum, 2017).

11 For some examples found in Kyrgyzstan, see Y.S. Hudiakov et al., 'Ancient Turkic Stone Statues at Tuura-Suu, Kyrgyzstan', *Archaeology, Ethnology and Anthropology of Eurasia*, vol. 43 (2015), pp. 109–15.

12 Jacobson-Tepfer 2023, pp. 220–21.

13 Information provided by the National Museum of the Republic of Kazakhstan.

14 Giles Dawkes and Gaygysyz Jorayev, 'A Case Study of an Early Islamic City in Transoxiana: Excavations at the Medieval Citadel in Taraz, Kazakhstan', *Archaeological Research in Asia*, vol. 4 (2015), pp. 17–24, at p. 18.

15 A. Onggaruly (ed.), *Великая степь: история и культура* (*The Great Steppe: History and Culture*), vol. 3: *Мир древних тюрков* (*The World of the Ancient Turks*) (Nur-Sultan: National Museum of the Republic of Kazakhstan, 2019), pp. 185–7.

16 Serik Sh. Akylbek, Erbulat A. Smagulov and Sergey A. Yatsenko, 'Décor of the Eighth-Century Turkic Rulers' Residence in the Citadel of Kulan Town', *The Silk Road*, vol. 15 (2017), pp. 65–82, at p. 79.

17 Ibid., p. 69.

18 Onggaruly (ed.) 2019, p. 187.

19 Ibid., p. 185.

20 James C.Y. Watt et al., *China: Dawn of a Golden Age, 200–750 AD* (New York: The Metropolitan Museum of Art, 2004), cat. no. 97, pp. 190–1.

21 Michael Fedorov, 'A Sogdian Incense-Burner of the Late VII–Early VIII c. AD from Koshoi Korgon Hillfort', *Iranica Antiqua*, vol. 36 (2001), pp. 361–81, at pp. 367–70.

22 More information on Kesken-Kuyuk Kala, Kazakhstan, is available at www.exploration-eurasia.com (accessed 15 June 2024). See Karl M. Baipakov, 'The Ancient Settlement of Kesken–Kuyuk–Kala in the Eastern Aral Region', in *Urban Cultures of Central Asia from the Bronze Age to the Karakhanids: Learnings and Conclusions from New Archaeological Investigations and Discoveries*, ed. Christoph Baumer and Mirko Novák (Wiesbaden: Harrassowitz Verlag, 2019), pp. 415–32, at pp. 422–3. Heinrich Härke and Irina Arzhantseva, 'Interfaces and Crossroads, Contexts and Communications: Early Medieval Towns in the Syr-Darya Delta (Kazakhstan)', *Journal of Urban Archaeology*, vol. 3 (2021), pp. 51–63.

23 J. Harmatta and B.A. Litvinsky, 'Tokharistan and Gandhara under Western Turk Rule (650–750)', in *History of Civilizations of Central Asia: The Crossroads of Civilizations A.D. 250 to 750*, ed. B.A. Litvinsky, Zhang Guang-da and R. Samghabadi (Paris: UNESCO, 1996), pp. 365–400, at p. 369.

24 Craig G.R. Benjamin, *Empires of Ancient Eurasia: The First Silk Roads Era, 100 BCE–250 CE* (Cambridge: Cambridge University Press, 2018), p. 260. On Buddhism and other religions at Merv, see Barbara Kaim and Maja Kornacka, 'Religious Landscape of the Ancient Merv Oasis', *Iran*, vol. 54, no. 2 (2016), pp. 47–72. On Mes Aynak, see Deborah Klimburg-Salter, 'Contextualizing Mes Aynak', *Afghanistan*, vol. 1, no. 2 (2018), pp. 213–38.

25 Valérie Zaleski, 'La diffusion du bouddhisme sur les terres du Tadjikistan', in *Tadjikistan: au pays des fleuves d'or*, ed. Musée Guimet (Paris: Éditions Snoeck Musée national des arts asiatiques-Guimet, 2020), pp. 199–230, at p. 200.

26 Baumer 2014, p. 203.

27 Zaleski 2020, p. 200.

28 Peter Zieme, 'Religions of the Turks in the Pre-Islamic Period', in Roxburgh (ed.) 2005, pp. 32–7, at p. 33.

29 Baumer 2014, p. 203.

30 Ball 2022, p. 370.

31 Matteo Compareti, 'Traces of Buddhist Art in Sogdiana', *Sino-Platonic Papers*, vol. 181 (Aug 2008), pp. 1–42.

32 B.A. Litvinsky, 'Ajina Tepe', *Encyclopaedia Iranica*, 1984 (updated 2011), available at iranicaonline.org/articles/ajina-tepe-the-present-day-name-of-the-mound-covering-the-ruins-of-an-early-medieval-buddhist-monastery-sarigharama (accessed 20 May 2024).

33 Zaleski 2020, p. 200; Baumer 2014, p. 204.

34 Ibid., p. 200; Litvinsky 2011.

35 Zaleski 2020, p. 200; Litvinsky 2011.

36 Zaleski 2020, p. 201.

37 Ibid., p. 202.

38 Ibid., p. 201.

39 B.A. Litvinsky and Tamara Ivanovna Zeymal, *Буддийский Монастырь Аджина-Тепа (Таджикистан): Раскопки, Архитектура, Искусство* (*Buddhist Monastery of Adjina-Tepa (Tajikistan): Excavations, Architecture, Art*) (St Petersburg: Nestor-Istoriâ, 2010), p. 191.

40 Peter Stewart, *Gandharan Art and the Classical World: A Short Introduction* (Oxford: Archaeopress, 2023), pp. 1–2.

41 Zaleski 2020, p. 200.

42 Ibid.

43 Stewart 2023, p. 2.

44 Zaleski 2020, p. 310.

45 Ibid., p. 204.

46 Valerii Kolchenko, trans. Gulzat Usubalieva, 'Buddhism in the Chuy Valley (Kyrgyzstan) in the Middle Ages', *Journal of Oriental Studies*, vol. 30 (2020) pp. 67–101, at p. 67.

47 Gregory Semenov, 'Suyab', *Encyclopaedia Iranica*, 20 July 2002, www.iranicaonline.org/articles/suyab (accessed 20 May 2024).

48 Shigeo Saito, 'Suiye (碎葉) and Ak-Beshim: A Historical Development at the Western Tien-shan in the 7th to the First Half of the 8th Century', *Protection and Research on Cultural Heritage in the Chuy Valley, the Kyrgyz Republic Ak-Beshim and Ken Bulun* (Bishkek and Tokyo: Institute of History and Cultural Heritage of the National Academy of Sciences of the Kyrgyz Republic/Tokyo National Research Institute for Cultural Properties, 2017), pp. 91–107.

49 Wang Wencai 王文才, '李白家世探微' ('Exploring Li Bai's family history'), 四川师院学报 (*Journal of Sichuan Normal University*), no. 4 (1979), pp. 50–54, 14.

50 Semenov 2002. To the Mongol period, see Valerii Kolchenko, 'Medieval Towns in the Chuy Valley', in *Protection and Research on Cultural Heritage in the Chuy Valley, the Kyrgyz Republic, Ak-Beshim and Ken-Bulun* (Tokyo: Tokyo National Research Institute for Cultural Properties, 2017), pp. 17–30, at p. 22; for the number of sites and their proposed dating see Kolchenko 2020, p. 75, table 2.

51 Kolchenko 2017, pp. 21–2.

52 Kolchenko 2020, pp. 85–6.

53 Valerii Kolchenko ヴァレリー・コルチェンコ, 'キルギスタン・チュー川流域における中世仏教の考古遺産 (前編)' ('Archaeological monuments of medieval Buddhism in the Chüy Valley, Kyrgyzstan'), 東洋学術研究 (*Journal of Oriental Studies*), vol. 59, no. 1 (2020), pp. 197–250, at p. 209.

54 Kolchenko 2020, p. 95.

55 Ibid.

56 Kolchenko 2017, p. 20. See also Wassilios Klein, 'A Christian Heritage on the Northern Silk Road: Archaeological and Epigraphic Evidence of Christianity in Kyrgyzstan', *Journal of the Canadian Society for Syriac Studies*, vol. 1 (2010), pp. 85–100, at p. 85.

57 Klein 2010, p. 86.

58 Ibid., pp. 20–1. Later in the wider context, Christianity continued with the discovery many tombstones with Syriac inscriptions from around 1250 onwards found the capital Bishkek and nearby Tokmak. But it is not clear whether it continued from Ak-Beshim or was re-introduced from elsewhere.

59 Kolchenko 2017, p. 21.

60 Klein 2010, p. 89.

61 On the Hindu Shahi dynasty, see Muhammad Zahir et al., 'Investigating the Hindu Shahi Kingdom in North-western Pakistan Through Systematic Landscape Survey', *Journal of Asian Civilisations*, vol. 44, no. 1, June 2021, pp. 135–70.

62 For the early history of this, see Simpson and Pankova 2017, pp. 262, 264.

63 Gani Omarov et al., 'Horse Equipment of Medieval Nomads of the Kazakh Altai (Based on Materials From the Tuyetas Burial Ground)', *Archaeological Research in Asia*, vol. 31 (2022), pp. 1–15.

64 Ibid., pp. 5–7, 13–14.

65 Ibid., p. 6; on the conservation of this bridle, see p. 12.

66 For a summary of the finds, see Zhalgas Zhalmaganbetov, Zainolla Samashev and Ulan Umitkaliev, 'Ancient Musicians' Monuments in the Kazakh Altai', *The Anthropologist*, vol. 22, no. 3 (2015), pp. 545–52.

67 Onggaruly (ed.) 2019, pp. 334–5.

68 Ibid., p. 331.

69 Zhalmaganbetov, Samashev and Umitkaliev 2015, p. 548.

70 Omarov et al. 2022.

71 Elena V. Stepanova, 'Saddles of the Hun-Sarmatian Period', in *Masters of the Steppe: The Impact of the Scythians and Later Nomad Societies in Eurasia*, ed. Svetlana V. Pankova and St John Simpson (Oxford: Archaeopress, 2020), pp. 561–87, at p. 586.

72 Ibid.

73 Ibid., p. 561.

74 Ibid., p. 582.

75 Ibid.

76 Ibid, pp. 561–87.

77 Sonja Marzinzik, *Masterpieces: Early Medieval Art* (London: The British Museum Press, 2013), pp. 280–1.

78 The development of stirrups, and the true extent of their impact, has been much debated: see Jessica Hemming, 'The Great Stirrup Controversy', in *The Ancient and Medieval World*, ed. Adrianna Bakos et al. (Surrey, BC: Kwantlen Polytechnic University) and Florin Curta, 'The Earliest Avar Stirrups, or the "Stirrup Controversy" Revisited', in *The Other Europe in the Middle Ages: Avars, Bulgars, Khazars and Cumans*, ed. Florin Curta (Leiden: Brill, 2007), pp. 237–62. Nevertheless, it was clearly of major significance, being rapidly and widely adopted.

79 Elfriede R. Knauer, 'A Quest for the Persian Riding-Coats: Sleeved Garments with Underarm Openings', in *Riding Costume in Egypt: Origin and Appearance*, ed. Cäcilia Fluck and Gillian Vogelsang-Eastwood (Leiden: Brill, 2004), pp. 7–28, at p. 8.

80 Ibid., p. 7.

81 Gillian Vogelsang-Eastwood, 'Sasanian "Riding Coats": The Iranian Evidence', in Fluck and Vogelsang-Eastwood (eds) 2004, pp. 209–29, at pp. 218–23.

82 Ulrike Beck et al., 'The invention of trousers and its likely affiliation with horseback riding and mobility: A case study of late 2nd millennium BC finds from Turfan in eastern Central Asia', *Quaternary International*, vol. 348 (2014), pp. 224–35.

83 Xinru Liu, 'Silk, Robes, and Relations Between Early Chinese Dynasties and Nomads beyond the Great Wall', in *Robes and Honor: The New Middle Ages*, ed. S. Gordon (New York: Palgrave Macmillan, 2001), pp. 23–34, at pp. 32–33. This is developed in Kyoko Nomoto, 'Dressing as Horsemen: The Universalisation of Steppe Dress in the First Half of Tang Dynasty China (618–755)', PhD dissertation, Oxford University, 2022. I am grateful to Dr Nomoto for sharing her thesis.

84 On the argument of cultural hybridisation in robes see Nomoto 2022, p. 170.

85 For an overview of the archaeological finds from the tombs of Moshchevaya Balka, see Anna A. Ierusalimskaja, *Die Gräber der Moščevaja Balka: frühmittelalterliche Funde an der nordkaukasischen Seidenstrasse* (Munich: Editio Maris, 1996).

86 Prudence O. Harper, 'A Man's Caftan and Leggings from the North Caucasus of the Eighth to Tenth Century: Introduction', *Metropolitan Museum Journal*, vol. 36 (2001), pp. 83–4, at p. 83.

87 Elfriede R. Knauer, 'A Man's Caftan and Leggings from the North Caucasus of the Eighth to Tenth Century: A Genealogical Study', *Metropolitan Museum Journal*, vol. 36 (2001), p. 131.

88 Ibid., pp. 125–54.

89 Yeonok Sim, 'Pearl Roundel Patterns: Regional Variations in Iconography', in *Textiles and Clothing along the Silk Roads*, ed. Zhao Feng and Marie Louise Nosch (Paris and Hangzhou: UNESCO and China National Silk Museum, 2022), pp. 173–87.

90 Knauer 2001.

91 Csete Katona, *Vikings of the Steppe: Scandinavians, Rus', and the Turkic World (c. 750–1050)* (London: Routledge, 2023), p. 31; Peter Golden, Haggai Ben-Shammai and András Roná-Tas (eds), *The World of the Khazars – New Perspectives: Selected Papers from the Jerusalem 1999 International Khazar Colloquium* (Leiden: Brill, 2007).

Vikings on the *austrvegr*

1 Csete Katona, *Vikings of the Steppe: Scandinavians, Rus' and the Turkic World (c. 750–1050)* (London: Routledge, 2023), pp. 36, 155–6; Helmer Gustavson, 'Runmonumentet i Rytterne', in *Nya Anteckningar om Rytterns Socken*, ed. Olle Ferm (Västerås: Västmanlands läns museum, 2002), pp. 145–7; Neil Price, Marianne Hem Eriksen and Carsten Jahnke (eds), *Vikings in the Mediterranean* (Athens: Norwegian Institute in Athens, 2023); Charlotte Hedenstierna-Jonson, John Ljungkvist and Neil Price, *The Vikings Begin* (Uppsala: Gustavianum, Uppsala University Museum, 2018), pp. 31–5.

2 Garnets: Charlotte Hedenstierna-Jonson, 'Archaeological Evidence of Contacts between Scandinavia and Central Asia in the Viking Age and the Tang Dynasty', *Bulletin of the Museum of Far Eastern Antiquities*, vol. 81 (2020), p. 58. Indian coin, known as a Jital: Historiska Museet, Stockholm 3000848, Eeva Jonsson, *En rik handelsmans silverskatt* (Stockholm: Kungliga Myntkabinettet, 2013), Hedenstierna-Jonson 2020, p. 58. Chinese silk: Historiska Museet, Stockholm 617937_HST, Hedenstierna-Jonson 2020, fig. 3.

3 Fedir Androshchuk, *Vikings in the East: Essays on Contacts along the Road to Byzantium* (Uppsala: Uppsala Universitetet, 2013); Neil Price, *The Children of Ash and Elm* (London: Penguin Books, 2022), pp. 423, 437; Cat Jarman, *River Kings: A New History of the Vikings from Scandinavia to the Silk Roads* (London: William Collins, 2021), p. 165; Marika Mägi, *In Austrvegr: The Role of the Eastern Baltic in Viking Age Communication across the Baltic Sea* (Leiden: Brill, 2018), pp. 97–117; Søren Sindbæk, 'Trading Towns and Market Sites: The "Small World" of the Viking Age', in *Rus: Vikings in the East*, ed. Pauline Asingh and Kristian Jensen (Moesgaard: Moesgaard Museum, 2022), p. 66; Hedenstierna-Jonson, Ljungkvist and Price 2018, pp. 22–7, 35–6; Hedenstierna-Jonson 2020, pp. 46–50, 59; Katona 2023, pp. 3, 24–9, 36, 160; T. Douglas Price et al., 'Human Remains, Context, and Place of Origin for the Salme, Estonia, Boat Burials', *Journal of Anthropological Archaeology*, vol. 58 (2020), e101149.

4 Þórir Jónsson Hraundal, 'The Rus in Arabic Sources: Cultural Contacts and Identity', PhD thesis, University of Bergen, 2013.

5 Katona 2023, pp. 28; Jarman 2021, pp. 114–15.

6 From grave Bj.581: Linda Wåhlander (ed.), *Begravd på Birka: Tre århundraden, fyra vikingaliv* (Stockholm: Åtta45, 2020), pp. 158–62; Katona 2023, p. 120.

7 Charlotte Hedenstierna-Jonson, 'Warriors Wearing Silk', in Price, Eriksen and Jahnke (eds) 2023, pp. 223–40, with references; Agnes Geijer, *Birka III: Die Textilfunde aus Gräbern* (Uppsala: Almquist & Wiksell, 1938); Marianne Vedeler, *Silk for the Vikings* (Oxford: Oxbow, 2014), pp. 27–8, 36, 56–7; Wåhlander (ed.) 2020, pp. 158–61.

8 Fredrik Lundström, Charlotte Hedenstierna-Jonson and Lena Holquist Olausson, 'Eastern Archery in Birka's Garrison', in *The Martial Society: Aspects of Warriors, Fortifications and Social Change in Scandinavia*, ed. Lena Holmquist Olausson and Michael Olausson (Stockholm: Stockholm University, 2009), p. 111; Wåhlander (ed.) 2020, pp. 160–1; Katona 2023, p. 120.

9 Lundström, Hedenstierna-Jonson and Olausson 2009, p. 111; Wåhlander (ed.) 2020, pp. 160–1; Katona 2023, p. 120; Ahmad ibn Fadlan, *Mission to the Volga*, trans. James E. Montgomery, (New York: New York University Press, 2017).

10 Price 2022, p. 424; Katona 2023, pp. 4–6, 120; Lars Grundvad, 'Fine Feathers Make Fine Birds: Middle Eastern Fashions in the Viking Homelands', in Asingh and Jensen (eds) 2022, pp. 139–46; Ibn Rustah, *Kitab Al-A'lq Al-Nafisa*, in *Ibn Fadlān and the Land of Darkness: Arab Travellers in the Far North*, trans. Paul Lunde and Caroline Stone (London: Penguin, 2012), III.13. A rider wearing baggy trousers appears on a picture-stone from Broa, dated to the eighth to ninth century: Sune Lindqvist, *Gotlands Bildsteine*, 2 vols (Stockholm: Wahlström and Widstrand, 1941/2), vol. 1, fig. 105 and vol. 2, fig. 384.

11 Archery equipment was also found at Birka's garrison, including a possible thumb ring similar to those used by archers in parts of Asia and southeast Europe, where the thumb, not the fingers, drew the bowstring. Lundström, Hedenstierna-Jonson and Olausson 2009, passim; Price 2022, p. 434; Kim Hjardar and Vegard Vike, *Vikings at War* (Oxford: Casemate, 2011), pp. 182, 195–6; Katona 2023, pp. 6–7, 96–8, 117–18.

12 Katona 2023, pp. 28, 96–8; Price 2022, p. 434.

13 Hedenstierna-Jonson 2020, p. 59; Price 2022, pp. 438–9; Ibn Khurradadhbih, *Kitāb al-Masālik wa-l-Mamālik*, in Lunde and Stone 2012, III.5; Hedenstierna-Jonson, Ljungkvist and Price 2018, pp. 36–8; Magnus Källström, 'Byzantium Reflected in the Runic Inscriptions of Scandinavia', in *Byzantium and the Viking World*, ed. Fedir Androshchuk, Jonathan Shepard and Monica White (Uppsala: Uppsala Universitetet, 2016), pp. 169–86.

14 Hedenstierna-Jonson 2020; Egil Mikkelsen, 'Islam and Scandinavia during the Viking Age', in *Byzantium and Islam in Scandinavia: Acts of a Symposium at Uppsala University, June 15–16 1996*, ed. Elisabeth Piltz (Oxford: Archaeopress, 1998), pp. 39–51; Matthew C. Delvaux, 'Transregional Slave Networks of the Northern Arc, 700–900 CE', PhD thesis, Boston College, Morrissey College of Arts and Sciences Graduate School, 2019; James H. Barrett, Natalia Khamaiko, Giada Ferrari, Angélica Cuevas, Catherine Kneale, Anne Karin Hufthammer, Albína Hulda Pálsdóttir and Bastiaan Star, 'Walruses on the Dnieper: New Evidence for the Intercontinental Trade of Greenlandic Ivory in the Middle Ages', *Proceedings of the Royal Society of London, Biological Sciences*, vol. 289 (2022); Richard L. Smith, 'Trade and Commerce', in *A Companion to the Global Middle Ages*, ed. Erik Hermans (Amsterdam: Amsterdam University Press, 2020), pp. 446–52; Andreas Hennius, *Outlanders? Resource Colonisation, Raw Material Exploitation and Networks in Middle Iron Age Sweden* (Uppsala: Uppsala Universitet, 2021), p. 72; Roman K. Kovalev, 'The Infrastructure of the Northern Part of the "Fur Road" between the Middle Volga and the East during the Middle Ages', *Archivum Eurasiae medii aevi*, vol. 11 (2000/1), pp. 25–64.

15 Price 2022, pp. 370–1, 440–1; Jane Kershaw et al., 'The Scale of Dirham Imports to the Baltic in the Ninth Century: New Evidence from Archaeometric Analyses of Early Viking Age Silver', *Fornvännen*, vol. 116 (2021), pp. 185–204; Jarman 2021, pp. 119, 167–9; Ann-Marie Pettersson (ed.), *The Spillings Hoard: Gotlands Role in Viking Age World Trade* (Visby: Fornsalens Förlag, 2009); Jonathan Shepard, 'Why Gotland?', in *Viking-Age Trade: Silver, Slaves and Gotland*, ed. Jacek Gruszczyński, Jonathan Shepard and Marek Jankowiak (London: Taylor & Francis, 2021), pp. 1–12; Dan Carlsson, 'Gotland: Silver Island', in Gruszczyński, Shepard and Jankowiak (eds) 2021, pp. 225–6; Sindbæk 2022, p. 67; Mikkelsen 1998, p. 45; Sunhild Kleingärtner and Gareth Williams, 'Contacts and Exchange', in *Vikings: Life and Legend*, ed. Gareth Williams, Peter Pentz and Matthias Wemhoff (London: The British Museum Press, 2014), p. 57.

16 Marek Jankowiak and Felix Biermann, 'Introduction: An "Invisible Commodity"?', in *The Archaeology of Slavery in Early Medieval Northern Europe: The Invisible Commodity*, ed. Marek Jankowiak and Felix Biermann (Cham: Springer International Publishing, 2021), p. 2; Marek Jankowiak, 'Tracing the Saqaliba: Slave Trade and the Archaeology of the Slavic Lands in the Tenth Century', in Jankowiak and Biermann (eds) 2021, pp. 161–82; Alice Rio, *Slavery after Rome* (Oxford: Oxford University Press, 2017), pp. 19, 22–5, 29; Price 2022, pp. 441–2; Michael McCormick, *Origins of the European Economy: Communications and Commerce, AD 300–900* (Cambridge: Cambridge University Press, 2001), pp. 734 ff., 745–6, 760–1, cf. pp. 775–6; Delvaux 2019, pp. 45–50.

17 Jankowiak 2021, pp. 162–3, 166; Delvaux 2019, pp. 20, 149, 219–20.

18 Jankowiak 2021, pp. 162–76.

19 *Vita Sancti Findani Confessoris*, trans. Reidar Thorolf Christiansen, 'The People of the North', *Lochlann: A Review of Celtic Studies*, vol. 2 (1962), pp. 156–8; Delvaux 2019, pp. 29–33, 40–1; Christopher Lowe, 'Image and Imagination: The Inchmarnock "Hostage Stone"', in *West Over Sea: Studies in Scandinavian Sea-borne Expansion and Settlement Before 1300: A Festschrift in Honour of Dr. Barbara E. Crawford*, ed. Gareth Williams, Beverley Ballin Smith and Simon Taylor (Leiden: Brill, 2007), pp. 53–68.

20 This restraint and other recorded examples of iron shackles are interpretatively ambiguous: Jankowiak 2021, p. 167; Janel M. Fontaine, 'Early Medieval Slave-trading in the Archaeological Record: Comparative Methodologies', *Early Medieval Europe*, vol. 25 (2017), pp. 466–88.

Central Asia to Arabia

1 Luk Yu-ping would like to thank Sue Brunning, Elisabeth O'Connell, Noorah Al-Gailani, St John Simpson and Arietta Papaconstantinou for their comments on drafts of this chapter. Dr Papaconstantinou also provided helpful references.

2 For an introduction see Hugh Kennedy, *The Great Arab Conquests: How the Spread of Islam Changed the World We Live In* (London: Weidenfeld & Nicolson, 2007).

3 Philippe Beaujard, *The Worlds of the Indian Ocean: A Global History*, vol. 2: *From the Seventh Century to the Fifteenth Century CE* (Cambridge: Cambridge University Press, 2019), p. 50.

4 For a brief introduction, see Touraj Daryaee, *Sasanian Persia: The Rise and Fall of an Empire* (London: I.B. Tauris, 2013).

5 Seth Priestman, 'The Silk Road or the Sea? Sasanian and Islamic Exports to Japan', *Journal of Islamic Archaeology*, vol. 3, no. 1 (2016), pp. 10–11.

6 Touraj Daryaee, 'Bazaars, Merchants, and Trade in Late Antique Iran', *Comparative Studies of South Asia, Africa and the Middle East*, vol. 30, no. 3 (2010), p. 4019.

7 Procopius, *History of the Wars*, vol. 1: *Books 1–2 (Persian War)*, trans. H.B. Dewing (Cambridge, MA: Harvard University Press, 1914), p. 193.

8 Alan Walmsley, *Early Islamic Syria: An Archaeological Assessment* (London: Duckworth, 2007), pp. 34–6.

9 Walmsley 2007, pp. 39–42. Fanny Bessard, *Caliphs and Merchants: Cities and Economies of Power in the Near East (700–950)* (Oxford: Oxford University Press, 2020).

10 Craig Benjamin, *Empires of Ancient Eurasia: The First Silk Roads Era, 100 BCE–250 CE* (Cambridge: Cambridge University Press, 2018), p. 254.

11 On Yazdegerd's death, see Kennedy 2007, pp. 186–91.

12 Kennedy 2007, p. 191.

13 Walter Scheidel, 'The Scale of Empire', in *The Oxford World History of Empire*, vol. 1, ed. Peter Fibiger Bang, C.A. Bayly and Walter Scheidel (New York: Oxford University Press, 2021), pp. 91–110, at p. 93.

14 Michael Shenkar, 'The Arab Conquest and the Collapse of the Sogdian Civilization', in *The History and Culture of Iran and Central Asia in the First Millennium CE: From the Pre-Islamic to the Islamic Era*, ed. D.G. Tor and Minoru Inaba (Notre Dame: Notre Dame University Press, 2022), pp. 95–125, at p. 110.

15 Etienne de la Vaissière, *Sogdian Traders: A History*, trans. James Ward (Leiden: Brill, 2005), p. 271.

16 Annabelle Collinet, 'Une nouvelle culture matérielle', in *Splendeurs des oasis d'Ouzbékistan*, ed. Rocco Rante and Yannick Lintz (Paris: Musée du Louvre, 2022), pp. 189–93, at p. 189, cat. no. 140.

17 Ladan Akbarnia et al., *The Islamic World: A History in Objects* (London: Thames & Hudson/The British Museum, 2018), pp. 50–1. Collinet 2022, p. 189.

18 Akbarnia et al. 2018, p. 50.

19 Shenkar 2022, p. 95.

20 Ibid., pp. 98–111.

21 Frantz Grenet, 'Varakhsha: les peintures de la "Salle Rouge" et les stucs', in Rante and Lintz (eds) 2022, pp. 138–42, at p. 138.

22 Aleksandr I. Naymark, 'Returning to Varakhsha', *The Silk Road Foundation Newsletter* 1, 2 (2003), pp. 9–22, at pp. 16–18.

23 Julie Bellemare and Judith A. Lerner, 'The Wall Paintings in the Palace at Varakhsha', Freer Gallery of Art, Smithsonian Institution online exhibition, www.sogdians.si.edu/varakhsah-wall-paintings (accessed 24 March 2024).

24 Naymark 2003, pp. 16–18.

25 Grenet 2022, p. 139.

26 Naymark 2003, p. 18.

27 Grenet 2022, p. 138.

28 Ibid.

29 Shenkar 2022, p. 95.

30 Glen W. Bowersock, *The Crucible of Islam* (Cambridge, MA: Harvard University Press, 2017), pp. 117–19.

31 Frank Harold, 'Bamiyan and Buddhist Afghanistan', Silk Road Seattle, depts.washington.edu/silkroad/cities/afghanistan/bamiyan.html (accessed 20 May 2024).

32 Sophie Makariou and Nicolas Engel (eds), *Afghanistan ombres et légendes. Un siècle de recherches archéologiques* (Paris: Musée Guimet: LienArt, 2022), p. 100. Llewelyn Morgan, *The Buddhas of Bamiyan* (London: Profile Books, 2012), pp. 96–7.

33 Morgan 2012, p. 97.

34 Ibid., pp. 97–8.

35 Deborah Klimburg-Salter, 'Entangled Narrative Biographies of the Colossal Sculptures of Bāmiyān: Heroes of the Mythic History of the Conversion to Islam', in *The Future of the Bamiyan Buddha Statues: Heritage Reconstruction in Theory and Practice*, ed. Masanori Nagaoka (Paris: UNESCO/Springer, 2020), pp. 215–37.

36 Joseph Hackin and Jean Carl, *Nouvelles Recherches archéologiques à Bāmiyān*, vol. 1 (Paris: G. van Oest, 1933), pp. 25–6, figs 48, 98.

37 Minoru Inaba, 'The Narratives on the Bāmiyān Buddhist Remains in the Islamic Period', *Encountering Buddhism and Islam in Premodern Central and South Asia*, ed. Blain Auer and Ingo Strauch (Berlin, Boston: De Gruyter, 2019), pp. 75–96; Morgan 2012, pp. 103–27; Finbarr Barry Flood, 'Between Cult and Culture: Bamiyan, Islamic Iconoclasm, and the Museum', *The Art Bulletin*, vol. 84, no. 4 (2002), pp. 641–59.

38 For instance, see Petra Sijpesteijn, *Shaping a Muslim State: The World of a Mid-eighth-century Egyptian Official* (New York: Oxford University Press, 2013).

39 Morgan 2012, pp. 100–1. On issues regarding the beginnings of Islam in Afghanistan, see Arezou Azad, 'The Beginnings of Islam in Afghanistan: Conquest, Acculturation, and Islamization', in *Afghanistan's Islam: From Conversion to the Taliban*, ed. Nile Green (Oakland, CA: University of California Press, 2017), pp. 41–55.

40 Kennedy 2007, pp. 238–41. Azad 2017, p. 42.

41 Kennedy 2007, p. 241.

42 M. Bates, 'Arab-Sasanian Coins', in *Encyclopaedia Iranica Online*, www.iranicaonline.org/articles/arab-sasanian-coins (accessed 25 May 2024).

43 Ibid. on counterstamps; Christopher I. Beckwith, *Empires of the Silk Road: A History of Central Eurasia from the Bronze Age to the Present* (Princeton, NJ: Princeton University Press, 2009), p. 132.

44 Melanie Michailidis, 'Dynastic Politics and the Samanid Mausoleum', *Ars Orientalis*, vol. 44 (2014), pp. 20–39, at p. 22.

45 Beaujard 2019, vol. 2, p. 67, no. 90.

46 Peter B. Golden, *Central Asia in World History* (New York: Oxford University Press), 2011, p. 64.

47 Ibid., p. 64.

48 Ibid., p. 65.

49 Melanie Michailidis, 'Samanid Silver and Trade along the Fur Route', in *Mechanisms of Exchange: Transmission in Medieval Art and Architecture of the Mediterranean, ca. 1000-1500* (Leiden: Brill, 2013), pp. 315–38.

50 Ibid. Roman K. Kovalev, 'The Infrastructure of the Northern Part of the "Fur Road" between the Middle Volga and the East during the Middle Ages', *Archivum Eurasiae medii aevi*, vol. 11 (2000/1), pp. 25–64.

51 Viola Allegranzi and Sandra Aube, 'Les décorations en stuc à Samarcande aux premiers siècles de l'Islam', in Rante and Lintz (eds) 2022, pp. 180–2, at p. 181.

52 Ibid., p. 182.

53 David Whitehouse, *Islamic Glass in the Corning Museum of Glass*, vol. 1 (New York: The Corning Museum of Glass, 2010), p. 92.

54 Akbarnia et al. 2018, pp. 90–1.

55 Sheila Blair, *Text and Image in Medieval Persian Art* (Edinburgh: Edinburgh University Press, 2014), p. 13.

56 Robert Hillenbrand, 'Content Versus Context in Samanid Epigraphic Pottery', in *Medieval Central Asia and the Persianate World*, ed. A.C.S. Peacock and D.G. Tor (London: I.B. Tauris, 2015), pp. 56–106, at p. 62.

57 Hillenbrand 2015, pp. 76–8; Akbarnia et al. 2018, p. 90.

58 Hayrettin Yücesoy, 'Language of Empire: Politics of Arabic and Persian in the Abbasid World', *PMLA* 130, no. 2 (2015), pp. 384–92, at p. 387.

59 Yücesoy 2015, p. 391, n. 5.

60 Michailidis 2014.

61 Kennedy 2007, p. 199.

62 Yücesoy 2015, pp. 387–8.

63 Akbarnia et al. 2018, pp. 236–7.

64 Djalal Khaleghi-Motlagh, 'Ferdowsi, Abu'l-Qasem', *Encyclopaedia Iranica Online*, www.iranicaonline.org/articles/ferdowsi-i (accessed 25 May 2024).

65 Ibid.

66 Susan Whitfield and Ursula Sims-Williams (eds), *The Silk Road: Trade, Travel, War and Faith* (London: The British Library, 2004), cat. no. 3, p. 119. The text is translated in Nicholas Sims-Williams, 'The Sogdian Fragments of the British Library', *Indo-Iranian Journal*, vol. 18, no. 1/2 (1976), pp. 43–82, at pp. 54–61.

67 Robert Hillenbrand, *Imperial Images of Persian Painting: A Scottish Arts Council Exhibition* (Edinburgh: Scottish Arts Council Gallery, 1977), cat. no. 64, p. 36. Hillenbrand notes that the caption and image do not match, and that this story does not seem to appear in Firdawsi's *Shahnama*, although Rustam and Zal are both featured in the epic.

68 Bilad al-Sham may be used interchangeably with Greater Syria, which encompasses Syria, Lebanon, Jordan, Israel and Palestine, as well as some regions in Turkey.

69 Akbarnia et al. 2018, pp. 32–3.

70 Finbarr B. Flood, 'Faith, Religion, and the Material Culture of Early Islam', in *Byzantium and Islam: Age of Transition, 7th–9th Century*, ed. Helen C. Evans and Brandie Ratliff (New York: The Metropolitan Museum of Art, 2012), pp. 244–57, at p. 248.

71 Akbarnia et al. 2018, p. 32.

72 Ibid., p. 32.

73 Ibid., p. 35.

74 Ibid., p. 29.

75 R.H. Pinder-Wilson, 'An Islamic Ewer in Sassanian Style', *The British Museum Quarterly*, vol. 22, no. 3/4 (1960), pp. 89–94.

76 Matteo Compareti, 'Composite Creatures in Sasanian Art according to Some Numismatic and Sphragistic Evidence', *Journal of Inter-cultural and Interdisciplinary Archaeology*, vol. 3 (2019), pp. 15–28.

77 Christopher Breward, Beverly Lemire and Giorgio Riello, *The Cambridge Global History of Fashion*, vol. 1 (Cambridge: Cambridge University Press, 2023), p. 647.

78 John Curtis, Ina Sarikhani Sandmann and Tim Stanley, *Epic Iran: 5000 Years of Culture* (London: V&A Publishing, 2021), cat. no. 108, pp. 130–1.

79 Denis Genequand, *Les établissements des élites omeyyades en Palmyrène et au Proche-Orient* (Beirut: IFPO, 2012); Denis Genequand, 'Umayyad Castles: The Shift from Late Antique Military Architecture to Early Islamic Palatial Building', in *Muslim Military Architecture in Greater Syria*, ed. Hugh Kennedy (Leiden: Brill: 2006), pp. 3–25; Evans and Ratliff (eds) 2012, p. 202.

80 Antoine Borrut, 'Pouvoir mobile et construction de l'espace dans les premiers siècles de l'islam', in *Le gouvernement en déplacement: Pouvoir et mobilité de l'Antiquité à nos jours*, ed. S. Destephen, J. Barbier et F. Chausson (Rennes: Presses Universitaires de Rennes, 2019), pp. 243–67.

81 Anna Ballian, 'Qasr al-Mshatta', in Evans and Ratliff (eds) 2012, p. 210.

82 Museum für Islamische Kunst, Staatliche Museen zu Berlin, inv. no. I. 6171.

83 Evans and Ratliff (eds) 2012, p. 211; Garth Fowden, *Qusayr 'Amra: Art and the Umayyad Elite in Late Antique Syria* (Berkeley, CA: University of California Press, 2004), p. 59.

84 On the Qusayr 'Amra, see Fowden 2004.

85 Flood 2012, p. 252.

86 Michael Greenhalgh, 'Islamic Re-use of Antique Mosaic

Tesserae', *Journal of Mosaic Research*, no. 1 (March 2008), pp. 55–81.

87 Louise Blanke and Alan Walmsley, 'Resilient Cities: Renewal after Disaster in Three Late Antique Towns of the East Mediterranean', in *Remembering and Forgetting the Ancient City*, ed. Javier Martínez Jiménez and Sam Ottewill-Soulsby (Havertown: Oxbow Books, 2022), pp. 69–109.

88 On the archaeology of Anjar, see Walmsley 2007, pp. 92–4.

89 The chronology is uncertain. See Vincent Lemire et al., *Jerusalem: History of a Global City*, trans. Juliana Froggatt (Oakland, CA: University of California Press, 2022), pp. 92–3.

90 Bowersock 2017, p. 119.

91 Lemire et al. 2022, p. 94.

92 Peter Frankopan, *The Silk Roads: A New History of the World* (London: Bloomsbury Publishing, 2015), pp. 80–4.

93 This event is depicted on the Franks Casket discussed in chapter 6 on northwest Europe.

94 Flood 2012, pp. 246–7.

95 Ibid., p. 247; Suleiman A. Mourad, 'Umayyad Jerusalem: From a Religious Capital to a Religious Town', in *The Umayyad World*, ed. Andrew Marsham (Abingdon: Routledge, 2021), pp. 393–408, at p. 393.

96 Ulrike Al-Khamis and Stefan Weber (eds), *Early Capitals of Islamic Culture. The Art and Culture of Umayyad Damascus and Abbasid Baghdad (650–950)* (Munich: Hirmer, 2014), pp. 30–1; Claus-Peter Haase, 'Qasr al-Mshatta and the Structure of Late Roman and Early Islamic Facades', *Age of Transition: Byzantine Culture in the Islamic World*, ed. Helen C. Evans (New York: The Metropolitan Museum of Art, 2015), pp. 112–31, at pp. 124–5 compares the decoration on the tray to the Mshatta façade.

97 Al-Khamis and Weber (eds) 2014, p. 30.

98 Flood 2012, p. 248.

99 Ibid., p. 249.

100 Evans and Ratliff (eds) 2012, cat. no. 186, p. 264.

101 Ibid.

102 Musée du Louvre, inv. no. AO 4087; more information about the inscription is available online at www.islamic-awareness.org/history/islam/inscriptions/malik1 (accessed 25 May 2024).

103 Calculated from measurements given in Lemire et al. 2022, p. 87.

104 Ibid.

105 Ibid.

106 On the House of Wisdom, see, for instance, Jim Al-Khalili, *The House of Wisdom: How Arabic Science Saved Ancient Knowledge and Gave Us the Renaissance* (New York: Penguin Press, 2011), pp. 68–72.

107 Jonathan M. Bloom, *Paper before Print: The History and Impact of Paper in the Islamic World* (New Haven, CT: Yale University Press, 2001); Al-Khalili 2011, p. 35.

108 Garth Fowden, 'Alexandria between Antiquity and Islam: Commerce and Concepts in First Millennium Afro-Eurasia', *Millennium*, vol. 16 (2019), pp. 233–70.

109 Frederick Starr, *Lost Enlightenment: Central Asia's Golden Age from the Arab Conquest to Tamerlane* (Princeton, NJ: Princeton University Press, 2013).

110 al-Khalili 2011, p. 110.

111 Ibid., p. 73.

112 Starr 2013, pp. 135, 136.

113 Jonathan Lyons, *The House of Wisdom: How the Arabs Transformed Western Civilization* (London: Bloomsbury, 2010), p. 38.

114 Anna Contadini, *A World of Beasts: A Thirteenth-Century Illustrated Arabic Book on Animals (the Kitāb Na't al-Ḥayawān) in the*

Ibn Bakhtīshū' Tradition (Leiden: Brill, 2012), p. 43.

115 Husain F. Nagamia, 'The Bukhtīshū' Family: A Dynasty of Physicians in the Early History of Islamic Medicine', *History of Medicine*, vol. 41, no. 1 (2009), pp. 7–12.

116 This is discussed in detail in Contadini 2012.

117 Zayde Antrim, *Mapping the Middle East* (London: Reaktion Books, 2018), p. 24.

118 Ibid., p. 24.

119 Ibid., p. 28.

120 Park Hyunhee, *Mapping the Chinese and Islamic Worlds: Cross-Cultural Exchange in Pre-Modern Asia* (Cambridge: Cambridge University Press, 2015), pp. 84–6; Antrim 2018, pp. 39–41.

121 An example of a world map stretching from Britain to Asia, but from a different perspective, is the Tabula Peutingeriana showing Roman roads, drawn in c. 1200 based on earlier maps, now lost. Discussed in Emily Albu, *The Medieval Peutinger Map: Imperial Roman Revival in a German Empire* (Cambridge: Cambridge University Press, 2014).

122 Akbarnia et al. 2018, p. 54.

123 Bloom 2001, pp. 42–5.

124 Ibid., p. 48.

125 Martin Lings and Jāsīn Ḥamīd Safadī, *The Qur'ān: Catalogue of an Exhibition of Qur'ān Manuscripts at the British Library* (London: World of Islam Publ. Co., 1976), p. 17.

126 Bloom 2001, p. 106.

127 Ibid., p. 108.

128 Fred Leemhuis, 'From Palm Leaves to the Internet', in *The Cambridge Companion to the Qur'ān*, ed. Jane Dammen McAuliffe (Cambridge: Cambridge University Press, 2006), pp. 145–62, at pp. 154–5.

129 Leemhuis 2006, p. 155.

130 Annabel Keeler, 'Exegesis iii. In Persian', *Encyclopaedia Iranica Online*, www.iranicaonline.org/articles/exegesis-iii (accessed 25 May 2024).

131 Akbarnia et al. 2018, p. 66.

132 Venetia Porter (ed.), *Hajj: Journey to the Heart of Islam* (London: The British Museum Press, 2012), p. 76.

133 Ibid., p. 92.

134 Ibid., p. 95.

135 John Guy, 'Rare and Strange Goods: International Trade in Ninth-Century Asia', in *Shipwrecked: Tang Treasures and Monsoon Winds*, ed. Regina Krahl et al. (Washington, DC, and Singapore: Arthur M. Sackler Gallery, Smithsonian Institution/Singapore Tourism Board, 2011), pp. 19–27.

136 Akbarnia et al. 2018, p. 80.

137 Marcus Milwright, 'Samarra and Abbasid Ornament', in *A Companion to Islamic Art and Architecture*, ed. Finbarr Barry Flood and Gülru Necipoğlu (Hoboken, NJ: Wiley Blackwell, 2017), pp. 177–96, at p. 178. I am grateful to Dr Rosalind Wade Haddon for this information.

138 Mariam Rosser-Owen and Rosalind Wade Haddon, 'A New Look at Samarra: Small Finds from the Herzfeld Excavation in the Victoria and Albert Museum', *Beiträge zur islamischen Kunst und Archäologie 7*, ed. Martina Müller-Wiener and Anne Mollenhauer (Wiesbaden: Dr. Ludwig Reichert Verlag, 2021), pp. 123–50, at pp. 132, 141.

139 Milwright 2017, p. 180.

140 Ibid., p. 181.

141 Rosser-Owen and Haddon 2021, p. 135.

142 Nadine Schibille et al., 'The Glass Walls of Samarra (Iraq): Ninth-Century Abbasid Glass Production and Imports', *PLOS ONE*, vol. 13, no. 8 (2018), e0201749. I am grateful to Dr Andrew Meek for this reference.

143 R.H. Brill, 'Appendix 3: Chemical analyses of some glass fragments from Nishapur in the Corning Museum of Art', *Nishapur: Glass of the Early Islamic Period*, ed. Jens Kröger (New York: The Metropolitan Museum of Art, 1995), pp. 211–33; Schibille et al. 2018; Mark T. Wypyski, 'Chemical Analysis of Early Islamic Glass from Nishapur', *Journal of Glass Studies*, vol. 57 (2015), pp. 121–36. I am grateful to Charlotte Nash for this information.

144 Regina Krahl, 'White Wares of Northern China', in Krahl et al. (eds) 2011, pp. 201–7, at p. 206.

145 Ibid.

146 Regina Krahl, 'Green, White, and Blue-and-white Stonewares: The Precious Part of the Ceramic Cargo', in *The Tang Shipwreck: Art and Exchange in the 9th Century*, ed. Alan Chong and Stephen A. Murphy (Singapore: Asian Civilisations Museum, 2017), pp. 80–104, at p. 85.

147 Oliver Watson, *Ceramics from Islamic Lands* (New York: Thames & Hudson, 2004), p. 24.

148 On the trade of flax from Egypt around 1000 CE, see A.L. Udovitch, 'International Trade and the Medieval Egyptian Countryside', in *Agriculture in Egypt: From Pharaonic to Modern Times*, ed. Alan K. Bowman and Eugene L. Rogan (Oxford: Oxford University Press, 1999), pp. 267–85.

149 Maryam Ekhtiar et al., *Masterpieces from the Department of Islamic Art in the Metropolitan Museum of Art* (New York: The Metropolitan Museum of Art, 2011), p. 23.

150 Stacey Pierson, *Chinese Ceramics* (London: V&A Publishing, 2009), p. 7.

151 Akbarnia et al. 2018, p. 84.

152 Watson 2004, p. 46. Krahl 2011, p. 205.

153 Krahl 2017, p. 85; Watson 2004, p. 28.

154 Ibid.

155 Michela Spataro et al., 'Pottery Technology in the Tang Dynasty (Ninth Century AD): Archaeometric Analyses of a Gongyi Sherd found at Siraf, Iran', *Archaeometry*, vol. 61 (2019), pp. 574–87.

156 Watson 2004, p. 47.

157 Ibid.

158 Akbarnia et al. 2018, pp. 122–3.

159 Watson 2004, p. 47.

Aksumites and their port city, Adulis

1 *Christian Topography* 2.54–67; Wanda Wolska-Conus, *Topographie chrétienne de Cosmas Indicopleustès*, vol. 1, books I–IV (Paris: Editions du Cerf, 1968), pp. 364–79. For a lively telling, see G.W. Bowersock, *Throne of Adulis: Red Sea Wars on the Eve of Islam* (Oxford: Oxford University Press, 2013). For the sources, see especially Iwona Gajda, *Le royaume de Himyar à l'époque monothéiste: L'histoire de l'Arabie du Sud ancienne de la fin du IVe siècle de l'ère chrétienne jusqu'à l'avènement de l'Islam* (Paris: De Boccard, 2009) and Paolo Marrassini (ed.), *Storia e leggenda dell'Etiopia tardoantica: le iscrizioni reali Aksumite* (Brescia: Paideia, 2014).

2 Bowersock 2013, pp. 34–43.

3 Ibid., pp. 44–62, p. 55.

4 Ibid., p. 21.

5 In Byzantine literary tradition, the emperor Justin is said to have urged Kaleb to 'go forth, whether by sea or by land against the abominable and criminal Jew' (ibid., p. 97). For the relative lack of direct contemporary evidence for Byzantine material support and encouragement, see Joëlle Beaucamp, 'Le rôle de Byzance en mer Rouge sous le règne de Justin : Mythe ou réalité', in *Juifs et chrétiens en Arabie aux Ve et VIe siècles: Regards croisés sur les sources. Actes du colloque de novembre 2008*, ed. Françoise Briquel-Chatonnet and Christian Robin

(Paris: Association des amis du Centre d'histoire et civilisation de Byzance, 2010), pp. 197–218; Antonella Brita and Jacopo Gnisci, 'Hagiography in Ge'ez', in *Treasures of Ethiopia and Eritrea in the Bodleian Library, Oxford*, ed. Jacopo Gnisci (Oxford: Manar al-Athar, University of Oxford, 2019), pp. 59–70.

6 George Hatke, 'Holy Land and Sacred Territory: A View from Early Ethiopia', in *Visions of Community in the Post-Roman World: The West, Byzantium and the Islamic World, 300–1100*, ed. Walter Pohl, Clemens Gantner and Richard E. Payne (Farnham: Ashgate, 2012), pp. 259–79. For a purely political and non-religious motivation for invasion, see Christian Julien Robin, 'The Judaism of the Ancient Kingdom of Himyar in Arabia: A Discreet Conversion', in *Diversity and Rabbinization: Jewish Texts and Societies between 400 and 1000 CE*, ed. Gavin McDowell, Ron Naiweld and Daniel Stökl Ben Ezravol (Cambridge: Open Book Publishers, 2021), pp. 165–270, at pp. 169–170.

7 George Hatke, 'The Aksumites in South Arabia: An African Diaspora of Late Antiquity', in *Migration Histories of the Medieval Afroeurasian Transition Zone: Aspects of Mobility between Africa, Asia and Europe, 300–1500 CE*, ed. Johannes Preiser-Kapeller, Lucian Reinfandt and Yannis Stouraitis (Leiden: Brill, 2020), pp. 311–15; Christian Julien Robin, 'Judaism in Pre-Islamic Arabia', *The Cambridge History of Judaism*, ed. Phillip I. Lieberman (Cambridge: Cambridge University Press, 2021), pp. 294–331, at pp. 319–22.

8 Briquel-Chatonnet and Robin 2010; Bowersock 2013, pp. 89–91.

9 Amelia Dowler, 'The Interaction of Aksumite and Roman Gold Coins in South Arabia in the 6th Century AD', *Journal of the Oriental Numismatic Society*, vol. 233 (2018), pp. 5–21.

10 Stuart Munro-Hay, 'The Al-Madhāriba Hoard of Gold Aksumite and Late Roman Coins', *The Numismatic Chronicle*, vol. 149 (1989a), pp. 83–100.

11 Robin 2021, pp. 320–1.

12 Hatke 2020, pp. 316–19.

13 D.W. Phillipson, *Foundations of an African Civilization: Aksum & the Northern Horn, 1000 BC–AD 1300* (Woodbridge and Rochester, NY: James Currey, 2012); Alessandro Bausi (ed.), *Languages and Cultures of Eastern Christianity: Ethiopian* (Burlington, VT: Ashgate, 2011).

14 Lionel Casson (ed.), *The Periplus Maris Erythraei: Text with Introduction, Translation and Commentary* (Princeton, NJ: Princeton University Press, 1989), pp. 52–3, 106–7; Roberta S. Tomber, *Indo-Roman Trade: From Pots to Pepper* (London: Duckworth, 2008), pp. 88–93; Phillipson 2012, pp. 195–207.

15 Tomber 2008, p. 92.

16 Ibid., pp. 92–3; Anna Filigenzi and Chiara Zazzaro, 'An Indian Terracotta Figurine from the Eritrean Port of Adulis', *Journal of Indian Ocean Archaeology*, no. 13–14 (2017), pp. 1–12.

17 Tomber 2008, pp. 140, 147, 163.

18 Procopius, *De bellis*, 1.20.9–13.

19 Phillipson 2012, pp. 209–23.

20 Bowersock 2013, pp. 63–77.

21 Eivind Heldaas Seland, 'Early Christianity in East Africa and Red Sea/Indian Ocean Commerce', *African Archaeological Review*, vol. 31, no. 4 (2014), pp. 637–47.

22 Gabriele Castiglia et al., 'For an Archaeology of Religious Identity in Adulis (Eritrea) and the Horn of Africa: Sources, Architecture, and Recent Archaeological Excavations', *Journal of African Archaeology*, vol. 19 (2021), pp. 25–56, at p. 28.

23 Bowersock 2013, pp. 63–77.

24 Wolfgang Hahn with Robert Keck, *Münzgeschichte der Aksumitenkönige in der Spätantike* (Vienna: Österreichische

Forschungsgesellschaft für Numismatik, 2020); Stuart Munro-Hay, *Catalogue of the Aksumite Coins in the British Museum* (London: The British Museum Press, 1999).

25 Judith McKenzie and Francis Watson, *The Garima Gospels: Early Illuminated Gospel Books from Ethiopia* (Oxford: Manar al-Athar, University of Oxford, 2016); Jacques Mercier, 'Les deux types d'édicules associés aux Canons d'Eusèbe. Apport des Évangiles d'Abba Gärima (c. 450–650) à leur histoire et symboliques byzantines et latines', *Cahiers Archéologiques*, vol. 58 (2021), pp. 29–54.

26 Alessandro Bausi et al., 'The Aksumite Collection or Codex Σ: Codicological and Palaeographical Observations. With a Note on Material Analysis of Inks', *Comparative Oriental Manuscript Studies Bulletin*, vol. 6, no. 2 (2020), pp. 127–71.

27 There is a lacuna in the manuscript so that the Sasanian conquest of Egypt does not appear.

28 Phil Booth, 'Severan Christians between the Roman and Arab Empires', in *Egypt and Empire: The Formation of Religious Identity after Rome*, ed. Elisabeth R. O'Connell (Leuven: Peeters, 2022), p. 353.

29 Maja Kominko, 'Beyond the Empire: Kosmas Indikopleustes, the Church of the East and the Indian Trade in the Sixth Century AD', in O'Connell (ed.) 2022, pp. 173–97.

30 For the different versions of the illustration in the three surviving manuscripts of the *Christian Topography* and manuscripts' dates of production, see Maja Kominko, *The World of Kosmas: Illustrated Byzantine Codices of the* Christian Topography (Cambridge: Cambridge University Press, 2013), pp. 24–35, 214–35.

31 Bowersock 2013, pp. 12–15.

32 D.P.S. Peacock and Lucy Katherine Blue, *The Ancient Red Sea Port of Adulis, Eritrea: Results of the Eritro-British Expedition, 2004–5* (Oxford: Oxbow Books, 2007), pp. 112–14.

33 Castiglia et al. 2021, p. 17.

34 Peacock and Blue 2007, pp. 122–4; Fabrizio Antonelli, 'Archaeometric Study of Marble Samples from Archaeological Artifacts of the British Museum of London' (LAMA – Laboratory for Analysing Materials of Ancient Origin, Iuav University of Venice, 2022).

35 For a nuanced view of evidence of 'prefabricated' church kits found in shipwrecks, see Justin Leidwanger, Elizabeth S. Greene and Andrew Donnelly, 'The Sixth-Century CE Shipwreck at Marzamemi', *American Journal of Archaeology*, vol. 125, no. 2 (2021), pp. 283–317.

36 Castiglia et al. 2021, p. 20.

37 Ibid.

38 For a recently excavated alabaster fragment which joins one in the British Museum, see ibid., p. 35, fig. 26.

39 Letter from Charles Thomas Newton to John Winter Jones, dated 9 Oct. 1867, in The British Museum Central Archive, Original Papers, vol. 92, Sept.–Dec. 1867, no. 9904; Richard Rivington Holmes, Final Report, 20 July 1868, in British Museum Central Archive, Original Papers, vol. 95, July–Oct. 1868, no. 7629. On the formation of the British Museum collection, see Stuart Munro-Hay, 'The British Museum Excavations at Adulis, 1868', *Antiquaries Journal*, vol. 69, no. 1 (1989b), pp. 43–52. On the larger context, see Volker Matthies, *The Siege of Magdala: The British Empire against the Emperor of Ethiopia* (Princeton, NJ: Markus Wiener Publishers, 2012); and Lucia Patrizio Gunning and Debbie Challis, 'Planned Plunder, the British Museum, and the 1868 Maqdala Expedition', *Historical Journal*, vol. 66, no. 3 (2023), pp. 550–72. I thank Zoe Cormack for sharing the results of her ongoing research.

40 Munro-Hay 1989b, pp. 43–52.

41 Timothy Power, *The Red Sea from Byzantium to the Caliphate: AD 500–1000* (Cairo and New York: American University in Cairo Press, 2012), p. 62.

42 Phillipson 2012, pp. 206, 209–23; Power 2012, pp. 89–96.

Mediterranean connections

1 For the distinctive history of the Mediterranean, see Fernand Braudel, *The Mediterranean and the Mediterranean World in the Age of Philip II*, 2 vols (rev. eds) (Berkeley, CA: University of California Press, 1949/1995); Henri Pirenne, *Mohammed and Charlemagne* (Mineola, NY: Dover Publications, 1935/2001); Peregrine Horden and Nicholas Purcell, *The Corrupting Sea: A Study of Mediterranean History* (Oxford: Blackwell Publishers, 2000); Chris Wickham, *Framing the Early Middle Ages: Europe and the Mediterranean 400–800* (Oxford: Oxford University Press, 2005), pp. 709–94; and Chris Wickham, *The Donkey and the Boat: Reinterpreting the Mediterranean Economy, 950–1180* (Oxford: Oxford University Press, 2023).

2 Wickham 2005 and Chris Wickham, *The Inheritance of Rome: A History of Europe from 400 to 1000* (London: Allen Lane, 2009).

3 Anthony Kaldellis, *Byzantium Unbound: Modernity, Imperial Bureaucracy and Islam* (Leeds: ARC Humanities Press, 2019). 'Byzantine' previously simply meant the inhabitants of Constantinople, ancient Byzantion, and the Carolingians already referred to them as 'Greeks'.

4 Jean-Jacques Aillagon and Yann Rivière (eds), *Rome and the Barbarians: The Birth of a New World* (Milan and New York: Skira, 2008); 'Migration Histories of the Medieval Afroeurasian Transition Zone: An Introduction', in Johannes Preiser-Kapeller, Lucian Reinfandt and Yannis Stouraitis (eds), *Migration Histories of the Medieval Afroeurasian Transition Zone: Aspects of Mobility between Africa, Asia and Europe, 300–1500 CE* (Leiden: Brill, 2020), pp. 5–15.

5 For the 'Eurasian hinge', see Garth Fowden, *Before and after Muhammad: The First Millennium Refocused* (Princeton, NJ: Princeton University Press, 2014), p. 104.

6 Robert G. Hoyland, *In God's Path: The Arab Conquests and the Creation of an Islamic Empire* (Oxford: Oxford University Press, 2015); John F. Haldon, *The Empire That Would Not Die: The Paradox of Eastern Roman Survival, 640–740* (Cambridge, MA: Harvard University Press, 2016); Petra M. Sijpesteijn, 'The Rise and Fall of Empires in the Islamic Mediterranean (600–1600 CE): Political Change, the Economy and Material Culture', in *The Routledge Handbook of Archaeology and Globalization*, ed. Tamar Hodos and Alexander Geurds (London: Routledge, 2017), pp. 652–68.

7 Jonathan Harris, *Byzantium and the Crusades* (London: Bloomsbury Academic, 2014).

8 Michael Maas (ed.), *The Cambridge Companion to the Age of Justinian* (Cambridge: Cambridge University Press, 2005); P.J. Heather, *Rome Resurgent: War and Empire in the Age of Justinian* (New York: Oxford University Press, 2018).

9 For the problematics of the term 'Germanic' to describe various peoples in this period, see Matthias Friedrich and James M. Harland (eds), *Interrogating the 'Germanic': A Category and its Use in Late Antiquity and the Early Middle Ages* (Berlin: De Gruyter, 2020).

10 The mortality figures are hotly contested by modern scholars. Lester K. Little (ed.), *Plague and the End of Antiquity: The Pandemic of 541–750* (New York: Cambridge University Press, 2007); John Haldon et al., 'Plagues, Climate Change, and the End of an Empire: A Response to Kyle Harper's *The Fate of Rome* (3): Disease, Agency, and Collapse', *History Compass*, vol. 16, no. 12 (2018), doi.org/10.1111/hic3.12507 (accessed 22 April 2024); Lee Mordechai and Merle Eisenberg, 'Rejecting Catastrophe: The Case of the Justinianic Plague', *Past & Present*, vol. 244, no. 1 (2019), pp. 3–50.

11 Horden and Purcell 2000.

12 For the Byzantine empire within its contemporary medieval world, see Wickham 2023, p. 269.

13 Excavation of the capital's harbour built at the end of the fourth century has unearthed the largest assemblage of medieval ship finds, some thirty-seven wrecks dating from the fifth to eleventh centuries, and a range of vessels from fishing boats to merchant vessels and war galleys. Ufuk Kocabaş, 'The Yenikapı Byzantine-Era Shipwrecks, Istanbul, Turkey: A Preliminary Report and Inventory of the 27 Wrecks Studied by Istanbul University', *International Journal of Nautical Archaeology*, vol. 44, no. 1 (2015), pp. 5–38.

14 Helen C. Evans and Brandie Ratliff (eds), *Byzantium and Islam: Age of Transition, 7th–9th Century* (New York: The Metropolitan Museum of Art, 2012), cat. no. 133, p. 193. For curated bead assemblages, see also pp. 212–13.

15 Wickham 2023.

16 Roberta S. Tomber, *Indo-Roman Trade: From Pots to Pepper* (London: Duckworth, 2008); Marlia Mundell Mango, 'Byzantine Maritime Trade with the East (4th–7th Centuries)', *Aram*, vol. 8 (1996), pp. 139–63; Timothy Power, *The Red Sea from Byzantium to the Caliphate: AD 500–1000* (Cairo and New York: AUC Press, 2012); and Rebecca R. Darley, 'Indo-Byzantine Exchange, 4th to 7th Centuries: A Global History', PhD dissertation, University of Birmingham, 2014.

17 Maja Kominko, 'Beyond the Empire: Kosmas Indikopleustes, the Church of the East and the Indian Trade in the Sixth Century AD', in *Egypt and Empire: The Formation of Religious Identity after Rome*, ed. Elisabeth R. O'Connell (Leuven: Peeters, 2022), pp. 173–97.

18 Ibid., pp. 182–4.

19 Eivind Heldaas Seland, *Gemstones and Mineral Products in the Red Sea/Indian Ocean Trade of the First Millennium* (Mainz: Verlag des Römisch-Germanischen Zentralmuseums, 2017).

20 Yvonne Stolz, 'Eine Kaiserliche Insignie? Der Juwelenkragen aus dem Sog. Schatzfund von Assiût', *Jahrbuch des Römisch-Germanischen Zentralmuseums*, vol. 53 (2006), pp. 521–603; Elizabeth Dospěl Williams, '"Into the Hands of a Well-Known Antiquary of Cairo": The Assiut Treasure and the Making of an Archaeological Hoard', *West 86th: A Journal of Decorative Arts, Design History, and Material Culture*, vol. 21, no. 2 (2014), pp. 251–72.

21 Anthony Cutler, *The Craft of Ivory: Sources, Techniques, and Uses in the Mediterranean World, AD 200–1400* (Washington, DC: Dumbarton Oaks, 1985), ch. 2.

22 Alan Cameron, 'The Origin, Context and Function of Consular Diptychs', *Journal of Roman Studies*, vol. 103 (2013), pp. 174–207, at p. 179.

23 Anthony Cutler, 'The Making of the Justinian Diptychs', *Byzantion*, vol. 54, no. 1 (1984), pp. 75–115.

24 Felicity Harley-McGowan, 'The Maskell Passion Ivories and Greco-Roman Art: Notes on the Iconography of Crucifixion', in *Envisioning Christ on the Cross: Ireland and the Early Medieval West*, ed. Juliet Mullins, Jenifer Ni Ghradaigh and Richard Hawtree (Dublin and Portland, OR: Four Courts Press, 2013), pp. 13–33.

25 Ivory objects have traditionally been attributed to workshops in Alexandria, but this cannot be assumed.

26 David Buckton, *Byzantium: Treasures of Byzantine Art and Culture from British Collections* (London: The British Museum Press, 1994), p. 74.

27 Katie A. Hemer et al., 'Ivory from Early Anglo-Saxon Burials in Lincolnshire: A Biomolecular Study', *Journal of Archaeological Science: Reports*, vol. 49 (2023), doi.org/10.1016/j.jasrep.2023.103943 (accessed 22 April 2024).

28 For a recent bibliography on the East African ivory trade to China and India in the ninth and tenth centuries, see Ashley Coutu and Kristoffer Damgaard, 'From Tusk to Town: Ivory Trade and Craftsmanship along the Red Sea', *Studies in Late Antiquity*, vol. 3, no. 4 (2019), pp. 508–46.

29 Elisabeth R. O'Connell et al., 'A Palimpsest Ivory Diptych in the British Museum' (forthcoming).

30 *Christian Topography* 2.45–47.

31 Julia Galliker, 'Silk in the Byzantine World: Technology and Transmission', in *Global Byzantium: Papers from the Fiftieth Spring Symposium of Byzantine Studies*, ed. Leslie Brubaker, Rebecca Darley and Daniel Reynolds (London: Routledge, Taylor & Francis Group, 2022), pp. 59–86, at p. 62.

32 Patricia Blessing, Elizabeth Dospěl Williams and Eiren L. Shea, *Medieval Textiles across Eurasia, c. 300–1400* (Cambridge: Cambridge University Press, 2023), p. 23; Gang Wu, 'Mapping Byzantine Sericulture in the Global Transfer of Technology', *Journal of Global History*, vol. 19 (2024), pp. 1–17.

33 Dated 18 March 325 CE, *P.Oxy.* 3758.

34 Linda Safran, 'Early Byzantine Art in China: A Test Case for Global Byzantium', in Brubaker, Darley and Reynolds (eds) 2022, pp. 289–315, at p. 291.

35 Procopius, *De bellis*, 1.20 (with the Aksumites) and 2.28–30 (with the Laz in Georgia).

36 David Jacoby, 'Silk Economics and Cross-Cultural Artistic Interaction: Byzantium, the Muslim World, and the Christian West', *Dumbarton Oaks Papers*, vol. 58 (2004), pp. 197–240, at p. 198; Wu 2024.

37 Annalisa Marzano, *Harvesting the Sea: The Exploitation of Marine Resources in the Roman Mediterranean* (Oxford: Oxford University Press, 2013).

38 Chris Entwistle, *A Catalogue of the Late Roman and Byzantine Weights and Weighing Equipment in the British Museum*, British Museum Research Publication (London: The British Museum, forthcoming).

39 Fedir Androshchuk, Jonathan Shepard and Monica White (eds), *Byzantium and the Viking World* (Uppsala: Uppsala Universitet, 2016).

40 Michael McCormick, *Origins of the European Economy: Communications and Commerce, AD 300–900* (Cambridge and New York: Cambridge University Press, 2001); Preiser-Kapeller, Reinfandt and Stouraitis (eds) 2020; Claudia Rapp, 'Mobility and Migration in Byzantium: Who Gets to Tell the Story?', *Early Medieval Europe*, vol. 31, no. 3 (2023), pp. 360–79.

41 Safran 2022, p. 292; see also a map of Byzantine coins found in China, p. 290, fig. 15.2.

42 R.A. Markus, 'How on Earth Could Places Become Holy? Origins of the Christian Idea of Holy Places', *Journal of Early Christian Studies*, vol. 2 (1994), pp. 257–73; Edward David Hunt, *Holy Land Pilgrimage in the Later Roman Empire: AD 312–460* (Oxford: Clarendon Press, 2002).

43 Youval Rotman, 'Migration and Enslavement: A Medieval Model', in Preiser-Kapeller, Reinfandt and Stouraitis (eds) 2020, pp. 399–400.

44 Walter Scheidel, 'The Roman Slave Supply', in *The Cambridge World History of Slavery*, vol. 1, ed. Keith Bradley and Paul Cartledge (Cambridge: Cambridge University Press, 2011), pp. 287–310.

45 Rotman 2020, p. 392, Noel Lenski, 'Slavery in the Byzantine Empire', in *The Cambridge World History of Slavery*, vol. 2, ed. Craig Perry et al. (Cambridge: Cambridge University Press, 2021), pp. 453–81.

46 Susanna Elm, 'Sold to Sin through Origo: Augustine of Hippo and the Late Roman Slave Trade', in *Papers Presented at the Seventeenth International Conference on Patristic Studies Held in Oxford 2015*, vol. 24: *St Augustine and his Opponents*, ed. Markus Vinzent (Leuven: Peeters, 2017), pp. 1–21.

47 Lenski 2021, p. 463. For Christian attitudes toward enslavement, see Jennifer A. Glancy, *Slavery in Early Christianity* (Minneapolis, MN: Fortress, 2006).

48 For prisoner exchanges, see Rotman 2020, pp. 394–5, 399; for evacuation of whole towns, p. 400; for new scale of trafficking, pp. 400–1.

49 Jeffrey Fynn-Paul, 'Empire, Monotheism and Slavery in the Greater Mediterranean Region from Antiquity to the Early Modern Era', *Past & Present*, vol. 205, no. 1 (2009), pp. 3–40; Rotman 2020, p. 405.

50 Jack Boulos Victor Tannous, *The Making of the Medieval Middle East: Religion, Society, and Simple Believers* (Princeton, NJ: Princeton University Press, 2019).

51 William Anderson, 'Menas Flasks in the West: Pilgrimage and Trade at the End of Antiquity', *Ancient West & East*, vol. 6 (2007), pp. 221–43.

52 For example, Michelle Brown (ed.), *In the Beginning: Bibles before the Year 1000* (Washington, DC: Freer Gallery of Art and Arthur M. Sackler Gallery, Smithsonian Institution, 2006).

53 Richard Stoneman et al., *Alexander the Great: The Making of a Myth* (London: The British Library, 2022).

54 For Arabic into Greek, see Maria Mavroudi, 'Byzantine Translations from Arabic into Greek: Old and New Historiography in Confluence and in Conflict', *Journal of Late Antique, Islamic and Byzantine Studies*, vol. 2, no. 1–2 (2023), pp. 215–88.

55 Constanza Cordoni, *Barlaam und Josaphat in der europäischen Literatur des Mittelalters. Darstellung der Stofftraditionen – Bibliographie – Studien* (Berlin: De Gruyter, 2014).

56 For a discussion, see Power 2012, pp. 19–101, and esp. pp. 76–86.

57 Timothy Dawson and Graham Sumner, *By the Emperor's Hand: Military Dress and Court Regalia in the Later Romano-Byzantine Empire* (Barnsley: Frontline Books, 2015), p. 7, pl. 3.

58 Matthew 2.1–12. For Mithras, see Philippa Adrych et al., *Images of Mithra (Visual Conversations in Art and Archaeology)* (Oxford and New York: Oxford University Press, 2017). For Christian art, see Felicity Harley-McGowan, 'Magi in Motion: The Making of an Image in Early Christian Rome', *Jahrbuch für Antike und Christentum*, vol. 63 (2022), pp. 188–216, at p. 192.

59 Elisabeth R. O'Connell et al, 'Remaking Martyrs: The Excavation, Conservation and Display History of a Late Antique Wall-Painting from Egypt (EA 73139)', in *Beyond Byzantium: Essays on the Medieval Worlds of Eastern Christianity and their Arts. In Honor of Helen C. Evans*, ed. Jennifer Ball et al. (Berlin: De Gruyter, forthcoming).

60 Frances Pritchard, *Clothing Culture: Dress in Egypt in the First Millennium AD. Clothing from Egypt in the Collection of the Whitworth Art Gallery, the University of Manchester* (Manchester: Whitworth Art Gallery, 2006), pp. 45–115.

61 Barbara Köstner, 'What Flaws Can Tell: A Case Study on Weaving Faults in Late Roman and Early Medieval Weft-Faced Compound Fabrics from Egypt', in *Egyptian Textiles and their Production: 'Word' and 'Object' (Hellenistic, Roman and Byzantine Periods)*, ed. Maria Mossakowska-Gaubert (Lincoln, NE: Zea Books, 2020).

62 For another fragment from the same tunic, see Marielle Martiniani-Reber (ed.), *Lyon, musée historique des tissus : Soieries sassanides, coptes et byzantines, Ve–XIe siècles* (Paris: Ministère de la Culture et de la Communication, Éditions de la Réunion des musées nationaux, 1986), no. 92.

63 Cäcilia Fluck and Gillian Vogelsang-Eastwood (eds), *Riding Costume in Egypt: Origin and Appearance* (Leiden: Brill, 2004).

64 Gillian Vogelsang-Eastwood, 'Sasanian "Riding Coats": The Iranian Evidence', in Fluck and Vogelsang-Eastwood (eds) 2004, p. 220; Kathrin Mälck, 'Technische Analyse der Berliner Reitermäntel und Beinlinge', in Fluck and Vogelsang-Eastwood (eds) 2004, pp. 163–73, see esp. fig. 68a–d.

65 Vogelsang-Eastwood 2004, p. 220.

66 Blessing, Dospěl Williams and Shea 2023.

67 Fluck and Vogelsang-Eastwood (eds) 2004. For other examples now identified at other sites, especially Naqlun, see Włodzimierz Godlewski, Petra Linscheid and Cäcilia Fluck, 'The Dress Ensemble of Naqlun Cemetery C Tomb 5', in *Dress – Continuity and Change in Egypt in the 1st millennium AD: Proceedings of the Twelfth Conference of the Research Group 'Textiles from the Nile Valley'*, ed. Antoine De Moor, Cäcilia Fluck and Petra Linscheid (Antwerp: Hannibal, 2023), pp. 36–43.

68 Cf. Florence Calament and Maximilien Durand (eds), *Antinoé, à la vie, à la mode. Visions d'élégance dans les solitudes* (Lyon: Fage éditions, 2013), nos 29, 34.

69 Dominique Bénazeth, 'Les tissus "sassanides" d'Antinoe au Musée du Louvre', in Fluck and Vogelsang-Eastwood (eds) 2004, pp. 117–28, at p. 120.

70 Fluck and Vogelsang-Eastwood (eds) 2004; Mälck 2004. The calibrated radiocarbon dates are 438 (95.4%) 558 cal. AD: Antoine De Moor, Mark Van Strydonck and Chris Verhecken-Lammens, 'Radiocarbon Dating of Two Sasanian Coats and Three Post-Sasanian Tapestries', in Fluck and Vogelsang-Eastwood (eds) 2004, pp. 181–7, at p. 184. The silk trimmings were removed and conserved separately, but were lost in the Second World War, when the building in which they were housed was bombed.

71 Achim Unger, 'Farbstoffanalyse an der Berliner Reitertracht', in Fluck and Vogelsang-Eastwood (eds) 2004, pp. 175–80, at p. 179.

72 For the gaiters, see Cäcilia Fluck, 'Zwei Reitermantel aus Antinoopolis im Museum für Byzantinische Kunst, Berlin: Fundcontext und Beschreibung', in Fluck and Vogelsang-Eastwood (eds) 2004, pp. 137–52; and Petra Linscheid, 'Gaiters from Antinoopolis in the Museum für Byzantinische Kunst, Berlin', in Fluck and Vogelsang-Eastwood (eds) 2004.

73 Fluck 2004; Evans and Ratliff (eds) 2012, cat. no. 114, pp. 171. For the construction and wearing of such coats, see Mälck 2004. For the radiocarbon dates c. 443 (95.4%) 637 cal. AD, see De Moor, Van Strydonck and Verhecken-Lammens 2004, p. 184.

74 De Moor, Van Strydonck and Verhecken-Lammens 2004, p. 184, and Dominique Bénazeth, 'Essai de datation par la méthode du Radiocarbon de vêtements à la mode orientale retrouvés à Antinoé et de quelques', in *Methods of Dating Ancient Textiles of the 1st Millennium AD from Egypt and Neighbouring Countries: Proceedings of the 4th Meeting of the Study Group 'Textiles from the Nile Valley'*, ed. Antoine De Moor, Cäcilia Fluck and Susanne Martinssen-von Falck (Tielt: Lannoo Publishers, 2007), pp. 115–28.

75 See Alexandra Fletcher, Daniel Antoine and JD Hill, *Regarding the Dead: Human Remains in the British Museum*, British Museum Research Publication 197 (London: The British Museum, 2014).

76 See, among others, Averil Cameron and Peter Garnsey, *The Cambridge Ancient History* (Cambridge: Cambridge University Press, 1998); Heather 2018.

77 Sonja Marzinzik, *Masterpieces: Early Medieval Art* (London: The British Museum Press, 2013), pp. 166–7.

78 Guy Halsall, *Barbarian Migrations and the Roman West, 376–568* (Cambridge: Cambridge University Press, 2007).

79 Judith Herrin, *Ravenna: Capital of Empire, Crucible of Europe* (Dublin: Penguin Books, 2021), p. 101.

80 Ibid, pp. 126–36.

81 Lauren A. Wainwright, 'Import, Export: The Global Impact of Byzantine Marriage Alliances during the Tenth Century', in Brubaker, Darley and Reynolds (eds) 2022.

82 Patrick Périn, 'The Treasure of Domagnano (Republic of San Marino)', in Aillagon and Rivière (eds) 2008, pp. 302–5, at p. 302.

83 Marzinzik 2013, pp. 180–1.

84 Périn 2008, p. 302.

85 Wickham 2009, p. 140.

86 Paul Williamson, *Medieval Ivory Carvings: Early Christian to Romanesque* (London: V&A Publishing, 2010), pp. 46–9. Some have suggested that the diptych has been recarved for Orestes, which Williamson discusses and finally refutes.

87 Herrin 2021, pp. 170, 172. For a survey challenging traditional identifications of figures and contemporary readings of the mosaics, see Liz James, 'Global or Local Art? The Mosaic Panels of Justinian and Theodora in S Vitale, Ravenna', in Brubaker, Darley and Reynolds (eds) 2022.

88 Herrin 2021, p. 166.

89 Ibid, pp. 166, 173.

90 Wickham 2009, pp. 140–2.

91 Marzinzik 2013, pp. 190–1.

92 Hugh Kennedy, 'Egypt as a Province in the Islamic Caliphate, 641–868', in *Islamic Egypt 640–1517*, ed. Carl F. Petry (Cambridge: Cambridge University Press, 1998), pp. 62–85; Peter Sheehan, *Babylon of Egypt: The Archaeology of Old Cairo and the Origins of the City* (Cairo: American University in Cairo Press, 2010); Tasha Vorderstrasse et al. (eds), *A Cosmopolitan City: Muslims, Christians, and Jews in Old Cairo* (Chicago: Oriental Institute of the University of Chicago, 2015).

93 For example, the Barghawata (744), the Rustamids (776), the Sufrites of Sijilmasa (758), the Idrisids (788), the Aghlabids (800), Almoravids (1050); in the context of the Aghlabids, see Glaire D. Anderson, Corisande Fenwick and Mariam Rosser-Owen, 'The Aghlabids and their Neighbors: An Introduction', in *The Aghlabids and Their Neighbors: Art and Material Culture in Ninth-Century North Africa*, ed. Glaire D. Anderson et al. (Leiden: Brill, 2018), pp. 1–30, at pp. 2–3.

94 As already suggested by the origins of the Tulunids and the Ikshidids, 'Arab' could include Persian or Türkic.

95 Mariam Rosser-Owen, 'Mediterraneanism: How to Incorporate Islamic Art into an Emerging Field', *Journal of Art Historiography*, vol. 6 (2012), pp. 1–33; Anderson, Fenwick and Rosser-Owen 2018, pp. 9–10; Barry W. Cunliffe, *Facing the Sea of Sand: The Sahara and the Peoples of Northern Africa* (Oxford: Oxford University Press, 2023).

96 Marina Rustow, *The Lost Archive: Traces of a Caliphate in a Cairo Synagogue* (Princeton, NJ: Princeton University Press, 2020), p. 35.

97 Wickham 2023, p. 31.

98 Stéphane Pradines, 'Islamic Archaeology in the Comoros: The Swahili and the Rock Crystal Trade with the Abbasid and Fatimid Caliphates', *Journal of Islamic Archaeology*, vol. 6, no. 1 (2019), pp. 109–35; Cynthia J. Hahn and Avinoam Shalem (eds), *Seeking Transparency: Rock Crystals across the Medieval Mediterranean* (Berlin: Gebr. Mann Verlag, 2020).

99 Jonathan Bloom, 'Gifts of the Fatimids', in *Gifts of the Sultan: The Arts of Giving at the Islamic Courts*, ed. Linda Komaroff (Los Angeles: Los Angeles County Museum of Art, 2011), pp. 95–111.

100 Petra Sijpesteijn, 'Visible Identities: In Search of Egypt's Jews in Early Islamic Egypt', in O'Connell (ed.) 2022, pp. 325–34, at pp. 331–2.

101 Yossef Rapoport and Emilie Savage-Smith, *Lost Maps of the Caliphs: Drawing the World in Eleventh-Century Cairo* (Oxford: Bodleian Library, 2018), pp. 249, 252.

102 Ibid., pp. 73–100.

103 Elżbieta Rodziewicz, *Fustat I: Bone Carvings from Fustat – Istabl Antar* (Cairo: Institut français d'archéologie orientale, 2012).

104 Ruth Barnes, *Indian Block-Printed Textiles in Egypt: The Newberry Collection in the Ashmolean Museum, Oxford* (Oxford: Clarendon Press, 1997), vol. 1, pp. 29, 34, 39; see cat. nos 241, vol. 2, p. 69; cat. no. 250, vol. 2, p. 72 and cat. no. 251, vol. 2, pp. 72–3.

105 Ibid., no. 241, vol. 2, p. 69.

106 Takahito Mikami, 'China and Egypt: Fustat', *Transactions of the Oriental Ceramic Society*, vol. 45, no. 81 (1980), pp. 67–87, at p. 70; Roland-Pierre Gayraud and Lucy Vallauri, *Fustat II : Fouilles d'Istabl Antar : céramiques d'ensembles des IXe et Xe siècles* (Cairo: Institut français d'archéologie orientale, 2017). For an up-to-date bibliography, see Wickham 2023, p. 42 n. 47, p. 43 n. 49; for Chinese ceramics from other sites in Egypt, see p. 90 n. 178.

107 Tsugio Mikami, 'Chinese Ceramics from Medieval Sites in Egypt', in *Cultural and Economic Relations between East and West: Sea Routes*, ed. Takahito Mikasa (Wiesbaden: Harrassowitz, 1988), pp. 8–44, at p. 12; for the ninth- and tenth-century finds, see Tadanori Yuba, 'Chinese Porcelain from Fustat Based on Research from 1988–2001', *Transactions of the Oriental Ceramic Society 2011–2012*, vol. 76 (2013), pp. 1–17, at pp. 4–5; for more recently excavated material dated to the tenth century, see Gayraud and Vallauri 2017.

108 Władysław B. Kubiak and George T. Scanlon, *Fustāt Expedition: Final Report*, vol. 2: *Fustāt-C* (Winona Lake, IN: Eisenbrauns, 1989), pp. 19, 47–9.

109 Jelle Bruning, 'Slave Trade Dynamics in Abbasid Egypt: The Papyrological Evidence', *Journal of the Economic and Social History of the Orient*, vol. 63, no. 5–6 (2020), pp. 682–742, at pp. 699–700.

110 Naïm Vanthieghem, 'Quelques contrats de vente d'esclaves de la Collection Aziz', *Journal of Juristic Papyrology*, vol. 44 (2014), pp. 163–87; Bruning 2020; Jane Rowlandson, Roger S. Bagnall and Dorothy J. Thompson (eds), *Slavery and Dependence in Ancient Egypt: Sources in Translation* (New York: Cambridge University Press, 2024).

111 Craig A. Perry, 'The Daily Life of Slaves and the Global Reach of Slavery in Medieval Egypt, 969–1250 CE', PhD dissertation, Emory University, 2014. For long-distance trade between northern Europe and Muslim territories with the Franks as intermediaries, see McCormick 2001, pp. 733–77; and Michael McCormick, 'New Light on the "Dark Ages": How the Slave Trade Fuelled the Carolingian Economy', *Past & Present*, vol. 177, no. 1 (2002), pp. 17–54.

112 See *P.Vente* 10–11; Bruning 2020, p. 701, n. 15.

113 Bruning 2020, p. 684.

114 Ibid., pp. 690–1.

115 Vanthieghem 2014, pp. 178, 189; Bruning 2020, p. 702.

116 Bruning 2020, p. 702.

117 Craig Perry et al., 'Slavery in the Medieval Millennium', in Perry et al. (eds) 2021, pp. 1–24, at p. 21.

118 For the Middle Egypt cemeteries, see Guy Brunton, *Qau and Badari*, 3 vols (London: British School of Archaeology in Egypt, 1927–30); Guy Brunton, *Mostagedda and the Tasian Culture* (London: B. Quaritch Ltd, 1937); Guy Brunton, *Matmar* (London: B. Quaritch Ltd, 1948); Alexandra D. Pleşa, 'The Late Antique and Early Islamic Necropolises at Matmar and Mostagedda, Middle Egypt. A Reassessment of the Excavation and Present State of the Collection', in *Excavating, Analysing, Reconstructing: Textiles of the 1st Millennium AD from Egypt and Neighbouring Countries. Proceedings of the 9th Conference of the Research Group 'Textiles from the Nile Valley'*, ed. Antoine De Moor, Cäcilia Fluck and Petra Linscheid (Tielt: Lannoo, 2017), pp. 72–87; Alexandra D. Pleşa, 'Religious Belief in Burial: Funerary Dress and Practice at the Late Antique and Early Islamic Cemeteries at Matmar and Mostagedda, Egypt (Late Fourth–Early Ninth Centuries CE)', *Ars Orientalis*, vol. 47 (2017), pp. 18–42; Joanna Then-Obłuska and Alexandra D. Pleşa, 'Roman to Islamic Beads and Pendants from Matmar and Mostagedda, Middle Egypt', *BEADS: Journal of the Society of Bead Researchers*, vol. 31, no. 1 (January 1, 2019), pp. 50–74. Ellen Swift, Jo Stoner and April Pudsey, *A Social Archaeology of Roman and Late Antique Egypt* (New York: Oxford University Press, 2022), pp. 8–20.

119 For circulation over generations, see Swift, Stoner and Pudsey 2022, p. 104; for women and girls, see pp. 103–4; for prestige of imports, see p. 105.

120 Mostagedda, tomb 1141; one of the beads was from a much earlier period, see Brunton 1937, p. 140.

121 Swift, Stoner and Pudsey 2022, pp. 104–6.

122 Rachel King, *Amber: From Antiquity to Eternity* (London: Reaktion Books, 2022), pp. 13, 45–58.

123 Swift, Stoner and Pudsey 2022, pp. 83–4, 104–7.

124 Ibid., p. 105.

125 For a hypothetical example drawing on evidence from a few different strings, see Swift, Stoner and Pudsey 2022, p. 108.

126 'A well-made figure of the god [Bes] in blue glaze, certainly not contemporary, was found on the wrist of a child strung with a Coptic cross' / 'come from Cemetery 600' (Brunton 1930, vol. 3, p. 27). For survival of ancient string, see Swift, Stoner and Pudsey 2022, pp. 89–103.

127 David Frankfurter, *Christianizing Egypt: Syncretism and Local Worlds in Late Antiquity* (Princeton, NJ: Princeton University Press, 2017).

128 Aksumite coins from Antaeopolis/Qaw al-Kebir, BM 1926,0108.82–83; for imported beads, see Swift, Stoner and Pudsey 2022, pp. 73–5.

129 Constantin Pion et al., 'Bead and Garnet Trade between the Merovingian, Mediterranean, and Indian Worlds', in *The Oxford Handbook of the Merovingian World*, ed. Bonnie Effros and Isabel Moreira (Oxford: Oxford University Press, 2020), pp. 818–59.

130 Joanna Then-Obłuska and Barbara Wagner, *Glass Bead Trade in Northeast Africa: The Evidence from Meroitic and Post-Meroitic Nubia* (Warsaw: University of Warsaw Press, 2019).

131 Ibid.

132 Joanna Then-Obłuska, 'Cross-Cultural Bead Encounters at the Red Sea Port Site of Berenike, Egypt: Preliminary Assessment', *Polish Archaeology in the Mediterranean*, vol. 24 (2015), pp. 735–77. Swift, Stoner and Pudsey 2022, p. 75.

133 Swift, Stoner and Pudsey 2022, pp. 38, 74–5, 348, 352.

134 Evans and Ratliff (eds) 2012, no. 173, pp. 238–41.

135 Petra Sijpesteijn, 'Request to Buy Coloured Silk', in *Gedenkschrift Ulrike Horak: P Horak*, ed. Hermann Harrauer and Rosario Pintaudi (Florence: Gonnelli, 2004), pp. 255–72.

136 David J. Mattingly and Martin Sterry, 'The First Towns in the Central Sahara', *Antiquity*, vol. 87, no. 336 (2013), pp. 503–18; David J. Mattingly et al. (eds), *Trade in the Ancient Sahara and Beyond* (Cambridge: Cambridge University Press, 2017); Martin Sterry and David J. Mattingly (eds), *Urbanisation and State Formation in the Ancient Sahara and Beyond* (Cambridge: Cambridge University Press, 2020).

137 Anna C. Kelley, 'Movement and Mobility: Cotton and the Visibility of Trade Networks across the Saharan Desert', in Brubaker, Darley and Reynolds (eds) 2022, pp. 138–54.

138 Richard W. Bulliet, *The Camel and the Wheel* (New York: Columbia University Press, 1990).

139 Douglas Post Park, 'Prehistoric Timbuktu and its Hinterland', *Antiquity*, vol. 84, no. 326 (2010), pp. 1076–88; Mamadou Cissé, 'The Trans-Saharan Trade Connection with Gao (Mali) during the First Millennium AD', in D. J. Mattingly et al. 2017, pp. 101–30; Sarah M. Guérin, 'Forgotten Routes? Italy, Ifrīqiya and the Trans-Saharan Ivory Trade', *Al-Masāq*, vol. 25, no. 1 (2013), pp. 70–91; Sterry and Mattingly 2020.

140 Shallow-mined gold may also have been available: research is ongoing. West Africa has little naturally occurring salt, the importation of which is required: Kathleen Bickford Berzock (ed.), *Caravans of Gold, Fragments in Time: Art, Culture, and Exchange across Medieval Saharan Africa* (Evanston, IL: Block Museum of Art, Northwestern University, 2019), p. 25.

141 Timothy Insoll and Thurstan Shaw, 'Gao and Igbo-Ukwu: Beads, Interregional Trade, and Beyond', *African Archaeological Review*, vol. 14, no. 1 (1997), pp. 9–23; Susan Keech McIntosh et al., 'Glass Beads from Medieval Gao (Mali): New Analytical Data on Chronology, Sources, and Trade', *Journal of African Archaeology*, vol. 18, no. 2 (2020), pp. 139–61; Susan Keech McIntosh, 'Igbo-Ukwu at 50: A Symposium on Recent Archaeological Research and Analysis', *African Archaeological Review*, vol. 39, no. 4 (2022), pp. 369–85.

142 Abidemi Babatunde Babalola, 'Medieval Glass Bead Production and Exchange', in Bickford Berzock (ed.) 2019, pp. 223–39, at p. 233.

143 Abidemi Babatunde Babalola et al., 'Chemical Analysis of Glass Beads from Igbo Olokun, Ile-Ife (SW Nigeria): New Light on Raw Materials, Production, and Interregional Interactions', *Journal of Archaeological Science*, vol. 90 (2018), pp. 92–105, at p. 104.

144 Thurstan Shaw, *Igbo-Ukwu: An Account of Archaeological Discoveries in Eastern Nigeria* (Evanston, IL: Northwestern University Press, 1970); Paul T. Craddock et al., 'Metal Sources and the Bronzes from Igbo-Ukwu, Nigeria', *Journal of Field Archaeology*, vol. 24, no. 4 (1997), pp. 405–29; Quanyu Wang, Paul Craddock and Julie Hudson, 'A Metallographic Study of Objects and Fragments from the Site of Igbo Isaiah, Igbo-Ukwu, Nigeria', *African Archaeological Review*, vol. 39, no. 4 (2022), pp. 419–35.

145 Nehemia Levtzion and J.F.P. Hopkins (eds), *Corpus of Early Arabic Sources for West African History* (Cambridge: Cambridge University Press, 2000).

146 Ibid., p. 21.

147 Ronald A. Messier, 'The Almoravids: West African Gold and the Gold Currency of the Mediterranean Basin', *Journal of the Economic and Social History of the Orient*, vol. 17, no. 1 (1974), p. 31; Sam Nixon, Thilo Rehren and Maria Filomena Guerra, 'New Light on the Early Islamic West African Gold Trade: Coin Moulds from Tadmekka, Mali', *Antiquity*, vol. 85, no. 330 (2011), pp. 1353–68; Thilo Rehren and Sam Nixon, 'Refining Gold with Glass: An Early Islamic Technology at Tadmekka, Mali', *Journal of Archaeological Science*, vol. 49 (2014), pp. 33–41.

148 Ibn-Hawqal, *Kitāb Sūrat al-Ard (La Configuration de la terre)*, 2 vols, trans. J.H. Kramers and G. Wiet (Paris and Beirut: Commission internationale pour la traduction des chefs-d'œuvre, 1964), vol. 1, pp. 58, 97–8; Robert Launay, 'Views from Afar: Reading Medieval Trans-Saharan Trade through Arabic Accounts', in Bickford Berzock (ed.) 2019, pp. 49–62, at pp. 50–3.

149 François-Xavier Fauvelle-Aymar, *The Golden Rhinoceros: Histories of the African Middle Ages* (Princeton, NJ: Princeton University Press, 2018), p. 51.

150 Jean D. Devisse, *Tegdaoust III : recherches sur Aoudaghost, Campagnes 1960–1965 : enquêtes générales* (Paris: Éditions Recherches sur les Civilisations, 1983).

151 Launay 2019, p. 51.

152 Fauvelle-Aymar 2018, pp. 75–80.

153 Sam Nixon (ed.), *Essouk-Tadmekka: An Early Islamic Trans-Saharan Market Town* (Leiden: Brill, 2017).

154 Sam Nixon, 'Essouk-Tadmekka: A Southern Saharan Center of the Early Islamic Camel Caravan Trade', in Bickford Berzock (ed.) 2019, pp. 123–37, at p. 123.

155 Cyrille Aillet, Patrice Cressier and Sophie Gilotte (eds), *Sedrata. Histoire et archéologie d'un carrefour du Sahara médiéval à la lumière des archives inédites de Marguerite van Berchem* (Madrid: Casa de Velázquez, 2017).

156 Patrice Cressier and Sophie Gilotte, 'Les décors de stuc de Sedrata : Essai de datation et de systématisation de la typologie', in ibid., pp. 397–431, at p. 430.

157 P.F. de Moraes Farias, *Arabic Medieval Inscriptions from the Republic of Mali: Epigraphy, Chronicles and Songhay-Tuāreg History* (Oxford: The British Academy/Oxford University Press, 2003), pp. 41–51; Nixon 2019, p. 132.

158 Nixon 2019, p. 129 (for nuance of comparison, p. 131).

159 Moraes Farias 2003; Nixon 2019, p. 133.

160 Nixon, Rehren and Guerra 2011; Nixon 2019, pp. 133–5, for the political neutrality of issuing 'blanks' without stamps bearing the name of a ruler, see p. 135.

161 For sources of gold see Nixon 2019, pp. 152–73; for pottery, p. 126; for steel, p. 128; for later imports, pp. 120–3, 126.

162 Wickham 2023, p. 180.

163 Ronald A. Messier, 'Dinars as Historical Texts', in Bickford Berzock (ed.) 2019, pp. 203–11, at p. 205.

164 Ibid., p. 207.

165 Guérin 2013.

166 Silvia Armando, 'Fatimid Ivories in Ifriqiya: The Madrid and Mantua Caskets between Construction and Decoration', *Journal of Islamic Archaeology*, vol. 2, no. 2 (2016), pp. 195–228, at p. 203.

167 Wickham 2023, p. 183.

168 Ibid., p. 191.

169 Rustow 2020, p. 14.

170 For this transition from papyrus to flax cultivation, see Wickham 2023, p. 5.

171 For the radiocarbon date, c. 774 (92.5%) 896 cal.AD, see Cäcilia Fluck, 'Fragments of a Tunic', in *Akhmim: Egypt's Forgotten City*, ed. Rafed El-Sayed et al. (Petersberg: Michael Imhof Verlag, 2021), pp. 246–7.

172 Yossef Rapoport, 'Where Did All the Christians Go? Peasants and Tribesman in the Fayum, AD 1060–1240', in O'Connell (ed.) 2022, pp. 199–214.

173 Luke B. Yarbrough, *Friends of the Emir: Non-Muslim State Officials in Premodern Islamic Thought* (Cambridge: Cambridge University Press, 2019).

174 Petra Sijpesteijn, *Shaping a Muslim State: The World of a Mid-Eighth-Century Egyptian Official* (New York: Oxford University Press, 2013).

175 Jean-Luc Fournet, *The Rise of Coptic: Egyptian versus Greek in Late Antiquity* (Princeton, NJ: Princeton University Press, 2020).

176 Tonio Sebastian Richter, *Writing and Practicing Alchemy in 8th to 10th-Century Egypt. The Coptic Alchemical Texts Edited and Translated*, Sources of Alchemy and Chemistry, Ambix Supplements (forthcoming).

177 Among others, Arietta Papaconstantinou, 'They Shall Speak the Arabic Language and Take Pride in It', *Le Muséon*, vol. 120, nos 3–4 (2007), pp. 273–99.

178 Arianna D'Ottone Rambach and Dario Internullo, 'One Script for Two Languages: Latin and Arabic in an Early Allographic Papyrus', *Rivista Degli Studi Orientali*, vol. 90 (2017), pp. 53–72.

179 Papaconstantinou 2007.

180 Jacques van der Vliet, 'Nubian Voices from Edfu: Egyptian Scribes and Nubian Patrons in Southern Egypt', in *Nubian Voices II: New Texts and Studies on Christian Nubian Culture*, ed. Adam Łajtar, Grzegorz Ochała and Jacques van der Vliet, *Journal of Juristic Papyrology*, Supplement vol. 27 (2015), pp. 263–77, at pp. 263–4.

181 Daniel King (ed.), *The Syriac World* (London: Routledge, 2019).

182 Volker L. Menze, *Justinian and the Making of the Syrian Orthodox Church* (Oxford: Oxford University Press, 2008).

183 Sebastian Brock, 'Without Mushê of Nisibis, Where Would We Be?', *Journal of Eastern Christian Studies*, vol. 56, no. 1 (2004), pp. 15–24.

184 Sebastian P. Brock, *An Inventory of Syriac Texts Published from Manuscripts in the British Library* (Piscataway, NJ: Gorgias Press, 2020); Sebastian P. Brock and Lucas van Rompay, *Catalogue of the Syriac Manuscripts and Fragments in the Library of Deir Al-Surian, Wadi Al-Natrun (Egypt)* (Leuven and Walpole, MA: Uitgeverij Peeters en Departement Oosterse Studies, 2014).

185 Siam Bhayro, 'Galen's *Simples* in Syriac', *Archives internationales d'histoire des sciences*, vol. 70, no. 184–5 (2020), pp. 114–28.

186 Irene Calà and Robert Hawley, 'Transliteration versus Translation of Greek Plant Names in the Syriac Medical Writings of Sergius of Reš 'Aynā: On the Tables of Contents in BL Add. 14,661', *Aramaic Studies*, vol. 15, no. 2 (2017), pp. 155–82.

187 Siam Bhayro et al., 'The Syriac Galen Palimpsest: Progress, Prospects and Problems', *Journal of Semitic Studies*, vol. 58, no. 1 (2013), pp. 131–48.

188 For Mount Sinai, see Claudia Rapp, 'A Cache of Palimpsests and Christian Manuscript Culture across the Medieval Mediterranean: First Results of the Sinai Palimpsests Project', in *Veröffentlichungen zur Byzanzforschung* (Vienna: Austrian Academy of Sciences Press, 2023), pp. 39–53.

189 For a recent survey, see Zina Cohen, *Composition Analysis of Writing Materials in Cairo Genizah Documents* (Leiden: Brill, 2022), pp. 5–16. Among others, Adina Hoffman and Peter Cole, *Sacred Trash: The Lost and Found World of the Cairo Geniza* (New York: Nextbook, 2011). For further considerations, see Rustow 2020, pp. 29–31.

190 Cohen 2022; Hoffman and Cole 2011; Rustow 2020, pp. 46–9.

191 S.D. Goitein, *A Mediterranean Society: The Jewish Communities of the Arab World as Portrayed in the Documents of the Cairo Geniza*, 6 vols (Berkeley, CA: University of California Press, 1967–93).

192 Marina Rustow, *Heresy and the Politics of Community: The Jews of the Fatimid Caliphate* (Ithaca, NY: Cornell University Press, 2008).

193 For example, the earliest texts are palimpsests, parchment books that were scraped of their ink and reused, such as a seventh-century copy of Church Father Origen's (*c.* 185–253 CE) *Hexapla*, which was identified under a tenth-century copy of a seventh-century liturgist Yannai, the first poet to introduce rhyme into Hebrew liturgy (Hoffman and Cole 2011, pp. 95–125).

194 Ben Outhwaite, 'The Oldest Hebrew Fragment in the Collection? T-S NS 3.21', *Genizah Research Unit, Fragment of the Month, November 2010*, 1 November 2010, doi.org/10.17863/CAM.55276 (accessed 22 April 2024).

195 Beatrice Gruendler et al., 'An Interim Report on the Editorial and Analytical Work of the AnonymClassic Project', *Medieval Worlds*, vol. 11 (2020), pp. 241–79, at pp. 243–5.

196 Goitein 1967–93.

197 Rustow 2020.

198 Goitein 1967–93, vol. 1, pp. 42–59; for a recent compilation of texts written in or concerning Southeast Asia, see Marina Rustow, 'Kalah in the Lands of Java: T-S Ar.30.42', *Genizah Research Unit, Fragment of the Month*, 1 November 2021, doi.org/10.17863/CAM.82612 (accessed 4 May 2024).

199 Rustow 2020, pp. 113–37.

200 S.D. Goitein and Mordechai Akiva Friedman, *India Traders of the Middle Ages: Documents from the Cairo Geniza: India Book* (Leiden: Brill, 2008), p. 61.

201 Rustow 2020.

202 For reuse, see Rustow 2020, pp. 77, 400; for Sitt al-Mulk, see pp. 51–4; for Fatimid decrees, see pp. 6, 12, 202, 381–401.

203 Rustow 2008, pp. 301–22.

204 For this and the following discussion, see Goitein 1967–93, vol. 1, pp. 52–3.

205 Ibid., p. 48.

206 Ibid, pp. 46, 50, vol. 3, pp. 12–31; Eve Krakowski, *Coming of Age in Medieval Egypt: Female Adolescence, Jewish Law, and Ordinary Culture* (Princeton, NJ: Princeton University Press, 2018).

207 Cambridge University Library, T-S Add. 3430; Goitein 1967–93, vol. 4, p. 305.

208 Mark R. Cohen, *Voice of the Poor in the Middle Ages: An Anthology of Documents from the Cairo Geniza* (Princeton, NJ: Princeton University Press, 2005a), p. 47; Mark R. Cohen, *Poverty and Charity in the Jewish Community of Medieval Egypt* (Princeton, NJ: Princeton University Press, 2005b), pp. 109–29.

209 Ibid., pp. 63–5; Ben Outhwaite, 'The Letter for a Man from Somewhere: T-S 10J10.9', *Genizah Research Unit, Fragment of the Month, December 2019*, 1 December 2019; T-S 10J10.9.

210 Norman Golb and Omeljan Pritsak, *Khazarian Hebrew Documents of the Tenth Century* (Ithaca, NY: Cornell University Press, 1982); Constantine Zuckerman, 'On the Kievan Letter from the Genizah of Cairo', *Ruthenica*, vol. 10 (2011), pp. 7–56, at pp. 12–14. For Khazars and the conversion of the royal house, see Dan Shapira, 'Khazars', in *Encyclopaedia Iranica Online*, vol. 16, no. 5 (2020), pp. 511–28. Cf. Shaul Stampfer, 'Did the Khazars Convert to Judaism?', *Jewish Social Studies*, vol. 19, no. 3 (2013), pp. 1–72.

211 Goitein 1967–93, vol. 4, p. 348; Hoffman and Cole 2011, pp. 181–7. For a copy of the *Khuzari*, see T-S Misc. 35.38; for a pen-trial, see T-S Ar. 40.126.

212 Hoffman and Cole 2011, p. 182.

213 Goitein 1967–93, vol. 1; Goitein and Friedman 2008; Roxani Margariti, *Aden & the Indian Ocean Trade: 150 Years in the Life of a Medieval Arabian Port* (Chapel Hill, NC: University of North Carolina Press, 2007); Jessica Goldberg, *Trade and Institutions in the Medieval Mediterranean: The Geniza Merchants and their Business World* (Cambridge: Cambridge University Press, 2012).

214 Goldberg 2012.

215 Ibid., p. 289; Elizabeth A. Lambourn, *Abraham's Luggage: A Social Life of Things in the Medieval Indian Ocean World* (Cambridge: Cambridge University Press, 2018), p. 53.

216 Goldberg 2012, p. 289; Lambourn 2018, p. 53.

217 Goldberg 2012, pp. 106–7.

218 Ibid. For an Aden-based shipowner see Roxani Margariti, 'Wrecks and Texts: A Judeo-Arabic Case Study', in *Maritime Studies in the Wake of the Byzantine Shipwreck at Yassiada, Turkey*, ed. Deborah N. Carlson, Justin Leidwanger and Sarah M. Kampbell (College Station, TX: Texas A&M University Press, 2015), pp. 189–202, at pp. 191–2.

219 Margariti 2007, pp. 94–6; and especially Goldberg 2012, pp. 106–7.

220 Goitein 1967–93, vol. 1, p. 154.

221 Goldberg 2012, pp. 33–5, 269, 288–90; Wickham 2023, pp. 44, 130.

222 Cohen 2005a, p. 68; Perry et al. (eds) 2021.

223 Goitein and Friedman 2008; for wonderful portraits of individual traders, see Margariti 2007 and Lambourn 2018.

224 Wickham 2023, pp. 194–5.

225 Lambourn 2018, pp. 43–8.

226 Ibid., pp. 98–103.

227 Ibid., pp. 59–63, 67–8.

228 Margariti 2015.

229 Lambourn 2018, p. 165.

230 Margariti 2007, pp. 184–6; Goitein and Friedman 2008, pp. 204–8.

231 Perry 2014, pp. 255–30.

232 Goitein 1967–93, vol. 1, pp. 130–47.

233 Perry 2014, p. 39.

234 Ibid., pp. 51–4.

235 Craig Perry, 'An Aramaic Bill of Sale for the Enslaved Nubian Woman Na'īm', *Jewish History*, vol. 32, no. 2/4 (2019), pp. 451–61.

236 See, among others, Erik Hermans, *A Companion to the Global Early Middle Ages* (Leeds: Arc Humanities Press, 2020); Brubaker, Darley and Reynolds (eds) 2022.

Peoples of al-Andalus

1 Patrice Cressier and Sonia Gutiérrez Lloret, 'Al-Andalus', in *The Oxford Handbook of Islamic Archaeology*, ed. Bethany J. Walker, Timothy Insoll and Corisande Fenwick (Oxford: Oxford University Press, 2020); Tawfiq ibn Hafiz Ibrahim, 'Nuevos documentos sobre la Conquista Omeya de Hispania: los precintos de plomo', in *711: Arqueología e historia entre dos mundos: Museo Arqueológico Regional, Alcalá de Henares, Madrid, del 16 diciembre de 2011 al 1 de abril de 2012*, vol. 1, ed. Luis A. García Moreno and Alfonso Vigil-Escalera (Madrid: Comunidad de Madrid, Consejería de Cultura y Deportes, 2011), pp. 149–50, fig. 2.

2 '... *clarum decus orbis*': Hrosvitha of Gandersheim, *Passio Sancti Pelagii* (author's translation).

3 Mariam Rosser-Owen, *Islamic Arts from Spain* (London: V&A Publishing, 2010), pp. 14–30; José C. Carvajal López, 'Introduction: Al-Andalus as a Common Ground', in *Al-Andalus: Archaeology, History and Memory*, ed. José C. Carvajal López (Edinburgh: UCL Qatar and Akkadia Press, 2016), pp. 1–6; Cressier and Gutiérrez Lloret 2020; Alejandra Gutiérrez et al., 'The Earliest Chinese Ceramics in Europe?', *Antiquity*, vol. 95 (2021), pp. 1213–30; Chris Wickham, *The Inheritance of Rome: A History of Europe from 400 to 1000* (London: Penguin, 2009), pp. 338–9; Daniel G. König, *Arabic-Islamic Views of the Latin West: Tracing the Emergence of Medieval Europe* (Oxford: Oxford University Press, 2015), pp. 43–4.

4 Sonia Gutiérrez Lloret, 'Early al-Andalus: An Archaeological Approach to the Process of Islamization in the Iberian Peninsula (7th to 10th centuries)', in *New Directions in European Archaeology: Spain and Italy Compared: Essays for Riccardo Francovich*, ed. Sauro Gelichi and Richard Hodges (Turnhout: Brepols, 2015), pp. 43–86; Victoria Amorós Ruiz and Sonia Gutiérrez Lloret, 'Ceramics in Transition from the First Islamic Period in the Western Mediterranean: The Example of al-Andalus', *Libyan Studies*, vol. 51 (2020), pp. 99–125.

5 Cressier and Gutiérrez Lloret 2020, p. 324; Sergio Vidal Álvarez et al., *Las artes del metal en al-Ándalus* (Madrid: P&M Ediciones, 2019), cat. no. 1; Ariza Armada, 'The Coinage of al-Andalus', *Shedet*, vol. 4 (2017), pp. 69–72; König 2015, p. 47.

6 Carolina Doménech Belda and Eduardo López Seguí, 'Los alifatos sobre hueso: un ejemplar del casco antiguo del Alicante', *LVCENTVM*, vol. 27 (2008), pp. 243–57; María Teresa Casal García, 'The First "Islamized" Urban Settlement in al-Andalus: The Archaeology of the Shaqunda's Suburb, Córdoba', paper delivered at Leeds International Medieval Congress, Session 1004, 7 July 2021; Juan Pedro Monferrer-Sala, 'The Fragmentary Ninth/Tenth Century Andalusi Arabic Translation of the Epistle to the Galatians Revisited (Vat. lat. 12900, olim Seguntinus 150 BC Sigüenza)', *Intellectual History of the Islamicate World*, vol. 7 (2019), pp. 125–91; Umberto Bongianino, *The Manuscript Tradition of the Islamic West: Maghribi Round Scripts and Andalusi Identity* (Edinburgh: Edinburgh University Press 2022), ch. 2, esp. pp. 108–11 and fig. 2.15.

7 Glaire D. Anderson, pers. comm., 19 October 2023; Carvajal López (ed.) 2016, p. 1; König 2015, pp. 44–7; Rosser-Owen 2010, pp. 16, 19–22; Richard Hitchcock, *Mozarabs in Medieval and Early Modern Spain: Identities and Influences* (Aldershot: Ashgate, 2008), pp. xii–xv; Cressier and Gutiérrez Lloret 2020, pp. 325–8; Wickham 2009, p. 342; Gutiérrez Lloret 2015, pp. 62–72; Marcos García García, 'Archaeozoology's Contribution to the Knowledge of al-Andalus', in Carvajal López (ed.) 2016, pp. 33–7; Carmen González Gutiérrez, 'Religious Spaces in Early al-Andalus: Mosques in Urban Contexts', paper delivered at Leeds International Medieval Congress, Session 504, 6 July 2021.

8 Hitchcock 2008, pp. xiv–xvii; Gutiérrez Lloret 2015, p. 70; Wickham 2009, p. 342; König 2015, p. 49.

9 Alternatively, the three arms could represent a pair of crosses, as the decoration on all three pieces may have been arranged for vertical viewing: Sophie Makariou, 'Deux bras de croix pattée', in *Les Andalousies de Damas á Cordoue*, ed. Marthe Bernus-Taylor (Paris: Hazan, L'Institut, 2000), pp. 172–3; Danielle Gaborit-Chopin, *Ivoires médiévaux: Ve–XVe siècle* (Paris: Éditions de la Réunion des musées nationaux, 2003), pp. 195–8.

10 Mariam Rosser-Owen, *Articulating the Hijāba: Cultural Patronage and Political Legitimacy in al-Andalus – The 'Āmirid*

Regency c. 970–1010 AD (Leiden: Brill, 2021), fig. 86; Victoria and Albert Museum, London, inv. no. 217-1865.

11 Glaire D. Anderson, 'Sign of the Cross: Contexts for the Ivory Cross of San Millán de la Cogolla', *Journal of Medieval Iberian Studies*, vol. 6 (2014), pp. 15–41; Rosser-Owen 2021, pp. 328–9; Rose Walker, *Art in Spain and Portugal from the Romans to the Early Middle Ages: Routes and Myths* (Kalamazoo, MI: Medieval Institute Publications, 2016), pp. 242–3. For the Christian-made interpretation, see Makariou 2000 and Gaborit-Chopin 2003, pp. 195–6.

12 Michael Toch, 'The Jews in Europe 500–1500', in *The New Cambridge Medieval History I: c.500–c.700*, ed. Paul Fouracre (Cambridge: Cambridge University Press, 2005), pp. 545–70; Peter Coe (trans. and ed.), *The Dream of the Poem: Hebrew Poetry from Muslim and Christian Spain 950–1492* (Princeton, NJ, and Oxford: Princeton University Press 2007), p. 5 ff.; Alexander Bar-Magen Numhauser, *The Jews of Hispania in Late Antiquity and the Early Middle Ages through their Material Remains* (Leiden: Brill, 2021), pp. 255–7.

13 Jerrilynn D. Dodds, 'The Great Mosque of Córdoba', in *Al-Andalus: The Arts of Islamic Spain*, ed. Jerrilynn D. Dodds (New York: Metropolitan Museum of Art, 1992), figs 3 and 6; Antonio Vallejo Triano, 'Madinat al-Zahra: The Triumph of the Islamic State', in Dodds (ed.) 1992, figs 4–6.

14 Mohammed Moain Sadeq, 'Architectural Overview of al-Andalus: Iberian Traditions and Islamic Innovations', in Carvajal López (ed.) 2016, pp. 7–11; Rosser-Owen 2010, pp. 19–25; Walker 2016, pp. 184–6; Juan Souto, 'Stonemasons' Identification Marks as a Prosopographical Source: The Case of Umayyad al-Andalus', *Medieval Prosopography*, vol. 23 (2002), pp. 229–45.

15 Glaire D. Anderson, *The Islamic Villa in Early Medieval Iberia: Architecture and Court Culture in Umayyad Córdoba* (Farnham: Ashgate, 2013), p. 12 and ch. 4; Miquel Forcada, 'The Garden in Umayyad Society in al-Andalus', *Early Medieval Europe*, vol. 27 (2019), pp. 349–73; Wendy Davies, 'Gardens and Gardening in Early Medieval Spain and Portugal', *Early Medieval Europe*, vol. 27 (2019), pp. 327–4; Rosser-Owen 2010, p. 25; D. Fairchild Ruggles, *Gardens, Landscape and Vision in the Palaces of Islamic Spain* (University Park, PA: Pennsylvania University Press, 2000), p. 42.

16 Information provided by Dr Antonio Vallejo Triano, who undertook research into the V&A's collection of archaeological material from Madinat al-Zahra in 2014 and 2015 thanks to funding received from the Office of Cultural and Scientific Affairs at the Spanish Embassy in London. See also Antonio Vallejo Triano, *La ciudad califal de Madinat Al-Zahrā': arqueología de su excavación* (Córdoba: Editorial Almuzara, 2010).

17 Forcada 2019, pp. 370–2; Davies 2019, pp. 331–3; Vidal Álvarez et al. 2019, cat. no. 153; Rosser-Owen 2021, pp. 104–5, 349ff; Anderson 2013, pp. 50ff, 74. See also Glaire D. Anderson, 'Aristocratic Residences and the Majlis in Umayyad Córdoba', in *Music, Sound, and Architecture in Islam*, ed. Michael Frishkopf and Federico Spinetti (Austin, TX: University of Texas Press, 2018), pp. 232–3 and fig. 9.5 for a visualisation of al-Rummaniyya.

18 Anderson 2013, pp. 111–18; Forcada 2019, pp. 352, 365; José María Martín Civantos, 'Intensive Irrigated Agriculture in al-Andalus', in Carvajal López (ed.) 2016, pp. 27–31; Cressier and Gutiérrez Lloret 2020, p. 321; Sonia Gutiérrez Lloret, 'The Case of Tudmīr: Archaeological Evidence for the Introduction of Irrigation Systems in al-Andalus', *European Journal of Archaeology*, vol. 27 (2019), pp. 394–415; Amorós Ruiz and Gutiérrez Lloret 2020, fig. 6.

19 Elena Salinas et al., 'From Glass to Glaze in al-Andalus: Local Invention and Technological Transfer', *European Journal of Archaeology*, vol. 25 (2022), pp. 22–41.

20 Rosser-Owen 2010, p. 22; Julio Samsó, *On Both Sides of the Strait of Gibraltar: Studies in the History of Medieval Astronomy in the Iberian Peninsula and the Maghrib* (Leiden: Brill, 2020), pp. 1–2, 23, 42; Glaire D. Anderson, pers. comm., 19 October 2023.

21 Samsó 2020, pp. 18–20, 380; Lena Wahlgren-Smith, 'Letter Collections in the Latin West', in *A Companion to Byzantine Epistolography*, ed. Alexander Riehle (Leiden: Brill, 2020), p. 94; Kocku von Stuckrad, *Locations of Knowledge in Medieval and Early Modern Europe: Esoteric Discourse and Western Identities* (Leiden: Brill, 2010), pp. 129–30.

22 Azucena Hernández Pérez, *Astrolabios en al-Andalus y los reinos medievales hispanos* (Madrid: Ediciones de la Ergástula, 2018); Glaire D. Anderson, 'Mind and Hand: Early Scientific Instruments from al-Andalus and 'Abbas ibn Firnas in the Córdoban Umayyad Court', *Muqarnas*, vol. 37 (2020), p. 14; Arianna Borelli, *Aspects of the Astrolabe: 'Architectonica Ratio' in Tenth- and Eleventh-Century Europe* (Stuttgart: Franz Steiner Verlag, 2008), pp. 16–19.

23 Samsó 2020, p. 390; David A. King, *Astrolabes from Medieval Europe* (London: Thames & Hudson, 2011), p. 382.

Northwest Europe

1 Michael McCormick, *Origins of the European Economy: Communications and Commerce, AD 300–900* (Cambridge: Cambridge University Press, 2001); Christopher Loveluck, *Northwest Europe in the Early Middle Ages, c. AD 600–1150: A Comparative Archaeology* (Cambridge: Cambridge University Press, 2013); Alice Hudson, 'Routes of North African Impact on Book Production in the British Isles before ca. 800', *Viator*, vol. 51 (2020), pp. 83–101; John D. Niles, 'Reassessing Anglo-Saxon Origins from a Eurasian Perspective', in *Global Perspectives on Early Medieval England*, ed. Karen Louise Jolly and Britton Elliot Brooks (Woodbridge: Boydell Press, 2022), pp. 139–70; Sam Ottewill-Soulsby, *The Emperor and the Elephant: Christians and Muslims in the Age of Charlemagne* (Princeton, NJ: Princeton University Press, 2023); Susan Whitfield (ed.), *Silk Roads: Peoples, Cultures, Landscapes* (London: Thames & Hudson, 2019). Recent major research projects exploring north and northwest Europe's wider connections include 'The Viking Phenomenon' at the University Uppsala, Sweden, 2015–25, and 'Nara to Norwich', developed at the Sainsbury Institute for the Study of Japanese Arts and Cultures (SISJAC) in 2016 (see the online exhibition *Nara to Norwich - Explore Arts and Beliefs at the Ends of the Silk Roads* at naratonorwich.org, accessed 3 April 2024).

2 McCormick 2001, pp. 77–9, 561–4.

3 Ibid., pp. 552, 561; Jan Bill and Else Roesdahl, 'Travel and Transport', in *The Archaeology of Early Medieval Europe*, ed. Magdalena Valor Piechotta, James A. Graham-Campbell and Jan Klápště (Aarhus: Aarhus University Press, 2007), pp. 261–3, 272.

4 Loveluck 2013, p. 3; Ian N. Wood, *The Merovingian Kingdoms 450–751* (London: Routledge, 2014), p. 1.

5 Two victims were recently identified in a sixth-century cemetery in Cambridgeshire: Marcel Keller et al., 'Ancient Yersinia Pestis Genomes from across Western Europe Reveal Early Diversification during the First Pandemic (541–750)', *PNAS*, vol. 116 (2019).

6 McCormick 2001, pp. 66, 501; Richard L. Smith, 'Trade and Commerce across Afro-Eurasia', in *The Cambridge World History*, vol. 5, ed. Benjamin Z. Kedar and Merry E. Wiesner-

Hanks (Cambridge: Cambridge University Press, 2017), pp. 242–3; Peter Sarris, 'Climate and Disease', in *A Companion to the Global Middle Ages*, ed. Erik Hermans (Amsterdam: Amsterdam University Press, 2020), pp. 521–6.

7 Loveluck 2013, pp. 179–81; McCormick 2001, pp. 695–6, 791–2; Paul Arthur and Søren M. Sindbæk, 'Trade and Exchange', in Piechotta, Graham-Campbell and Klápště (eds) 2007, pp. 301–7; Julia M.H. Smith, *Europe After Rome: A New Cultural History 500–1000* (Oxford: Oxford University Press, 2007), pp. 188–9.

8 McCormick 2001, pp. 501–22, 549; Chris Wickham, *Framing the Early Middle Ages: Europe and the Mediterranean, 400–800* (Oxford: Oxford University Press, 2005), pp. 707–8, 819.

9 Aldhelm, Riddle 40, in *Saint Aldhelm's Riddles*, trans. A.M. Juster (Toronto: University of Toronto Press, 2015), p. 23.

10 McCormick 2001, pp. 733–77; cf. Alice Rio, *Slavery After Rome, 500–1100* (Oxford: Oxford University Press, 2017), pp. 19–28.

11 Duncan Sayer, Dominic Powlesland and Allison Stewart, 'Individual Encounters: Capturing Personal Stories with Ancient DNA', *Current Archaeology*, vol. 392 (November 2022), www.the-past.com/feature/individual-encounters-capturing-personal-stories-with-ancient-dna (accessed 11 August 2023); Katie A. Hemer et al., 'Evidence of Early Medieval Trade and Migration between Wales and the Mediterranean Sea Region', *Journal of Archaeological Science*, vol. 40 (2013), pp. 2352–9; Yves Gleize et al., 'Early Medieval Muslim Graves in France: First Archaeological, Anthropological and Palaeoenomic Evidence', *PLoSONE*, vol. 11 (2016), e0148583.

12 Wood 2014, pp. 1–2; Bonnie Effros and Isabel Moreira, 'Pushing the Boundaries of the Merovingian World', in *The Oxford Handbook of the Merovingian World*, ed. Bonnie Effros and Isabel Moreira (Oxford: Oxford University Press, 2020), p. 4; McCormick 2001, pp. 704–7; Wickham 2005, p. 818; Constantin Pion et al., 'Bead and Garnet Trade between the Merovingian, Mediterranean, and Indian Worlds', in Effros and Moreira (eds) 2020, pp. 819–60; Jörg Drauschke, 'Archaeological Perspectives on Communication and Exchange between the Merovingians and the Eastern Mediterranean', in *East and West in the Early Middle Ages: The Merovingian Kingdoms in Mediterranean Perspective*, ed. Stefan Esders et al. (Cambridge: Cambridge University Press, 2019), pp. 9–31.

13 McCormick 2001, pp. 574–5, 613, 647–51; Jennifer R. Davis, 'Western Europe', in Hermans (ed.) 2020, pp. 351, 363–4; Janet L. Nelson, *King and Emperor: A New Life of Charlemagne* (Berkeley, CA: University of California Press, 2019); Christoph Stiegemann and Matthias Wemhoff, *799: Kunst und Kultur der Karolingerzeit – Karl der Große und Papst Leo III in Paderborn*, 3 vols (Mainz: Philipp von Stabern, 1999), vol. 2, p. 6.

14 Loveluck 2013, pp. 114, 122–3; Einhard, *Vita Karoli Magni*, III.23, in Einhard and Notker the Stammerer, *Two Lives of Charlemagne*, trans. David Ganz, (Harmondsworth: Penguin, 2008); Rosamond McKitterick, 'Charlemagne, the Carolingian Empire, and its Successors', in *The Oxford World History of Empire*, vol. 2: *The History of Empires*, ed. Peter Fibiger Bang, C.A. Bayly and Walter Scheidel (Oxford: Oxford University Press, 2021), p. 468; Leslie Webster, 'Charlemagne: The Material Culture of Court and Church', online version of a paper given at the conference 'Charlemagne: The First 1200 Years, King's College London, 28 January 814', 28 January 2014, www.charlemagneeurope.ac.uk/leslie-webster-charlemagne-the-material-culture-of-court-and-church (accessed 9 August 2023).

15 Joanna Story, *Charlemagne and Rome: Alcuin and the Epitaph of Pope Hadrian I* (Oxford: Oxford University Press, 2023), p. 247 ff.; Stiegemann and Wemhoff 1999, p. 9; Adeo Batozzi, 'Aachener Dom war Einst Rot Verputzt', *Baugewerbe*, 27 October 2003, www.baugcewbe.ch/de/Aachener+Dom+war+einst+rot+verputzt/155549/detail.htm (accessed 10 August 2023); Peter Lasko, *Ars Sacra, 800–1200*, 2nd edn (New Haven: Yale University Press, 1994), pp. 14–16. A lion-headed door handle appears on a fifth-century CE casket panel from Rome in the British Museum, 1856,0623.6.

16 Michael Greenhalgh, *Marble Past, Monumental Present: Building with Antiquities in the Mediaeval Mediterranean* (Leiden: Brill, 2009), ch. 8.

17 Webster, 'Charlemagne: The Material Culture'; Lawrence Nees, *Early Medieval Art* (Oxford: Oxford University Press, 2002), p. 163 ff.; Stiegemann and Wemhoff 1999, p. 7.

18 Brigitte Buettner, *The Mineral and the Visual: Precious Stones in Medieval Secular Culture* (University Park, PA: Pennsylvania State University Press, 2022), p. 12; see also chapter 5 of this book.

19 Guido Alberto Gnecchi-Ruscone, Anna Szécsényi-Nagy, István Koncz et al., 'Ancient Genomes Reveal Origin and Rapid Trans-Eurasian Migration of 7th Century Avar Elites', *Cell*, vol. 185 (2022), pp. 1402–13; Tivadar Vida, 'Conflict and Coexistence: The Local Population of the Carpathian Basin under Avar Rule (Sixth to Seventh Century)', in *The Other Europe in the Middle Ages: Avars, Bulgars, Khazars and Cumans*, ed. Florin Curta (Leiden: Brill, 2007), pp. 13–46; Walter Pohl, *The Avars: A Steppe Empire in Central Europe, 567–811* (Ithaca, NY: Cornell University Press, 2018), ch. 8; Falko Daim, 'The Gold of the Avars: Three Case Studies', in *Dalle steppe al Mediterraneo: Popoli, culture, integrazione – Atti del Convegno internazionale di studi Fondazioni e rituali funerari delle aristocrazie germaniche nel contesto mediterraneo: Cimitile-Santa Maria Capua Vetere, 18–19 giugno 2015*, ed. Carlo Ebanista and Marcello Rotili (Naples: Guida editori, 2017), pp. 407–8.

20 Csanád Bálint, 'Der Goldschatz von Nagyszentmiklós/Sânnicolau Mare: Bemerkungen zum Forschungsstand', in *Der Goldschatz von Sânnicolau Mare (ungarisch: Nagyszentmiklós)*, ed. Falko Daim et al. (Mainz: RGZM, 2015), pp. 1–8; Ádám Bollók, 'The Visual Arts of the Sasanian Empire and the Nagyszentmiklós/Sânnicolau Mare Treasure', in Daim et al. (eds) 2015, pp. 43–70; Karoline Zhuber-Okrog, 'The Nagyszentmiklós Gold Treasure', in *The Nagyszentmiklós Gold Treasure*, ed. Metodi Daskalov et al. (Sofia: National Archaeological Institute with Museum, 2017), pp. 32–5; Falko Daim, 'Bilder für den Herrscher: Der Goldschatz von Sânnicolau Mare/Nagyszentmiklós', in *Reiternomaden in Europa: Hunnen, Awaren, Ungarn*, ed. Harald Meller, Falko Daim and Thomas Puttkammer (Halle: Landesmuseum für Vorgeschichte Halle, 2022), pp. 210–11; Sarah Bergner and Karoline Zhuber-Okrog, 'The Catalogue', in Daskalov et al. (eds) 2017, pp. 77–161, cat. nos 21 (bowl) and 18 (shell); Daim 2017, p. 416; Raimar W. Kory, 'Die nautilusförmige Schale Nr. 18 von Nagyszentmiklós: Erwägungen zu Parallelen und Provenienz', in *Zwischen Byzanz und der Steppe: Archäologische und historische Studien, Festschrift für Csanád Bálint zum 70. Geburtstag*, ed. Ádám Bollók, Gergely Csiky and Tivadar Vida (Budapest: Institute of Archaeology, Research Centre for the Humanities, Hungarian Academy of Sciences, 2016), pp. 371–92.

21 Bergner and Zhuber-Okrog 2017, p. 35; *Annales Northumbrani*, quoted in Pohl 2018, n. 262; Joanna Story, pers. comm., 10 March 2023; Chris Wickham, *The Inheritance of Rome: A History of Europe from 400 to 1000* (London: Penguin, 2009), p. 381.

22 McCormick 2001, fig. 11.1, pp. 320, 675–8, 792–3; Wickham 2009, pp. 378–80; Clemens Gantner, 'A Brief Introduction to Italian Political History until 875', in *After Charlemagne: Carolingian Italy and its Rulers*, ed. Clemens Gantner and Walter Pohl (Cambridge: Cambridge University Press, 2020), pp. 5–18.

23 McCormick 2001, p. 725, nn. 136–7; Loveluck 2013, pp. 121–2.

24 Courtney Luckhardt, *The Charisma of Distant Places: Travel and Religion in the Early Middle Ages* (London: Routledge, 2020), ch. 2; McCormick 2001, p. 718; Huneberc of Heidenheim, *Hodoeporicon*, in *The Anglo-Saxon Missionaries in Germany*, trans. C.H. Talbot (London: Sheed and Ward, 1954), p. 170.

25 Claire Burridge, 'Incense in Medicine: An Early Medieval Perspective', *Early Medieval Europe*, vol. 28 (2020), pp. 219–55; McCormick 2001, pp. 709–8.

26 Robin Fleming, 'Acquiring, Flaunting and Destroying Silk in Late Anglo-Saxon England', *Early Medieval Europe*, vol. 15 (2007), pp. 127–58. On the reliquary fragments specifically: Joanne Dyer, Diego Tamburini and Caroline Cartwright, 'Analysis of Four Textile Relic Wrappings from the St Eustace Head Reliquary', British Museum Scientific Research Analytical Request report AR2023-18 (London: The British Museum, 5 April 2024, unpublished); Diego Tamburini, 'Dyes along the Silk Roads', in *Textiles and Clothing along the Silk Roads*, ed. Zhao Feng and Marie-Louise Nosch (Paris and Hangzhou: UNESCO and China National Silk Museum, 2022), pp. 53–71, at p. 59; Hero Granger-Taylor, 'Textile Fragments from the Basel Reliquary Head, British Museum ML&A 50,11-27,1', unpublished internal report, 10 May 1989, British Museum; John Cherry, 'Kopfreliquiar des hl. Eustachius', in *Der Basler Münsterschatz*, ed. Brigitte Meles (Basel: C. Merien, 2001), no. 13, pp. 60–4. The dates given here are from recent observations by Hero Granger-Taylor, who has also suggested a potential Khotanese origin for the pinkish fragment (pers. comm., 18 May 2024).

27 Cristina Borgioli, 'Wearing the Sacred: Images, Space, Identity in Liturgical Vestments (13th to 16th Centuries)', *Espacio, Tiempo y Forma*, vol. 6 (2018), pp. 172–3; Elizabeth Coatsworth and Gale Owen-Crocker, *Clothing the Past: Surviving Garments from Early Medieval to Early Modern Western Europe* (Leiden: Brill, 2018), pp. 120–8.

28 Ottewill-Soulsby 2023, esp. ch. 3; Abdurrahman A. El-Hajji, 'Andalusian Diplomatic Relations with the Franks during the Umayyad Period', *Islamic Studies*, vol. 30 (1991), pp. 241–62; McCormick 2001, pp. 675–8; Sam Ottewill-Soulsby, 'Charlemagne's Asian Elephant: India in Carolingian-Abbasid Relations', in *Levant, Cradle of Abrahamic Religions: Studies on the Interaction of Religion and Society from Antiquity to Modern Times*, ed. Catalin-Stefa Popa (Münster: LIT Verlag, 2022), pp. 187–8, 197–8.

29 Bibliothèque nationale de France, Paris, lat. 2195, fol. 9v.

30 Dicuil, *Liber De Mensura Orbis Terrae*, VII.35, trans. James J. Tierney (Dublin: Dublin Institute for Advanced Studies, 1967); Ottewill-Soulsby 2022, pp. 188, 191.

31 Venetia Porter and Barry Ager, 'Islamic Amuletic Seals: The Case of the Carolingian Cross Brooch from Ballycotton', *Res Orientales*, vol. 12 (1999), pp. 211–18; Venetia Porter, *Arabic and Persian Seals and Amulets in the British Museum* (London: The British Museum Press, 2011), pp. 1–6, 14, 62; Egon Wamers, *Die frühmittelalterlichen Lesefunde aus der Löhrstrasse (Baustelle Hilton II) in Mainz* (Mainz: Archäologische Denkmalpflege, Amt Mainz, 1994), pp. 134–42. The brooch's findspot in Ballycotton Bog, County Cork, Ireland has also been attributed to Viking activity between the North and Irish Seas. However, cultural, political and religious connections between Ireland and Carolingian Francia offer alternative channels. Griffin Murray, 'Early Medieval Shrine Fragments from Park North Cave, Co. Cork and Kilgreany Cave, Co. Waterford', in *Underground Archaeology: Studies on Human Bones and Artefacts from Ireland's Caves*, ed. Marion Dowd (Oxford: Oxbow, 2016), p. 156; Sean Duffy (ed.), *Medieval Ireland: An Encyclopaedia* (Abingdon: Taylor & Francis, 2005), pp. 105–6.

32 These ideas are part of ongoing research by the author and will be published at a future date. With thanks to Venetia Porter and Sam Ottewill-Soulsby for discussions on this topic.

33 Sonja Marzinzik, *Masterpieces: Early Medieval Art* (London: The British Museum Press, 2013), p. 234; Ottewill-Soulsby 2023, pp. 52–3; Daniel G. König, *Arabic-Islamic Views of the Latin West: Tracing the Emergence of Medieval Europe* (Oxford: Oxford University Press, 2015), pp. 66–8; Bayard Dodge (ed. and trans.), *The Fihrist of al-Nadīm: A Tenth-Century Survey of Muslim Culture* (New York: Columbia University Press, 1970), 2 vols, vol. I, p. 38.

34 El-Hajji 1991, p. 247; British Museum, AF.3041: Marzinzik 2013, pp. 204–5.

35 The British Library, Cotton MS Vitellius A.XV; Karen Louise Jolly and Britton Elliot Brooks, 'Introduction: Global Perspectives on Early Medieval England', in Jolly and Brooks (eds) 2022, pp. 1–2; Rory Naismith, *Early Medieval Britain, c. 500–1000* (Cambridge: Cambridge University Press, 2021), pp. 43–4, 211–2.

36 Marzinzik 2013, p. 103; László Kovács with Gyula Radócz, *Vulvae, Eyes, Snake Heads: Archaeological Finds of Cowrie Amulets* (Oxford: Archaeopress, 2008); Katie A. Hemer et al., 'Ivory from Early Anglo-Saxon Burials in Lincolnshire: A Biomolecular Study', *Journal of Archaeological Science: Reports*, vol. 49 (2023); Katie Danielle Haworth, '"Most Precious Ornaments": Necklaces in Seventh-Century England', PhD thesis, Durham University, 2021, pp. 43–5; Christopher J. Arnold, *An Archaeology of the Early Anglo-Saxon Kingdoms* (London: Routledge, 1997), p. 113–14, 119–20; Christopher Scull, 'Social Transactions, Gift Exchange, and Power in the Archaeology of the Fifth to Seventh Centuries', in *The Oxford Handbook of Anglo-Saxon Archaeology*, ed. David A. Hinton, Sally Crawford and Helena Hamerow (Oxford: Oxford University Press, 2011), pp. 848–64.

37 Arnold 1997, pp. 115, 123–4.

38 Rupert Leo Scott Bruce-Mitford, *The Sutton Hoo Ship Burial*, vol. 3.1: *Late Roman and Byzantine Silver, Hanging Bowls, Drinking Vessels, Cauldrons and Other Containers, Textiles, the Lyre, Pottery Bottle and Other Items* (London: The British Museum Press, 1983), pp. 4–69; Gregory of Tours, *Historiae Francorum*, II.38, IV.38, in Gregory of Tours, *The History of the Franks*, trans. Lewis Thorpe (Harmondsworth: Penguin, 1974); Bede, *Historia Ecclesiastica*, I.25, in Bede, *Ecclesiastical History of the English People*, trans. Leo Sherley-Price (London: Penguin, 2003).

39 Helen Gittos, 'Sutton Hoo and Syria: The Anglo-Saxons Who Served in the Byzantine Army?', *English Historical Review* (forthcoming); Benjamin Fourlas, 'Early Byzantine Church Silver Offered for the Eternal Rest of Framarich and Karilos: Evidence of "the Army of Heroic Men" Raised by Tiberius II Constantine?', in Esders et al. (eds) 2019, pp. 87–107. For Rendlesham, see Chris Scull, Faye Minter and Jude Plouviez, 'Social and Economic Complexity in Early Medieval England: a Central Place Complex of the East Anglian Kingdom at Rendlesham, Suffolk', *Antiquity*, vol. 90, issue 354 (2016), pp. 1594–1612.

40 Bitumen: Pauline Burger et al., 'Identification, Geochemical Characterisation and Significance of Bitumen among the Grave Goods of the 7th Century Mound 1 Ship-Burial at Sutton Hoo (Suffolk, UK)', *PLoS ONE*, vol. 11 (2016): e0166276. Mahdi Shahriari, Farzaneh Zare and Majid Nimrouzi, 'The Curative Role of Bitumen in Traditional Persian Medicine', *Acta medico-historica Adriatica*, vol. 16 (2018), pp. 283–92; St John Simpson, 'Sutton Hoo, St. Sergius and the Sasanians: Anglo-Saxon Finds Re-Interpreted from an Eastern Perspective', *Ash-sharq*, vol. 8 (2024), pp. 1–35, esp. pp. 5–14. Woollen garments: Bruce-Mitford 1983, vol. 3.1, pp. 453–6. Mail-armour: Simon Timothy James, 'The Arms and Armour from Dura-Europos, Syria: Weaponry Recovered from the Roman Garrison Town and the Sassanid Siegeworks during the Excavations, 1922–37, vol. 1 – Texts, Catalogues and Published Papers', PhD thesis, Institute of Archaeology, University College London, 1990, pp. 39, 139; Rupert Leo Scott Bruce-Mitford, *The Sutton Hoo Ship Burial*, vol. 2: *Arms, Armour and Regalia* (London: The British Museum Press, 1978), ch. 4.

41 Marlia Mundell Mango, 'The East Mediterranean Flagon', in *The Prittlewell Princely Burial: Excavations at Priory Crescent, Southend-on-Sea, Essex, 2003*, ed. Lyn Blackmore et al. (London: Museum of London Archaeology, 2019), pp. 182–4; Simpson 2024, pp. 17ff.

42 Gale R. Owen-Crocker, *Dress in Anglo-Saxon England* (Woodbridge: Boydell, 2010), pp. 180–1; Penelope Walton Rogers, *Cloth and Clothing in Early Anglo-Saxon England, AD 450–700* (York: Council for British Archaeology, 2007), pp. 211–4; Ulla Mannering, *Iconic Costumes: Scandinavian Late Iron Age Costume Iconography* (Oxford: Oxbow, 2017), pp. 159–60; Noël Adams, 'Rethinking the Sutton Hoo Shoulder-Clasps', in *Intelligible Beauty: Recent Research on Byzantine Jewellery*, ed. Christopher Entwistle and Noël Adams (London: The British Museum Press, 2010), pp. 83–112; Bruce-Mitford 1978, vol. 2, p. 186, fig. 140.

43 Eleanor Blakelock and Chris Fern, 'Workshop Practice', in *The Staffordshire Hoard: An Anglo-Saxon Treasure*, ed. Chris Fern, Tania Dickinson and Leslie Webster (London: Society of Antiquaries of London, 2019), p. 166; Noël Adams, 'Garnet Inlays in the Light of the Armaziskhevi Dagger Hilt', *Medieval Archaeology*, vol. 43 (2003), pp. 167–97; Niles 2022.

44 The clasp's form may draw upon Roman or Byzantine models from the eastern reaches of the empire: Adams 2010.

45 The analysis, involving the Particle-Induced X-Ray Emission (PIXE) method, is part of ongoing research that will be published at a future date. It was undertaken by Thomas Calligaro and Quentin Lemasson via the Grand Louvre Accelerator for Elemental Analysis (AGLAE) at the Centre de recherche et de restauration des musées de France (C2RMF) in Paris in February–March 2023. With thanks to both for their expertise and for discussions that have informed the preliminary observations made here. The analysis was funded by IPERION-HS, a project funded by the European Union, H2020-INFRAIA-2019-1, under GA 871034, with additional support from the British Museum Research Fund.

46 Naismith 2021, p. 68; Nancy Edwards, *Life in Early Medieval Wales* (Oxford: Oxford University Press, 2023), pp. 251–2; Aidan O'Sullivan et al., *Early Medieval Ireland, AD 400–1100: The Evidence from Archaeological Excavations* (Dublin: Royal Irish Academy, 2013), pp. 249–67; Maria Duggan, *Links to Late Antiquity: Ceramic Exchange and Contacts on the Atlantic Seaboard in the 5th to 7th Centuries AD* (Oxford: BAR Publishing, 2020); Ewan Campbell, 'Peripheral Vision: Scotland in Early Medieval Europe', in *Scotland in Early Medieval Europe*, ed. Alice Blackwell (Edinburgh: National Museums Scotland, 2019), pp. 21–2; Gordon Noble and Nicholas Evans, *Picts: Scourge of Rome, Rulers of the North* (Edinburgh: Birlinn, 2022), pp. 137–9.

47 Lynda Mulvin, 'West-to-East Migration and the Dynamics of Celtic Monasteries in a European Context', in *Migration und Baukultur: Transformation des Bauens durch individuelle und kollektive Einwanderung*, ed. Heiderose Kilper (Berlin: Birkhäuser, 2019), pp. 77–88; Naismith 2021, p. 47.

48 Leslie Webster, *Anglo-Saxon Art: A New History* (London: The British Museum Press, 2012a), p. 110.

49 John Gillis, *The Faddan More Psalter: The Discovery and Conservation of a Medieval Treasure* (Dublin: National Museum of Ireland, 2021), pp. 124–64.

50 Bede, *Historia Ecclesiastica*, I.29, in Bede 2003.

51 Bede, *Historia Abbatum*, in *The Age of Bede*, trans. David H. Farmer (London: Penguin, 1983); Webster 2012a, pp. 69–70; Rosemary Cramp, *Wearmouth and Jarrow Monastic Sites*, 2 vols (Swindon: English Heritage, 2005), vol. 1: pp. 222–30, vol. 2: p. 67; Vincent Daniels, 'Sample from inside a Censer ML&A 1986,0705.1', unpublished report 1991/3, Conservation Research Section, British Museum; Leslie Webster and Janet Backhouse, *The Making of England: Anglo-Saxon Art and Culture, AD 600–900* (London: The British Museum Press, 1991), p. 68.

52 Michael Lapidge, 'The School of Theodore and Hadrian', *Anglo-Saxon England*, vol. 15 (1986), pp. 45–72; Naismith 2021, p. 60; Bernhard Bischoff and Michael Lapidge (eds), *Biblical Commentaries from the Canterbury School of Theodore and Hadrian* (Cambridge: Cambridge University Press, 1995).

53 Webster 2012a, p. 112; Michelle P. Brown, *Art of the Islands: Celtic, Pictish, Anglo-Saxon and Viking Visual Culture, c. 450–1050* (Oxford: Bodleian Library, 2016), pp. 129–30; Richard Henry Iliffe Jewell, 'The Anglo-Saxon Friezes at Breedon-on-the-Hill, Leicestershire', *Archaeologia* 108 (1986), pp. 95–115.

54 Warwick Rodwell et al., 'The Lichfield Angel: A Spectacular Anglo-Saxon Painted Sculpture', *Antiquaries Journal*, vol. 88 (2008), pp. 1–28.

55 Including Boniface and Alcuin: Katharine Scarfe Beckett, *Anglo-Saxon Perceptions of the Islamic World* (Cambridge: Cambridge University Press, 2003), pp. 165–6.

56 Ibid., pp. 6, 43, 117, 124, 225; Bede, *Historia Ecclesiastica*, V.15, in Bede 2003; Brown 2016, p. 133; Naismith 2021, pp. 65–7.

57 Barry Ager, 'The Carolingian Cup from the Vale of York Viking Hoard: Origins of its Form and Decorative Features', *Antiquaries Journal*, vol. 100 (2020), pp. 86–108; Martin Goldberg and Mary Davis, *The Galloway Hoard: Viking-Age Treasure* (Edinburgh: National Museums Scotland, 2021), pp. 65–8; Martin Goldberg, pers. comm., 4 July 2023. The metallurgical analysis, undertaken by Jane Kershaw and Stephen Merkel, will feature in a forthcoming publication and is referenced here with their kind permission.

58 Marzinzik 2013, p. 132; Scarfe Beckett 2003, p. 224; Naismith 2021, p. 67.

59 Leslie Webster, *The Franks Casket* (London: The British Museum Press, 2012b); Marzinzik 2013, p. 128; James Paz, *Nonhuman Voices in Anglo-Saxon Literature and Material Culture* (Manchester: Manchester University Press, 2017).

Select bibliography

This represents a general reading list. Full references can be found in the notes to the chapters (pp. 274–95).

Silk Roads, 500–1000

Frankopan, Peter, *The Silk Road: A New History of the World* (London: Bloomsbury, 2015)

Hansen, Valerie, *The Silk Road: A New History* (Oxford: Oxford University Press, 2012)

Hermans, Erik (ed.), *A Companion to the Global Early Middle Ages* (Leeds: Arc Humanities Press, 2020)

Preiser-Kapeller, Johannes, Lucian Reinfandt and Yannis Stouraitis (eds), *Migration Histories of the Medieval Afroeurasian Transition Zone: Aspects of Mobility between Africa, Asia and Europe, 300– 1500 C.E.* (Leiden: Brill, 2020)

Whitfield, Susan, *Life along the Silk Road* (Oakland: University of California Press, 2015)

————, *Silk, Slaves, and Stupas: Material Culture of the Silk Road* (Oakland: University of California Press, 2018)

———— (ed.), *Silk Roads: Peoples, Cultures, Landscapes* (London: Thames & Hudson, 2019)

Three capitals in East Asia

Hu, Jun, 'Global Medieval at the "End of the Silk Road" circa 756 ce: The Shōsō-in Collection in Japan', in *Re-Assessing the Global Turn in Medieval Art History*, ed. Christina Normore (Leeds: ARC Humanities Press, 2018), pp. 177–202

Lee Insook, 'The Silk Road Treasures of Ancient Korea: Glass and Gold', in *The Eastern Silk Road Story, 2015 Conference Proceeding* (Paris, Bangkok: UNESCO, 2016), pp. 53–60

Lee Soyoung and Denise Patry Leidy (eds), *Silla: Korea's Golden Kingdom* (New York: The Metropolitan Museum of Art, 2013)

Lewis, Mark Edward, *China's Cosmopolitan Empire: The Tang Dynasty* (Cambridge, MA: Belknap Press of Harvard University Press, 2012)

Rong Xinjiang, *The Silk Road and Cultural Exchanges between East and West*, ed. and trans. Sally K. Church et al. (Leiden: Brill, 2023)

Schafer, Edward H., *The Golden Peaches of Samarkand: Study of T'ang Exotics* (Berkeley and Los Angeles, CA: University of California Press, 1985)

Wang Zhenping, *Ambassadors from the Islands of Immortals: China–Japan Relations in the Han–Tang Period* (Honolulu, HI: University of Hawai'i Press, 2005)

Verschuer, Charlotte von, *Across the Perilous Sea: Japanese Trade with China and Korea from the Seventh to the Sixteenth Centuries*, trans. Kristen Lee Hunter (Ithaca, NY: Cornell University, 2006)

Seafarers in the Indian Ocean

Chong, Alan, and Stephen A. Murphy (eds), *The Tang Shipwreck: Art and Exchange in the 9th Century* (Singapore: Asian Civilisations Museum, 2017)

Krahl, Regina, et al. (eds), *Shipwrecked: Tang Treasures and Monsoon Winds* (Washington, DC and Singapore: Arthur M. Sackler Gallery, Smithsonian Institution/Singapore Tourism Board, 2011)

Pearson, Natali, *Belitung: The Afterlives of a Shipwreck* (Honolulu: University of Hawai'i Press, 2023)

Southeast Asia to the Tarim Basin

Akasoy, Anna, Charles Burnett and Ronit Yoeli-Tlalim (eds), *Islam and Tibet: Interactions along the Musk Routes* (Farnham: Ashgate, 2011)

Beaujard, Philippe, *The Worlds of the Indian Ocean: A Global History*, vol. 2: *From the Seventh Century to the Fifteenth Century CE*, trans. Tamara Loring, Frances Meadows and Andromeda Tait (Cambridge: Cambridge University Press, 2019)

Klokke, Marijke J., 'Central Javanese Empire (Early Mataram)', in *The Encyclopedia of Empire*, vol. 1, ed. John M. MacKenzie et al. (Chichester: John Wiley & Sons, 2016), pp. 450–5.

Rong Xinjiang, *Eighteen Lectures on Dunhuang* (Leiden: Brill, 2013)

Galambos, Imre, *Dunhuang Manuscript Culture: End of the First Millennium* (Berlin: De Gruyter, 2020)

Sen, Tansen, *Buddhism, Diplomacy, and Trade: The Realignment of India–China Relations, 600–1400* (Honolulu, HI: Association for Asian Studies and University of Hawai'i Press, 2003)

Wen, Xin, *The King's Road: Diplomacy and the Remaking of the Silk Road* (Princeton, NJ: Princeton University Press, 2023)

Whitfield, Roderick, and Anne Farrer, *Caves of the Thousand Buddhas: Chinese Art from the Silk Route* (London: The British Museum Press, 1990)

Whitfield, Susan, and Ursula Sims-Williams (eds), *The Silk Road: Trade, Travel, War and Faith* (London: The British Library, 2004)

Sogdians from Central Asia

Freer Gallery of Art, Smithsonian Institution, *The Sogdians: Influencers on the Silk Roads* (online exhibition)

Azarpay, Guitty, et al., *Sogdian Painting: The Pictorial Epic in Oriental Art* (Berkeley, CA: University of California Press, 1981)

Shenkar, Michael, 'The Religion and the Pantheon of the Sogdians (5th–8th centuries CE) in Light of their Sociopolitical Structures', *Journal Asiatique*, no. 2 (2017), pp. 191–209

Vaissière, Étienne de la, *Sogdian Traders: A History*, trans. James Ward (Leiden: Brill, 2005)

Central Asia and the steppe

Ball, Warwick, *The Eurasian Steppe: People, Movement, Ideas* (Edinburgh: Edinburgh University Press, 2021)

Baumer, Christoph, *The History of Central Asia*, vol. 2: *The Age of the Silk Roads* (London: I.B. Tauris, 2012)

Golden, Peter, Haggai Ben-Shammai and András Roná-Tas (eds), *The World of the Khazars – New Perspectives: Selected Papers from the Jerusalem 1999 International Khazar Colloquium* (Leiden: Brill, 2007)

Kolchenko, Valery A., 'Buddhism in the Chuy Valley (Kyrgyzstan) in the Middle Ages', *Journal of Oriental Studies*, vol. 30 (2020), pp. 67–101

Litvinsky, B.A., and Tamara Ivanovna Zeymal, *The Buddhist Monastery of Ajina Tepa, Tajikistan: History and Art of Buddhism in Central Asia* (Rome: IsIAO, 2004)

Omarov, Gani, et al., 'Horse Equipment of Medieval Nomads of the Kazakh Altai (Based on Materials from the Tuyetas Burial Ground)', *Archaeological Research in Asia*, vol. 31 (2022), pp. 1–15

Pankova, Svetlana and St John Simpson (eds), *Masters of the Steppe: The Impact of the Scythians and Later Nomad Societies in Eurasia* (Oxford: Archaeopress, 2020)

Vikings on the *austrvegr*

Asingh, Pauline, and Kristian Jensen (eds), *Rus: Vikings in the East* (Moesgaard: Moesgaard Museum, 2022)

Jankowiak, Marek, and Felix Biermann (eds), *The Archaeology of Slavery in Early Medieval Northern Europe: The Invisible Commodity* (Cham: Springer International Publishing, 2021)

Jarman, Cat, *River Kings: A New History of the Vikings from Scandinavia to the Silk Roads* (London: William Collins, 2021)

Katona, Csete, *Vikings of the Steppe: Scandinavians, Rus', and the Turkic World (c. 750–1050)* (London: Routledge, 2023)

Price, Neil, *The Children of Ash and Elm* (London: Penguin Books, 2022)

Vedeler, Marianne, *Silk for the Vikings* (Oxford: Oxbow, 2014)

Central Asia to Arabia

Antrim, Zayde, *Mapping the Middle East* (London: Reaktion Books, 2018)

Bessard, Fanny, *Caliphs and Merchants: Cities and Economies of Power in the Near East (700-950)* (Oxford: Oxford University Press, 2020).

Bloom, Jonathan M., *Paper before Print: The History and Impact of Paper in the Islamic World* (New Haven, CT: Yale University Press, 2001)

Golden, Peter B., *Central Asia in World History* (New York: Oxford University Press, 2011)

Kennedy, Hugh, *The Great Arab Conquests: How the Spread of Islam Changed the World We Live In* (Philadelphia, PA: Da Capo Press, 2007)

Morgan, Llewelyn, *The Buddhas of Bamiyan* (London: Profile Books, 2012)

Ratliff, Brandie, and Helen C. Evans (eds), *Byzantium and Islam: Age of Transition, 7th–9th Century* (New York: The Metropolitan Museum of Art, 2012)

Starr, S. Frederick, *Lost Enlightenment: Central Asia's Golden Age from the Arab Conquest to Tamerlane* (Princeton, NJ: Princeton University Press, 2013)

Aksumites and their port city, Adulis

Bausi, Alessandro (ed.), *Languages and Cultures of Eastern Christianity: Ethiopian* (Burlington, VT: Ashgate, 2011)

Bowersock, G.W., *Throne of Adulis: Red Sea Wars on the Eve of Islam* (Oxford and New York: Oxford University Press, 2013)

Castiglia, Gabriele, et al., 'For an Archaeology of Religious Identity in Adulis (Eritrea) and the Horn of Africa: Sources, Architecture, and Recent Archaeological Excavations', *Journal of African Archaeology*, vol. 19 (2021), pp. 1–32

Phillipson, D.W., *Foundations of an African Civilization: Aksum & the Northern Horn, 1000 BC–AD 1300* (Woodbridge, NY: James Currey, 2012)

Mediterranean connections

Berzock, Kathleen Bickford (ed.), *Caravans of Gold, Fragments in Time: Art, Culture, and Exchange across Medieval Saharan

Africa (Evanston, IL: Block Museum of Art, Northwestern University, 2019)

Cunliffe, Barry W., *Facing the Sea of Sand: The Sahara and the Peoples of Northern Africa* (Oxford: Oxford University Press, 2023)

Goitein, S.D., *A Mediterranean Society: The Jewish Communities of the Arab World as Portrayed in the Documents of the Cairo Geniza*, 6 vols (Berkeley, CA: University of California Press, 1967–93)

Goldberg, Jessica, *Trade and Institutions in the Medieval Mediterranean: The Geniza Merchants and their Business World* (Cambridge: Cambridge University Press, 2012)

Herrin, Judith, *Ravenna: Capital of Empire, Crucible of Europe* (Dublin: Penguin Books, 2021)

Perry, Craig, et al. (eds), *The Cambridge World History of Slavery*, vol. 2: *AD 500–AD 1420* (Cambridge: Cambridge University Press, 2021)

Rustow, Marina, *The Lost Archive: Traces of a Caliphate in a Cairo Synagogue* (Princeton, NJ: Princeton University Press, 2020)

Preiser-Kapeller, Johannes, Lucian Reinfandt and Yannis Stouraitis (eds), 'Migration Histories of the Medieval Afroeurasian Transition Zone: An Introduction', in *Migration Histories of the Medieval Afroeurasian Transition Zone: Aspects of Mobility between Africa, Asia and Europe, 300–1500 CE* (Leiden: Brill, 2020), pp. 5–15

Vorderstrasse, Tasha, et al. (eds), *A Cosmopolitan City: Muslims, Christians, and Jews in Old Cairo* (Chicago: Oriental Institute of the University of Chicago, 2015)

Wickham, Chris, *The Donkey and the Boat: Reinterpreting the Mediterranean Economy, 950–1180* (Oxford: Oxford University Press, 2023)

Peoples of al-Andalus

Anderson, Glaire D., 'Sign of the Cross: Contexts for the Ivory Cross of San Millán de la Cogolla', *Journal of Medieval Iberian Studies*, vol. 6 (2014), pp. 15–41

Borelli, Arianna, *Aspects of the Astrolabe: 'Architectonica Ratio' in Tenth- and Eleventh-Century Europe* (Stuttgart: Franz Steiner Verlag, 2008)

Cressier, Patrice, and Sonia Gutiérrez Lloret, 'Al-Andalus', in *The Oxford Handbook of Islamic Archaeology*, ed. Bethany J. Walker, Timothy Insoll and Corisande Fenwick (Oxford: Oxford University Press, 2020), pp. 311–34

Davies, Wendy, 'Gardens and Gardening in Early Medieval Spain and Portugal', *Early Medieval Europe*, vol. 27 (2019), pp. 327–4

Rosser-Owen, Mariam, *Islamic Arts from Spain* (London: V&A Publishing, 2010)

Northwest Europe

Bruce-Mitford, Rupert Leo Scott (ed.), *The Sutton Hoo Ship Burial*, 3 vols (London: The British Museum Press, 1978–1983)

Daskalov, Metodi, et al. (eds), *The Nagyszentmiklós Gold Treasure* (Sofia: National Archaeological Institute with Museum, 2017)

Duggan, Maria, *Links to Late Antiquity: Ceramic Exchange and Contacts on the Atlantic Seaboard in the 5th to 7th Centuries AD* (Oxford: BAR Publishing, 2018)

Goldberg, Martin, and Mary Davis, *The Galloway Hoard: Viking-Age Treasure* (Edinburgh: National Museums Scotland, 2021)

McCormick, Michael, *Origins of the European Economy: Communications and Commerce, AD 300–900* (Cambridge: Cambridge University Press, 2001)

Naismith, Rory, *Early Medieval Britain, c. 500–1000* (Cambridge: Cambridge University Press, 2021)

Ottewill-Soulsby, Sam, *The Emperor and the Elephant: Christians and Muslims in the Age of Charlemagne* (Princeton: Princeton University Press, 2023)

Wickham, Chris, *The Inheritance of Rome: A History of Europe from 400 to 1000* (London: Penguin, 2009)

Acknowledgements

We would like to begin by thanking our generous donors: the exhibition's lead supporter The Huo Family Foundation; the additional support from James Bartos and The Ruddock Foundation for the Arts; and further support from The Ministry of Culture, Sports and Tourism of the Republic of Korea, Unicorn Publishing Group, the International Foundation for Arts and Culture Japan, the National Museum of Tajikistan, Rodolphe Olard and Susan Sinclair, The Huang Yao Foundation, and Dr Michael Watts and Jolanda Watts. We are also extremely grateful to the twenty-nine lenders to the exhibition for their support and collaboration. Our thanks to the Art and Culture Development Foundation of the Republic of Uzbekistan for their support of loans from Uzbekistan. We also thank the National Museum of the Republic of Kazakhstan, the East Kazakhstan Regional Local Historical Museum, the Zhambyl Regional Local Historical Museum, and the National History Museum of the Kyrgyz Republic, for their help with images in the book.

Sincere thanks are due to those who have provided thoughtful comments on drafts of the narrative, book and/or label text: Glaire D. Anderson, Alessandro Bausi, Siam Bhayro, Phil Booth, Leslie Brubaker, Gabriele Castiglia, Cäcilia Fluck, Helen Gittos, Charlotte Hedenstierna-Jonson, Julia Hillner, Liz James, Hugh Kennedy, Sophie Lunn-Rockliffe, B.M. Outhwaite, Arietta Papaconstantinou, Neil Price, Mariam Rosser-Owen, Claudia Rapp, Petra Sijpesteijn, Joanna Story, Ellen Swift, Naïm Vanthieghem, Chris Wickham, and colleagues who are acknowledged in the endnotes of each of the chapters.

We warmly appreciate the many curators, other scholars and colleagues who kindly supported the exhibition and shared their expertise: Tuija Ainonen, Shahboz Ahmadov, Saltanat Amirova, Fabrizio Antonelli, Arezou Azad, Claire Breay, Sebastian Brock, Florence Calament, Katie Campbell, Beatriz Campdera, Annabelle Collinet, Gemma Cruikshanks, Ishbel Curr, Felipa Diaz, Mélodie Doumy, Motoko Endo, Nicolas Engel, Michael Erdman, José Escudero Aranda, Yasmin Faghihi, Gwenaëlle Fellinger, Imre Galambos, Anna Garnett, Libby Gavin, Martin Goldberg, Hero Granger-Taylor, Jessica Hallett, Kayley Harrison, Rebekah Higgit, Philippa Hoskin, Said Reza Huseini, Gai Jorayev, Sven Kalmring, Simon Kaner, Shimizu Ken, Valerii Kolchenko, Miriam Kühn, Kevin Lam, Hyun-tae Lee, Francesca Leoni, Li Baoping, Xiaoxin Li, Kristen Lippincott, Daniel Lowe, Kathrin Mälck, Roxani Eleni Margariti, Luisa Mengoni, Florian Meunier, María Jesús

Moreno Garrido, Stephen Murphy, Gordon Noble, Suzanne Paul, Ciara Phipps, Johannes Preiser-Kappeller, Frances Pritchard, Rocco Rante, Claire Reed, Vittorio Ricchetti, T.S. Richter, Rebecca Roberts, Catherine Robertson, Lilla Russell-Smith, Marina Rustow, Melonie Schmierer-Lee, Maeve Sikora, Nicholas Sims-Williams, Ursula Sims-Williams, Ilana Tahan, Carmen Ting, Hamish Todd, Peter Tóth, Katherine Turchin, Shelagh Vainker, Sam van Schaik, Dmitriy Voyakin, Johanna Ward, Alasdair Watson, Antje Wendt, Elizabeth Dospěl Williams, Catriona Wilson, Maggie Wilson, Ronit Yoeli-Tlalim, Yoon Sang-deok, Valérie Zaleski, Hongxing Zhang and Karoline Zhuber-Okrog. We are also grateful to the many individuals who have participated in research workshops, as well as colleagues in institutions who have provided images and other information – regretfully too many to name individually, but whose contribution was invaluable.

We would especially like to thank Tim Williams for his contribution and Susan Whitfield for her comments, advice and support as the book came together.

At the British Museum, we would like to thank Nicholas Cullinan, Jill Maggs, Rosalind Winton and Ruth Cribb, and our Keepers – Daniel Antoine, Jill Cook, Jane Portal and Jessica Harrison-Hall – for their guidance and support throughout the exhibition process. We are indebted to colleagues across the Museum who shared their expertise and commented on the narrative, book and/or label text: Awet Teklehimanot Araya, Richard Blurton, Rosina Buckland, Zoe Cormack, Paul Collins, Jill Cook, Amelia Dowler, Noorah Al-Gailani, Alexandra Green, Jessica Harrison-Hall, Richard Hobbs, Julie Hudson, Sang-ah Kim, Zeina Klink-Hoppe, Sam Nixon, St John Simpson and Akiko Yano. We thank the following colleagues for their advice and support: Richard Abdy, Tim Clark, Chen Ze, Barrie Cook, Vesta Curtis, Alfred Haft, JD Hill, Sushma Jansari, Marta Mroczek, Imma Ramos, Ruiliang Liu, Venetia Porter, Rebecca Scott, Naomi Speakman, Helen Wang, Craig Williams, Gareth Williams and Xin Wenyuan.

In the Department of Scientific Research, thanks to Carl Heron, Alessandro Armigliato, Caroline Cartwright, Joanne Dyer, Andrew Meek, Aude Mongiatti, Charlotte Nash, Lucía Pereira-Pardo, Laura Perucchetti, Michela Spataro, Rebecca Stacey, Antony Simpson and Diego Tamburini. Thanks to Amy Drago and the team of conservators working on the exhibition – Rachel Berridge, Duygu Camurcuoglu, Holly Daws, David

Green, Michelle Hercules, Joanna Kosek, Kyoko Kusunoki, Valentina Marabini, Shoun Obana, Kathryn Oliver, Alex Owen, Pippa Pearce, Emily Phillips, Qiu Jin Xian, Rachel Reynolds, Nicole Rode, Rebecca Snow, Matthias Sotiras, Tracey Sweek, Stephanie Vasiliou, Carol Weiss, Keeley Wilson – and Joanna Fernandes and her team of photographers: David Agar, Marco Borsato, Stephen Dodd, Isabel Marshall and Bradley Timms.

Special thanks to Senior Project Manager Jane Bennett for calmly steering the *Silk Roads* exhibition process with a steady hand; to Interpretation Manager Asha McLoughlin for her patience, support and her brilliant work on the exhibition text and graphics; to Vicci Ward and the excellent team of exhibition designers and contractors as well as the most helpful team of collection managers. The exhibition would not have been possible without our indefatigable Project Curator Zumrad Ilyasova, whom we'd especially like to thank for her hard work, diligence, composure and good humour. All have been dauntless and dependable companions on this epic journey. Further thanks to the rest of the *Silk Roads* core exhibition team: Mica Benjamin Mannix, Shani Crawford, Lydia Fellgett, Luminita Holban, Lucy Holmes, Matthew Hutt, Keith Lyons, Danny Kane, Deklan Kilfeather, Rebekah Manning, Jekaterina Paronjan, Clara Potter, Angela Pountney, Hannah Scully, Lindsey Snook, Chris Stewart, Philip Woods, Sam Wyles, Keeley Wilson and Yiman Lin.

This book could not have come to fruition without the hard work of Lydia Cooper, Senior Development Editor, and Lilly Phelan, Project Editor. Thank you to Beata Kibil for her work on the production with Jules Bettinson and Harry King at Altaimage, and to Toni Allum, Sales and Marketing Manager, and Claudia Bloch, Head of Publishing. We would also like to thank Michelle Noel and Lana Zoppi at Studio Noel for the book design and copyeditor Robert Sargant, proofreader Sarah Waldram, indexer Amanda Speake, and map designer Martin Brown.

Finally, we would like to thank our families for their unwavering support: Nathan Hadfield, Chrissie Monroe, Bob Brunning and Michael Brunning; Luk Siu Luen, Lam Oi Wai and Luk Yu Man; and Ethan and Ayla Thomas, and their father, Ross, whom we lost too soon.

Sue Brunning, Curator: European Early Medieval Collections
Luk Yu-ping, Basil Gray Curator: Chinese Paintings, Prints and Central Asian Collection
Elisabeth R. O'Connell, Curator: Byzantine World

Credits

The publisher would like to thank the copyright holders for granting permission to reproduce the images illustrated. Every attempt has been made to trace accurate ownership of copyrighted images in this book. Any errors or omissions will be corrected in subsequent editions provided notification is sent to the publisher.

Further information about the Museum and its collection can be found at britishmuseum.org. Registration numbers for British Museum objects are included in the image captions. Unless otherwise stated, copyright in photographs belongs to the institution mentioned in the caption. All images of British Museum objects are © 2024 The Trustees of the British Museum, courtesy the Department of Photography and Imaging.

10, 141 (top and middle), 145 (middle) Myrin, Ola, The Swedish History Museum / SHM (CC BY 4.0)

12 SOAS Library, Ferdinand Richthofen, *China: Ergebnisse eigener Reisin und darauf gregundeter Studien*, 1877, L EM49 /31478.

14 Courtesy of Kulturhistorisk museum, University of Oslo. Photo: Kirsten Helgeland.

16 *Excavations at Helgö I. Report for 1954–1956*, ed. Holmqvist, Arrhenius and Lundström, Kungl. Vitterhets Historie och Antikvitets Akademien (Uppsala: Almqvist & Wiksell, 1961), p. 112, fig. 18. Photography by Nils Lagergren, Harald Holmqvist and Marianne Bratt / Cambridge University Library

19 (top) © Floydian / Dreamstime.com

19 (bottom) Adel Newman/Shutterstock.com

20 (top) Vilion Fok/Shutterstock.com

20 (bottom) Joshua Davenport/Shutterstock.com

21 (top) marcovarro/Shutterstock.com

21 (bottom) © Yevgeniy Domashev

22 Oleg Belyakov/Shutterstock.com

23 (top) Kasbah/Shutterstock.com

23 (bottom) Sibag / Alamy Stock Photo

24 (top) Berkomaster/Shutterstock.com

24 (middle) © Sam Nixon

24 (bottom) Jose Miguel Sanchez/Shutterstock.com

25 coxy58/Shutterstock.com

29 The Shosoin Treasures, courtesy of the Imperial Household Agency

32, 36 TNM Image Archives. The work may not be reproduced without permission

34 (top) Richie Chan/Shutterstock.com

34 (bottom), 83 (bottom), 85 (top), 88 (top and bottom), 100, 159 (top), 166, 167 (bottom), 169 (left), 170 (left and right), 223 (right), 224, 248, 268 From The British Library Collection

37 (bottom) Public domain / The Metropolitan Museum of Art, New York, 30.47a-c. Gift of Benjamin Strong, 1930

38, 39 (top and bottom), 40, 41, 43 (left and right), 44 (top and bottom) © National Gyeongju Museum, Korea 국립경주박물관

39 (right) JIPEN/Shutterstock.com

42 jksz.photography/Shutterstock.com

48, 54 (bottom), 56, 57 (top), 75 (top), 161 (top), 176 (bottom), 201 (left), 206, 209, 215 (top), 222, 238 (bottom) © Victoria and Albert Museum, London

50 (top) Pictures from History / Bridgeman Images

50 (bottom) Courtesy of Sotheby's

54 (top) jejim/Shutterstock.com

58 (EA1991.59, ea1991.58), 78 (EA1999.98), 164 (1949.144.a), 211 (EA1990.250) © Ashmolean Museum, University of Oxford

62, 65 (top and bottom), 66 (top and bottom), 68 (top and bottom), 69 (top and bottom), 70, 71 (top and bottom) Asian Civilisations Museum, Tang Shipwreck Collection

64 © Foreign Ministry, Sultanate of Oman

67 © Dr Michael Flecker

76 (bottom) Hadi_design/Shutterstock.com

77 (top) PeoGeo/Shutterstock.com

91 (right) The China National Silk Museum

96 (III 4524), Staatliche Museen zu Berlin, Museum für Asiatische Kunst / Dietmar Katz

97 (III 4624), 97 (III 6916) Staatliche Museen zu Berlin, Museum für Asiatische Kunst / Jürgen Liepe

104, 112–13 Art and Culture Development Foundation of Uzbekistan, Samarkand State Museum Reserve

106 (top and bottom), 110, 152, 156 (top) Art and Culture Development Foundation of Uzbekistan, Samarkand State Museum Reserve. Photos: Andrey Arakelyan

109 Art and Culture Development Foundation of Uzbekistan, Samarkand State Museum Reserve. Photo: Andrey Arakelyan. Illustration: M. Sultanova

117 (top and bottom) East Kazakhstan Regional Local Historical Museum

118 (left) © Zhambyl Regional Local Historical Museum, Kazakhstan

118 (right), 120, 126 (bottom), 127 (bottom), 128, 129, 130–1 National History Museum of the Kyrgyz Republic

119, 121, 132, 133 (top and bottom), 134 (top) National Museum of the Republic of Kazakhstan

123, 124–5 State Institution 'National Museum' of the Executive Office of the President of the Republic of Tajikistan

126 (top) © Gai Jorayev, CAAL project, UCL Institute of Archaeology

127 (top) © Archaeological Museum at the Kyrgyz-Russian Slavic University

137 (left and right) Public domain / The Metropolitan Museum of Art, New York, 1996.78.1. Harris Brisbane Dick Fund, 1996

138 © Magnus Binnerstam / Dreamstime.com

140 Illustration by Craig Williams

141 (bottom) Hildebrand, Gabriel, Swedish History Museum/SHM (CC BY 4.0)

142 (top and bottom) Kalmring, Sven, Swedish History Museum/SHM (CC BY 4.0)

145 (top), 242, 270 (bottom) © National Museums Scotland

153 Collection of the State Museum of Arts of Uzbekistan. Photo by Andrey Arakelyan

154 © MNAAG, Paris, Dist. GrandPalaisRmn / image Musée Guimet

155 (bottom) Oybek Ostanov/Shutterstock.com

161 (bottom) Museum für Islamische Kunst-Staatliche Museen zu Berlin, photo: Johannes Kramer

162 (top) Museum für Islamische Kunst–Staatliche Museen zu Berlin, photo: Nico Becker

162 (bottom) Lev Levin/Shutterstock.com

163 (top) Mikhail Markovskiy/Shutterstock.com

163 (bottom) Museum für Islamische Kunst – Staatliche Museen zu Berlin

164 (bottom) © Musée du Louvre, Dist. GrandPalaisRmn / Hughes Dubois

165 (left), 243 Bibliothèque nationale de France

165 (right), 168, 169 (right), 180, 210, 217 The Bodleian Libraries, University of Oxford

167 (top) Copyright © The al-Sabah Collection, Dar al-Athar al-Islamiyyah, Kuwait.

171 Omarfox ali / CC BY-SA, Wikipedia

175 Museum für Islamische Kunst-Staatliche Museen zu Berlin, photo: Christian Krug

178 Florence, Laurentian Library, Ms. Plut. 9.28, f. 38r. Courtesy of the MiC. Any further reproduction by any means is prohibited.

183 © Michael Gervers, 2004

189 © Dumbarton Oaks, Byzantine Collection, Washington, DC

199, 212, 225 (top and bottom), 227, 228, 230 Reproduced by kind permission of the Syndics of Cambridge University Library

202, 203, 220 © Berlin, Bode-Museum, Museum für Byzantinische Kunst / Antje Voigt; CC BY-SA 4.0

207 (top) Roger Culos / CC BY-SA, Wikipedia by permission of Opera di Religione of the Diocese di Ravenna

207 (bottom) Petar Milošević / CC BY-SA, Wikipedia by permission of Opera di Religione of the Diocese di Ravenna

213 (top), 214 (right) © Petrie Museum, London / Photograph by Catriona Wilson

218 © Musée du Louvre, Dist. GrandPalaisRmn / Claire Tabbagh / Collections Numériques

219 (Inv. 50887), 237 (Inv. 63935), 241 (Inv. 63049) Museo Arqueológico Nacional, Madrid. Photographs by Ángel Martínez Levas

223 (left) © Musée du Louvre, Dist. GrandPalaisRmn / Georges Poncet

232 Bisual Photo/Shutterstock.com

235 (Inv. 2004/117/1, Inv. 2004/117/14 and Inv. 104279) Museo Arqueológico Nacional, Madrid. Photograph by Alberto Rivas Rodríguez

235 (Inv. 1986/60/V-4), 241 (Inv. 50955) Museo Arqueológico Nacional, Madrid. Photographs by Ariadna González Uribe

236 © 2024 Biblioteca Apostolica Vaticana

237 © GrandPalaisRmn (musée du Louvre) / Stéphane Maréchalle

238 (top and middle), 240 (top and bottom) © Museo Arqueológico de Córdoba. Photographs by Lucía Rivas

251, 252 KHM-Museumsverband

254 Wyvern Collection, UK

255 Parker Library, Corpus Christi College, Cambridge

257 Albuin chasuble, Byzantine purple silk, 10th century, from the Bressanone Cathedral Treasury, Diocesan Museum Hofburg Bressanone, © Hofburg Brixen Bressanone

260 (bottom) Courtesy of Southend Museums. Photograph: Tessa Hallmann

265 University of Aberdeen

266 (top) © National Museum of Ireland. This image is reproduced with the kind permission of the National Museum of Ireland

266 (bottom) Caroline Cartwright; © 2024 The Trustees of the British Museum

267 Courtesy of Jarrow Hall Anglo-Saxon Farm, Village and Bede Museum. Photography by Phoebe Lenderyou

269 Lichfield Cathedral. Photograph by Clive Allerton

Index